ssional
Programm

D0523761

Professional
XNA™ Game Programming
For Xbox 360™ and Windows®

Benjamin Nitschke

BICENTENNIAL
1807
WILEY
2007
BICENTENNIAL

Wiley Publishing, Inc.

Professional XNA™ Game Programming
For Xbox 360™ and Windows®

Published by
Wiley Publishing, Inc.
10475 Crosspoint Boulevard
Indianapolis, IN 46256
www.wiley.com

For general information on our other products and services or to obtain technical support, please contact our Customer Care Department within the U.S. at (800) 762-2974, outside the U.S. at (317) 572-3993 or fax (317) 572-4002.

Library of Congress Cataloging-in-Publication Data

Nitschke, Benjamin, 1980-
    Professional XNA game programming: for Xbox 360 and Windows / Benjamin Nitschke.
        p. cm.
    Includes bibliographical references and index.
    ISBN 978-0-470-12677-6 (pbk.)
    1. Computer games--Programming. 2. Microsoft XNA (Computer file) 3. Computer games. I. Title.
    QA76.76.C672N58 2007
    794.8'1526--dc22
                                    2007007059

This book is dedicated to all people that helped me in becoming a game programmer, especially all the programmers out there creating engines and libraries, sharing knowledge, and writing reusable code to help out fellow programmers.

About the Author

Benjamin Nitschke is the founder, lead programmer, and game designer at exDream entertainment. He is 26 years old, lives in Hannover, Germany, and also became a DirectX MVP of Microsoft in 2006 for his outstanding work in the DirectX community, especially with the free game Rocket Commander.

He started young—at the age of 9 he bought his first computer, a C64. He did not have many games, but he was very eager to type in commands on the C64, and from that to writing the first applications and games in Basic was not a big step. A few years later he finally got a PC (386) and started some small game projects (Tetris clones, shoot-em-up games, and so on). exDream entertainment was founded 10 years ago, and they released a couple of smaller games until the first RTS game Arena Wars was created. Arena Wars was the first commercial .NET game ever and was released in 2004, where it received more than 20 awards worldwide, especially for the great multiplayer modes.

Recently Benjamin has developed a couple of free open source games like Rocket Commander and the XNA Racing Game Starter Kit and many game modifications for these games. These games feature many video tutorials and a good documentation and code style to help beginners create their first video games. The video tutorials were watched more than 100,000 times and the games were downloaded and played even more often than that.

Credits

Executive Editor
Chris Webb

Development Editor
Kenyon Brown

Technical Editor
Jim Perry

Production Editor
Angela Smith

Copy Editor
Kim Cofer

Editorial Manager
Mary Beth Wakefield

Production Manager
Tim Tate

Vice President and Executive Group Publisher
Richard Swadley

Vice President and Executive Publisher
Joseph B. Wikert

Composition
Craig Johnson, Happenstance Type-O-Rama

Proofreading
Sossity Smith

Indexing
Johnna VanHoose Dinse

Anniversary Logo Design
Richard Pacifico

Contents

Contents

Contents

Contents

Contents

Acknowledgments

First and foremost I would like to thank my parents for not supporting me at first in my childhood to work with computers. Only in this way did I become insanely interested and motivated in programming even without knowing anyone else that even had a computer.

I want to thank Chris Webb for giving me the opportunity to become an author. I also want to thank Kenyon Brown, Jim Perry, and everyone else at Wiley. It was an absolute pleasure to work with all of you.

I would also like to thank my colleagues and friends supporting me in my game projects. Thanks to Enrico Ciesiek for helping me out with the chapters and thanks to Christoph Rienaecker for giving me so many cool 3D models for my games. Thanks also fly out to Boje Holtz, Leif Griga, and Manuel Nitschke for testing and feedback.

Without the hard work of the XNA team, and also the .NET, DirectX, and Xbox 360 teams at Microsoft this book would not have been possible. They are not only responsible for creating XNA, DirectX, .NET, and many other frameworks that made this book and the games in it as useful as they are, but they are also incredibly cool guys, who are easy to talk to and very supportive. I especially want to thank Christina Storm, Tom Miller, Mitch Walker, Dave Mitchell, Dirk Primbs, and Uwe Baumann at Microsoft.

Finally, I also want to thank my family and friends for supporting me throughout the time I wrote this book. They may be used to the fact that I sometimes do not sleep for a couple of days just focusing on my projects, but it might not have been easy for them during that time. In a way, this is my gift to all of you.

Introduction

Up until recently, the concept for the Xbox 360 as a platform for creating homebrew games was not even thinkable. For most people creating console games was just a pure impossibility, not just because SDKs are expensive, but because you won't even get one or access to any development information to create console games.

This has all changed. Microsoft's new XNA Framework makes homebrew cross-platform games for Windows and the Xbox 360 possible. XNA is not only just a new framework, but it is also the best framework available today to create games. With no other language or tool you will be able to create powerful games with little effort. You will see throughout this book why this statement is true when you take a look at all the great games it covers. I would never have been able to create a great game like the Racing Game in such a short time frame if it was not for XNA.

Who This Book Is For

This book is aimed at a variety of audiences. You should have knowledge of the programming language C#, but if you already know C++ or Java, it will be very easy to switch. If you have not worked with any high-level programming language before I suggest you pick up a C# book first. Even without knowledge of programming this book has many tips and tricks in it for upcoming game programmers, but for a more practical use of this book you should follow all examples and code right along. Most of the chapters are organized in a way that is equally useful to both beginners and experienced game programmers. All you need to write successful games is your willingness to learn the game programming techniques presented in this book and the desire to explore the world of computer games and keep improving over and over again.

What This Book Covers and How It's Structured

Part I, "XNA Framework Basics," covers the basics of XNA. You will learn all about the XNA Framework and XNA Game Studio Express. Even if you already know some of the basics there are many useful tips and tricks in the first chapter. The second chapter already explains the creation process of your first game; it is a simple one, but the lessons learned here will help you out later. In Chapters 3 and 4 two more games are created, but more importantly the foundation for your game engine is built.

Thanks to the many helper classes of Part I, writing the game engine in Part II, "Basic Graphics Engine," is much easier and can focus on the hard parts of getting 3D models and shaders to work. Because everything in XNA is based on shaders because there is no more fixed function rendering, most of the time is spent talking about shaders, normal mapping, post-screen effects, and more. At the end of Part II the Rocket Commander XNA game is shown as a great example of a game combining all the shaders and the game engine from the previous chapters.

Part III, "Improving Your Game Engine," goes back to the basics and talks about audio, UI, input handling, and managing your game engine in a meaningful way. Based on the XNA Graphics Engine and the Rocket Commander game you also create a new game called XNA Shooter, which is a really fun old-school shoot-'em-up game with cool 3D graphics and advanced shader effects.

In Part IV, "Writing a Racing Game," you pull in all the knowledge you've gained to create full-blown racing game in XNA. This part features the most advanced topics like landscape and 3D track rendering, creating and handling physics engines, and many new shader technologies like shadow mapping, detail mapping, and rendering in an optimized way for optimal performance.

If you are ready to begin learning XNA game development, I suggest reading on and start with Chapter 1, "Introducing XNA." Good luck creating your first XNA games and, above all, have fun! I hope you enjoy reading this book as much as I enjoyed writing it.

Source Code

As you work through the examples in this book, you may choose either to type in all the code manually or to use the source code files that accompany the book. All of the source code used in this book, including all the code to create a full racing game in XNA, is available for download at http://www.wrox.com. Once at the site, simply locate the book's title (either by using the Search box or by using one of the title lists) and click the Download Code link on the book's detail page to obtain all the source code for the book.

> *Because many books have similar titles, you may find it easiest to search by ISBN; this book's ISBN is 978-0-470-12677-6.*

Once you download the code, just decompress it with your favorite compression tool. Alternatively, you can go to the main Wrox code download page at http://www.wrox.com/dynamic/books/download.aspx to see the code available for this book and all other Wrox books.

Errata

We make every effort to ensure that there are no errors in the text or in the code. However, no one is perfect, and mistakes do occur. If you find an error in one of our books, like a spelling mistake or faulty piece of code, we would be very grateful for your feedback. By sending in errata you may save another reader hours of frustration and at the same time you will be helping us provide even higher quality information.

To find the errata page for this book, go to http://www.wrox.com and locate the title using the Search box or one of the title lists. Then, on the book details page, click the Book Errata link. On this page you can view all errata that has been submitted for this book and posted by Wrox editors. A complete book list including links to each book's errata is also available at www.wrox.com/misc-pages/booklist.shtml.

If you don't spot "your" error on the Book Errata page, go to www.wrox.com/contact/techsupport.shtml and complete the form there to send us the error you have found. We'll check the information and, if appropriate, post a message to the book's errata page and fix the problem in subsequent editions of the book.

p2p.wrox.com

For author and peer discussion, join the P2P forums at p2p.wrox.com. The forums are a Web-based system for you to post messages relating to Wrox books and related technologies and interact with other readers and technology users. The forums offer a subscription feature to e-mail you topics of interest of your choosing when new posts are made to the forums. Wrox authors, editors, other industry experts, and your fellow readers are present on these forums.

At http://p2p.wrox.com you will find a number of different forums that will help you not only as you read this book, but also as you develop your own applications. To join the forums, just follow these steps:

1. Go to p2p.wrox.com and click the Register link.

2. Read the terms of use and click Agree.

3. Complete the required information to join as well as any optional information you wish to provide and click Submit.

4. You will receive an e-mail with information describing how to verify your account and complete the joining process.

    You can read messages in the forums without joining P2P but in order to post your own messages, you must join.

Once you join, you can post new messages and respond to messages other users post. You can read messages at any time on the Web. If you would like to have new messages from a particular forum e-mailed to you, click the Subscribe to this Forum icon by the forum name in the forum listing.

For more information about how to use the Wrox P2P, be sure to read the P2P FAQs for answers to questions about how the forum software works as well as many common questions specific to P2P and Wrox books. To read the FAQs, click the FAQ link on any P2P page.

Part I: XNA Framework Basics

Introducing XNA

Welcome to the world of XNA. As a game programmer you probably know about DirectX and maybe even the basics of the XNA Framework. This chapter explains how to install XNA Game Studio Express and how to use it in a productive way. It also contains quite a lot of tips that might even be useful for anyone who already knows the basics.

In the next few chapters you will directly start developing some cool smaller games. This section contains the basic foundation and helper classes you will use later in this book to develop a full-blown graphics engine for more advanced game projects. To keep things simple you start with 2D programming in Part I and then advance to 3D in Part II.

Let's get started.

Introduction to the XNA Framework

XNA is developed by Microsoft and was started a few years ago, but kept very secret. At the GDC (annually biggest Game Developers Conference) in 2004 Microsoft announced XNA for the first time. XNA is not just a framework like DirectX; it also contains a lot of tools and even a custom IDE derived from Visual Studio to make the game programmer's life easier. Because no tools or bits were released until 2006, DirectX developers only noticed the "XNA" logo in the upper-right corner of the DirectX SDK documentation from 2004 to 2006 (see Figure 1-1). (XNA just means "XNAs Not Acronymed.")

Figure 1-1

This means Microsoft was working on the XNA Framework for quite a while, but the developers did not really know what to expect. It could be a successor of the DirectX Framework, but when Direct3D 10 Beta for Windows Vista was released in the end of 2005, it seemed that DirectX was still the preferred graphics framework even for this new operating system. Then early in 2006 at the GDC the Microsoft XNA Build March 2006 CTP was released. XNA Build is a tool that allows you to manage complex build processes, similar to Msbuild and tools like Ants, but more complex and powerful. Because Microsoft's MechCommander 2 was also released as a Shared Source Release, a lot of people downloaded it and tried to rebuild the MechCommander 2 game. But after a while not much happened, and especially small to mid-sized teams don't really need a complex build management tool.

Then it was quiet for a while and only Microsoft personnel and DirectX MVPs (luckily I am one) got to know about the upcoming XNA Framework and XNA Game Studio releases. The rest of the world found out about that at the Gamefest conference in August (a new game developer conference by Microsoft), where Microsoft announced the XNA Game Studio Express beta 1 release on August 30, 2006. The first beta only contained one starter kit, "Space Wars," and XNA did not include much 3D functionality. Many developers and hobbyists tried out XNA and wrote many small 2D games with the help of the Sprite classes in XNA. Although you could quickly create your Pong clone or some simple shoot-'em-up game, it was very hard to write your own 3D model importer and render code.

XNA Game Studio Express was initially targeted at beginners, hobbyists, and students to allow them to quickly develop their own games for the Windows and Xbox 360 platform. But this does not mean professional game studios cannot use XNA yet. A special XNA Game Studio Professional version targeted to professional game studios will be released in the summer of 2007, but if you want to start developing in Visual Studio 2005 Professional, follow the tricks I describe later in this chapter on how to work with VS and XNA productively.

Gladly, Microsoft released another beta a few months later in November 2006 before the final release of XNA Game Studio Express happened in December 2006, which includes the content pipeline and many new features you will learn about in Chapters 2 and 3.

XNA is completely free and allows developers to create games for both the Windows platform and for the Xbox 360 platform simultaneously for the first time. But if you want to run your XNA game on the Xbox 360 console you have to join the "Creators Club" for an annual fee of $99.

XNA Game Studio Express

Figure 1-2 shows you XNA Game Studio Express. You learn how to install it in a second.

The screen does not only look similar to Visual C# 2005 Express, it actually is just that. There are only some minor changes to your project settings if you create an XNA project. There is also an extra option in Tools ➪ Options, which allows you to select your Xbox 360 device and enter the encryption key. Additionally, there are some new features inside the IDE; for example, the content pipeline that allows you to import textures, models, and shaders very quickly into your project. More about all that in a little bit.

Figure 1-2

XNA Game Studio Express is currently the only available IDE for developing games with the XNA Framework, but Microsoft will ship XNA Game Studio Pro sometime in 2007 (summer or later). XNA Game Studio Professional will be based on the Visual Studio 2005 Professional Edition and allows you to use all Visual Studio plugins and features. If you own Visual Studio 2005 and try to create an XNA project, there will be no templates in it. Even worse: If you try to open a .csproj file you created with XNA Game Studio Express, Visual Studio cannot open the project. It is not supported. Read on for a few tips on how to get XNA working with Visual Studio 2005 in the section "What about Visual Studio 2005 Professional?"

Microsoft also mentions another version of the XNA IDE called just XNA Studio, which is based on the Visual Studio Team System version and is targeted to large AAA studios. Read more about the XNA Framework at http://msdn.microsoft.com/directx/xna/faq.

Application Model

The XNA Framework is divided into three essential parts (see Figure 1-3):

❑   **XNA Graphic Engine** in the Microsoft.Xna.Framework.dll

❑   **XNA Game Application Model** in the Microsoft.Xna.Framework.Game.dll

❑   **XNA Content Pipeline** in the Microsoft.Xna.Framework.Content.Pipeline.dlls

Figure 1-3

All of these dlls are written in C# and are completely managed dlls. This means you can open them up with a tool like Reflection (get it from http://www.aisto.com/roeder/dotnet/) and see directly how they work (see Figure 1-4). Most internal functionality just calls to the DirectX dlls and simplifies things a little bit. The content pipeline is discussed in a little bit.

Figure 1-4

Take a look at the Application Model. Each XNA project uses a `Game` class, which contains all the important game components, the graphic device, the window settings, and the content manager. You can also add the input and sound handling here. Basically everything that your game does on a very high level somehow roots in the game class or at least is in some component that can be accessed from the game class.

The following are the three most important methods in the game class (see Figure 1-5). For the final release Microsoft also added the `LoadGraphicsContent` and `UnloadGraphicsContent` helper methods by default to the `Game1.cs` class, which is created automatically for you when you create a new XNA project, but these methods will never be used in this book because it is much simpler to have all initialization and loading code at one place in the `Initialize` function.

- ❑   `Initialize ()`
- ❑   `Update (GameTime time)`
- ❑   `Draw (GameTime time)`

Figure 1-5

You can probably already guess what all these do. `Initialize` loads all your game content, sets all your startup settings, and initializes everything you need. If you want to follow the design patterns Microsoft provides for XNA you would do all the loading in the `LoadGraphicsContent` method. `Update` is called before each frame is drawn to update your game time, input, sound, and everything else that is not visible on the screen. If your game is GPU limited it can very well happen that `Update` is called more often than `Draw`, but your update code should run separate from the drawing code anyway and none of the samples in this book will need special care for the number of times `Update` and `Draw` are called. And finally, `Draw` is called each frame to draw everything to the screen. The separation of `Update` and `Draw` might not always be important and can almost always be ignored for unit tests, but for the final game it is quite important to make sure the game logic runs independent of the draw code. For example, on the Windows platform the user could press Alt and Tab or minimize the game, in which case `Draw` does not need to be called anymore, but maybe you want the game to continue to run in the background. This is especially important for network games to make sure the player is still synchronized.

Additionally, you can add `GameComponent` classes to your game class, which again have an `Update` and a `Draw` method. Both these methods are automatically called from your game `Update` and `Draw` methods. The initialization can happen directly in the constructor there. Initially Microsoft wanted the developers to create and add game components with the designer of Visual Studio, which can be seen in the first beta of XNA Game Studio Express (30 August, 2006). The designer feature was later removed because it did not work well, was not supported for the Xbox 360 platform, and not many developers used it anyway.

The idea with the game components is to reuse parts of your code and make it very easy to just plug them into your games. Examples would be a frame counter or maybe a sky cube mapping renderer for the 3D background. In my opinion there are two major drawbacks: No standard game components are shipped with XNA, and it is not really hard to code such an application model yourself and even extend it. I will not use many `GameComponent` classes in this book, but feel free to plug them in on your own. Read Chapter 4 for more details of the `GameComponent` class and learn about its advantages and disadvantages. Because the game class has a `Components` property, it is very easy to add more components.

Don't get me wrong, the basic idea of game components is really great; there was a small webcast from Mitch Walker, the Program Manager of the XNA Framework at Microsoft, at the time the first XNA beta was released about the game components and how to combine them. At first I was not very sure what to think of the content pipeline and the game components idea; it looked cool in the webcasts, but when I started coding my first game projects in XNA I did not find it very useful to work with the designer that was presented in the first beta. In the second beta and the final release, most of the initial game component code was removed as well as the graphical designer component in XNA Game Studio. This happened because Microsoft was not able to find a way to implement the designer and game components idea in a useful way for the Xbox 360 console (it only worked on the Windows platform before). This just confirmed my first feeling that the game component idea is not very useful and may even limit you in certain respects, like having to worry about the drawing yourself (see Chapter 4 for more details).

This is similar to the fact that every game implements its own UI and menu logic, which is quite a hassle. But if you think about it, just some standard menu system like Windows uses for every app is very boring and it is always a nice experience to see a new way in which menus are created in every game. You can still extract code very easily and create your own game components if you want to create a new game, and then you can just reuse the code (for example, the `SkyCubeMapping` class). Some game components like the camera and screenshot capturer classes from Chapter 4 are good examples for components that can be reused in many other games, but almost everything else in the games from this book is implemented without using game components.

One of the hopes Microsoft has with this application model is that the community of game developers can create and share their game components quite easily and improve the community aspect of XNA. For more information you can check out the eXperience project on `www.codeplex.com`.

Content Pipeline

The content pipeline is used to import, compile, and load game assets like textures, 3D models, shaders, and sound files to your game project (see Figure 1-6). It greatly reduces the amount of custom code you have to do to get graphics, 3D data, and shaders into your game. For example, if you drop a model file into your project and it uses two textures and a specific shader, the content pipeline will process your model file and automatically find and add the required textures and shaders. You don't have to do this for yourself; the content importer "compiles" the data into a binary format and in the process it picks up everything you need.

Say the shader you added through the model you dropped into your project contains an error. In the past you would have to start your game project, and then get an exception telling you that the shader could not be compiled and the game would crash. Now the shader is compiled in the build process and you don't have to start your game to see that it does not work yet. You can quickly fix the error through the line and error message from the build output in XNA Game Studio Express and then rebuild.

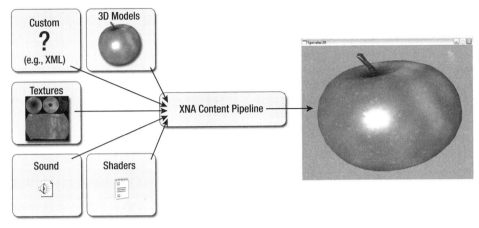

Figure 1-6

The content pipeline does not just consist of one dll; there are five different dlls:

❑ **Microsoft.Xna.Framework.Content.Pipeline.dll** contains the basic functions for the content pipeline.

❑ **Microsoft.Xna.Framework.Content.Pipeline.EffectImporter.dll** is used to compile and import shaders.

❑ **Microsoft.Xna.Framework.Content.Pipeline.FBXImporter.dll** is the biggest of all dlls and contains a lot of code to import .fbx 3D model files and supports many features, for example skinning and bones.

❑ **Microsoft.Xna.Framework.Content.Pipeline.TextureImporter.dll** is used to import texture files to your game. These files can be dds files already in the DirectX format (which is the best format for textures and supports hardware compression), but .png, .jpg, .bmp, and .tga files are also supported. 2D sprites are just textures too and usually use the uncompressed 32-bit format.

❑ **Microsoft.Xna.Framework.Content.Pipeline.XImporter.dll** allows you to import .x 3D model files, a format that was used by many DirectX applications and samples.

Your game itself will never require any of these dlls; they are just used to build and compile the content into .xnb (XNA Binary) files in your build process. This makes the distribution easier because you don't have to worry about the game content files anymore; it is easier to make sure all the content files are there when you start your game. Don't modify the .xnb files, they are just the output format like .exe files and should not be modified directly. The data can also not be converted back to textures, models, or shaders (well it might be possible, but there are no tools for that). The .xnb files are also very different on the Windows platform and the Xbox 360 platform, whereas the game source code and the content files might be exactly the same.

Additionally you can create your own custom content processors, which allow you to compile any other game asset you have (for example, another model format) into .xnb files. You explore that in Part II when you have to make sure all your 3D models have tangent data for the normal mapping shaders.

Ok, that's all the basics you need for now. It is time to get going and code your first game.

Get the Free XNA Game Studio Express

To start coding right away you have to make sure that you have the correct tools installed, the IDE is an especially important tool to get started quickly. If you already have XNA Game Studio Express installed and configured you can skip this chapter. This part was written just in case anyone needs additional tips and tricks. For example, how to get XNA running in Visual Studio 2005 Professional is covered here, which is not supported out of the box, but quite useful if you use Visual Studio plugins or tools like SourceSafe (to work better in a team, for example).

Requirements

XNA Game Studio Express targets just Windows XP SP2 (SP means Service Pack) at the time of this writing. SP2 is important because of the requirements of the .NET 2.0 Framework. Other platforms like Windows 2003 or Windows Vista run .NET 2.0 too, but are not supported. XNA is also only tested on 32-bit platforms, but I tested it on Windows XP x64 and Windows Vista too and it runs fine, even as a development platform.

Because XNA Game Studio Express is based on Visual C# Express it has the same basic requirements. You basically need a computer, nothing fancy. But for game development you have much higher basic requirements anyway, which I talk about in a second. Visual C# Express runs on Windows 2000 SP4, Windows XP SP2, Windows 2003 SP1, Windows XP x64, and Windows Vista. As you can see the older the operating system is, the more service packs you need.

And finally you also need the most current DirectX runtimes, and if you are serious about game development, better get the full DirectX SDK. The DirectX SDK is not required by XNA Game Studio Express because the dlls just call the underlying DirectX dlls, but it is always useful to have some more documentation on your system and DirectX contains many samples and tutorials, which are useful if you run into trouble. For example, the DirectX SDK contains tools to help you generate DDS texture files, which are optimized for the best graphic card texture formats that are available today.

Because XNA does not support the fixed function pipeline anymore like DirectX or Managed DirectX do, it is important that you have a graphic card that supports at least Shader Model 1.1 or even better, Shader Model 2.0. The first graphic cards with shader support were shipped back in 2001 (GeForce 3 and ATI 7000); the next generation with Shader Model 2.0 (GeForce 5x, ATI 9x00 Series) was introduced in 2003 and made popular by the many games in 2004 that made good use of shaders (Far Cry, Doom 3, Half-Life 2). Shader Model 3.0 (GeForce 6x, ATI x1000 Series) is the standard today and new cards with Shader Model 4.0 (GeForce 8x) will be shipped late 2006/early 2007. The Xbox 360 uses an extended version of Shader Model 3.0.

So this is what you need at minimum before attempting to install XNA Game Studio Express:

- ❑ **Windows XP SP2** or Windows Vista
- ❑ **512 MB Ram**, but better to have more — 1 or 2 GB
- ❑ **1 GHz CPU**, the faster the better, compiling gets faster
- ❑ **Shader Model 1.1 graphic card** (Nvidia GeForce 3 or 4, ATI Radeon 7x) or better Shader Model 2.0

Installing

Get the latest version of XNA Game Studio Express for free at `http://msdn.microsoft.com/directx/xna/`.

The beta versions still require that you install Visual C# Express and the latest version of DirectX 9.0c first; this will most likely still be the fact when the final version is shipped. All of these downloads are completely free and it is really a nice thing to have all these tools available without any costs involved. This enables many more people, especially students, hobbyists, and normal players, to check out the development environment and maybe get even more excited about game development than they already are.

If you want a step-by-step introduction to the install process and see which steps I took you can also watch the video tutorials I made for my the official XNA Starter Kit Racing Game on `http://www.xnaracinggame.com`.

Start with installing XNA Game Studio Express (see Figure 1-7). There are no special options you have to select; the installer will do everything for you (for example, adding firewall rules for Xbox 360 testing). The installer also adds the XNA help, the starter kits, and the project templates to get you started.

Figure 1-7

You will not really need the DirectX SDK, but as suggested before it is recommended to install it anyway. You will have additional documentation available and a great repertoire of tutorials and samples in case you need more information about common techniques for your graphic engine.

You can download DirectX from the Microsoft DirectX Developer Center page on `http://msdn.microsoft.com/directx/`.

When installing it you should select installing the Redistributable in the custom setup step too. You will need it if you want to install your game on other computers. When DirectX is installed you can check out the newest features by taking a look at the samples with the DirectX Sample Browser. If you haven't worked much with Managed DirectX before and are interested, check out the documentation and tutorials.

If you want to use an Xbox 360 controller on your Windows machine (which works just fine thanks to the fact that the controller uses USB) you can just plug it into your PC and it should work fine on Windows XP and Vista after it automatically installs all required drivers. If that does not work automatically for you can also download the drivers yourself and follow the instructions from the official hardware site of Microsoft products at http://www.microsoft.com/hardware/gaming/download.mspx.

Last but not least, you will do a lot of unit testing in this book, and for that I usually recommend NUnit and TestDriven.NET, but because NUnit is an external dll and TestDriven.NET is not supported in the Express Editions anymore, you will implement your own kind of unit testing with a special class later on.

If you use Visual Studio 2005 I suggest using TestDriven.NET, and if you are using Visual Studio 2005 Team System you can also use the Unit Testing features implemented directly in VS there. Alternatively there are also other Unit Testing Frameworks around (for example, MbUnit, csUnit, and so on). Most of the samples in this book try to keep things simple and only use very basic features of unit testing and make it look like many little test programs.

You can certainly do all your work inside the XNA Game Studio Express IDE, and Microsoft encourages you to do so. All samples in this book work fine with the Express editions and I did not use any external dlls (which was also one of the requirements for the XNA Starter Kits). However, some people already have Visual Studio 2005 and may feel more comfortable doing their coding over there. Read on for a couple of tricks on how to get XNA working with Visual Studio 2005 Professional.

What about Visual Studio 2005 Professional?

XNA Game Studio Express is fine and a nice environment to work in. However, if you are used to tools like SourceSafe or any other CMS (Content Management System) or plugins like CodeRush, TestDriven.NET, and other productivity tools, you will run into a bunch of problems. As I said earlier it is not even possible to open your XNA projects from Visual Studio 2005.

The XNA Framework uses the .NET 2.0 Framework and DirectX 9.0c. This means to run games on any Windows PC, it needs the .NET 2.0 Framework, DirectX 9.0c, and the XNA dlls. If you are a game developer you will have the latest DirectX SDK anyway and if you have Visual Studio 2005, you will have the .NET 2.0 Framework too, so the only thing you need for running and even compiling XNA applications are the two XNA dlls:

❑   Microsoft.Xna.Framework.dll

❑   Microsoft.Xna.Framework.Game.dll

These dlls are referenced in all XNA projects, so if you just add them to a project in Visual Studio 2005, you can directly start coding. To get started just copy over the Game1.cs and Program.cs files from an empty XNA project you created with XNA Game Studio Express.

Another problem could arise if you work on a 64-bit operating system like Windows XP x64 or Windows Vista x64. Though DirectX 9.0c has had 64-bit dlls for some time now and the .NET Framework runs fine on 64 bit too, the problem lies in the XNA Framework, which is only available in a 32-bit version (called x86, by the way). People using the 64-bit operating systems of Windows had the same problem in the past with Managed DirectX, which is only available for 32 bit too. Using a 64-bit operating system does not mean you cannot use 32-bit applications anymore; quite the contrary. Almost all applications that exist today are written for 32-bit operating systems, but they run fine in the 32-bit mode of Windows XP x64 or Windows Vista x64.

Why do I even bring this up if you can run 32-bit and 64-bit applications on 64-bit operating systems? Well, you cannot use 64-bit assemblies (dlls) from 32-bit applications or vice versa. The reason for that is that a Windows process has to be run either in 64 bit or 32 bit; emulating 32 bit from 64 bit would be too slow and is not even supported. Now how do you get XNA working in 64-bit mode? You don't, it is just not supported. Instead you have to make sure that the .NET Framework and your application run in 32-bit mode, then Windows will start the whole process in 32-bit mode and you can load the XNA dlls just fine. If you don't do that your game cannot even be started on any x64-bit platform.

In Visual Studio 2005 you can just select "x86" platform instead of "All CPUs" in the Project ⇨ Properties ⇨ Build screen. In XNA Game Studio Express there is no such option and if you want the same setting you have to add a line to your .csproj file in each PropertyGroup section:

```
<PlatformTarget>x86</PlatformTarget>
```

I also wrote a little tool that converts XNA Game Studio Express projects to Visual Studio 2005 projects and back, and it also handles the x64 bit issue. You can download it on my blog at http://abi.exdream.com.

Configuring Your Xbox 360

To connect your Xbox 360 to your PC you have to install the XNA Framework on your Xbox 360 first via the Xbox Live Service. Unlike the Windows platform the download of the XNA Framework for the Xbox 360 is not free. You will have to join the "Creator's Club" subscription on the Xbox 360 through the Xbox Live Marketplace for $99 a year or $49 for four months. Microsoft does this to have a little control over the developers. Console development is usually very closed off and there is no open source thinking like in the Windows or Linux world. We can all just hope this is going to change.

First of all make sure your PC and the Xbox 360 are connected to the same network. You don't have to connect the Xbox 360 directly to your PC; just plug it into the same network (router or modem). It is important that you always have access to the Internet from the console and not just to your PC because XNA requires an Xbox Live connection on your console. Once you have installed the XNA Framework on the Xbox 360, which also includes a custom version of the .NET 2.0 Compact Framework to make it run on the console, you can start the XNA Game Launcher (see Figure 1-8).

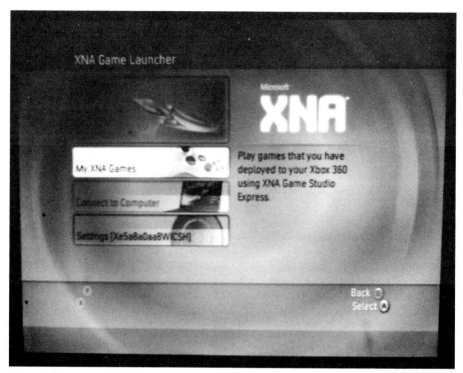

Figure 1-8

In the XNA Game Launcher you can now start your game projects or copy over XNA games from your friends or the Internet and start them on your console. Before you can connect to the PC you will have to make an encryption key first by clicking Settings and then "Create Encryption Key." You will now see the encryption key; don't close this window. On your PC open up XNA Game Studio Express and go to Tools ⇨ Options and scroll down. You will see the new XNA Game Studio option. Here you can add your Xbox 360 and enter your encryption key, and just click Add (see Figure 1-9).

Figure 1-9

After you have successfully entered the encryption key, you can click OK on both the PC and the console. If this failed or you reinstall XNA Game Studio, you can always get a new encryption key and enter it again here.

From now on you can create Xbox 360 projects and deploy them to your console, which can be done in the XNA Studio build menu. If you start to debug a project with F5 it will get deployed too and you can directly debug it on your console, which is pretty cool because you can step through code on your PC and immediately see the results on your Xbox 360 (kind of multi-monitor developing for free). Read more about running your first game in Chapter 2.

Getting Started

You have everything set up now and it is time to finally do some coding and get your hands dirty. In this chapter you will just create a simple project with the help of the XNA Studio templates. Then you will change the code a little and add a little functionality to the `Update` and `Draw` methods. In the next chapter you will create your first game after you learn about the `SpriteBatch` class.

Your First Project

Create a new XNA project in XNA Studio by clicking File ➪ New Project. Now select Windows Game and enter a name for your first project — for example, "Hello World" — or just leave it as "WindowsGame1" (see Figure 1-10). As you can see you can also create games based on the starter kits quite easily from here too.

Figure 1-10

You can see now that a new project was created and it contains two source files: Game1.cs and Program.cs. The Program file basically just contains the following three lines of code:

```
using (Game1 game = new Game1())
{
..game.Run();
} // using
```

The Game1 class contains the Initialize, Update, and Draw methods mentioned a little bit earlier. Initialize does nothing for now and Update just checks if the back button on the first connected gamepad was pressed.

For now you are just interested in the Draw method, which basically just executes the following line to clear the background to a specific color:

```
graphics.GraphicsDevice.Clear(Color.CornflowerBlue);
```

F5 and Go

If you press F5, the project starts (same as Debug ⇨ Start Debugging) and you see the screen shown in Figure 1-11, which shows the blue color that is specified in the Draw method.

Figure 1-11

To feel like you are actually doing something, change the Color to Color.Green and press F5 again. The window now has a green background. The Clear method of the graphics device has other overloads that can be used to clear the depth and stencil buffers, which will be done automatically if you just set the color. For example, later in this book you will just need to clear the depth buffer, but not the color of the background. To do that you just write the following line:

```
graphics.GraphicsDevice.Clear(ClearOptions.DepthBuffer,
   Color.Green, 1, 0);
```

By default the ClearOptions are set to ClearOptions.Target | ClearOptions.DepthBuffer, which means both the background color and the depth buffer are cleared. By the way, if you don't know it already the | operator between the ClearOptions flags will combine both settings.

Changing the Code

Ok, instead of giving up here, think about some ways you can modify the code in a useful manner. First of all you should be able to quit your program by pressing Escape. By default XNA just adds the following lines to the Update method, which quits the program when the Xbox 360 controller's back button is being pressed:

```
// Allows the default game to exit on Xbox 360 and Windows
if (GamePad.GetState(PlayerIndex.One).Buttons.Back ==
ButtonState.Pressed)
   this.Exit();
```

To learn more about the Input classes go to Chapter 3, "Helper Classes." For now you will just use a quick and dirty way to access the keyboard. If you modify the code in the following way you can also press Escape now to quit the application:

```
// Get current gamepad and keyboard states
GamePadState gamePad = GamePad.GetState(PlayerIndex.One);
KeyboardState keyboard = Keyboard.GetState();
// Back or Escape exits our game on Xbox 360 and Windows
if (gamePad.Buttons.Back == ButtonState.Pressed ||
   keyboard.IsKeyDown(Keys.Escape))
   this.Exit();
```

As you can see you put the gamepad and keyboard states in extra variables to have easier access. If you press F5 again, you can quit the game with Escape now.

Next you are going to jump a little bit ahead and load a graphic into your game. More details about sprites are discussed in Chapter 2. The idea is to display a small background texture and tile it over the whole screen. Then you implement some simple keyboard and gamepad controls to move the background like in a top-down racing game or a tile engine, which is often used in 2D role playing games. For a more complex tile engine you would need more textures like stones, grass, water, mud, and so on, and then even transition textures you can put between grass and water, for example. This would require a little bit more textures and custom code, but overall this is not a very hard topic. You can also find a lot of information about this topic on the Internet if you are really interested in tile engines.

For your simple first project you just add the texture shown in Figure 1-12.

Figure 1-12

To load this texture (`CityGroundSmall.jpg`) into your game, just drag it into your project on the Solution Explorer. Then click the file in the project and select Properties. You should now see the screen shown in Figure 1-13.

Figure 1-13

Normally you would just see the build action and some options for copying the content file to the output directory (e.g. if you want to include a .dll or .xml file). But if XNA Studio detects one of the supported content file formats, you will see the advanced XNA properties. There are three important new settings: Asset Name, Content Importer, and Content Processor. The Asset Name is used to load the content later; each content file must have a unique Asset Name. For the Content Importer you can select a Texture as in this case or a Model Importer for .x files or an Effect Importer for .fx files.

The Content Processor contains more options; for example, you could select DXT, DXT mip-mapped, or Sprite 32bpp for your texture here. DXT is a compression format, which is also used in dds files and it is very good for textures in games because they get compressed down in a 1:6 ratio (or 1:4 if they contain transparent pixels). This means you can have up to six times as many textures for the same space on the hard disk and graphic memory. For 2D sprites it is usually better not to compress them because you see them in their full size, and using 32bpp (bits per pixel) guarantees the best possible sprite quality. For more information about the content pipeline read the next part of this chapter.

If you press F5 or build the project (F6) the content is processed and a new file, CityGroundSmall.xnb, will be created in your output directory. The build output window also shows the following new line:

```
Building CityGroundSmall.jpg -> bin\x86\Debug\CityGroundSmall.xnb
```

The final thing you have to do now is to load the imported texture. You will do that in the Initialize method and use a new variable backgroundTexture in your class. To load the texture you use the asset name you specified earlier (it was actually generated automatically from the filename of the file you dragged into your project). To render the texture on the screen you need a SpriteBatch, which is discussed in the next chapter. Basically it sets up the alpha blending, then draws textures into the sprite and finally draws everything on the screen:

```
Texture2D backgroundTexture;
SpriteBatch sprites;
protected override void Initialize()
{
  backgroundTexture = content.Load<Texture2D>("CityGroundSmall");
  sprites = new SpriteBatch(graphics.GraphicsDevice);
  base.Initialize();
} // Initialize()
```

To display the background texture you have to start the sprite batch and render the texture to your sprites in the Draw method:

```
protected override void Draw(GameTime gameTime)
{
  graphics.GraphicsDevice.Clear(Color.Green);

  sprites.Begin();
  sprites.Draw(backgroundTexture, Vector2.Zero, Color.White);
  sprites.End();
  base.Draw(gameTime);
} // Draw(gameTime)
```

This renders the background texture at the location (0, 0) on top of your green background. With the color parameter you can also recolor a sprite, but for now this is not important.

If you press F5 you will now see the result shown in Figure 1-14.

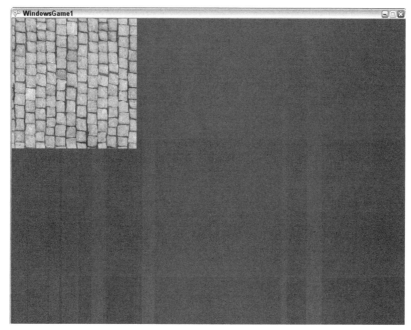

Figure 1-14

One final thing you are going to add for this first project is the ability to scroll the background with the cursor keys or a gamepad and then you render the scrollable tiles to the whole background. To capture the gamepad and keyboard input you modify the Update method a little:

```
float scrollPosition = 0;
protected override void Update(GameTime gameTime)
{
    // Get current gamepad and keyboard states
    GamePadState gamePad = GamePad.GetState(PlayerIndex.One);
    KeyboardState keyboard = Keyboard.GetState();
    // Back or Escape exits our game on Xbox 360 and Windows
    if (gamePad.Buttons.Back == ButtonState.Pressed ||
        keyboard.IsKeyDown(Keys.Escape))
        this.Exit();
    // Move 400 pixels each second
    float moveFactorPerSecond = 400 *
    (float)gameTime.ElapsedRealTime.TotalMilliseconds / 1000.0f;
    // Move up and down if we press the cursor or gamepad keys.
    if (gamePad.DPad.Up == ButtonState.Pressed ||
        keyboard.IsKeyDown(Keys.Up))
        scrollPosition += moveFactorPerSecond;
    if (gamePad.DPad.Down == ButtonState.Pressed ||
        keyboard.IsKeyDown(Keys.Down))
        scrollPosition -= moveFactorPerSecond;
    base.Update(gameTime);
} // Update(gameTime)
```

The first few lines are the same as before. Then you calculate how many pixels you would move this frame. If a frame would take 1 second, moveFactorPerSecond would be 400; for 60 frames it would be 400/60. Because you use floats here instead of just integers you can have a couple of thousand frames and the movement is still 400 pixels per frame if you press up or down.

The variable scrollPosition is changed if the user presses up or down. In your draw method you can now render each tile and add the scrollPosition to the y position to move the background up and down:

```
protected override void Draw(GameTime gameTime)
{
  graphics.GraphicsDevice.Clear(Color.Green);

  sprites.Begin();
  int resolutionWidth = graphics.GraphicsDevice.Viewport.Width;
  int resolutionHeight = graphics.GraphicsDevice.Viewport.Height;
  for (int x = 0; x <= resolutionWidth / backgroundTexture.Width;
    x++)
  for (int y = -1; y <= resolutionHeight / backgroundTexture.Height;
    y++)
  {
    Vector2 position = new Vector2(
      x * backgroundTexture.Width,
      y * backgroundTexture.Height +
      ((int)scrollPosition) % backgroundTexture.Height);
    sprites.Draw(backgroundTexture, position, Color.White);
  } // for for
  sprites.End();
  base.Draw(gameTime);
} // Draw(gameTime)
```

Now you can start your project and move around with up and down. This is pretty good for your first little application, isn't it?

Notes about XNA

To finish this chapter, here are some additional tips and tricks about the XNA Framework and XNA Game Studio Express. As you saw, you can just start coding and it works great, but it is always good to have a couple of bookmarks for your browser you can rely on when you run into problems or don't know how to solve a specific issue. Additionally, this section discusses the advantages of .NET and C# a little and checks out the differences between XNA and Managed DirectX.

Important Links

Just a couple of links for your bookmarks:

❑   **http://msdn.microsoft.com/directx/xna/** — XNA Developer Center on Microsoft's MSDN page with the XNA Game Studio Forum and the XNA Framework Forum, which are the most active XNA forums you will find on the Internet. You can also download the latest XNA version here, read the FAQ, and see what's new.

❏ **http://en.wikipedia.org/wiki/Microsoft_XNA** — Entry on Wikipedia about XNA, constantly updated and contains many links to other topics. On the bottom of the page a few useful external links are listed.

❏ **http://xnadevelopment.com** — Nice new site with many links, tutorials, and tips to get you started in the XNA world.

❏ **http://xnaresources.com** — Another new site with lots of news and some really useful tutorials on tile engines. Also contains a lot of game components you might like.

❏ **http://learnxna.com** — XNA news site in form of a blog, also contains some video tutorials and focuses on learning XNA and tips and tricks with graphic tools.

❏ **http://abi.exdream.com** — Official website of the author. You can find more games I made here, as well as Rocket Commander XNA, the XNA Shooter, or the Racing Game from this book, and all the documentation and video tutorials I made for them. Additionally I suggest checking out the Rocket Commander Video Tutorials, which were pretty popular on Coding4Fun.

Is C# Good for Game Development?

There are constantly forum threads on sites like `www.GameDev.net` discussing the differences between C++ and C#. Usually after a few posts they all end in a senseless language war. Back in the early days of .NET (2002) I discussed quite a lot in those threads, but it was way too depressing when 99.9% of the programmers were on the C++ side and there was no way to convince anyone because they didn't even take you seriously. The language war does not really have anything to do with C# as a language, except it might have some bad taste because Java failed as a game programming platform except for cell phone games, because both Java and C# are managed languages and look very similar. But if you think about it the same kind of wars happened in the days when C replaced Assembler and C++ replaced C. Even to this day, more than 20 years after C++ was developed by *Bjarne Stroustrup*, some game programmers still use C and do not really take full advantage of C++. Even if you take a look at the source code for popular game engines like Quake or Half-Life it looks more like C than C++.

This is something really strange in the game programming world; everyone is afraid of losing too much performance by switching to a new language, and additionally might also lose their old code base or have a lot of work converting it to a new language. However, game programmers quickly adopt new techniques and scripting languages, and are always on the very latest hardware developments. One year before Shader Model 4 cards are even available we game developers had Direct3D 10 available and many people checked this out without even having the hardware to run it.

I adopted .NET and C# pretty quickly in the beginning of 2002 after checking out the early betas at the end of 2001. I just started a new game engine and our team had a new project we wanted to do. There were absolutely no graphic engines or anything but some simple 2D games around in the early years of .NET. This made it very hard to use OpenGL or DirectX directly in C#. It required a lot of calls to unmanaged dlls and involved a lot of nasty pointer logic, which is only available in the unsafe mode of C#. In 2003 Microsoft finally released the first beta of Managed DirectX, which made it possible to program new DirectX applications quite easily in .NET. It proved that using Managed DirectX instead of the native DirectX dlls has only a performance impact of 1%–2%, which is really not important if you think about it (just the CPU has a little more work; most games are GPU bound anyway).

However, this did not mean that game developers were jumping on C#; everyone was still very skeptical and even after I released the first commercial .NET game ever, *Arena Wars*, in 2004, it took another year until more and more developers finally gave .NET another chance. Students and beginners especially really appreciate the simplicity of C#, and more and more people started to develop games in .NET. C++ versus C# discussions still exist and the discussion points are still the same, but the result is more balanced right now (I stopped looking at any topic that has "vs" in the name a long time ago; it is just a waste of time reading the same arguments over and over again).

Always remember this when you run into guys that might tell you C++ is superior and that C# is only for newbies. The same thing happened with Assembler and C++ few years ago, and in the future there will be new languages that make our life easier and there will still be people hesitant to adopt them right away. Most big game studios also can't just adopt every new technology right away; they might be in the middle of some big project and they also have a very big code base, which is not easy to port. In the long run, however, code will get converted and we will move up the ladder of high-level languages.

Figure 1-15 is an old picture I did to show the differences between DirectX with C++ and Managed DirectX in C#. As you can see, MDX code can be half the size of unmanaged code. For XNA the code would even be shorter and it gets much easier to load textures and show them on the screen, but the comparison to MDX gets harder because the concepts are different.

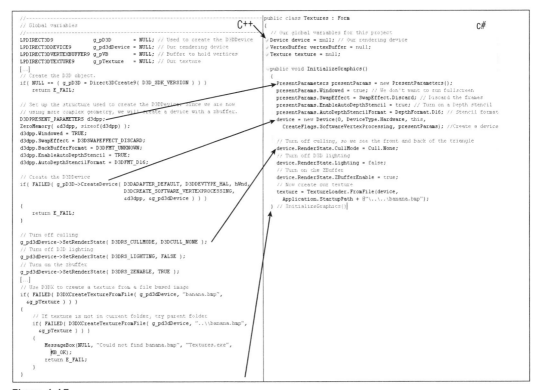

Figure 1-15

Getting Used to the Content Pipeline

As you saw earlier with your first XNA project it is quite easy to just drag and drop a texture into your game project inside XNA Studio. Although it is nice to have all your game content in one place and directly side by side with the code, there are a couple of things you have to remember. Most projects I saw in my life did not put the textures, models, or shaders directly in the Visual Studio project. The reason for that is the fact that it is much easier to just copy a few files over and then let the game load them directly. By default Visual Studio will also not copy any content files to your output directory; you have to change the Build Action from *None* to *Content* and set the Copy to Output Directory setting to *Copy if newer*. This is quite a hassle and XNA makes it a little easier.

You might even ask why change the way you loaded textures before. If you just want your game to run on the Windows platform, you can certainly load textures and shaders dynamically and without importing them first into your project as XNA content files. This has the advantage that you can change textures or shaders while the game is running (a feature that is not supported by the XNA content pipeline). However, for model files this will not work because there are no load methods other than from the `ContentManager` class, which only loads compiled .xnb content files.

On the Xbox 360 you can only load content files; there is no support to load textures or shaders directly. If you use direct texture or shader loading, make sure you exclude that code from the Xbox 360 platform; the dlls for the Xbox will not support loading anything but the content files.

For more details about important model files, read the chapters in Part II of this book. This topic is not as easy as using textures. For that reason this section sticks with sprites and 2D textures and keeps things simple. For simple 2D games it is nice and easy, but to write a serious game you will need 3D models and many cool shader effects. I also suggest that you get an artist to do the textures and 3D models for you. It is a quite complex topic and you might waste a lot of time doing all this yourself. Other people might also be more talented doing textures and 3D models; take advantage of your coding skills and let other people do the painting. If you don't have any artists available, try to use some of the models and textures from this book and the XNA starter kits to get started.

Differences with MDX

If you are coming from MDX (Managed DirectX) and want to migrate your game to the XNA Framework, there is a great guide on the official XNA pages at `http://msdn.microsoft.com/directx/xna/migration/`.

You can find the same help in the XNA documentation. I won't repeat all that here, but basically you have to remember that XNA uses right-handed matrices and MDX was left handed by default. Also there are some new classes and structures to make sure you don't need the Windows.Forms namespace anymore. Because there is no fixed function pipeline support, the old way of working with Windows Forms and handles and thinking of supporting older PC configurations is no longer necessary. Graphics and shaders are discussed in Part II of this book.

Additional Tools and Tips

Additionally you should take a look at the *Getting Started* help topics in the XNA documentation, which can be accessed from XNA Studio ➪ Help ➪ Contents ➪ XNA Game Studio Express. You can find more information about connecting to your Xbox 360, writing your first project, and about all the starter kits.

As I mentioned before, TestDriven.NET is a nice tool for Visual Studio and test-driven development is a very important methodology in this book (see Chapter 3). Another great tool for .NET development is the Ants Profiler. Unlike all other tools and programs I mentioned so far it is not free, but there are alternatives available on the net, which might help you as well. The Ants Profiler can be used to directly see how much time every single line of your project takes. In my opinion this is much more useful than using some high-level application performance tool like NvPerf from Nvidia, PIX from the DirectX SDK, or using the Performance Counters of Windows. You can quickly figure out why parts of your render code gets slow, detect bugs that call slow methods way too often, and it is always good to review your code by having some new interesting information available.

For more links on the Internet, check out the great collection of XNA links at `http://xnadevelopment .com/links.shtml`.

There are many more sites about XNA and it seems every day you see a couple of new community sites and more resources. Do a Google search to find out which site is the most popular.

Troubleshooting

You have now read everything you need to know to get started with your first XNA project. If you just read through this chapter, I highly recommend you at least open up the project for this chapter (download it from `www.wiley.com`) and run it.

If you run into problems installing DirectX, .NET 2.0, or XNA, try to search for help on the XNA Forums — `http://msdn.microsoft.com/xna/forums`. It is hard to give tips in the form of a book because of the many errors that can happen. Generally, make sure you meet the minimum requirements. For example, if you try to install on an unsupported platform and it does not work out, try to find help on that issue on the Internet or switch to a supported platform.

For .NET 2.0 it is important that you have the most recent service pack for your operating system. For DirectX make sure you have the most recent graphics driver and a decent graphic card to even work on 3D graphics, and finally for XNA, make sure you have everything correctly installed before starting the XNA setup.

Getting XNA to work on Windows isn't very hard. On the Xbox 360 a lot of things go can go wrong. Here are a couple of tips to make sure you meet the requirements for running XNA games on your 360:

❑ You need an Xbox 360 Live Account on your Xbox 360, which must be connected at all times when you develop and test your XNA games.

❑ Make sure your PC and the Xbox 360 are on the same network and they can "see" each other. You can test ping-ing the Xbox 360 IP from your PC or connecting to your PC as a media center from the Xbox 360.

❑ If the Xbox 360 XNA Framework could not be installed, search for more help on the Internet to see if your Xbox 360 meets the minimum requirements (you need a hard disk, for example).

❑ When you create an encryption key in Settings of the XNA Game Launcher and it is not accepted by your PC because you maybe mistyped it or it contained 0 (the number zero) and O letters, which almost look the same, just try it again; you can always create a new encryption key. See earlier in the chapter for details.

❑   If the XNA Game Launcher does not start or all buttons are grayed out or if you receive some error like 0xffffffff, it means that your profile is not connected to Xbox Live or it has some wrong settings. If you had an older version of the XNA Framework installed before, uninstall it, delete your profile, and create a new profile and reinstall the XNA Framework again.

Chapter 2 talks in greater detail about every single step required to get a game running on the Xbox 360, but the sample of this chapter does also work on the console out of the box. Just start the project, switch to the Xbox 360 output, and press F5. If you have set up everything correctly you can see the same output on the Xbox 360. Congratulations, you just started your first Xbox 360 game!

Last but not least if you run into compiler errors from the code in this chapter, here are some final tips:

❑   Make sure you have all required variables defined: graphics, content, `backgroundTexture`, sprites, and `scrollingPosition`.

❑   Read the compiler error message and change the code accordingly. Maybe you are trying to use some obsolete method; either replace it with the new method or just comment it out to see how the rest of the code behaves.

❑   If the compiling works, but the program crashes or throws an exception, it is most likely that you have some content file missing (the `CityGroundSmall.jpg` texture in this project) or that your graphic hardware does not support at least Shader Model 1.1.

Summary

This chapter covered a lot about the background of XNA and how to get XNA Game Studio Express working on your PC, and even how to install XNA on your Xbox 360 if available. You also wrote your first little project — I wouldn't really call it a game, but it has a texture, the Xbox 360 controller input and keyboard input is handled, and you have a response on the screen by scrolling the background texture up and down.

The following chapters focus more on programming cool little games. Here's a recap of what you have learned so far:

❑   Background of the XNA Framework

❑   Installing XNA Game Studio Express

❑   Tips and tricks how to get XNA running on Visual Studio 2005

❑   Additional tools that might be useful like TestDriven.NET, SourceSafe, and Ants Profiler

❑   Writing your first XNA project

❑   Concept of the Application Model and the `Initialize`, `Update`, and `Draw` methods

❑   Clearing the background

❑   Drawing a texture with help of a sprite batch

❑   Handling gamepad and keyboard input

❑   Drawing a tiled background based on your input

2

Creating Your First Game: Pong

This chapter talks about designing and creating a simple Pong game. Pong was the first video game ever and even before there were the first Pong versions in the sixties there was a version that could be played on an oscilloscope (Tennis for Two, 1958, by William A. Higinbotham). This shows how easy it is to implement a very basic version of Pong. A TV engineer named Ralph Baer claims that he had the idea of implementing Pong even before that in 1951, but not until 1966 was he able to produce the first prototypes. Atari licensed Pong in the eighties and even fought a court case with another company claiming they were the first to invent Pong. If you think about it today it sounds really crazy for such a simple game. You can read the whole Pong story at www.pong-story.com.

Implementing a very simple Pong clone doesn't take much time, but you will also learn about the sprite classes of XNA in this chapter. You start by writing the concept of your game and go through the full design phase of game projects. In future projects you can make the same choices, and after a while you won't have to think about the process of writing concepts first anymore because you will do it naturally to get the ideas for the first unit tests. Then you learn about an effective way to organize and use textures for your games. Additionally you will fine-tune the game, make it more fun, add 2-player support, and even test it on the Xbox 360 console.

Though this chapter focuses on the Pong game, it is not the only thing you are going to learn. The Pong game is used to learn more about the Agile Methodology I will mention later in this chapter. You will learn why it is important to write unit tests first and design the game up front in a very quick process and then improve it as you go along. In the next chapters you will use unit tests for additional classes too. For this game you just have one simple class and a couple of unit tests added at the end of it to test out the graphics, the collision testing, and to position everything correctly.

The kinds of unit tests used in this chapter are referred to as static unit tests as opposed to the dynamic unit tests you learn about in the next chapter. The difference is that you have to start static unit tests by hand and check the results yourself by watching the result on the screen. Dynamic unit tests, on the other hand, are executed automatically with help of a Unit Testing Framework like NUnit. For more details about the Unit Testing Framework, read Chapter 3.

Game Ideas

Talking about the game concept for a game like Pong seems to be a little ridiculous, but I will try to keep things as general as possible. The important thing is that you think about what the game should look and feel like before you start coding. The bigger the game project is, the more important the design phase is. I'm not saying that you can't write games or applications without any concept at all. In fact, most beginners will just start writing something and then improve it again and again until it looks good. The problem with this approach is that it is highly unlikely to find the best solution on the first try.

The game logic is very simple and it does not require much text or graphics (see Figure 2-1). This makes both the game code and your concept very simple to write. Just think about all the components required for this game (ball, paddles, and the screen borders) and write down your initial ideas.

Figure 2-1

Write Down Your Ideas!

Writing a concept does not necessarily mean you have to write down all your ideas, draw UML diagrams like crazy, and only start working when everything is fully planned. I'm completely against that approach because you can't know how everything will work out. Additionally, beginners probably have no idea what the best way is to design a full game up front. Instead you can have a very clear picture of the game in your mind and after you think you have spent enough time on the design in your mind, you can start working.

If you have other people working on your game project too, it becomes harder to explain ideas and keep everyone in sync. Just for this reason alone you should make it a habit to write down your game idea on just one single page. You can not only show this to other people and get more input, but you will also think about things while writing down some parts of your game idea — and when you see it on paper it might seem more complex than in your mind and you have to think about additional dependencies.

For example, for your Pong game you know that you need two paddles and a ball, which moves between the paddles. But maybe only after you write down the initial ideas and think about the sprite textures might you think about the more detailed game play — how many lives does each player have, how do you find out if the ball hits the paddle edges, and how do you handle that? Does the speed of the paddle influence the ball speed and direction? What about increasing the ball speed after a while to speed up the game if both players are bored? Sure, many of these things can be improved after you finish the first version of your game. But it is a lot easier to take all these things into consideration before you write complicated code and then later see that you don't even need that.

As an example, I will write down the design concept for the Pong game you will develop in this chapter. You might want to take 5–10 pages for more complex games, but don't write 100 pages of concept text without coding anything. It will take too much time and it will get very hard to manage the concept. For the Agile Methodology you will often update the concept and change details. I usually don't start with UML diagrams until at least 50% of the code is done, and the overview diagrams and the documentation gets updated later when the project goes final.

Game Idea: Pong

The game is a simple Pong clone for one or two players. In the singleplayer mode the computer will control the other paddle. In the multiplayer mode, two players can either control their paddles with two gamepads, with different keys on the keyboard on the same PC, or on the Xbox 360 console.

The game features a few 2D graphics for the ball and the paddles and a few sound files for the ball hitting one of the paddles or for losing a life. There is a very simple menu allowing you to select the following:

- ❏ Singleplayer
- ❏ Multiplayer
- ❏ Exit

The menu is implemented with a simple texture, the background is just a dark space, and most graphics are bright. You will try to make the game as much fun as possible.

Features and Game Play

The game has two screen modes: Menu and Game. The menu just contains the menu items that were mentioned in the preceding section, and the game consists basically of the ball and the two paddles and a simple scoring system. Take a look at a simple drawing for what you are trying to accomplish (see Figure 2-2).

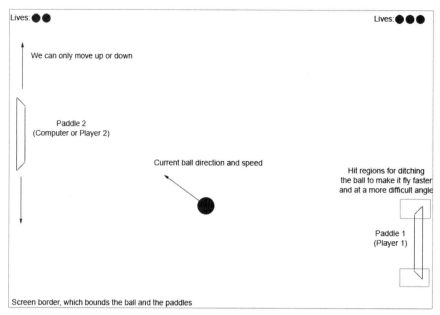

Figure 2-2

Technology

Obviously you are going to use XNA Game Studio Express; there are no additional libraries you are going to use and because you will just render some simple sprites, there are no 3D models or shaders involved here. The game should run on both the Windows platform and the Xbox 360 console.

As you can see I managed to fit everything on a single page, which is one of my rules I use when I write game concepts: First fit everything on one single page, then get a little bit into coding and if required by your team or an external partner (for example, if you want to show the concept to a game publisher), write a whitepaper with 5–10 pages from the initial idea and add some early sketches.

I never talked about the programming itself in the concept; I just made sure that you know which technology to use. Now it is time to think about the implementation. Don't think about your abilities when writing the game concept, it will just limit you too much. Keep it in the back of your mind.

A more complete example of a game concept is the Rocket Commander concept (see Figure 2-3). You can check it out from the PDF file in the directory for this chapter. It contains four pages and a cover and it features all the ideas for the Rocket Commander game. As you can see from the cover, the game looks very different from the concept, but the general game ideas are there.

Agile Methodology

The Agile Methodology is a conceptual framework for software development. The basic idea is to avoid big planning phases, which can often lead to risky and unrealistic project schedules that are hard to keep. For smaller projects you will use short time iterations anyway, but as projects grow bigger you might see yourself standing in front of problems that require months or even years to finish, and that is very hard to plan.

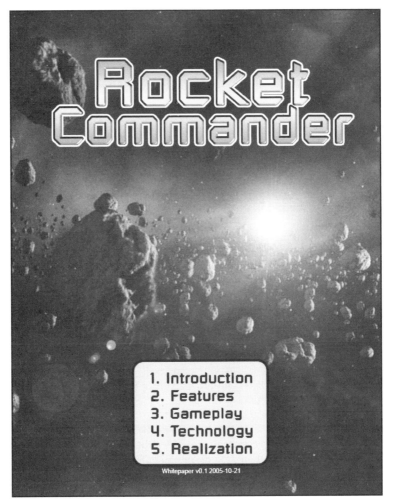

Figure 2-3

Instead of planning everything down to the most detailed level, only a very rough concept is done. Each part of the concept is then iterated through the agile process of planning this feature in greater detail, designing the code with help of unit tests, then doing the actual code implementation, and finally testing and documenting this part. This iteration should not take longer than a few weeks and is repeated for all parts of the big project.

Agile methods also include some other ideas about working better together, teaming up developers with the customers, testers, managers and designers, and so on. There are several rules that can be used to bring some structure into this agile framework to avoid having total chaos. Because of the shortened planning phase it looks like there is no detailed plan for the project, similar to a chaotic brute force coding approach. But in reality the planning process continues throughout the whole project and is much more useful than planning everything just at the beginning and having to live with all the mistakes made in that stage for the whole project.

I will not talk much about the Agile Methodologies in this book, but I will use unit testing and the short concept first, unit test design, then code iteration throughout all projects in this book. If you want to read more about unit testing I recommend reading the website of Martin Fowler at `http://martinfowler.com`.

Martin has also written several books and I can recommend his *Refactoring: Improving the Design of Existing Code* book, which you can also find on the website. You can find many more links and information about the agile software development process on his site too.

Solving Initial Difficulties

Ok, now you have an idea about your game, but you have not spent much time about where you get the graphics from, what you do about the sound files, and how to implement them. What about the problem with the ball hitting the sides of the paddle? Do you even need a simple physics engine for the ball?

All these questions usually arise after the design phase and for more complex projects it can take weeks, if not months to just figure out some of the basic problems. For example, the first .NET 2.0 game I did was Rocket Commander and I had a nice idea to have thousands of asteroids on the screen, and millions in the level as a whole. I had some cool ideas about letting them collide and bounce off each other; it was not really clear how to implement it in an optimized manner. After some initial tests I found out that I couldn't even render 100 asteroids without a significant performance drop. Instead of rewriting the game concept and making a really boring game without many asteroids at all (which is the game principle of Rocket Commander — without the many asteroids you don't really have a game at all), I tried to solve this problem by rendering a lot of asteroids sorted by shaders and material settings, doing very early skipping of asteroids if they were not visible, and having the physics only apply to the nearby asteroids.

Even after working and optimizing the asteroids for a week until they rendered at a great performance, the physics were still way too slow. Just updating 5 to 10 thousand asteroids in viewable range every single frame to see if any of them hit any other asteroid was just way too much, even with the best optimizations applied. I still wanted the asteroids to collide and behave correctly after collisions. If I did just check a certain amount of asteroids each frame, the algorithm often missed collisions and only caught up when both asteroids had already penetrated each other, causing even more troubles than removing the physics altogether. I was close to giving up because I had already spent 50% of the total project time just solving this single problem, but then I got the idea to separate the space into sectors. Each sector had a certain amount of asteroids and every time an asteroid left a sector it was removed and added to the new sector. For collision checks asteroids had only to check their own and all neighboring sectors, which still sounds like a lot of collision checks, but the sector logic did improve the physics performance by a factor of 100 and even more after more optimizations.

In most game projects I do nowadays I spend more than half of the time solving the initial problems and then dividing them up into smaller problems, which again have to be solved. The game itself is then later assembled by just putting these pieces together, and almost like magic the whole game is done in a matter of days. Though this is the best approach to finish a game as quickly as possible, it can be frustrating to see no results for a very long time, and in the past I always iterated the game until I was pleased with the results. This did take a very long time. Thanks to the agile development process, I'm now able to work on the problems and not iterate an almost endless loop of improvements.

What does this mean for your Pong game? Well, the game is very simple and you won't spend a lot of time improving it 100 times. But say you just implement a basic version of Pong with a hard-coded paddle for the computer on the left side moving up and down depending on the ball position and controlling the right paddle. Then later after improving and testing the single-player game you might want to add 2-player support and it gets hard because you hard-coded the computer code. You might comment the computer code out or even remove it and restructure the game play code. Then a little bit later after testing the 2-player mode you might want to add the menu and again you have put the code at a different location, re-implement the computer game code, and so on.

Though this is all good practice and forces you to refactor (refactoring means changing the layout of your code without changing the functionality to improve maintenance; see Martin Fowler's book, *Refactoring*) it is a lot easier to just focus on one part of the game at a time and have several game versions and tests running side by side. You will do exactly that in the next part of this chapter, and hopefully you can grasp what I mean. Refactoring will occur more naturally and makes your code more usable and lets you see the result much quicker thanks to unit testing.

One of the problems you will solve in the next part is how to handle the ball physics and how to detect which part of the paddle you hit.

Creating Some Textures

Before you start coding you need some textures to display stuff on the screen. Even if you use dummy bitmaps here or get some graphics from somewhere else, it is still important to think about the final graphics, which dimensions the ball and paddles should have, and things like that.

Again for your Pong game it is pretty simple, but more complex games might require an art concept, a lot of sketches and someone who has a good idea how to manage all this artwork and how to get them all done in time for the game programmer to implement them. Back in the early days of computer games almost all games were created by one individual, and though this is the easiest way, today no serious game is developed by just one person. Most good artists are not programmers and most programmers are not good artists. If you do a simple game it does not matter so much, but the bigger your project gets, the more time you will spend with finding teammates, skilled artists, and modelers and putting everything together.

Take a look at the graphics for your game (see Figure 2-4). You will use three textures: (1) `PongBackground.dds` for the background, (2) `PongMenu.png`, which contains the logo, menu items, and all other texts for your game, and finally, (3) `PongGame.png` for the paddles and the ball.

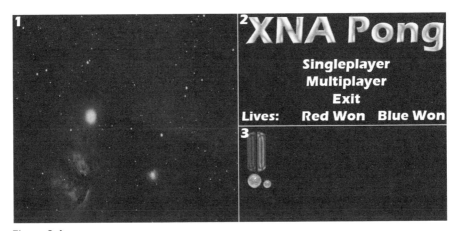

Figure 2-4

Additionally you will import two sound files (`PongBallHit.wav` and `PongBallLost.wav`) into your project and add a simple XACT project to play the sounds. To learn more about sounds and XACT, please read Chapter 9.

Let's Write Pong

You got the concept all figured out and have all the files you need to get started. It's time to do some actual coding. First take a look at the `SpriteBatch` class and see how you can easily manage all the sprites. The `SpriteBatch` class is not only useful to render sprites in the same format as the graphics were saved, but it is possible to scale them up or down, recolor them, and even rotate them around.

After putting the menu together you will add the paddles and move them with help of the input capabilities you already saw in Chapter 1. The ball itself moves with help of some simple variables, and every time you hit one of the paddles you bounce the ball back and play the `PongBallHit.wav` sound. If the ball goes out of the screen on the left or right side, the `PongBallLost.wav` sound is played and the player loses one life.

A few unit tests will be used to make sure that the menu and the basic game work. Then you will add additional unit tests to handle the complicated parts like hitting the ball from the sides of the paddle and fine-tuning the game play. For multiplayer support you will have a unit test to test out the controls, which are then wired up to the main menu option to support the multiplayer mode.

In the next part of this chapter you will then test the whole game on the Xbox 360 and think about more improvements you can make to the game.

Sprites

As you saw in Chapter 1 the `SpriteBatch` class is used to render your textures directly on the screen. Because you don't have any helper classes yet you will render everything the same way. For more information about helper classes to make your everyday game programming life easier, check out Chapter 3. For your Pong game you use two layers: the Space Background, which is loaded from the `PongBackground.dds` texture, and the menu and game textures showing the menu texts and the game components (paddles and ball).

To load all textures you use the following lines. First of all you have to define the textures you are using here:

```
Texture2D backgroundTexture, menuTexture, gameTexture;
```

Then load everything in the `Initialize` method:

```
// Load all our content
backgroundTexture = content.Load<Texture2D>("PongBackground");
menuTexture = content.Load<Texture2D>("PongMenu");
gameTexture = content.Load<Texture2D>("PongGame");
```

And finally you can render the background with the `SpriteBatch` methods you learned about in Chapter 1:

```
// Draw background texture in a separate pass, else it gets messed up
// with our other sprites, the ordering does not really work great.
spriteBatch.Begin();
spriteBatch.Draw(backgroundTexture,
   new Rectangle(0, 0, width, height),
   Color.LightGray);
spriteBatch.End();
```

`LightGray` for the color means that you darken down the background a little bit for a better contrast to the foreground items (menu text and game elements). As you can see it is not just one line to render a sprite on the screen, and it will get a lot more complicated to render just parts of your sprite textures. Take a look at the rectangles you use for the game:

```
static readonly Rectangle
   XnaPongLogoRect = new Rectangle(0, 0, 512, 110),
   MenuSingleplayerRect = new Rectangle(0, 110, 512, 38),
   MenuMultiplayerRect = new Rectangle(0, 148, 512, 38),
   MenuExitRect = new Rectangle(0, 185, 512, 38),
   GameLifesRect = new Rectangle(0, 222, 100, 34),
   GameRedWonRect = new Rectangle(151, 222, 155, 34),
   GameBlueWonRect = new Rectangle(338, 222, 165, 34),
   GameRedPaddleRect = new Rectangle(23, 0, 22, 92),
   GameBluePaddleRect = new Rectangle(0, 0, 22, 92),
   GameBallRect = new Rectangle(1, 94, 33, 33),
   GameSmallBallRect = new Rectangle(37, 108, 19, 19);
```

That is quite a lot of rectangles, but it is still simpler to just use these constant values than to import some xml data, for example. Static read-only is used instead of constants here because constants can't be assigned to structs and static read-only behaves the same way as constants. You might ask how to get these values and how to make sure they are correct.

Unit Testing in Games

This is where unit testing comes into play. Unit testing for game programming basically means to split up your problems into small, easily manageable problems. Even for this very simple game it is still a good idea to write unit tests. Unit testing is perfect to align textures on the screen, test sound effects, and add collision testing. Originally I planned to write this chapter and the Pong game without using unit testing, but as soon as I programmed the game I couldn't stop myself and before I knew it I had already written six unit tests, and I was convinced that this is the way to go and it would not make sense to delete the very useful tests.

For example, to test out the menu graphics rectangles you use the following unit test:

```
public static void TestMenuSprites()
{
  StartTest(
    delegate
    {
      testGame.RenderSprite(testGame.menuTexture,
        512-XnaPongLogoRect.Width/2, 150,
        XnaPongLogoRect);
      testGame.RenderSprite(testGame.menuTexture,
        512-MenuSingleplayerRect.Width/2, 300,
        MenuSingleplayerRect);
      testGame.RenderSprite(testGame.menuTexture,
        512-MenuMultiplayerRect.Width/2, 350,
        MenuMultiplayerRect, Color.Orange);
      testGame.RenderSprite(testGame.menuTexture,
        512-MenuExitRect.Width/2, 400,
        MenuExitRect);
    });
} // TestMenuSprites()
```

Please note: This is not the final way you will do unit testing in this book. You just use the very basic idea here to execute unit tests. The delegate holds the code you will execute each frame in the Draw method.

You might ask yourself: What is StartTest? What about testGame or the RenderSprite method? Where do they come from? Well, this is one of the main differences between the old way of game programming and using an agile approach with unit testing. All these methods do not exist yet. Similar to how you planned your game, you also plan your unit tests by just writing down how you want to test something; in this case displaying the game logo and the three menu entries (Singleplayer, Multiplayer, and Exit).

After writing a unit test and all syntax errors are fixed you can immediately start testing by compiling your code — just press F5 and you will see a couple of errors. These errors have to be fixed step by step and then the unit test can be started. Static unit tests do not use Assert functions very often, but it is possible to add some code to throw exceptions if some values are not as expected. For your unit tests you will just test them by looking at the result on the screen and then modify the RenderSprite method until everything works the way you want.

The next chapter talks in greater detail about unit testing. For the Pong game, you just derive from the PongGame class and add a simple delegate to render custom code in your unit tests:

```
delegate void TestDelegate();
class TestPongGame : PongGame
{
  TestDelegate testLoop;
  public TestPongGame(TestDelegate setTestLoop)
  {
    testLoop = setTestLoop;
  } // TestPongGame(setTestLoop)
```

```
    protected override void Draw(GameTime gameTime)
    {
      base.Draw(gameTime);
      testLoop();
    } // Draw(gameTime)
  } // class TestPongGame
```

Now you can write the very simple StartTest method to create an instance of TestPongGame and then call Run to execute the Draw method with your custom testLoop code:

```
  static TestPongGame testGame;
  static void StartTest(TestDelegate testLoop)
  {
    using (testGame = new TestPongGame(testLoop))
    {
      testGame.Run();
    } // using
  } // StartTest(testLoop)
```

The static instance testGame is used to make writing the unit tests easier, but it can be confusing if you use it somewhere else because it will only be valid after StartTest is called. In the next chapters you will see a better way to do all this.

Now two of the errors from the first version of the unit test are fixed; only the RenderSprite method is missing now. It is ok to add an empty method just to make the unit test work:

```
  public void RenderSprite(Texture2D texture, int x, int y,
    Rectangle sourceRect, Color color)
  {
    //TODO
  } // RenderSprite(texture, rect, sourceRect)
  public void RenderSprite(Texture2D texture, int x, int y,
    Rectangle sourceRect)
  {
    //TODO
  } // RenderSprite(texture, rect, sourceRect)
```

After adding these two methods you can now execute the TestMenuSprites method. How to do that? With TestDriven.NET you can just right-click and select "Start Test," but XNA Game Studio Express does not support plugins and you have to write your own way of unit testing by changing the Main method in the Program.cs file:

```
  static void Main(string[] args)
  {
    //PongGame.StartGame();
    PongGame.TestMenuSprites();
  } // Main(args)
```

As you can see I have also extracted the `StartGame` method to make the `Main` method easier to read and to make it easy to change unit tests. `StartGame` uses just the standard code:

```
public static void StartGame()
{
  using (PongGame game = new PongGame())
  {
    game.Run();
  } // using
} // StartGame()
```

If you press F5 now the unit test is executed instead of the normal game code. Because `RenderSprite` does not contain any code yet you will just see the space background that is drawn in the `Draw` method of `PongGame`. Now you add the code to make the menu work. You already know how to render sprites, but it is highly ineffective to start and end a `SpriteBatch` for every single `RenderSprite` call. Create a simple list of sprites you want to render each frame and add a new entry every time you call `RenderSprite`. Then at the end of the frame you will just draw all sprites:

```
class SpriteToRender
{
  public Texture2D texture;
  public Rectangle rect;
  public Rectangle? sourceRect;
  public Color color;
  public SpriteToRender(Texture2D setTexture, Rectangle setRect,
    Rectangle? setSourceRect, Color setColor)
  {
    texture = setTexture;
    rect = setRect;
    sourceRect = setSourceRect;
    color = setColor;
  } // SpriteToRender(setTexture, setRect, setColor)
} // SpriteToRender
List<SpriteToRender> sprites = new List<SpriteToRender>();
```

By the way: You added all this code, including the unit tests, to your `PongGame` class. Usually you would want to reuse code and extend games later and it is better to split everything up in multiple classes. To keep things simple and because you won't use much of this code later, everything is just written down in the fastest way possible. Though this is clearly not the cleanest and most elegant way to code, it is usually the fastest and most efficient way to make your unit tests run. At a later point you can refactor your code to make it more elegant and reusable. Thanks to unit testing you always have a strong tool to make sure everything is still functioning after changing the layout of the code several times.

You might have seen that "`Rectangle?`" is used instead of just "`Rectangle`" for the `sourceRect` in the preceding code. "`Rectangle?`" means that this type is null-able and you can just pass in null for this argument, which makes it possible to create overloads of `RenderSprite` that don't use `sourceRect` to just render the full texture:

```
public void RenderSprite(Texture2D texture, Rectangle rect,
  Rectangle? sourceRect, Color color)
{
  sprites.Add(new SpriteToRender(texture, rect, sourceRect, color));
} // RenderSprite(texture, rect, sourceRect, color)
```

That's pretty straightforward. The `DrawSprites` method, which is called at the end of the `Draw` method, is also not very complicated:

```
public void DrawSprites()
{
  // No need to render if we got no sprites this frame
  if (sprites.Count == 0)
    return;
  // Start rendering sprites
  spriteBatch.Begin(SpriteBlendMode.AlphaBlend,
    SpriteSortMode.BackToFront, SaveStateMode.None);
  // Render all sprites
  foreach (SpriteToRender sprite in sprites)
    spriteBatch.Draw(sprite.texture,
      // Rescale to fit resolution
      new Rectangle(
      sprite.rect.X * width / 1024,
      sprite.rect.Y * height / 768,
      sprite.rect.Width * width / 1024,
      sprite.rect.Height * height / 768),
      sprite.sourceRect, sprite.color);
  // We are done, draw everything on screen with help of the end method.
  spriteBatch.End();

  // Kill list of remembered sprites
  sprites.Clear();
} // DrawSprites()
```

Though it is not very important for this game, at least on the Windows platform where you use 1024×768 as the default resolution anyway, you will rescale all sprites from 1024×768 to the current resolution. Please note that all textures for this game and all upcoming games in this book are usually stored in the 1024×768 resolution. The code in `DrawSprites` makes sure that all sprites are scaled correctly to the currently used resolutions. For example, on the Xbox 360 several resolutions are possible and will force the game to run in these resolutions, which you can't know beforehand. For this reason Xbox 360 games should be resolution independent and allow HDTV-like 1080p (1920×1080) formats if possible.

Basically, `DrawSprites` checks if there are any sprites to render, else just exit the function. Then render all sprites with the default alpha blend mode and sorted from back to front without saving the states, which means that if you change any render state of XNA it will not be restored when `End` is called. Usually you will always want to use `SaveStateMode.None` because it is the fastest, and through your unit tests you make sure everything works out and is not changed in a way that messes up your rendering done after this method.

You might think "All that just to render the main menu graphics?" but if you press F5 now you can see the screen shown in Figure 2-5. Because you have implemented the basic code for your game, all the sprite rendering code, and everything you need for your unit tests, you have almost completed 50% of the work already. You now just need to add the game graphics, the controls, and some simple ball collision code and you are done.

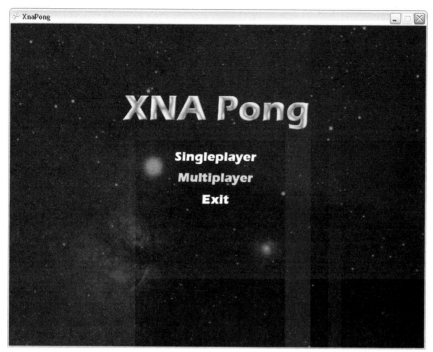

Figure 2-5

Adding the Ball and Paddles

To add the ball, paddles, and all other game components you need you use another unit test called
TestGameSprites:

```
public static void TestGameSprites()
{
  StartTest(
    delegate
    {
      // Show lives
      testGame.ShowLives();
      // Ball in center
      testGame.RenderBall();
      // Render both paddles
      testGame.RenderPaddles();
    });
} // TestGameSprites()
```

This unit test represents the methodology of the agile development process even better than the last unit
test. As you can see you just took a look at the design concept and implemented everything at a very

high level. At the top you see the number of lives each player has. Then there is the ball in the middle and each player has his paddle. The screen border does not use any special graphics and you already have the background.

Just to make sure you understand the way these unit tests are done, add them and press F5 after adding this to the Main method and commenting out the old unit test:

```
//PongGame.StartGame();
//PongGame.TestMenuSprites();
PongGame.TestGameSprites();
```

You will get three error messages because none of the three new methods of TestGameSprites is implemented yet. Now after you see these errors you know exactly that these are your next three steps, and if all of them are implemented and tested, this test is complete and you continue with the next part of your game. I cannot mention this often enough: This really makes the overall process much more straightforward and it seems like you planned everything from start to finish, but as you saw earlier you just wrote down one simple page of your game idea. Everything else was just designed and created as you go from the top-level design down to the implementation at the lowest level. Take a look at the three new methods:

```
public void ShowLives()
{
  // Left players lives
  RenderSprite(menuTexture, 2, 2, GameLivesRect);
  for (int num = 0; num < leftPlayerLives; num++)
    RenderSprite(gameTexture, 2+GameLivesRect.Width+
      GameSmallBallRect.Width*num-2, 9,
      GameSmallBallRect);
  // Right players lives
  int rightX = 1024-GameLivesRect.Width-GameSmallBallRect.Width*3-4;
  RenderSprite(menuTexture, rightX, 2, GameLivesRect);
  for (int num = 0; num < rightPlayerLives; num++)
    RenderSprite(gameTexture, rightX+GameLivesRect.Width+
      GameSmallBallRect.Width*num-2, 9,
      GameSmallBallRect);
} // ShowLives()
```

ShowLives just shows the "Lives:" text for both players and adds the number of lives as small balls from the game texture. RenderBall is even simpler:

```
public void RenderBall()
{
  RenderSprite(gameTexture,
    (int)((0.05f+0.9f*ballPosition.X)*1024)-
    GameBallRect.Width/2,
    (int)((0.02f+0.96f*ballPosition.Y)*768)-
    GameBallRect.Height/2,
    GameBallRect);
} // RenderBall()
```

And finally you have `RenderPaddles` to show the left and right paddles at the current position:

```
public void RenderPaddles()
{
  RenderSprite(gameTexture,
    (int)(0.05f*1024)-GameRedPaddleRect.Width/2,
    (int)((0.06f+0.88f*leftPaddlePosition)*768)-
    GameRedPaddleRect.Height/2,
    GameRedPaddleRect);
  RenderSprite(gameTexture,
    (int)(0.95f*1024)-GameBluePaddleRect.Width/2,
    (int)((0.06f+0.88f*rightPaddlePosition)*768)-
    GameBluePaddleRect.Height/2,
    GameBluePaddleRect);
} // RenderPaddle(leftPaddle)
```

Before you even wonder about the all the floating-point numbers in `RenderBall` and `RenderPaddles`, these are the new variables you need for your game to keep track of the current ball and paddles positions:

```
/// <summary>
/// Current paddle positions, 0 means top, 1 means bottom.
/// </summary>
float leftPaddlePosition = 0.5f,
  rightPaddlePosition = 0.5f;
/// <summary>
/// Current ball position, again from 0 to 1, 0 is left and top,
/// 1 is bottom and right.
/// </summary>
Vector2 ballPosition = new Vector2(0.5f, 0.5f);
/// <summary>
/// Ball speed vector, randomized for every new ball.
/// Will be set to Zero if we are in menu or game is over.
/// </summary>
Vector2 ballSpeedVector = new Vector2(0, 0);
```

Now it might be a little bit clearer why you work with floating-point numbers in the render methods. This way you don't have to deal with screen coordinates, multiple resolutions, and checking screen borders. Both the ball and the paddles just stay between 0 and 1. For the x coordinate 0 means you are at the left border, and 1 means you are at the right border of the screen. Same thing for the y coordinate and the paddles; 0 is the topmost position and 1 is the bottom of the screen. You also use a speed vector to update the ball position each frame, which is discussed in a minute.

The paddles are just rendered on the screen; you put the left paddle (red) to the left side and add 5% to make it more visible and add a little area behind it where the ball can move to lose a life for this player. The same thing happens for the right paddle (blue) at the right side at 95% (which is 0.95f) of the screen width. Take a look at the output you see after pressing F5 now (see Figure 2-6).

Figure 2-6

That does look like the game is almost done right now. Although unit testing is great and gives you great results in a quick manner, it does not mean you are done yet. The input and the collision testing still have to be done.

Handling Player Input

As you saw in Chapter 1, capturing the keyboard and gamepad input is quite easy in XNA. Writing an extra unit test just for that would be overkill; you already know how this works and you just want to test controlling the paddles here. You don't even need a new unit test; you can just use the `TestGameSprites` test and maybe rename it to `TestSingleplayerGame`. The content of the unit test stays the same; you will now just change input handling and update the paddle positions in the `Update` method of `PongGame`:

```
// Get current gamepad and keyboard states
gamePad = GamePad.GetState(PlayerIndex.One);
gamePad2 = GamePad.GetState(PlayerIndex.Two);
keyboard = Keyboard.GetState();
gamePadUp = gamePad.DPad.Up == ButtonState.Pressed ||
    gamePad.ThumbSticks.Left.Y > 0.5f;
gamePadDown = gamePad.DPad.Down == ButtonState.Pressed ||
    gamePad.ThumbSticks.Left.Y < -0.5f;
gamePad2Up = gamePad2.DPad.Up == ButtonState.Pressed ||
    gamePad2.ThumbSticks.Left.Y > 0.5f;
gamePad2Down = gamePad2.DPad.Down == ButtonState.Pressed ||
    gamePad2.ThumbSticks.Left.Y < -0.5f;
```

```
// Move half way across the screen each second
float moveFactorPerSecond = 0.5f *
  (float)gameTime.ElapsedRealTime.TotalMilliseconds / 1000.0f;
// Move up and down if we press the cursor or gamepad keys.
if (gamePadUp ||
  keyboard.IsKeyDown(Keys.Up))
  rightPaddlePosition -= moveFactorPerSecond;
if (gamePadDown ||
  keyboard.IsKeyDown(Keys.Down))
  rightPaddlePosition += moveFactorPerSecond;
// Second player is either controlled by player 2 or by the computer
if (multiplayer)
{
  // Move up and down if we press the cursor or gamepad keys.
  if (gamePad2Up ||
    keyboard.IsKeyDown(Keys.W))
    leftPaddlePosition -= moveFactorPerSecond;
  if (gamePad2Down ||
    keyboard.IsKeyDown(Keys.S))
    leftPaddlePosition += moveFactorPerSecond;
} // if
else
{
  // Just let the computer follow the ball position
  float computerChange = ComputerPaddleSpeed * moveFactorPerSecond;
  if (leftPaddlePosition > ballPosition.Y + computerChange)
    leftPaddlePosition -= computerChange;
  else if (leftPaddlePosition < ballPosition.Y - computerChange)
    leftPaddlePosition += computerChange;
} // else
// Make sure paddles stay between 0 and 1
if (leftPaddlePosition < 0)
  leftPaddlePosition = 0;
if (leftPaddlePosition > 1)
  leftPaddlePosition = 1;
if (rightPaddlePosition < 0)
  rightPaddlePosition = 0;
if (rightPaddlePosition > 1)
  rightPaddlePosition = 1;
```

You might see a few new variables here (multiplayer, gamePad, gamePad2, keyboard, and ComputerPaddleSpeed), but this section focuses on the code that changes the paddle positions for now. To make sure you always move the ball and the paddles at the same speed no matter how many frames you get, moveFactorPerSecond is calculated. moveFactorPerSecond will be 1 for 1 fps (frame per second), 0.1 for 10 fps, 0.01 for 100 fps, and so on.

Next you will change the right paddle position if up or down buttons or cursor keys are pressed. The left paddle is either controlled by player 2 using a second gamepad if available or the W and S keys. If multiplayer is not true you are in singleplayer mode and the left paddle is controlled by the computer, which just follows the ball limited by the ComputerPaddleSpeed, which is 0.5f. The ball will initially move much slower, but the speed gets increased at each contact and you can also hit the ball with the edge of the paddles to make it speed up. Then the computer will not catch up and you can win.

To make the new `Update` method work, add the new variables and constants:

```
/// <summary>
/// Ball speed multiplicator, this is how much screen space the ball
/// will travel each second.
/// </summary>
const float BallSpeedMultiplicator = 0.5f;
/// <summary>
/// Computer paddle speed. If the ball moves faster up or down than
/// this, the computer paddle can't keep up and finally we will win.
/// </summary>
const float ComputerPaddleSpeed = 0.5f;
/// <summary>
/// Game modes
/// </summary>
enum GameMode
{
  Menu,
  Game,
  GameOver,
} // enum GameMode
GamePadState gamePad, gamePad2;
KeyboardState keyboard;
bool gamePadUp = false,
    gamePadDown = false,
    gamePad2Up = false,
    gamePad2Down = false;
/// <summary>
/// Are we playing a multiplayer game? If this is false, the computer
/// controls the left paddle.
/// </summary>
bool multiplayer = false;
/// <summary>
/// Game mode we are currently in. Very simple game flow.
/// </summary>
GameMode gameMode = GameMode.Menu;
/// <summary>
/// Currently selected menu item.
/// </summary>
int currentMenuItem = 0;
```

For the current test you just need the variables I mentioned before. However, take a look at all the rest of the variables you need for the game. `BallSpeedMultiplicator` determinates how fast the ball is and therefore how fast the game is. The game mode is used to handle all the three game modes you can be in. Either you just started the game and are in the menu or you are in the game. When you are in the game, but one player lost, the mode is changed to the game over state, showing the winner.

You don't need this code yet, but it is the last part of input you have to handle, so take a look at the input for the menu:

```
// Show screen depending on our current screen mode
if (gameMode == GameMode.Menu)
{
    // Show menu
    RenderSprite(menuTexture,
        512-XnaPongLogoRect.Width/2, 150, XnaPongLogoRect);
    RenderSprite(menuTexture,
        512-MenuSingleplayerRect.Width/2, 300, MenuSingleplayerRect,
        currentMenuItem == 0 ? Color.Orange : Color.White);
    RenderSprite(menuTexture,
    512-MenuMultiplayerRect.Width/2, 350, MenuMultiplayerRect,
    currentMenuItem == 1 ? Color.Orange : Color.White);
    RenderSprite(menuTexture,
    512-MenuExitRect.Width/2, 400, MenuExitRect,
    currentMenuItem == 2 ? Color.Orange : Color.White);
    if ((keyboard.IsKeyDown(Keys.Down) ||
        gamePadDown) &&
        remDownPressed == false)
    {
        currentMenuItem = (currentMenuItem + 1)%3;
    } // else if
    else if ((keyboard.IsKeyDown(Keys.Up) ||
        gamePadUp) &&
        remUpPressed == false)
    {
        currentMenuItem = (currentMenuItem + 2)%3;
    } // else if
    else if ((keyboard.IsKeyDown(Keys.Space) ||
        keyboard.IsKeyDown(Keys.LeftControl) ||
        keyboard.IsKeyDown(Keys.RightControl) ||
        keyboard.IsKeyDown(Keys.Enter) ||
        gamePad.Buttons.A == ButtonState.Pressed ||
        gamePad.Buttons.Start == ButtonState.Pressed ||
        // Back or Escape exits our game
        keyboard.IsKeyDown(Keys.Escape) ||
        gamePad.Buttons.Back == ButtonState.Pressed) &&
        remSpaceOrStartPressed == false &&
        remEscOrBackPressed == false)
    {
        // Quit app.
        if (currentMenuItem == 2 ||
            keyboard.IsKeyDown(Keys.Escape) ||
        gamePad.Buttons.Back == ButtonState.Pressed)
        {
            this.Exit();
        } // if
        else
        {
            // Start game
.. handle game, etc. ..
```

There are a few new variables like `remDownPressed` or `gamePadUp`, which are used to make handling the input a little easier. Check out the source code for additional details. The next chapter discusses the `Input` helper class in more detail, and that will simplify the process even more.

That's all you need to know for handling the input in this Pong game. If you execute the unit test again you can still see the same screen as before, but you can now control the paddles.

Collision Testing

To move the ball away from the middle, the following method has to be called in your unit test `TestSingleplayerGame`. The ball moves to a random location (at least randomly in the four directions you have defined here):

```
/// <summary>
/// Start new ball at the beginning of each game and when a ball is
/// lost.
/// </summary>
public void StartNewBall()
{
   ballPosition = new Vector2(0.5f, 0.5f);
   Random rnd = new Random((int)DateTime.Now.Ticks);
   int direction = rnd.Next(4);
   ballSpeedVector =
      direction == 0 ? new Vector2(1, 0.8f) :
      direction == 1 ? new Vector2(1, -0.8f) :
      direction == 2 ? new Vector2(-1, 0.8f) :
      new Vector2(-1, -0.8f);
} // StartNewBall()
```

In the `Update` method the ball position gets updated based on the `ballSpeedVector`:

```
// Update ball position
ballPosition += ballSpeedVector *
   moveFactorPerSecond * BallSpeedMultiplicator;
```

If you start the game now with your unit test the ball will move away from the center and go out of the screen, which is not really cool. This is why you need collision testing. Take a look at the concept again (see Figure 2-7) and add some improvements for the collision code. This is one of the times it makes sense to go back to the concept and make improvements based on your new ideas and knowledge. There are three kinds of collisions that can happen:

❑ **Collision with Screen Border** at the top and bottom screen borders

❑ **Collision with a Paddle** to push the ball back to the other player

❑ **Lose life if collision with screen border behind paddle happens.** Player will lose a life when this happens and the ball is reset with the help of `StartNewBall`.

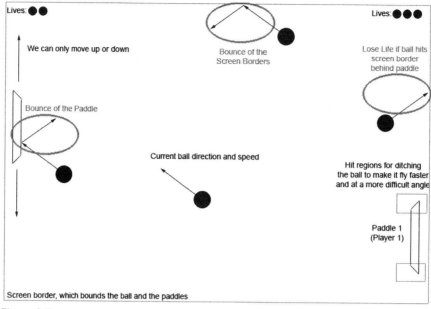

Figure 2-7

You could continue using TestSingleplayerGame to check out the collisions, but it is far easier to construct a few tests and have every single issue tested. Again, unit testing is great for exactly this kind of problem. You have a clear idea on what you have to do now, but you don't know yet how to do it. Just write a unit test and then work on the implementation:

```
public static void TestBallCollisions()
{
  StartTest(
    delegate
    {
      // Make sure we are in the game and in singleplayer mode
      testGame.gameMode = GameMode.Game;
      testGame.multiplayer = false;
      testGame.Window.Title =
        "Xna Pong - Press 1-5 to start collision tests";
      // Start specific collision scene based on the user input.
      if (testGame.keyboard.IsKeyDown(Keys.D1))
      {
        // First test, just collide with screen border
        testGame.ballPosition = new Vector2(0.6f, 0.9f);
        testGame.ballSpeedVector = new Vector2(1, 1);
      } // if
      else if (testGame.keyboard.IsKeyDown(Keys.D2))
      {
        // Second test, straight on collision with right paddle
        testGame.ballPosition = new Vector2(0.9f, 0.6f);
        testGame.ballSpeedVector = new Vector2(1, 1);
        testGame.rightPaddlePosition = 0.7f;
      } // if
```

```
            else if (testGame.keyboard.IsKeyDown(Keys.D3))
            {
                // Thrid test, straight on collision with left paddle
                testGame.ballPosition = new Vector2(0.1f, 0.4f);
                testGame.ballSpeedVector = new Vector2(-1, -0.5f);
                testGame.leftPaddlePosition = 0.35f;
            } // if
            else if (testGame.keyboard.IsKeyDown(Keys.D4))
            {
                // Advanced test to check if we hit the edge of the right paddle
                testGame.ballPosition = new Vector2(0.9f, 0.4f);
                testGame.ballSpeedVector = new Vector2(1, -0.5f);
                testGame.rightPaddlePosition = 0.29f;
            } // if
            else if (testGame.keyboard.IsKeyDown(Keys.D5))
            {
                // Advanced test to check if we hit the edge of the right paddle
                testGame.ballPosition = new Vector2(0.9f, 0.4f);
                testGame.ballSpeedVector = new Vector2(1, -0.5f);
                testGame.rightPaddlePosition = 0.42f;
            } // if
            // Show lifes
            testGame.ShowLives();
            // Ball in center
            testGame.RenderBall();
            // Render both paddles
            testGame.RenderPaddles();
        });
    } // TestBallCollisions ()
```

The idea here is to press 1–5 to set up custom collision test scenes. For example, if 1 is pressed the ball is moved to (0.6, 0.9), which is near the center at the bottom of the screen. The ball speed is set to (1, 1) to make sure it moves to the screen border, where the ball should bounce off as described in the concept. If you press 4 or 5 the advanced paddle tests are started to check if you hit the edges of the right paddle, which requires a little bit more fine-tuning than the other quite simple collision tests. Collision testing is done in the Update method of PongGame.

Now you can start testing. Obviously if you just start the test now, it will not work because you have not implemented any collision testing yet.

Testing if you hit the top or bottom screen borders is the easiest test; all of the following code is added to the Update method just before you update the ball position for the next frame:

```
// Check top and bottom screen border
if (ballPosition.Y < 0 ||
  ballPosition.Y > 1)
{
  ballSpeedVector.Y = -ballSpeedVector.Y;
  // Move ball back into screen space
  if (ballPosition.Y < 0)
    ballPosition.Y = 0;
  if (ballPosition.Y > 1)
    ballPosition.Y = 1;
} // if
```

The important part here is to just invert the y part of the ball speed vector. Sometimes it can happen that in the next frame the moveFactorPerSecond is smaller than in this frame. Then the ball position can be still out of the screen border and you would invert the y part of the speed vector every frame. To fix this issue you make sure the ball position is always inside the screen and does not goes outside. The same adjustment is done for the paddles too.

The paddle collisions are a little bit more complicated. If you just want to test the top and bottom screen collision, just start the unit test with F5 now. To do the paddle collisions, bounding boxes are constructed to perform the intersection tests, which are available in the BoundingBox class of XNA. The BoundingBox struct uses Vector3 struct and works in 3D space, but you can just ignore the z value and always use 0 and use it just fine in 2D space of your Pong game:

```
// Check for collisions with the paddles.
// Construct bounding boxes to use the intersection helper method.
Vector2 ballSize = new Vector2(
  GameBallRect.Width / 1024.0f, GameBallRect.Height / 768.0f);
BoundingBox ballBox = new BoundingBox(
  new Vector3(ballPosition.X - ballSize.X / 2,
  ballPosition.Y - ballSize.Y / 2, 0),
  new Vector3(ballPosition.X + ballSize.X / 2,
  ballPosition.Y + ballSize.Y / 2, 0));
Vector2 paddleSize = new Vector2(
  GameRedPaddleRect.Width / 1024.0f,
  GameRedPaddleRect.Height / 768.0f);
BoundingBox leftPaddleBox = new BoundingBox(
  new Vector3(-paddleSize.X/2,
  leftPaddlePosition-paddleSize.Y/2, 0),
  new Vector3(+paddleSize.X/2,
  leftPaddlePosition+paddleSize.Y/2, 0));
BoundingBox rightPaddleBox = new BoundingBox(
  new Vector3(1-paddleSize.X/2,
  rightPaddlePosition-paddleSize.Y/2, 0),
  new Vector3(1+paddleSize.X/2,
  rightPaddlePosition+paddleSize.Y/2, 0));
// Ball hit left paddle?
if (ballBox.Intersects(leftPaddleBox))
{
  // Bounce of the paddle
  ballSpeedVector.X = -ballSpeedVector.X;
  // Increase speed a little
  ballSpeedVector *= 1.05f;
  // Did we hit the edges of the paddle?
  if (ballBox.Intersects(new BoundingBox(
    new Vector3(leftPaddleBox.Min.X - 0.01f,
      leftPaddleBox.Min.Y - 0.01f, 0),
    new Vector3(leftPaddleBox.Min.X + 0.01f,
      leftPaddleBox.Min.Y + 0.01f, 0))))
    // Bounce of at a more difficult angle for the other player
    ballSpeedVector.Y = -2;
  else if (ballBox.Intersects(new BoundingBox(
    new Vector3(leftPaddleBox.Min.X - 0.01f,
      leftPaddleBox.Max.Y - 0.01f, 0),
    new Vector3(leftPaddleBox.Min.X + 0.01f,
      leftPaddleBox.Max.Y + 0.01f, 0))))
```

```
      // Bounce of at a more difficult angle for the other player
      ballSpeedVector.Y = +2;
      // Move away from the paddle
      ballPosition.X += moveFactorPerSecond * BallSpeedMultiplicator;
    } // if
```

The bounding boxes are constructed in a similar way as the rendering code is handled in `RenderBall` and `RenderPaddles`. The edge detection code makes it a little bit more complicated and it is just a quick and dirty way to speed up the ball if you hit it with the edge of your paddle. But these few lines make the game a lot more fun.

Exactly the same code you use for the left paddle is also used for the right paddle; you just have to replace all left paddle variables with right paddle variables and negate the move away code.

The final thing you have to do for your game to handle all the game play and the final collision test is to check when the ball gets behind the players paddle and the player loses a life. The code for that is quite simple. You can also directly handle if one of the players loses all his lives and the game is over then. Displaying the "Red Won" or "Blue Won" messages is done in the `Draw` method. If the user presses Space or Escape, he will return to the main menu and the game can start again:

```
    // Ball lost?
    if (ballPosition.X < -0.065f)
    {
      // Play sound
      soundBank.PlayCue("PongBallLost");
      // Reduce number of lives
      leftPlayerLives -- ;
      // Start new ball
      StartNewBall();
    } // if
    else if (ballPosition.X > 1.065f)
    {
      // Play sound
      soundBank.PlayCue("PongBallLost");
      // Reduce number of lives
      rightPlayerLives -- ;
      // Start new ball
      StartNewBall();
    } // if
    // If either player has no more lives, the other player has won!
    if (gameMode == GameMode.Game &&
      (leftPlayerLives == 0 ||
      rightPlayerLives == 0))
    {
      gameMode = GameMode.GameOver;
      StopBall();
    } // if
```

Well, this was the hardest part for this game; the bounding box collision tests were a little bit complicated, but the rest of the game was very straightforward and could be implemented quite easily. You also learned a bit about unit testing and how to handle sprites in an effective manner. You can now test the game with your unit test by pressing F5 and fine-tune the collisions a bit (see Figure 2-8).

Figure 2-8

Adding Sound

To add sound to your game you would usually just drop a couple of .wav files into your project and play them back. In XNA, loading .wav files is not supported and the reason for that is that the Xbox 360 and Windows use different formats for sound and music. To overcome this issue Microsoft invented the XACT tool, which has been available in the DirectX SDK and the Xbox 360 SDK for quite some time now. XACT is short for "Microsoft Cross-Platform Audio Creation Tool." XNA also makes use of this tool and Microsoft decided to make this the only way to play sound files.

Although XACT is a great tool for adding effects, making a lot of adjustments, and having all sound files managed in one place, it can overcomplicate things a little for a project like this one. There is a full chapter on XACT in this book; check it out in Chapter 9. For your Pong game you will just use two simple sound files:

❑   **PongBallHit.wav** is played every time you collide with something (border or paddle) and it is also used for the menu as the sound for changing the selection.

❑   **PongBallLost.wav** is used when a player lost a life because he didn't catch the ball in time.

To add these files to your game, you have to create a new XACT project. You can find XACT at Start ➪ All Programs ➪ Microsoft XNA Game Studio Express ➪ Tools.

In the new XACT project add a wave bank by clicking Wave Banks ⇨ Create Wave Bank and then add a sound bank by clicking Sound Banks ⇨ Create Sound Bank. Now drag the two .wav files into the new XACT wave bank (see Figure 2-9).

Figure 2-9

Next drag the two new wave bank entries over to the sound bank, and then drag them over to the cues. If you are confused or run into problems, check out Chapter 9 for more details.

These are the main components used in XACT for sounds:

❑ **Wave Bank** stores all your .wav files; you can't add anything but wav files here. No support for .mp3, .wma, or any format other than .wav. Importing compressed files is also not an option; ACPCM for Windows and XMA compression for the Xbox 360 is possible, but you have to follow the rules, which are described in Chapter 9.

❑ **Sound Bank** is used to play back sounds later in the game with help of the cues. You can modify the sound settings here by changing the volume and pitch, adding categories, and attaching sound effects (RPC). You can also define multiple tracks here. Usually you will just set the volume here.

❑   **Sound Cues** are used to play sounds. A sound cue has at least one sound bank entry attached, but you can assign multiple sound files to one cue and set rules — if one of the sounds should be played randomly, if you can only play one sound of this kind at a time, and rules for replacing sounds. The important thing here is the cue name, which is used in the game to access the cue and finally play the sound.

Figure 2-10 shows how your XACT project should look like now. You will set the volume of `PongBallHit` to –8 and the `PongBallLost` to –4; the default value of –12 is too silent and your hit sound is a little bit to loud, so reducing it sounds nicer in the game. The rest can use the default values and you can just save the project as `PongSound.xap`. Then add this file to your XNA Studio project and it will use the XNA content pipeline to automatically compile and build all files for both the Windows and Xbox 360 platform for you. Also make sure the two wav files are in the same directory as the `PongSound.xap` file, otherwise the content pipeline might not be able to find these files and it won't be able to build your XACT project.

Figure 2-10

The code to play back the sounds is quite easy, and just to make sure the sounds work fine and the volume is correct, here is simple unit test for the sounds:

```
public static void TestSounds()
{
  StartTest(
    delegate
    {
      if (testGame.keyboard.IsKeyDown(Keys.Space))
        testGame.soundBank.PlayCue("PongBallHit");
      if (testGame.keyboard.IsKeyDown(Keys.LeftControl))
        testGame.soundBank.PlayCue("PongBallLost");
    });
} // TestSounds()
```

Now all you have to do to implement the sounds to the game is to add a couple of lines at the locations where you want the sound to happen. First of all, add the hit sound to the menu and every time a ball collision occurs with the screen borders or the paddles (see the earlier collision tests).

Then add the lost sound like this to the part where you find out if a player lost a life:

```
// Ball lost?
if (ballPosition.X < -0.065f)
{
  // Play sound
  soundBank.PlayCue("PongBallLost");
  // Reduce life
  leftPlayerLives -- ;
  // Start new ball
  StartNewBall();
} // if
else if (ballPosition.X > 1.065f)
{
  // Play sound
  soundBank.PlayCue("PongBallLost");
  // Reduce life
  rightPlayerLives -- ;
  // Start new ball
  StartNewBall();
} // if
```

After adding these lines you can re-enable the TestSingleplayerGame unit test and see if the sounds are played correctly. For more complex games a better system for checking when to play sounds might be required, but most simple games will work fine just with the PlayCue method, which just plays the sound and holds the cue as long as it is needed. You can also get a sound cue and manage it yourself; this has the advantage of being able to stop it and resume it, and so on.

How This Looks on the Xbox 360

Ok, the game is now finished and you tested it quite a bit on the Windows platform. As I already explained in the first chapter there are several steps required to get the Xbox 360 up and running for the XNA Framework. If the XNA Game Launcher is started on the Xbox 360 you can try to compile your XNA Pong game and deploy it to the console.

There are a few important things to remember for the Xbox 360:

❑ **Do not use any external dlls if not required** — Although it is supported to use XNA Game library dlls, most dlls you will have on the Windows platform will call system dlls that are not available on the Xbox 360, or even worse, call unmanaged dlls with P-Invoke, which is absolutely not supported on the Xbox 360 for security reasons. Also don't use unsafe code or make any attempts to call external code, access devices, or use unsupported features. It will be a waste of time and you are better off just playing by the rules.

❑ **Don't wait with the testing** — In the middle of the project test if your code compiles if you change the output settings to the Xbox 360. Often methods you might get used to might be missing on the Xbox 360. For example, there are no `TryParse` methods in the System.dll on the Xbox 360, and some XNA methods and classes like the `MouseState` classes are even missing and unsupported.

❑ **Don't load content directly** — On the Windows platform it is possible to load textures or shaders directly with help of the `Texture2D` or `CompiledEffect` constructors. These methods are completely missing from the Xbox 360; you can only load content from the content pipeline. If you use code that dynamically loads or reloads textures or shaders, it will only work on your Windows platform, so exclude the code with `#if !XBOX360 … #endif` for the Xbox 360 build.

❑ **Save Games and loading other content** — For save games you can use the Content namespace and the many available helper classes. To load content you will always have to make sure you use the correct path with the help of `StorageContainer.TitleLocation`, which works on the Windows platform too and just uses your output directory there. Loading from other locations on the Xbox 360 results in Access Denied exceptions for IO operations.

❑ **Test resolutions** — The Xbox 360 supports many different resolutions from the PC and you should test at least 2–3 different resolutions to make sure the game runs fine with it.

❑ **Allow controlling everything with a gamepad** — Most XNA games I've seen to this point made the mistake of only allowing keyboard input or only gamepad input, which means it runs either only on Windows or only if you have an Xbox 360 controller. Always add support to as many input devices as you can think of and that make sense for your game.

❑ **Debug and unit test on the Xbox 360** — Debugging and unit testing is no different on your console; the same rules apply. It might be a little harder to trace errors and log messages, but stepping through code and testing unit tests works great with XNA. Take advantage of that. By the way: edit and continue works only on the Windows platform, you can't do that with Xbox 360 games, which can be annoying, but you will probably do the major part of your development on the Windows platform anyway.

XNA Pong was always coded with the Xbox 360 in mind; all methods and features you used are supported on the Xbox 360. Therefore testing the game on the Xbox 360 is no big deal, you can just deploy it and start it and it will work fine (see Figure 2-11).

Figure 2-11

Challenge: Improve the Pong Game

It is now your turn to improve the game a little bit; maybe you can exchange the graphics or sounds or you can adjust the game play. Also try to add Rumble support for your Gamepad controller if you have one. You really should have one if you read this book, even if you don't have an Xbox 360; a lot of XNA samples will require an Xbox 360 controller and some of the games are more fun with an Xbox 360 controller than having to play with the keyboard.

Here is the method to add Rumble support for a specific gamepad:

```
GamePad.SetVibration(PlayerIndex.One, leftRumble, rightRumble);
```

Use that code to rumble a bit for a short while if the ball hits your paddle (use the same value for left and right rumble, then the whole controller just shakes). And also rumble if you lost a life, this time longer and stronger.

As always you can check out the project for this chapter and see a solution to the challenge. Your solution does not have to be the same, but it might be useful to see another or maybe even an easier way to solve a specific problem.

Have fun with XNA Pong.

Troubleshooting

Hopefully there is not much that can go wrong in this chapter. This chapter only touched on two major issues: unit testing and sprites. You also might have problems getting the game to run on your Xbox 360, but I already wrote down a bunch of tips and tricks on this issue at the end of Chapter 1; check them out if you still have problems setting up your Xbox 360.

Another problem most of you will probably not have, but for the few readers that are not experienced with exceptions, especially with the ones from XNA, is to understand why an exception is thrown and what exactly has to be done to fix it. Always read the exception very closely and try to review the full stack trace and check out if there are inner exceptions with more detailed information.

Similar to Managed DirectX, sometimes you get exceptions from the underlying DirectX framework, which can be confusing sometimes. Try to search for help on specific error numbers on the Internet and MSDN. In those cases the context is usually more important than the error message itself. For example, if compiling a shader fails you might get strange error codes, but instead of trying to find out what these error codes mean make sure the shader file exists, it can be compiled, and your hardware can handle it. A good tool to check if shader files are valid is FX Composer from Nvidia.

If you run into trouble using unit testing please also read the troubleshooting section of the next chapter, because it talks a lot about unit testing too. Basically always remember that the kind of unit tests you used here behave like normal programs; treat them the same way. Debug them and step through them like you would with the final application.

Last but not least, some tips about using sprites in XNA:

❏ If you render a lot of sprites on top of each other there might be many issues in XNA showing random sorting order, problems when using different textures, and often the background sprite might kill everything in front of it. As you can see in XNA Pong you rendered the background in an extra spritebatch call. This way it was separated and cannot interfere with any of the sprites in the game or menu.

❏ Try to render all sprites at once, especially if you can sort them by the blend mode. It is a lot faster if you render all sprites at once in one big call to spritebatch. Check out the DrawSprites method as an example. If you use different blend modes like additive for light effects and alpha blending for all other sprites, try to render in two passes, first the alpha blended stuff, then the additive lights on top. Performance can improve to 200%–300% if you do that.

❏ Think about resolutions and how to handle different widths and heights; you can get the used resolution in the Initialize method with the following two lines:

```
width = graphics.GraphicsDevice.Viewport.Width;
height = graphics.GraphicsDevice.Viewport.Height;
```

❏ You cannot force a specific resolution; it will not work on the Xbox 360 at all and on Windows it is only used as a suggestion. For example, if you want to test the 720p 16:9 resolution (1280×720) on your PC, you must have a monitor that supports this resolution either in windowed mode or in fullscreen mode depending on what you are testing. Add the following lines to the constructor of your main game class (PongGame in this Chapter) to suggest the 720p resolution. You can check if that worked in the `Initialize` method by checking the width and height as described earlier:

```
graphics.PreferredBackBufferWidth = 1280;
graphics.PreferredBackBufferHeight = 720;
```

❑ There is no font support in XNA — to show text you can either create textures like in this game with all the text already written down or write your own font support like in Chapter 5. For both solutions you will use sprites to render text or just a letter at a time on the screen.

❑ Sprites are not the only way to display 2D data in XNA; you can write your own shaders and even do much more advanced effects than is possible with the sprite class. As an example check out Chapter 5 and see how 2D lines are rendered with help of shaders.

Summary

I hope you enjoyed this chapter and tried to follow the process of creating a game closely. Pong might not be the most exciting game, but it was a great example to really cover everything from start to finish that would usually happen for any game project. Bigger projects would be impossible to cover in just one chapter and this way you already learned about concepts, unit tests, and the basic terminology of agile development. After learning about the helper classes in the next chapter and then diving into the details of the game class and game components, you will be ready to do a rocking 3D engine with lots of cool effects for the final part of this book to write nice big game with XNA. In the meantime you will see a couple of other small fun game projects.

The most important point of this chapter is the proof that agile programming works great for games, and though you are able to dynamically change things and have a very easy top-down approach to solve problems, it is still very important to make a concept, even if it is just one-page long. Unit tests also helped a lot, but as you will see in the next chapter unit tests can also be automated and they are very useful for the helper classes, which are used all over the place in the projects later in this book.

Take a look what you have learned in this chapter:

❑ It is important to write down your ideas and to develop a small concept.

❑ Just one page of concept can be quite useful.

❑ To solve problems you use a top-down approach and you use unit testing to stay at just the top level without even thinking of the implementation. This way you can quickly adopt ideas from the concept and write them down in unit tests, making it easier to see exactly what methods you have to implement.

❑ You created some textures, loaded them into the project, and displayed them as sprites.

❑ Rendering many sprites at once gives better performance.

❑ Using a clever formula helped you to make the game resolution-independent. This way the game works fine on the Xbox 360 and any resolution that is possible.

❑ You added sound using XACT and learned some basics; you can find more details in Chapter 9.

❑ Handling game input using two gamepads controllers and using the keyboard for multiple players.

❑ Collision testing in 2D with help of the `BoundingBox` structure.

❑ Using `Vector3` instead of `Vector2` works fine if you always set the z component to 0.

❑ Using unit tests for collision testing is very important and greatly reduces the amount of testing you have to do. You can also always switch back to the unit test and test the collisions again, even if you are currently working on a completely different part of the game.

3

Helper Classes

In the Helper namespace I usually put a lot of helpful little tools and classes, which become quite useful over time. For a single project it might not be the most important or valuable code, but because it is used again and again, no matter whether other parts of the engine change, helper classes will be the most consistent part of your engines and projects. Most of the helper classes don't have much to do with game programming, and they are useful in other projects or even in websites.

You just saw in the previous chapter that you can write a whole game without any helper classes and without even using any extra files or classes at all. But as the projects become bigger and bigger you will see that there are a lot of repeating patterns and similar problems occur, which were already solved in the past. Usually most of the reused functionality in XNA is graphic components. In the next chapter and especially in the second part of this book you learn more about game components and the graphic engine. For now this chapter keeps the focus on the very basic functionality to log messages, access the game content, do unit testing effectively, how to generate random numbers, and many other smaller issues.

To make this chapter a little bit more exciting, you also create another little game just for the fun of it. Not all of the helper classes will be used, but building a game engine is not an easy task. For that reason, this and the next chapter start with the helper classes and the game components to make developing your graphic engine in Part II of this book a little easier. Please note that I did not write the helper classes in the way they are presented in this chapter; they evolved over the course of the past couple of years. Just add functionally or your own helper classes whenever you need them. If you solve a problem once and think it might not be useful again, just leave it where it is. But if you find yourself copying that solution over to a new project or maybe just to another class several times, you should seriously consider extracting the logic and putting it into a special class.

Additionally, you learn a little bit more about the content pipeline you already used in the previous chapters to support the Xbox 360. It is possible to directly load textures or shaders without using the content pipeline, but all these methods work only on the Windows platform. If you want to create a cross-platform game you should make sure everything compiles and works on both the Windows and the Xbox 360 platforms. You will continue to do that throughout this book.

At the end of this chapter you will quickly develop a fun Breakout clone game. It will be a lot easier than in the previous chapter because you will write all the helper classes first. For example, sprite rendering is very easy with the help of the SpriteHelper class. You can find more helper classes and game components to improve both the Pong and Breakout games in the next chapter.

Managing the Content Pipeline

As you learned in Chapter 1, the content pipeline is used to import game assets like textures, models, shaders, and sound files. Instead of just adding them to your project like any other unsupported files for Visual Studio (or XNA Studio), the content files get processed and then are compiled into binary content files, which can be loaded from your game (see Figure 3-1).

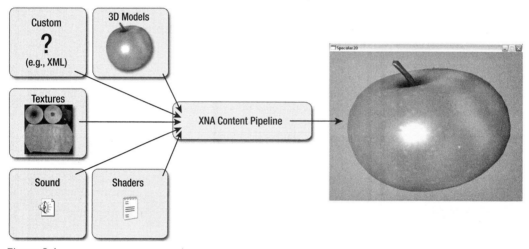

Figure 3-1

In the past a game programmer had to write his own importer to load game content data or use one of the available formats like the .x file format in DirectX for model files. But often the available formats are insufficient, too slow, or just too inflexible when trying to add new features to a game. This is the reason why almost every commercial game has its own file formats and custom logic programmed behind it. This has the advantage that only the developers of a game know the layout of their internal format and they can extend it or change it as often as they want. However, it is usually a lot of work to get 3D content in your game this way. Loading textures is usually not that complicated because many libraries exist and even when writing your own file format, it basically just contains pixels, which are stored as 24- or 32-bit color values. It can become a little bit more difficult if you try using compression or if you want to use hardware-compressed textures like with the DXT format, but DirectX has a great repertoire of helpful methods to assist you with that.

On the other hand, loading 3D model data is a lot more complicated, especially in XNA, where you have to have not only the geometry data, but also shaders to render a 3D object and then, of course, material data to tell the shaders which colors, textures, and parameters to use. In DirectX most tutorials and samples just use the .x file format, but the .x file format might not be sufficient for many projects. Especially if you use normal napping and require the geometry data to contain tangents, the .x file format will not be very helpful. You would have to generate tangents in your application and work around problems this might introduce. For example, one of my older games, Rocket Commander, had this exact problem and it required a complex model loading process and tangent regeneration process.

Other game data like loading sound files (.wav), shaders (.fx), or custom (for example, .xml) data might be straightforward because your game or the framework you are using provides enough helpful classes to load everything quickly, but then you might run into problems running your game with the same content on another platform. You can, for example, use ACPCM sound files on the Windows platform and use compiled Pixel Shader 1.1 files or just load a couple of .jpg files as textures, but there is no ACPCM support on the Xbox 360; sound is either PCM or in the custom XMA format for the Xbox. Shader code has to be in the format the Xbox 360 accepts, and loading textures might work differently too. This problem would even get more complicated if more platforms are supported in the future.

To simplify loading the game content, XNA allows you now to just drop the raw content files into your XNA Studio project and they will be processed and compiled to the correct output format for the currently selected platform. For example, your sound files can be processed and based on your XACT project settings — you will have different output formats and compressions, but all the raw sound files in the wave bank are the same and only have to be updated in one place. This idea is great, but it would require that *any* raw content file format is supported, which is not practical because there are so many file formats available and you don't know which ones are going to be used. For example, one of your graphic artists might use Photoshop and store .psd files, and other teams might use Gimp or Paint-Shop or just the Paint program of Windows. And there are thousands of other graphic tools and programs around. Additionally, you don't really know which data to extract; many formats can have multiple layers and maybe the artist wants to have each layer available or just have everything merged down.

Supported File Formats

Instead of just dropping anything, use one of the available processors and supported formats or try to write your own content processors (see Chapter 7) if you think you will need it:

❑ **Texture formats: .dds, .png, .jpg, .bmp, .tga** — Basically everything you can load with the .NET Framework or DirectX. The input format should usually be uncompressed for the best quality. Highly compressed .jpg files are bad, especially if you compress them again with DXT for your game. Alternatively, you can use the correct output compression in your input files (dds files with DXT compression) and set the same settings for the content properties again to leave them that way (which is the way I process most of the content in all my projects).

❑ **Sound and Music formats: .xap (XACT Audio Project)** — In XACT you can only import .wav files, but you can set a lot of effects, set parameters, and choose ACPCM compression on the Windows platform or XMA on the Xbox 360 platform. Read more about this in Chapter 9.

❑ **3D Model formats: .fbx and .x model files** — .x files are known from the DirectX SDK and many samples and tutorials. DirectX provides classes to easily load .x files. Most .x files should work fine with XNA too; the main difference is that DirectX usually doesn't use shaders for .x files and XNA always uses shaders. To export models from 3D Studio Max, use the Panda DirectX Exporter. You can find the Panda Exporter plugin at http://www.andytather.co.uk/Panda/directxmax.aspx.

.fbx files are a little bit newer and were originally developed by Alias, the makers of Maya, also a 3D modeling tool. Alias was acquired by Autodesk, the makers of 3D Studio Max and many CAT programs. .fbx stands for "Universal 3D Asset Exchange" and is Autodesk's free format for cross-platform content interchanging. In the new version of 3D Studio Max 9 it is included by default and Maya supports it too. There are also many other 3D content creation programs that support importing and exporting the .fbx format. In XNA it is especially useful for animated models, bones, and skinning. It supports more options for that, but it is especially bad for shaders, because no material or any shader settings can be exported.

Another problem with the .fbx format is the missing format specification, and to access the SDK you have to join the Autodesk Developer Network for an annual membership fee, which really sucks. If you take a look at other interchange formats like Collada, you can see that they are much more open and extensible, and because they are not just developed by one company many new additions and features are added constantly. In the past Collada did not support shader settings, but the current versions are very good for 3D data; you can export tangents, shader settings, and everything else you need for a game. Sadly, Collada is not supported by XNA and I was not able to convince Microsoft to include it. XNARacer initially used Collada files for all models, track, and landscape data, but this was changed later to support the content pipeline.

❑ **Other formats** — You can import custom file formats, for example xml files, binary files, or even write your own custom processor. This can be useful if you have a bigger project and it is worth the effort or you need a special model format and it is not supported yet by XNA. For example, Quake3/Doom3 uses md3/md5 files and if you just used to import some models for testing and playing around, an md5 importer would be nice.

In case you have more content files or some custom data for your game you can either decide to write a custom processor and then use the imported and compiled data in your project or just do it the old way by loading the content files yourself. For example, the racer game you will write in the last chapters of this book uses a landscape with landscape height values imported from a bitmap file. Processing the bitmap file and outputting the landscape height data for the game would be possible, but it is too much work — just loading the height data is much simpler and only required once.

Advantages and Disadvantages

Another disadvantage of the content pipeline is the fact that your compiled content cannot be changed anymore. Once you start your game or have your game deployed on client computers or the Xbox 360, all the content files have only the compiled data in them. Say you have just written a particle editor with shader support for all particles. If you want to change the textures, shaders, and other particle settings dynamically while the editor is running, you would have to reload the textures, shaders, and so on. But because you need to have the content compiled first inside of XNA Studio you have to stop your application, add all the files to your XNA Studio project, recompile and wait until all the content is rebuilt, and then start again. Especially in the case of just testing and tweaking effects or particles, this can be very annoying and slows down your work process a lot. It would be more useful to just load textures, shaders, and your particle settings dynamically and not use the content pipeline for programs like that.

Last but not least, here is a trick I use in most projects with many content files: compile them all and make sure you don't change them very often (only every couple of days). Now you can use a dummy project to compile all your game content and copy over all compiled content files to your real project.

Especially when using unit testing and the Agile Methodology talked about in the last chapter, you will start the application several hundred times a day and each run should be as fast as possible.

The good thing about the content pipeline is that the compiled data (.xnb files) cannot be read by any programs except from an XNA engine and the loading process is usually also a lot faster because all the data is already in the exact format you need for your game. For example, textures are always stored as DXT files and use mip-maps if you specified that in the content properties. This way the game just has to load the texture data in one quick call and then send it to the graphic card for rendering, again a very fast process. This is even more important for 3D model data. If you take a look at Rocket Commander and profile it a little bit, you can see that loading the 3D models and generating all the extra data and tangents takes most of the initialization time (over 90%), whereas XNA games with 10 times as many models load a lot faster. Loading all data as quickly as possible is also a good thing for the Xbox 360 console; console games usually have a short loading time.

Handling Content Directories

Okay, you learned a lot about the advantages and disadvantages of using the content pipeline; here you focus on the game programming a little bit more and the everyday problems. If you take a look at the content directories for the Rocket Commander game and Racing game (see Figure 3-2) you can see that Rocket Commander has a lot of directories, whereas just two simple directories are used in XNARacer.

Figure 3-2

From the looks of it you would expect that Rocket Commander has a lot more content, but in reality XNARacer uses almost 10 times as many 3D model files and also has a lot more textures, music, and sound files.

You might ask why Rocket Commander uses so many directories. There is no content pipeline in the game, and to keep everything organized and easy to find directories are used for each part of the game. For example, the Textures folder holds all the 2D textures for the menu and game interface, the Models sub-directory holds the textures for the 3D models, the Effects sub-directory contains the effect textures, and so on.

In XNA you cannot use this kind of directory structure because most content files, especially the 3D models, can require a lot of other content files to be loaded recursively (see Figure 3-3).

Content Processor Dependencies

Figure 3-3

As you can see, the Apple model is loaded from the `Apple.x` file, which recursively loads `Apple.dds`, `AppleNormal.dds`, and `NormalMapping.fx`. The content processor expects all these files in the same directory, which forces you to use one directory for all the 3D models and the textures and shaders you use for them. Additionally, most shaders are used for other 3D data as well and it would be very confusing duplicating the shaders and having them in another directory too. You also sometimes load the textures for custom 3D data too (for example, the guard rail holder model uses the same texture as the generated guard rail object in XNARacer).

Anyway, it is important to remember that each piece of content must have a unique name. You can't have an Apple model and an Apple texture. As you can see in the Input File line of Figure 3-3 you only add the `Apple.x` file; all the other files are added automatically through the model processor. Additionally XNA is clever enough to rename all the recursive files because they often use textures with the same names as the model files. Recursive files will end with ~0. You also can't set the content properties of these recursive files because you don't add them into your project. For that reason make sure the input files already use the correct format (DXT1 and DXT5 in the preceding example).

Importing and Accessing Content

You now know enough to import some content and access it from your game. In the previous chapters you already accessed some content files and took a quick look at the content pipeline. Now you will take a closer look at the actual process and how to use content files. In Chapter 7 you learn how to write your own content processors by extending the X Model File Processor with some useful features for your graphics engine.

Back in Chapter 1 you learned how to add textures; just take a texture file (.dds, .jpg, .bmp, or .png) and drop it onto your XNA Studio project. Now you can click the texture and configure the Texture Content Processor settings (see Figure 3-4).

For textures it is important to set the correct Content Processor mode. For 2D data like sprites, text, and all user interface (UI) graphics you have in your game it is usually best to use the 32bpp Sprite format (uncompressed, which means it takes 4 MB for a 1024x1024 texture with 32bbp).

Figure 3-4

3D texture data will be used a lot more in a 3D game than 2D UI textures, and textures and levels are getting bigger with every game. For this reason it is very important to keep the texture sizes small. Instead of just reducing the resolution for your textures and making your games look very bad, use hardware texture compression instead. You can simply select DXT1 for a 1:6 compression ratio for color textures and DXT5 for a 1:4 compression ratio for textures with alpha information (or compressed normal maps). This means with DXT1 textures you can have six times as many textures in your game consuming the same amount of video memory as uncompressed textures without losing much of its quality. Another trick is to combine or even generate textures inside your shaders; for example, detail textures can improve land-scape details for almost no extra video memory cost.

For models you can currently only select the X Model Importer or the FBX Model Importer (see Figure 3-5). Maybe more formats will be available in the future. If you write custom model processors like you will do in Chapter 7, you can select them the same way you select texture processors. For normal mapping you want to select your custom XNARacer Tangent Model Processor from Chapter 7. For the next few chapters just leave the default value.

Figure 3-5

If you followed the way you loaded textures in the last two chapters you will probably already know how to load content in XNA. Textures are loaded with:

```
backgroundTexture = content.Load<Texture2D>("CityGroundSmall");
```

And 3D models can be loaded the same way — just change the generic type of the Load method:

```
appleModel = content.Load<Model>("apple");
```

Displaying a model is a little bit more complicated; there is no simple draw method, you have to go through all model meshes and update all shader effects, and then you can render each part. For more details see Chapters 5 and 6. Later in this book in Chapter 7 you will see a new class just for loading and rendering models, which makes it even easier to just show the 3D model in our 3D world with just one single line of code:

```
appleModel.Render(Vector3.Zero);
```

You now know all the basics about the content pipeline. You learn more about the content pipeline in the upcoming chapters when adding 3D models with your custom tangent model processor in your graphics engine, and in Chapter 9 when you learn in detail about XACT.

Logging Error Messages

Debugging game code can be very complicated, especially if you don't get any exceptions, but something in your render loop goes wrong. Just setting a few breakpoints might not be enough and especially if you experience errors after running the game for a while, debugging is not the right option. You want to know what is going on each frame, but you don't want to step through 500 frames to find it out. For these kinds of problems you can just throw some text to the console, but this will only work inside Visual Studio and you will lose all the console content the next time you start your project.

One of the most important classes in all bigger projects I have done is the Log class, which just writes information, warning, error, or debugging texts to a simple text file. The class itself is very short and simple, but if you use it in the right way it will make your debugging and testing sessions much more enjoyable. There are also more advanced logging classes and frameworks available like Log4Net, which you can find at http://logging.apache.org/log4net/. Logging can be more than just writing a few lines to a text file. Logging data from your application can be used to find out about user errors remotely with a web service, you can fire Windows error events, and you can do a lot more things. This is not covered in this book because it is a very complex topic. For the simple games in this book, using Log class should be sufficient.

Take a look at the Log class (a more complex version can be found in the Breakout game):

```
public class Log
{
  #region Variables
  private static StreamWriter writer = null;
  private const string LogFilename = "Log.txt";
  #endregion
```

The Log class uses the Log.txt file to store all the log messages with the help of the StreamWriter object stored as a static object to have easy access from your static methods. The first time this class is called it gets instantiated through the static constructor:

```
#region Static constructor to create log file
static Log()
{
  // Open file
  FileStream file = new FileStream(
    LogFilename, FileMode.OpenOrCreate,
    FileAccess.Write, FileShare.ReadWrite);
  writer = new StreamWriter(file);
  // Go to end of file
  writer.BaseStream.Seek(0, SeekOrigin.End);
  // Enable auto flush (always be up to date when reading!)
  writer.AutoFlush = true;

  // Add some info about this session
  writer.WriteLine("/// Session started at: "+
    StringHelper.WriteIsoDateAndTime(DateTime.Now));
} // Log()
#endregion
```

FileShare.ReadWrite makes sure you can always read and write the file from outside while the game is running. Other than that the writer is set to the end of the file, auto flush is enabled to make sure writing new data is immediately saved to the log file, and finally you add a little text indicating that this session started. For the time stamp you will use a helper method from the StringHelper class you learn about in a second.

And finally, here is the most important method and the only one you will ever call from this class:

```
#region Write log entry
static public void Write(string message)
{
  DateTime ct = DateTime.Now;
  string s = "[" + ct.Hour.ToString("00") + ":" +
    ct.Minute.ToString("00") + ":" +
    ct.Second.ToString("00") + "] " +
    message;
  writer.WriteLine(s);

#if DEBUG
  // In debug mode write that message to the console as well!
  System.Console.WriteLine(s);
#endif
} // Write(message)
#endregion
```

First, a simple time stamp is added in front of the message. Then the message is written to your Log.txt file and finally you also add the message to the console if the project is in debug mode. Now you can add a new line to the Log.txt file every time you complete a level in the Breakout game from Chapter 2 by just adding the following line:

```
Log.Write("Level " + level + " completed.");
```

Unit Testing in XNA

Before going into greater detail about the helper classes for the upcoming projects in this book, this section talks a little bit about unit testing. You already learned about static unit tests in the last chapter. Static unit tests are great for quickly checking visual results, testing physics and the controllers, and building your game in a quick manner. But helper classes and components that do not require user input would require you to think about interfacing with them. That makes no sense because unit testing is all about improving the maintainability of your application and making sure everything runs as errorless as possible. For example, to test if the Log class works you could call the following lines of code:

```
FileHelper.DeleteFile(Log.LogFilename);
Log.Write("New log entry");
```

This code can only be executed inside the Log *class because* Log.LogFilename *is private.*

Now you could go into the application directory and check if the log file exists and has an entry with the "New log entry" text in it. But checking this file yourself over and over again is a bit of a hassle. Instead of logging every error here you should only put the less important warning messages (e.g. user is not connected to the internet) into the log and throw exceptions when fatal errors occur (e.g. texture not found, no shaders available, etc.). This is especially true if the problems become bigger and the tests are much more complex and involve a very lengthy check process. You can avoid checking for errors yourself by letting these tests check themselves and let them be executed automatically instead of calling them yourself from the Program class like static unit tests.

NUnit and TestDriven.Net

To do this you can use the popular NUnit Framework, which you can download at http://www .nunit.org/.

Alternatively you can also use TestDriven.NET from http://www.testdriven.net/ if you are using Visual Studio 2005 Professional or better. It supports many cool features and you can start tests directly with hotkeys or the popup menu, which is really cool and simple. TestDriven.Net does not work in VC# Express or XNA Studio Express (it did work a year ago, but the developer had to remove the plugin support for Express because Microsoft wants developers to use the Professional Edition for serious programmers). See Chapter 1 on how to get XNA working in Visual Studio 2005; use a dummy project from XNA Studio Express for processing your content, which is not possible in Visual Studio 2005.

It does not matter which one you install, just add the NUnit.Framework.dll from the installation folder to your project (right-click your project references and add a new reference; use Browse if you can't find it in the Global Assembly Cache (GAC), which is represented in the first tab). Now you can add the following using directive:

```
#if DEBUG
using NUnit.Framework;
#endif
```

I usually add this at the very top of the using directives region and the reason why this is used only in debug mode is the fact that you will only use the unit tests in your debug build; for the final game you don't want the extra NUnit.Framework.dll and all the testing code, because it is not required for your game.

As an example, take a look at the first unit test in the `StringHelper` class, which checks if the `IsInList` helper method works as expected:

```
[TestFixture]
public class StringHelperTests
{
  /// <summary>
  /// Test IsInList
  /// </summary>
  [Test]
  public void TestIsInList()
  {
    Assert.IsTrue(IsInList("whats",
      new string[] { "hi", "whats", "up?" }, false));
    Assert.IsFalse(IsInList("no way",
      new string[]
      { "omg", "no no", "there is no way!" }, false));
  } // TestIsInList()
...
```

`Assert` is a helper class inside the NUnit framework and it contains methods to check if the return values are as expected. If the value is not as expected an exception will be thrown and you can immediately see which line of your test failed. For example, `Assert.IsTrue` checks if the return value of `IsInList` is true. If the return value is false, an exception will be thrown. Luckily the string list contains "whats" and the test should pass. The next test checks for "no way" and that string is not in the second string list and therefore the second test line should return false as it does. Note: "there is no way!" contains "no way," but you were not checking the `Contains` method, which also exists in the `StringHelper` class. `IsInList` only returns true if the exact string was found in the list.

Starting Unit Tests

You can run the test in TestDriven.Net by clicking the right mouse button and selecting "Run Test" (see Figure 3-6) or you can use the NUnit GUI program if you don't have or cannot use TestDriven.Net. You can also test static unit tests the same way with TestDriven.Net, but the NUnit GUI does not support static unit tests. For this reason I added the unit tests in `Program.cs` (or the `UnitTesting.cs` class in later projects) to support all users and XNA Studio Express. TestDriven.Net can be used to start both dynamic and static unit tests, but since version 2.0 you will have to remove the [Test] attribute from static unit tests in order to work properly (you don't use the [Test] attributes for static unit tests in this book anyway).

Figure 3-6

The test will execute without any error, but if you were to change the test by changing "whats" to "whats up" the first Assert test would fail and you would see the following results from TestDriven.Net:

```
TestCase 'M:XnaBreakout.Helpers.StringHelper.StringHelperTests.TestIsInList' failed:
  NUnit.Framework.AssertionException
  at NUnit.Framework.Assert.DoAssert(IAsserter asserter)
  at NUnit.Framework.Assert.IsTrue(Boolean condition, String message, Object[] args)
  at NUnit.Framework.Assert.IsTrue(Boolean condition)
  C:\code\XnaRacer\Helpers\StringHelper.cs(1387,0): at
    XnaBreakout.Helpers.StringHelper.StringHelperTests.TestIsInList()


0 passed, 1 failed, 0 skipped, took 0,48 seconds.
```

This tells you exactly where to look (you can even double-click the error and jump to the line 1387) and what you should change. The error becomes even more visible if using the NUnit GUI (see Figure 3-7).

Figure 3-7

The NUnit GUI is a good tool to run many unit tests at once and quickly see which ones did not work properly and then investigate further in the source code. You can use File ➪ Load to select your program or just drag and drop any .NET .exe or .dll file onto the NUnit GUI program. Then you see all the tests in that assembly and can test them by clicking Run. The program is nice, but I usually don't go outside of my programming environment when coding and testing, and therefore I like TestDriven.Net a lot more and use it all the time. To fix the error you just change the "whats up" line back to "whats" and all your tests will pass and you get a green light.

Golden Rules

I did not go much into writing unit tests here because Chapter 2 already discussed the basic rules, which of course also apply for dynamic unit tests. Keep these guidelines in mind when you start writing your first unit tests:

❑ Think about your problems and divide them into small manageable parts.

❑ Write the tests first and do not think about the implementation, just write them down like you think the final code should look or like you want to have your game code.

❑ Try to make sure you test as much as possible. For example, the `TestIsInList` method tests both a successful call to `IsInList` and a failure from the `IsInList` call. Spend time with your unit tests, but never more than 50% — you should not have to write 30 checks for a method that has only two lines of code.

❑ Start the test constantly from this point on, even when you think it does not make sense. It will force you to see what has to be done and how far you are in the implementation process. At first the test will not even compile because you haven't implemented anything. Then after implementing empty methods the test should fail because you are not doing anything yet. Later when everything works you will feel much better.

❑ Though you will not test your static unit tests very often, dynamic unit tests can be tested every single time you compile your code (if they all run quick enough). Always try to run all unit tests once a day or once a week to make sure your latest code changes did not add new bugs or errors.

RandomHelper Class

Take a look at one of the helper classes. `RandomHelper` will not be used often in a single project, but almost any game uses some random number generation to make the game content appear less periodic and to add more variation to the game.

In the Breakout game you will write in a little bit, the blocks are generated randomly. For level 1 you use a probability of 10%, level 2 uses a probability of 20%, and so on. This way the level gets more filled and the game gets harder. You could just use the `Random` class and call the `Next` method to get a new random number, but in case you want to generate a random normalized vector you would have to write the following lines of code:

```
Random randomGenerator = new Random((int)DateTime.Now.Ticks);
Vector3 randomNormalVector = new Vector3(
   (float)randomGenerator.NextDouble() * 2.0f - 1.0f,
   (float)randomGenerator.NextDouble() * 2.0f - 1.0f,
   (float)randomGenerator.NextDouble() * 2.0f - 1.0f);
randomNormalVector.Normalize();
```

Instead of repeating this code over and over again, a helper class like `RandomHelper` might be very useful. Figure 3-8 shows the basic layout of the `RandomHelper` class.

Figure 3-8

As you can see the methods are very simple and it would only take a couple of minutes to write the whole class. However, the class is still useful and thanks to the internal globalRandomGenerator instance of the Random class, the RandomHelper class is much quicker generating random values than creating a new Random class every time you need a random number.

Generate Random Vectors

Here you can see a method from the RandomHelper class:

```
/// <summary>
/// Get random Vector2
/// </summary>
/// <param name="min">Minimum for each component</param>
/// <param name="max">Maximum for each component</param>
/// <returns>Vector2</returns>
public static Vector2 GetRandomVector2(float min, float max)
{
  return new Vector2(
    GetRandomFloat(min, max),
    GetRandomFloat(min, max));
} // GetRandomVector2(min, max)
```

It does not make sense to unit test any method in the RandomHelper class because all return values are random and you don't really have to check if GetRandomVector2 returns a Vector2; it just does that. There is not much that can go wrong.

StringHelper Class

The StringHelper class is one of the biggest helper classes and I guess it was the first helper class I ever wrote because working with strings involves so many things, it is very easy to think about many ways to improve performance, handle lists of strings easier, output string data easily, and so on.

If you take a look at the StringHelper class (see Figure 3-9) you will immediately notice the many methods and all the method overloads supporting many different parameter types. It also contains quite a lot of unit tests; you just saw a unit test from the StringHelper class a few minutes ago.

continued ..

Figure 3-9

You might ask yourself why there are only a couple of unit tests, but so very many methods in this class. The reason for this is that I started coding this class many years ago, a long time before I started using unit testing. Some methods don't make much sense in .NET 2.0 because the framework implements them now, but I got used to my own methods. I just hope you can find some useful methods in this class. It might take a while to get used to the many methods, but when you need a complicated string operation you will thank me (or yourself if you have your own helper class) for a useful method.

Extracting Filenames

Many of the GetDirectory, CutExtension, and so on methods are available in the Path class from the System.IO namespace too, but one of the most useful methods in StringHelper for filenames is the ExtractFilename method, which cuts off both the path and the extension to just get the name of a file, nothing else. Path.GetFileNameWithoutExtension does a similar thing, but I like my own method better for some reason. It might also be interesting if you want to implement your own methods and need some working code you can start with. Again: You don't have to write your own Path methods, but sometimes you don't know what the framework provides or you just want to investigate yourself.

It's been a long time since I tested the performance of these methods, but I would still guess that most of the StringHelper methods are faster than some of the Path methods.

```
/// <summary>
/// Extracts filename from full path+filename, cuts of extension
/// if cutExtension is true. Can be also used to cut of directories
/// from a path (only last one will remain).
/// </summary>
static public string ExtractFilename(string pathFile, bool cutExtension)
{
  if (pathFile == null)
    return "";

  // Support windows and unix slashes
  string[] fileName = pathFile.Split(new char[] { '\\', '/' });
  if (fileName.Length == 0)
  {
    if (cutExtension)
      return CutExtension(pathFile);
    return pathFile;
  } // if (fileName.Length)

  if (cutExtension)
    return CutExtension(fileName[fileName.Length - 1]);
  return fileName[fileName.Length - 1];
} // ExtractFilename(pathFile, cutExtension)
```

Writing a unit test for a method like this is also very simple. Just check if the expected result is returned:

```
Assert.AreEqual("SomeFile",
  StringHelper.ExtractFilename("SomeDir\\SomeFile.bmp"));
```

Writing Lists

A little bit more unique is the WriteArrayData method in the StringHelper class, which writes any type of lists, arrays, or IEnumerable data to a text string, which then can be used for logging. The implementation is again quite simple:

```
/// <summary>
/// Returns a string with the array data, ArrayList version.
/// </summary>
static public string WriteArrayData(ArrayList array)
{
  StringBuilder ret = new StringBuilder();
  if (array != null)
    foreach (object obj in array)
      ret.Append((ret.Length == 0 ? "" : ", ") +
        obj.ToString());
  return ret.ToString();
} // WriteArrayData(array)
```

Lists, even generic ones, are derived from the ArrayList class and therefore you can call this method with any dynamic list. For arrays a special overload exists, also for special collections and byte or integer arrays, which would work with IEnumerable too, but it is faster to use overloads that don't use the object class.

To test the WriteArrayData method you could write a method like the following one:

```
/// <summary>
/// Test WriteArrayData
/// </summary>
[Test]
public void TestWriteArrayData()
{
  Assert.AreEqual("3, 5, 10",
    WriteArrayData(new int[] { 3, 5, 10 }));
  Assert.AreEqual("one, after, another",
    WriteArrayData(new string[] { "one", "after", "another" }));
  List<string> genericList = new List<string>();
    genericList.Add("whats");
    genericList.AddRange(new string[] { "going", "on" });
  Assert.AreEqual("whats, going, on",
    WriteArrayData(genericList));
} // TestWriteArray()
```

Other Helpers

The Helpers namespace contains a few more helper classes; most of them are simple like the RandomHelper class. It is not very exciting to go through all of them, so please review the ones that are not mentioned in this chapter yourself and test them out with the included unit tests if you want to know more about them.

Before you go into the Breakout game at the end of this chapter, take a quick look at some of the remaining helper classes, which will be used more frequently in the next chapters: SpriteHelper, EnumHelper, and ColorHelper.

SpriteHelper Class

You used a lot of sprite rendering in the previous chapter and because of the unit tests you forced yourself to write an easy way to handle sprites in XNA. This approach and the fact that you should put useful code that is used more than once into reusable classes leads us to the SpriteHelper class (see Figure 3-10). Basically it provides a constructor to create new SpriteHelpers storing the texture and graphic rectangle data and a few Render methods to easily draw the sprites to the screen like you did in the last chapter with a list of SpriteToRender classes.

Figure 3-10

Most methods here don't do much; the constructor just sets the values, `Render` just adds a new `SpriteToRender` instance to the sprites list, `RenderCentered` renders the sprite centered at the specified location, and `DrawSprites` finally draws all the sprites on the screen. Take a look at the `DrawSprites` method, which will look similar to the `DrawSprites` method from the previous chapter, but with some improvements:

```
public static void DrawSprites(int width, int height)
{
  // No need to render if we got no sprites this frame
  if (sprites.Count == 0)
    return;

  // Create sprite batch if we have not done it yet.
  // Use device from texture to create the sprite batch.
  if (spriteBatch == null)
    spriteBatch = new SpriteBatch(sprites[0].texture.GraphicsDevice);

  // Start rendering sprites
  spriteBatch.Begin(SpriteBlendMode.AlphaBlend,
    SpriteSortMode.BackToFront, SaveStateMode.None);

  // Render all sprites
  foreach (SpriteToRender sprite in sprites)
    spriteBatch.Draw(sprite.texture,
      // Rescale to fit resolution
      new Rectangle(
      sprite.rect.X * width / 1024,
      sprite.rect.Y * height / 768,
      sprite.rect.Width * width / 1024,
      sprite.rect.Height * height / 768),
      sprite.sourceRect, sprite.color);
```

```
        // We are done, draw everything on screen.
        spriteBatch.End();

        // Kill list of remembered sprites
        sprites.Clear();
    } // DrawSprites(width, height)
```

This method is called with the current width and height of the render window resolution to scale all sprites up and down depending on the resolution, which is important to support all Xbox 360 screen resolutions. In the `DrawSprites` method you first check if there is something to render. Then you make sure the static sprite batch was created, which will be used for all sprites you draw here. After beginning the sprite batch you go through all sprites for this frame and rescale their rectangles to fit correctly on the screen, and finally you let everything draw on the screen by calling `End`. The sprites list is also killed to start fresh the next frame. As an example on how this class works see the Breakout game at the end of the chapter.

EnumHelper Class

The `EnumHelper` class (see Figure 3-11) is useful when you want to enumerate through any enum or quickly find out the number of enum values contained in an enum. For the Pong and Breakout games you are not using any enums, but in the next chapter the `Enum` class becomes useful when going through the types of blocks for the game there. Please also note that the `EnumHelper` class uses some methods of the `Enum` class, which are not implemented in the .NET Compact Framework. To avoid any compilation errors the whole class is usually left out of the Xbox 360 project, but you can still use it on the Windows platform if you like.

Figure 3-11

The unit test for `TestGetAllEnumNames` looks like this and also explains how `GetAllEnumNames` works. It goes through each enum value with help of the `EnumEnumerator` helper class inside of `EnumHelper`:

```
[Test]
public void TestGetAllEnumNames()
{
  Assert.AreEqual(
    "Missions, Highscore, Credits, Help, Options, Exit, Back",
    EnumHelper.GetAllEnumNames(typeof(MenuButton)));
} // TestGetAllEnumNames()
```

And the `GetAllEnumNames` just uses the `WriteArrayData` helper method of the `StringHelper` class just talked about:

```
public static string GetAllEnumNames(Type type)
{
  return StringHelper.WriteArrayData(GetEnumerator(type));
} // GetAllEnumNames(type)
```

ColorHelper Class

Initially the `ColorHelper` class (see Figure 3-12) was a lot longer and had many methods, but because the new `Color` class in XNA is much more powerful than the `Color` class from `System.Drawings` that is used in Managed DirectX, many of the methods were not required anymore. It still contains some useful methods you use for color manipulation.

Figure 3-12

For example, the `Color.Empty` field is used to initialize shader effect parameters to unused values — 0, 0, 0, 0 is usually not a valid color; it is completely transparent. Even black has 255 for the alpha value.

```
/// <summary>
/// Empty color, used to mark unused color values.
/// </summary>
public static readonly Color Empty = new Color(0, 0, 0, 0);
```

The Breakout Game

Alright, this chapter talked a lot about helper classes and it is finally time to put them to some use. I will skip the concept phase here and basically just say that Breakout is an abbreviation of Pong for just one player to play against a wall of blocks. Breakout was initially created by Nolan Bushnell and Steve Wozniak and released by Atari in 1976. In this early version it was just a black and white game like Pong, but to make it more "exciting" transparent stripes were placed over the monitor to color the blocks (see Figure 3-13).

Figure 3-13

You will actually go a similar road by reusing some of the Pong components and using the helper classes you learned about in this chapter. Breakout is a more complex game than Pong; it can have many levels and can be improved quite a lot. For example, Arkanoid is a clone of Breakout and there were many games in the 1980s and 1990s that still used this basic game idea and added weapons, better graphic effects, and many levels with different block placements.

As you can see in Figure 3-14, the BreakoutGame class is structured in a similar way to the Pong class from the last chapter. The sprite handling is missing because it is done now with help of the SpriteHelper class. Some other internal methods and calls are also replaced by some of the helper classes. For example, StartLevel generates a random new level based on the level value, and to generate the random values you will use the RandomHelper class.

Please also note that many test methods are visible in the class. This will be improved similar to the helper classes in the next chapter, which introduces the BaseGame and TestGame classes that make handling the game class and especially unit testing a lot easier and more organized.

Figure 3-14

Take a look at Figure 3-15 for a quick overview of the Breakout game you are going to develop in the next few pages. It is quite a lot of fun and certainly has a greater replay value than Pong, which is only fun with two human players anyway. The Breakout game uses the same background texture and the two sound files from the Pong project, but you also add a new texture (`BreakoutGame.png`) for the paddle, ball, and blocks and you have new sounds for winning a level (`BreakoutVictory.wav`) and for destroying blocks (`BreakoutBlockKill.wav`).

Figure 3-15

Unit Testing in Breakout

Before you start copying and pasting code over from the last project, using your new helper classes, and drawing the new game elements, you should think about the game and the problems you might run into. Sure you can just go ahead and implement the game, but it will be much harder to test the collisions, for example, which are the hardest part of this game. The unit tests help you out and provide you with an easy way to at least check all the basic parts of your game, and they also help you to organize your code and force you to program only what is really required. As always start with the most obvious part of the game and unit test it, then add more unit tests until you are done, and finally put everything together and test the final game.

Here is a quick overview of the unit tests for the Breakout game; check the full source code for this chapter for more details. You don't have the TestGame class yet, so you still use the same kind of unit testing you used in the last chapter. Check out the next chapter on a better way to do static unit tests. You only have three unit tests, but they were used and changed a lot as I implemented the game.

❑ **TestSounds** — Just a quick test to check out all the new sounds for your project. Press space, Alt, Control, and Shift to play the sounds. I also added a little pause after playing the next sound to make it a little easier to hear the sounds. This test was used to check out the new XACT project I created for this game.

❑ **TestGameSprites** — This test was initially used to test the SpriteHelper class, but then all the code was moved to the Draw method of the game. The test was also used to initialize all the blocks in the game; the code was moved to the constructor, which is shown at the end of this chapter. This test shows you that it is not important to have a complicated test at the end because it is now only four lines of code, but the important part is to make your life easier while you are coding the game. Copy and paste useful parts of unit tests to your code as often as you need. Static unit tests also don't have to be intact like dynamic unit tests for the helper classes because you only use them to build and test your game. When the game works you don't need the static unit tests anymore except for testing parts of the game at a later point in time.

❑ **TestBallCollisions** — Like in the previous chapter testing the ball collisions is the most useful unit test. Here you check if the collisions happen with the screen borders and paddle as expected. Only minor changes were required to get this to work. Then you can go to the more complicated block collision code, which is explained in more detail a bit later. You might even be able to think of more ways to test the collision and improve the game if you like. For example, it would make sense to trap the ball behind the wall of blocks and see if it destroys all the blocks correctly.

Breakout Levels

Because you are using many of the existing Pong ideas, you can skip the code that is similar or identical. You should focus on the new variables for now:

```
/// <summary>
/// How many block columns and rows are displayed?
/// </summary>
const int NumOfColumns = 14,
  NumOfRows = 12;
```

```
/// <summary>
/// Current paddle positions, 0 means left, 1 means right.
/// </summary>
float paddlePosition = 0.5f;

/// <summary>
/// Level we are in and the current score.
/// </summary>
int level = 0, score = -1;

/// <summary>
/// All blocks of the current play field. If they are
/// all cleared, we advance to the next level.
/// </summary>
bool[,] blocks = new bool[NumOfColumns, NumOfRows];

/// <summary>
/// Block positions for each block we have, initialized in Initialize().
/// </summary>
Vector2[,] blockPositions = new Vector2[NumOfColumns, NumOfRows];

/// <summary>
/// Bounding boxes for each of the blocks, also precalculated and
/// checked each frame if the ball collides with one of the blocks.
/// </summary>
BoundingBox[,] blockBoxes = new BoundingBox[NumOfColumns, NumOfRows];
```

First you define how many columns and blocks you can have at maximum; in the first levels you will not fill all the lines and only use 10% of the blocks. The paddle position is also a little bit easier than in Pong because you have just one player. Then you store the current level and the score, which is new. In Pong each player just had three balls and the game was over if all balls were lost. In Breakout the player starts at level 1 and works his way up until he finally loses a ball. You don't have a high score here or any game font, so the level and score data is just updated in the title of the window.

Then all the blocks are defined; the most important array is *blocks*, which just tells you which block is currently used. The blocks are initialized before each level starts, whereas the blockPositions and blockBoxes are initialized only once in the constructor of the game; blockPositions is used to determine the centered position of the block for rendering and blockBoxes defines the bounding box of the block for collision testing. It is important to note that none of these lists or position values use screen coordinates. All position data is stored in the 0-1 format: 0 is left or top, and 1 is right or bottom. This way the game stays resolution-independent and makes both rendering and collision checking easier.

The levels are generated in the StartLevel method, which is called at the beginning of the game and every time you advance one level:

```
void StartLevel()
{
  // Randomize levels, but make it more harder each level
  for (int y = 0; y < NumOfRows; y++)
    for (int x = 0; x < NumOfColumns; x++)
      blocks[x, y] =
        RandomHelper.GetRandomInt(10) < level+1;
```

```
          // Use the lower blocks only for later levels
          if (level < 6)
            for (int x = 0; x < NumOfColumns; x++)
              blocks[x, NumOfRows - 1] = false;
          if (level < 4)
            for (int x = 0; x < NumOfColumns; x++)
              blocks[x, NumOfRows - 2] = false;
          if (level < 2)
            for (int x = 0; x < NumOfColumns; x++)
              blocks[x, NumOfRows - 3] = false;

          // Halt game
          ballSpeedVector = Vector2.Zero;

          // Wait until user presses space or A to start a level.
          pressSpaceToStart = true;

          // Update title
          Window.Title =
            "XnaBreakout - Level " + (level+1) +
            " - Score " + Math.Max(0, score);
        } // StartLevel
```

In the first `for` loop you just fill the whole block array with new values depending on the level. In level 1 the level value is 0 and you will only fill 10% of the blocks. `RandomHelper.GetRandomInt(10)` returns 0–9, which is smaller than 1 in only 10% of the cases. In level 2 this goes up to 20% until you reach level 10 or higher, where 100% of the level is filled. The game actually has no limit; you can play as long as you want.

Then you clear the lower three lines for the first levels to make the first levels easier. At level 3 only two lines are removed and at level 5 just one line is removed until you reach level 7 where all the lines are used.

Unlike Pong the ball speed vector is not immediately started for a new game. The ball stays on the paddle until the user presses space or A. Then the ball bounces off the paddle to a random location and the ball goes between the wall blocks, the screen borders, and the player paddle until either all blocks are removed to win a level or the player loses by not catching the ball.

Finally the window's title is updated to show the current level number and the score the player has reached so far. In this very simple game the player only gets one point for every block he destroys; reaching a score of 100 is really good, but as I said before, there is no limit. Try to go higher and have fun with the game.

The Game Loop

The game loop in Pong was quite easy and contained mostly input and collision code. Breakout is a little bit more complicated because you have to handle two states of the ball. It is either still on the paddle and awaits the user to press space or you are in the game and have to check for any collisions with the screen borders, the paddle, or any of the blocks in the game.

Most of the `Update` method looks the same way as in the previous chapter; the second player was removed and a little bit of new code was added at the bottom:

```
// Game not started yet? Then put ball on paddle.
if (pressSpaceToStart)
{
  ballPosition = new Vector2(paddlePosition, 0.95f - 0.035f);

  // Handle space
  if (keyboard.IsKeyDown(Keys.Space) ||
    gamePad.Buttons.A == ButtonState.Pressed)
  {
    StartNewBall();
  } // if
} // if
else
{
  // Check collisions
  CheckBallCollisions(moveFactorPerSecond);

  // Update ball position and bounce off the borders
  ballPosition += ballSpeedVector *
    moveFactorPerSecond * BallSpeedMultiplicator;

  // Ball lost?
  if (ballPosition.Y > 0.985f)
  {
    // Play sound
    soundBank.PlayCue("PongBallLost");
    // Game over, reset to level 0
    level = 0;
    StartLevel();
    // Show lost message
    lostGame = true;
  } // if

  // Check if all blocks are killed and if we won this level
  bool allBlocksKilled = true;
  for (int y = 0; y < NumOfRows; y++)
    for (int x = 0; x < NumOfColumns; x++)
      if (blocks[x, y])
      {
        allBlocksKilled = false;
        break;
      } // for for if

  // We won, start next level
  if (allBlocksKilled == true)
  {
    // Play sound
    soundBank.PlayCue("BreakoutVictory");
    lostGame = false;
    level++;
    StartLevel();
```

```
    } // if
  } // else
```

First you check if the ball was not started yet. If not update the ball position and put it on the center of the player's paddle. Then check if space or A was pressed and start the ball then (just randomizes the `ballSpeedVector` for you and bounces the ball off to the wall of blocks).

The most important method is `CheckBallCollisions`, which you will check out in a second. Then the ball is updated like in the Pong game and you check if the ball is lost. If the player did not catch the ball, the game is over and the player can start over at level 1.

Finally you check if all blocks were removed and the level is complete. If all blocks are killed you can play the new victory sound and start the next level. The player sees a "You Won!" message on the screen (see `Draw` method) and can press space to start the next level.

Drawing Breakout

Thanks to the `SpriteHelper` class the `Draw` method of the Breakout game is short and easy:

```
protected override void Draw(GameTime gameTime)
{
  // Render background
  background.Render();
  SpriteHelper.DrawSprites(width, height);

  // Render all game graphics
  paddle.RenderCentered(paddlePosition, 0.95f);
  ball.RenderCentered(ballPosition);
  // Render all blocks
  for (int y = 0; y < NumOfRows; y++)
    for (int x = 0; x < NumOfColumns; x++)
      if (blocks[x, y])
        block.RenderCentered(blockPositions[x, y]);

  if (pressSpaceToStart &&
    score >= 0)
  {
    if (lostGame)
      youLost.RenderCentered(0.5f, 0.65f, 2);
    else
      youWon.RenderCentered(0.5f, 0.65f, 2);
  } // if

  // Draw all sprites on the screen
  SpriteHelper.DrawSprites(width, height);

  base.Draw(gameTime);
} // Draw(gameTime)
```

You start by rendering the background; you don't have to clear the background because the background texture fills the complete background. To make sure everything is rendered on top of the background, you draw it immediately before rendering the rest of the game sprites.

Next you draw the paddle and the ball, which is very easy to do because of the RenderCentered helper method in the SpriteHelper class, which works like this (the three overloads are just for a more convenient use of this method):

```
public void RenderCentered(float x, float y, float scale)
{
  Render(new Rectangle(
    (int)(x * 1024 - scale * gfxRect.Width/2),
    (int)(y * 768 - scale * gfxRect.Height/2),
    (int)(scale * gfxRect.Width),
    (int)(scale * gfxRect.Height)));
} // RenderCentered(x, y)

public void RenderCentered(float x, float y)
{
  RenderCentered(x, y, 1);
} // RenderCentered(x, y)

public void RenderCentered(Vector2 pos)
{
  RenderCentered(pos.X, pos.Y);
} // RenderCentered(pos)
```

RenderCentered takes a Vector2 or x and y float values and rescales the positions from 0 to 1 (the format you use in your game) to 1024×768. The Draw method of SpriteHelper then rescales everything to the current screen resolution from 1024×768. It may sound complicated, but it is really easy to use.

Then all the blocks of the current level are rendered and again that is very easy thanks to the position you have calculated in the constructor of your game. Take a look at the code on how to initialize all block positions at the upper part of the screen:

```
// Init all blocks, set positions and bounding boxes
for (int y = 0; y < NumOfRows; y++)
  for (int x = 0; x < NumOfColumns; x++)
  {
    blockPositions[x, y] = new Vector2(
      0.05f + 0.9f * x / (float)(NumOfColumns - 1),
      0.066f + 0.5f * y / (float)(NumOfRows - 1));
    Vector3 pos = new Vector3(blockPositions[x, y], 0);
    Vector3 blockSize = new Vector3(
      GameBlockRect.X/1024.0f, GameBlockRect.Y/768, 0);
    blockBoxes[x, y] = new BoundingBox(
      pos - blockSize/2, pos + blockSize/2);
  } // for for
```

The blockBoxes bounding boxes are used for the collision testing discussed in a second. The calculation of the position is also no big deal; the x coordinate goes from 0.05 to 0.95 in as many steps as you have columns (14 if I remember correctly). You can try to change the NumOfColumns constant to 20 and the field will have many more blocks.

Finally a small message is rendered on the screen with a scaling factor of two in case the player has won a level or lost the game. Then you just call the Draw method of SpriteHelper to render all game elements on the screen. Check out the unit tests in the game for how the rendering of the blocks, paddle, and game messages was developed. I started with the unit tests again and then wrote the implementation.

Collision Testing

The collision testing for the Breakout game is a little bit more complicated than just checking the paddles and the screen border in Pong. The most complicated part is to correctly bounce off the blocks the ball hits. For the complete code check the source code for this chapter.

Like the last game you have a ball with a bounding box, screen borders, and the paddle. The blocks are new and to check for any collisions you have check all of them each frame. See Figure 3-16 for an example collision happening with a block in the game.

Figure 3-16

Take a closer look at the basic collision code with the blocks. The collision with the screen border and paddle is pretty much the same as in the Pong game and is checked with the help of the TestBallCollisions unit test. To check for collisions with the blocks you iterate through all of them and check if the bounding box of the ball hits the bounding box of the blocks. The actual game code is a little bit more complicated to check which side of the bounding box you hit and in which direction you have to bounce off, but the rest of the code and the general idea is still the same.

```
// Ball hits any block?
for (int y = 0; y < NumOfRows; y++)
  for (int x = 0; x < NumOfColumns; x++)
    if (blocks[x, y])
    {
      // Collision check
      if (ballBox.Intersects(blockBoxes[x, y]))
      {
        // Kill block
        blocks[x, y] = false;
```

```
            // Add score
            score++;
            // Update title
            Window.Title =
                "XnaBreakout - Level " + (level + 1) + " - Score " + score;
            // Play sound
            soundBank.PlayCue("BreakoutBlockKill");
            // Bounce ball back
            ballSpeedVector = -ballSpeedVector;
            // Go outta here, only handle 1 block at a time
            break;
        } // if
    } // for for if
```

Challenge: Improve the Breakout Game

Try to improve the game by giving the player more than one life, and maybe also add a menu like in the previous chapter. You can also use the Breakout game as a test platform to check out the helper classes you implemented so far. For example, you could write a log message every time the player completes a level or destroys a block and then check out the log file.

The next chapter introduces the Input class to make it easier to catch all controller inputs. A nice improvement to the game would be to implement rumble support for gamepads like in the last chapter and also shake the screen or add simple explosion graphics when blocks get destroyed. The sky is the limit; if you really like arcade games there are many ways you can improve this game and make it much more fun.

Maybe you are more interested in the helper classes and have several of your own helper classes you would like to add and test using your new knowledge. Now is the time to do that. The next chapter focuses more on reusability; the chapters after that only talk about creating a 3D engine and you might forget about all the useful helper classes until you miss some feature. The good thing about helper classes is that it is easy to improve them all the time. They may become a little bit big like the StringHelper class, but you can always refactor them.

Anyway, have fun with XNA Breakout and relax for a while. Try to get to level 5 without cheating — it is not easy.

Summary

You covered a lot of classes in this chapter, which will be useful in your later projects. Unit testing is also an important point and I hope I convinced you that writing unit tests first is the way to go. The Breakout game got a little attention at the end of the chapter. The chapter is long enough as it is and luckily you could skip a few points of the Breakout game because many parts of the game could be reused from the Pong game of the last chapter.

The next chapter focuses a little bit more on game programming and how to build a game with several components. In this chapter you saw the usefulness of the helper classes and now you are ready to extend this idea to your game code, which is important for creating more complex games.

Here's a recap of what you have learned in this chapter:

❏   Use helper classes wherever possible, put code to methods or helper classes especially if you have used it more than twice.

❏   Always write unit tests first and then work on the implementation.

❏   Keep the unit tests simple. You don't have to waste time writing overly complex unit tests for helper classes or make static unit tests more complex than the game itself. Unit tests are not important for the final game (in fact they are not even included thanks to the `#if DEBUG` directives) and they are only used to make your life easier and help you to test and reuse new and existing code.

❏   When changing code, always run the tests to make sure everything still works correctly:

   ❏   Use TestDriven.Net to run single tests or run every test of a class or namespace in the Solution Explorer.

   ❏   Alternatively, use the NUnit GUI to test all unit tests of your assembly. For static unit tests use the `Program` class and start the tests manually.

   ❏   Test the most complicated parts of your game as much as possible, like the collision testing in Breakout.

Game Components

This chapter talks about the concept behind the Game class and the game components you can add to it. To get your graphic engine up and running in the next chapter you still need some new helper classes before starting with 3D concepts. The BaseGame class is used to implement more features and to include all the other classes you have written so far. It is derived from the Game class to take advantage of all the existing XNA features. In the same way our main test class TestGame is derived from BaseGame to help you execute static unit tests in your game. Then you will add the TextureFont class to your Helpers namespace to allow you to draw text on the screen, which is not possible out of the box in XNA. Finally, you also add some of the existing functionality from the previous chapters such as input, controller handling, and sound output into special classes to make it much easier to write a new game. Instead of just making some general assumptions, this chapter takes the game you are going to develop later in this chapter as a prime example.

In contrast to the previous chapter you are not going to write any helper classes first, but instead you are going to write the unit tests and the game class first and then add all the game components you need to your project. In the last few projects the problems were fairly simple and once you resolved them there was no need to go through them again. For the game you are going to develop in this chapter many improvements can be made and you will see this becomes even more true the bigger the game projects become. Refactoring is still the most important thing you have to remember when working over existing code and improving your game. Sometimes you will even see the code used in the unit tests ending up somewhere else in the final game code.

As an example game a simple Tetris clone is used. It will feature a big play field with colored blocks falling down, support for keyboard and gamepad input, a next block field showing you what comes next, and a little scoreboard containing the current level, score, highscore, and lines you destroyed. If you are a Tetris fan like me and like to play it every once in a while this game is great fun. Tetris is one of the most popular puzzle arcade games ever. It was invented by the Russian Alexey Pazhitnov in 1985 and became very popular ever since Nintendo released it on the Game Boy system in 1989.

The Game Class

You already used the Game class in the previous chapters, but other than starting the game by calling the Run method from the Program class and your unit tests and using the Initialize, Update, and Draw methods, those chapters did not talk about the underlying design. Well, you don't really need to know anything else if you are just creating a few simple games, but as games become bigger and have more features you might want to think about the class overview and class design of your game.

The Game class itself is used to hold the graphics device in the GraphicsDeviceManager instance and the content manager in the content field. From the Program class you just have to create an instance of your game class and call the Run method to get everything started. Unlike in the old days with Managed DirectX or OpenGL you don't have to manage your own window, create your game loop, handle Windows messages, and so on. XNA does all that for you, and because it is handled in such a way it is even possible to run your game on the Xbox 360 platform where no window classes or Windows events are available.

It is still possible to access the window of the game through the Window property of the game class. It can be used to set the window's title, specify if the user is allowed to resize the window, get the under-lying Windows handle for interop calls, and so on. All these methods do nothing on the Xbox 360 platform. There is no window, there is no window title, and it can certainly not be resized. As you already saw in the previous game, you used the Window.Title property to set some simple text to the title for showing the current level and score to the user. The reason you did that is because there is no font support in XNA; to render text on the screen you have to create your own bitmap font and then render every letter yourself. In the next games and even for the Tetris game you will need that feature, and therefore the TextureFont class is introduced in a few minutes.

Additionally, it is worth mentioning that it is possible to set the preferred resolution in the game class constructor by setting the graphics properties like in the following example, which tries to use the 1024×768 resolution in fullscreen mode:

```
graphics.PreferredBackBufferWidth = 1024;
graphics.PreferredBackBufferHeight = 768;
graphics.IsFullScreen = true;
```

There is no guarantee that the game will actually run in that mode; for example, setting 1600×1200 on a system that just supports up to 1024×768 will only use the maximum available resolution.

You already know that Update and Draw are called every frame, but how do you incorporate new game components without overloading the game class itself? It's time to look at the game classes and components overview of the Tetris clone game (see Figure 4-1).

The first thing you will notice is that you have now three game classes instead of just one like in the previous game examples. The reason for that is to make the main game class shorter and simpler. The BaseGame class holds the graphics manager with the graphics device, the content manager, and it stores the current width and height values of the current resolution you use in the game. The Update and Draw methods also handle the new Input, Sound, and TextureFont classes to avoid having to update them in the main game class. Then the TetrisGame class is used to load all the graphics from the content pipeline and initialize all sprites and game components, which you learn about in a second.

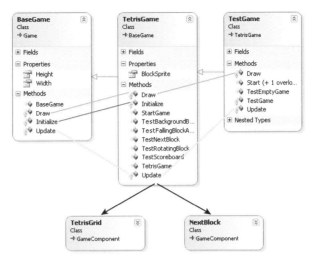

Figure 4-1

Finally, the `TestGame` class derives itself from the `TetrisGame` class to have access to all the textures, sprites, and game components, and it is only used in debug mode to start unit tests. The functionality of the `TestGame` class is very similar to the previous chapters, but this time it is organized in a nice way and separate from your main game class. The `TetrisGame` class uses several unit tests to make sure each part of the game works as you have planned.

Game Components

The `TetrisGame` class also holds all game components in the `Components` property derived from the game class. You can add any class that is derived from the `GameComponent` class to this list and it will automatically be called when your game is started and when it is updated. It will not be called when you draw your game because the `GameComponent` does not have a `Draw` method. You can, however, implement your own drawing methods or just use the `DrawableGameComponent` class, which does have a `Draw` method. XNA does not have a direct `Draw` support for the game components; you have to call it yourself to make sure all components are called in the correct order. Because of this and for several other reasons (forcing you to use this model with almost no advantages, makes unit tests harder, your own game classes might be more effective or specific, and so on), you will not use many game components later in this book. It is generally a nice idea, but you can live without it because you have to create game components yourself anyway and you have to call `Draw` for them yourself too. Just for the `Update` method, it does not make much sense to use them.

As I mentioned in Chapter 1 the basic idea is to have users collaborate and share their game components to allow others to use parts of their game engine. For example, a frame counter component or even a full-blown 3D landscape rendering engine could be implemented as a game component, but just because someone does not use a game component does not mean it is harder to copy over. For example, if you have a complicated game component like a landscape rendering module, it will probably involve some other classes too and use its own rendering engine, which might not work out of the box in your engine if you just copy one file over. Either way, plugging in external code often requires quite a bit of refactoring until it is usable in your own game engine. In beta 1 of the XNA Framework a graphical designer was available in XNA Game Studio Express for the game components and you could easily drag and drop components into your game class or even into other game components to add features to your game without writing a single line of code. Because this feature was very complicated, buggy, and did not work on the Xbox 360, it was abandoned in the beta 2 release of the XNA Framework.

It is not a sure thing that game components will not be used, and maybe it does not matter to most programmers that the designer is missing and you have to call the Draw methods yourself. Then a lot of game components might be available and it would be useful to know all the basics about them. In the case of the Tetris game a few components come to mind:

❑   The grid itself with all the colored blocks and the current falling block

❑   The scoreboard with the current level, score, highscore, and number of lines you destroyed

❑   The next block type box for the game

❑   More simple things like a frame counter, handling the input, and so on

I decided to just implement the Tetris grid and the next block feature as game components; all the code is just way too simple for implementing several new classes just for them. If you will reuse the scoreboard, for example, you could always put it in a game component, but I cannot think of any other game I would like to write that uses that scoreboard.

Take a closer look at the Game class and the components that were added to it (see Figure 4-2).

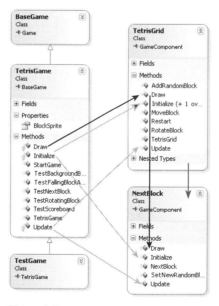

Figure 4-2

The gray arrows indicate that these methods are called automatically through the fact that `TetrisGrid` and `NextBlock` were added to the `Components` list of the `Game` class. In `TetrisGame.Draw` the `Draw` method of `TetrisGrid` is called, which again calls the `NextBlock.Draw` method. `TetrisGame` itself holds just an instance of `TetrisGrid`. The `NextBlock` instance is only used inside of the `TetrisGrid` class.

You can see that using the game components for these three classes forced you to think about the calling order and it made your game more organized just by the fact that you did not put everything into one big class. This is a good thing and, though you can do all this by yourself if you are an experienced programmer, it might be a good idea for beginners to anticipate the idea of the game components in XNA.

More Helper Classes

Didn't talk enough about helper classes in the last chapter? Yes we did. The two new classes you are going to use for the Tetris game are not discussed here in great detail and they are just stripped-down versions of the real classes you use later in this book. But they are still useful and help you to make the programming process of your game easier.

TextureFont Class

You already learned about the missing font support in XNA and you know that using bitmap fonts is the only option to display text in XNA (apart from using some custom 3D font rendering maybe). In the first games of this book you just used some sprites to display fixed text in the game or menu. This approach was very easy, but for your scoreboard you certainly need a dynamic font allowing you to write down any text and numbers the way you need it in the game.

Let's go a little bit ahead and take a look at the `TestScoreboard` unit test in the `TetrisGame` class, which renders the background box for the scoreboard and then writes down all the text lines to display the current level, score, highscore, and number of lines you destroyed in the current game:

```
int level = 3, score = 350, highscore = 1542, lines = 13;
TestGame.Start("TestScoreboard",
  delegate
  {
    // Draw background box
    TestGame.game.backgroundSmallBox.Render(new Rectangle(
      (512 + 240) - 15, 40 - 10, 290 - 30, 190));

    // Show current level, score, etc.
    TextureFont.WriteText(512 + 240, 50, "Level: ");
    TextureFont.WriteText(512 + 420, 50, (level + 1).ToString());
    TextureFont.WriteText(512 + 240, 90, "Score: ");
    TextureFont.WriteText(512 + 420, 90, score.ToString());
    TextureFont.WriteText(512 + 240, 130, "Lines: ");
    TextureFont.WriteText(512 + 420, 130, lines.ToString());
    TextureFont.WriteText(512 + 240, 170, "Highscore: ");
    TextureFont.WriteText(512 + 420, 170, highscore.ToString());
  });
```

You might notice that you are now using the TestGame class to start your unit test. For this test you use a couple of variables (level, score, and so on), which are replaced by the real values in the game code. In the render loop you first draw the background box and display it immediately to avoid display errors with sprites you draw later. Then you write down four lines of text with help of the WriteText method in the new TextureFont class at the specified screen positions. You actually call WriteText eight times to properly align all the numbers at the right side of your background box, which looks much nicer than just writing down everything in four lines.

After writing this unit test you will get a compiler error telling you that the TextureFont class does not exist yet. After creating a dummy class with a dummy WriteText method you will be able to compile and start the test. It will just show the background box, which is drawn in the upper-right part of the screen with help of the SpriteHelper class you learned about in the last chapter.

Before you even think about implementing the TextureFont class you will need the actual bitmap texture with the font in it to render text on the screen. Without a texture you are just doing theoretical work, and unit testing is about practical testing of game functionality. You will need a texture like the one in Figure 4-3 to display all the letters, numbers, and signs. You can even use more Unicode letters in bigger textures or use multiple textures to achieve that, but that would go too far for this chapter. Please check out the websites I provided at the top of the TextureFont class comment in the source code to learn more about this advanced topic.

Figure 4-3

Take a look at the implementation of the TextureFont class (see Figure 4-4). Calling the TextureFont class is very easy; you just have to call the WriteText method like in the unit test shown earlier. But the internal code is not very easy. The class stores rectangles for each letter of the GameFont.png texture, which is then used in WriteAll to render text by drawing each letter one by one to the screen. The class also contains the font texture, which is GameFont.png, a sprite batch to help render the font sprites on the screen, and several helper variables to determine the height of the font. For checking how much width a text will consume on the screen you can use the GetTextWidth method.

The internal FontToRender class holds all the text you want to render each frame, which is very similar to the process the SpriteHelper class uses to render all sprites on the screen at the end of each frame. In the same way SpriteHelper.DrawAll is called by BaseGame, TextureFont.WriteAll is also called and flushes everything on the screen and clears all lists. To learn more about the TextureFont class, check out the source code and run the unit tests or try stepping through the WriteAll method.

Figure 4-4

Input Class

Another new class that is used in the Tetris game is the `Input` class, which encapsulates all the input handling, checking, and updating you did in the previous chapters yourself. Chapter 10 talks about the `Input` class in greater detail and some nice classes that really need all the features from the `Input` class (see Figure 4-5).

Figure 4-5

As you can see, the `Input` class has quite a lot of properties and a few helper methods to access the keyboard, the gamepad, and the mouse data. It will be updated every frame with the help of the static `Update` method, which is called directly from the `BaseGame` class. For this game you are mainly going to use the key press and gamepad press methods like `GamePadAJustPressed` or `KeyboardSpaceJustPressed`. Similar to the `RandomHelper` class it is not hard to figure out how this class works, and you already implemented much of the functionally in the previous chapter. For more details and uses you can check out Chapter 10.

Sound Class

Well, you already had sound in the first game in Chapter 2 and you also used it in Chapter 3 for the Breakout game. To keep things simple and to allow you to add more sound functionally later without having to change any of the game classes, the sound management is now moved to the `Sound` class. Take a quick look at the class (see Figure 4-6). It looks very simple in this version, but in Chapter 9, which also talks about XACT in greater detail, you will extend the `Sound` class quite a bit and make it ready for your great racing game at the end of this book.

Figure 4-6

As you can see, all the sound variables are now in this class and the `Game` class no longer contains any sound variables. The `Sound` constructor is static and will be called automatically when you play a sound for the first time with the `Play` method. The `Update` method is called automatically from the `BaseGame` class.

The `Sounds` enum values and the `TestPlayClickSound` unit test depend on the actual content in your current game. These values will change for every game you are going to write from here on, but it is very easy to change the `Sounds` enum values. You might ask why you don't just play the sounds with help of the cue names stored in XACT. Well, many errors could occur by just mistyping a sound cue and it is hard to track all changes in case you remove, rename, or change a sound cue. The `Sounds` enum also makes it very easy to quickly add a sound effect and see which ones are available through IntelliSense.

The Tetris game uses the following sounds:

- ❑ **BlockMove** for moving the block left, right, or down. It is a very silent sound effect.

- ❑ **BlockRotate** is used when you rotate the current block and it sounds very "whooshy."

- ❑ **BlockFalldown** is used when the current block reaches the ground and finally lands.

- ❑ **LineKill** is played every time you manage to kill a line in the game.

- ❑ **Fight** is played at the start of each game to motivate the player.

- ❑ **Victory** is used when the player reaches the next level and contains an applause sound.

- ❑ **Lose** is an old school dying sound and is played when the player loses the game.

Tetris, Tetris, Tetris!

Enough with all the helper classes and game components discussions. It is time to write another cool game. Thanks to the many classes available in the little game engine it is now easy to write text on the screen, draw sprites, handle input, and play sounds.

Before going into the details of the Tetris game logic, it would be useful to think about the placement of all game elements in a similar way you did in the previous games. Instead of drawing all game components on the screen, you just show the background boxes to see what is going to be displayed. For the background you use the space background once again (I promise, this will be the last time). The background box is a new texture and exists in two modes (see Figure 4-7). It is used to separate the game components and make everything fit much nicer on the screen. You could also just reuse the same box for both parts of the game, but because the aspect ratio is so different for them it would either look bad for the background box or for the extra game components, which are smaller, but also need the background box graphic, just a smaller version of it.

BackgroundBigBox.png, used for the Tetris Grid background

Both textures are 50% transparent

BackgroundSmallBox.png, used for smaller boxes

Figure 4-7

Rendering the Background

To render these boxes on the screen you use the `SpriteHelper` class again and test everything with help of the following unit test:

```
public static void TestBackgroundBoxes()
{
  TestGame.Start("TestBackgroundBoxes",
    delegate
    {
  // Render background
  TestGame.game.background.Render();

      // Draw background boxes for all the components
      TestGame.game.backgroundBigBox.Render(new Rectangle(
        (512 - 200) - 15, 40 - 12, 400 + 23, (768 - 40) + 16));
      TestGame.game.backgroundSmallBox.Render(new Rectangle(
        (512 - 480) - 15, 40 - 10, 290 - 30, 300));
      TestGame.game.backgroundSmallBox.Render(new Rectangle(
        (512 + 240) - 15, 40 - 10, 290 - 30, 190));
    });
} // TestBackgroundBoxes()
```

This unit test will produce the output shown in Figure 4-8.

Figure 4-8

You might ask why the right box is a little bit smaller and where I got all these values from. Well, I just started with some arbitrary values and then improved the values until everything in the final game fit. First, the background is drawn in the unit test because you will not call the Draw method of TetrisGame if you are in the unit test (otherwise the unit tests won't work anymore later when the game is fully implemented).

Then three boxes are drawn. The upper-left box is used to show the next block. The center box shows the current Tetris grid. And finally, the upper-right box is used to display the scoreboard. You already saw the unit test for that earlier.

Handling the Grid

It is time to fill the content of these boxes. Start with the main component: the TetrisGrid. This class is responsible for displaying the whole Tetris grid. It handles the input and moves the falling block and it shows all the existing data as well. You already saw which methods are used in the TetrisGrid class in the discussion about the game components. Before rendering the grid you should check out the first constants defined in the TetrisGrid class:

```
#region Constants
public const int GridWidth = 12;
public const int GridHeight = 20;
..
```

There are a couple more interesting constants, but for now you only need the grid dimensions. So you have 12 columns and 20 lines for your Tetris field. With help of the Block.png texture, which is just a simple quadratic block, you can now easily draw the full grid in the Draw method:

```
// Calc sizes for block, etc.
int blockWidth = gridRect.Width / GridWidth;
int blockHeight = gridRect.Height / GridHeight;

for ( int x=0; x<GridWidth; x++ )
  for ( int y=0; y<GridHeight; y++ )
  {
    game.BlockSprite.Render(new Rectangle(
      gridRect.X + x * blockWidth,
      gridRect.Y + y * blockHeight,
      blockWidth-1, blockHeight-1),
      new Color(60, 60, 60, 128)); // Empty color
  } // for for
```

The gridRect variable is passed as a parameter to the Draw method from the main class to specify the area where you want the grid to be drawn to. It is the same rectangle as you used for the background box, just a little bit smaller to fit in. The first thing you are doing here is calculating the block width and height for each block you are going to draw. Then you go through the whole array and draw each block with the help of the SpriteHelper.Render method using a half transparent dark color to show an empty background grid. See Figure 4-9 to see how this looks. Because of the fact that you use game components you also don't have to do all this code in your unit test. The unit test just draws the background box and then calls the TetrisGrid.Draw method to show the results (see the TestEmptyGrid unit test).

Figure 4-9

Block Types

Before you can render anything useful on your new grid you should think about the block types you can have in your game. The standard Tetris game has seven block types; all of them consist of four small blocks connected to each other (see Figure 4-10). The most favorite block type is of course the line type because you can kill up to four lines with that giving you the most points.

Figure 4-10

These block types have to be defined in the TetrisGrid class. One way of doing that is to use an enum holding all the possible block types. This enum can also hold an empty block type allowing you to use this data structure for the whole grid too because each grid block can contain either any part of the pre-defined block types or it is empty. Take a look at the rest of the constants in the TetrisGrid class:

```
/// <summary>
/// Block types we can have for each new block that falls down.
/// </summary>
```

```
public enum BlockTypes
{
  Empty,
  Block,
  Triangle,
  Line,
  RightT,
  LeftT,
  RightShape,
  LeftShape,
} // enum BlockTypes

/// <summary>
/// Number of block types we can use for each grid block.
/// </summary>
public static readonly int NumOfBlockTypes =
  EnumHelper.GetSize(typeof(BlockTypes));

/// <summary>
/// Block colors for each block type.
/// </summary>
public static readonly Color[] BlockColor = new Color[]
  {
    new Color( 60, 60, 60, 128 ), // Empty, color unused
    new Color( 50, 50, 255, 255 ), // Line, blue
    new Color( 160, 160, 160, 255 ), // Block, gray
    new Color( 255, 50, 50, 255 ), // RightT, red
    new Color( 255, 255, 50, 255 ), // LeftT, yellow
    new Color( 50, 255, 255, 255 ), // RightShape, teal
    new Color( 255, 50, 255, 255 ), // LeftShape, purple
    new Color( 50, 255, 50, 255 ), // Triangle, green
  }; // Color[] BlockColor

/// <summary>
/// Unrotated shapes
/// </summary>
public static readonly int[][,] BlockTypeShapesNormal = new int[][,]
  {
    // Empty
    new int[,] { { 0 } },
    // Line
    new int[,] { { 0, 1, 0 }, { 0, 1, 0 }, { 0, 1, 0 }, { 0, 1, 0 } },
    // Block
    new int[,] { { 1, 1 }, { 1, 1 } },
    // RightT
    new int[,] { { 1, 1 }, { 1, 0 }, { 1, 0 } },
    // LeftT
    new int[,] { { 1, 1 }, { 0, 1 }, { 0, 1 } },
    // RightShape
    new int[,] { { 0, 1, 1 }, { 1, 1, 0 } },
    // LeftShape
    new int[,] { { 1, 1, 0 }, { 0, 1, 1 } },
    // Triangle
    new int[,] { { 0, 1, 0 }, { 1, 1, 1 }, { 0, 0, 0 } },
  }; // BlockTypeShapesNormal
```

BlockTypes is the enum we talked about; it contains all the possible block types and also is used to randomly generate new blocks in the NextBlock game component. Initially all of the grid fields are filled with the empty block type. The grid is defined as:

```
/// <summary>
/// The actual grid, contains all blocks,
/// including the currently falling block.
/// </summary>
BlockTypes[,] grid = new BlockTypes[GridWidth, GridHeight];
```

By the way, NumOfBlockTypes shows you the usefulness of the enum class. You can easily determine how many entries are in the BlockTypes enum.

Next the colors for each block type are defined. These colors are used for the NextBlock preview, but also for rendering the whole grid. Each grid has a block type and you can easily use the BlockColors by converting the enum to an int number, which is used in the Draw method:

```
BlockColor[(int)grid[x,y]]
```

And finally the block shapes are defined, which looks a little bit more complicated, especially if you take into consideration that you have to allow these block parts to be rotated. This is done with help of the BlockTypeShapes, which is a big array of all possible blocks and rotations calculated in the constructor of TetrisGrid.

To add a new block to the Tetris grid you can just add each of the block parts to your grid, which is done in the AddRandomBlock method. You keep a separate list called floatingGrid to remember which parts of the grid have to be moved down (see the following section, "Gravity"; you can't just let everything fall down) each time Update is called:

```
// Randomize block type and rotation
currentBlockType = (int)nextBlock.SetNewRandomBlock();
currentBlockRot = RandomHelper.GetRandomInt(4);

// Get precalculated shape
int[,] shape = BlockTypeShapes[currentBlockType,currentBlockRot];
int xPos = GridWidth/2-shape.GetLength(0)/2;
// Center block at top most position of our grid
currentBlockPos = new Point(xPos, 0);

// Add new block
for ( int x=0; x<shape.GetLength(0); x++ )
  for ( int y=0; y<shape.GetLength(1); y++ )
    if ( shape[x,y] > 0 )
    {
      // Check if there is already something
      if (grid[x + xPos, y] != BlockTypes.Empty)
      {
        // Then game is over dude!
        gameOver = true;
```

```
      Sound.Play(Sound.Sounds.Lose);
   } // if
   else
   {
      grid[x + xPos, y] = (BlockTypes)currentBlockType;
      floatingGrid[x + xPos, y] = true;
   } // else
} // for for if
```

First you determine which block type you are going to add here. To help you do that you have a helper method in the NextBlock class, which randomizes the next block type and returns the last block type that was displayed in the NextBlock window. The rotation is also randomized; say "Hi" to the RandomHelper class.

With that data you can now get the precalculated shape and put it centered on the top of your grid. The two for loops iterate through the whole shape. It adds each valid part of the shape until you hit any existing data in the grid. In case that happens the game is over and you hear the lose sound. This will happen if the pile of blocks reaches the top of the grid and you cannot add any new blocks.

You now have the new block on your grid, but it is boring to just see it on the top there; it should fall down sometimes.

Gravity

To test the gravity of the current block the TestFallingBlockAndLineKill unit test is used. The active block is updated each time you call the Update method of TetrisGrid, which is not very often. In the first level the Update method is called only every 1000ms (every second). There you check if the current block can be moved down:

```
// Try to move floating stuff down
if (MoveBlock(MoveTypes.Down) == false ||
   movingDownWasBlocked)
{
   // Failed? Then fix floating stuff, not longer moveable!
   for ( int x=0; x<GridWidth; x++ )
      for ( int y=0; y<GridHeight; y++ )
         floatingGrid[x,y] = false;
   Sound.Play(Sound.Sounds.BlockFalldown);
} // if
movingDownWasBlocked = false;
```

Most of the Tetris logic is done in the MoveBlock helper method, which checks if moving in a specific direction is possible at all. If the block can't be moved anymore it gets fixed and you clear the floatingGrid array and play the sound for landing a block on the ground.

After clearing the `floatingGrid` array there is no active block you can move down and the following code is used to check if a line was destroyed:

```
// Check if we got any moveable stuff,
// if not add new random block at top!
bool canMove = false;
for ( int x=0; x<GridWidth; x++ )
  for ( int y=0; y<GridHeight; y++ )
    if ( floatingGrid[x,y] )
      canMove = true:

if (canMove == false)
{
  int linesKilled = 0;
  // Check if we got a full line
  for ( int y=0; y<GridHeight; y++ )
  {
    bool fullLine = true;
    for ( int x=0; x<GridWidth; x++ )
      if ( grid[x,y] == BlockTypes.Empty )
      {
        fullLine = false;
        break;
      } // for if

    // We got a full line?
    if (fullLine)
    {
      // Move everything down
      for ( int yDown=y-1; yDown>0; yDown- )
        for ( int x=0; x<GridWidth; x++ )
          grid[x,yDown+1] = grid[x,yDown]:

      // Clear top line
      for ( int x=0; x<GridWidth; x++ )
        grid[0,x] = BlockTypes.Empty:

      // Add 10 points and count line
      score += 10;
      lines++;
      linesKilled++;
      Sound.Play(Sound.Sounds.LineKill);
    } // if
  } // for

  // If we killed 2 or more lines, add extra score
  if (linesKilled >= 2)
    score += 5;
  if (linesKilled >= 3)
    score += 10;
  if (linesKilled >= 4)
    score += 25;

  // Add new block at top
  AddRandomBlock();
} // if
```

The first thing that is done here is to check if there is an active moving block. If not you go into the "if block," checking if a full line is filled and can be destroyed. To determine if a line is filled you assume it is filled and then check if any block of the line is empty. Then you know that this line is not fully filled and continue checking the next line. If the line is filled, however, you remove it by copying all the lines above it down. This is the place where a nice explosion could occur. Anyway, the player gets 10 points for this line kill, and you hear the line kill sound.

If the player was able to kill more than one line he gets awarded more points. And finally the AddRandomBlock method you saw before is used to create a new block at the top.

Handling Input

Handling the user input itself is no big task anymore thanks to the Input helper class. You can easily check if a cursor or gamepad key was just pressed or is being held down. Escape and Back are handled in the BaseGame class and allow you to quit the game. Other than that you only need four keys in your Tetris game. To move to the left and right the cursor keys are used. The up cursor key is used to rotate the current block and the down cursor key or alternatively the space or A keys can be used to let the block fall down faster.

Similar to the gravity check to see if you can move the block down, the same check is done to see if you can move the current block left or right. Only if that is true do you actually move the block; this code is done in the TetrisGame Update method because you want to check for the player input every frame and not just when updating the TetrisGrid, which can only happen every 1000ms as you learned before. The code was in the TetrisGrid Update method before, but to improve the user experience it was moved and improved quite a lot also allowing you to move the block quickly left and right by hitting the cursor buttons multiple times.

Well, you have learned a lot about all the supporting code and you are almost done to run the Tetris game for the first time. But you should take a look at the MoveBlock helper method because it is the most integral and important part of your Tetris game. Another important method is the RotateBlock method, which works in a similar way testing if a block can be rotated. You can check it out yourself in the source code for the Tetris game. Please use the unit tests in the TetrisGame class to see how all these methods work:

```
#region Move block
public enum MoveTypes
{
  Left,
  Right,
  Down,
} // enum MoveTypes

/// <summary>
/// Remember if moving down was blocked, this increases
/// the game speed because we can force the next block!
/// </summary>
public bool movingDownWasBlocked = false;
/// <summary>
/// Move current floating block to left, right or down.
/// If anything is blocking, moving is not possible and
/// nothing gets changed!
/// </summary>
```

```
/// <returns>Returns true if moving was successful, otherwise false</returns>
public bool MoveBlock(MoveTypes moveType)
{
  // Clear old pos
  for ( int x=0; x<GridWidth; x++ )
    for ( int y=0; y<GridHeight; y++ )
      if ( floatingGrid[x,y] )
        grid[x,y] = BlockTypes.Empty;
  // Move stuff to new position
  bool anythingBlocking = false;
  Point[] newPos = new Point[4];
  int newPosNum = 0;
  if ( moveType == MoveTypes.Left )
  {
    for ( int x=0; x<GridWidth; x++ )
      for ( int y=0; y<GridHeight; y++ )
        if ( floatingGrid[x,y] )
        {
          if ( x-1 < 0 ||
            grid[x-1,y] != BlockTypes.Empty )
            anythingBlocking = true;
          else if ( newPosNum < 4 )
          {
            newPos[newPosNum] = new Point( x-1, y );
            newPosNum++;
          } // else if
        } // for for if
  } // if (left)
  else if ( moveType == MoveTypes.Right )
  {
    for ( int x=0; x<GridWidth; x++ )
      for ( int y=0; y<GridHeight; y++ )
        if ( floatingGrid[x,y] )
        {
          if ( x+1 >= GridWidth ||
            grid[x+1,y] != BlockTypes.Empty )
            anythingBlocking = true;
          else if ( newPosNum < 4 )
          {
            newPos[newPosNum] = new Point( x+1, y );
            newPosNum++;
          } // else if
        } // for for if
  } // if (right)
  else if ( moveType == MoveTypes.Down )
  {
    for ( int x=0; x<GridWidth; x++ )
      for ( int y=0; y<GridHeight; y++ )
        if ( floatingGrid[x,y] )
        {
          if ( y+1 >= GridHeight ||
            grid[x,y+1] != BlockTypes.Empty )
            anythingBlocking = true;
```

```
        else if ( newPosNum < 4 )
            {
                newPos[newPosNum] = new Point( x, y+1 );
                newPosNum++;
            } // else if
        } // for for if
        if ( anythingBlocking == true )
            movingDownWasBlocked = true;
    } // if (down)

    // If anything is blocking restore old state
    if ( anythingBlocking ||
        // Or we didn't get all 4 new positions?
        newPosNum != 4 )
    {
        for ( int x=0; x<GridWidth; x++ )
            for ( int y=0; y<GridHeight; y++ )
                if ( floatingGrid[x,y] )
                    grid[x,y] = (BlockTypes)currentBlockType;
        return false;
    } // if
    else
    {
        if ( moveType == MoveTypes.Left )
            currentBlockPos =
                new Point( currentBlockPos.X-1, currentBlockPos.Y );
        else if ( moveType == MoveTypes.Right )
            currentBlockPos =
                new Point( currentBlockPos.X+1, currentBlockPos.Y );
        else if ( moveType == MoveTypes.Down )
            currentBlockPos =
                new Point( currentBlockPos.X, currentBlockPos.Y+1 );

        // Else we can move to the new position, lets do it!
        for ( int x=0; x<GridWidth; x++ )
            for ( int y=0; y<GridHeight; y++ )
                floatingGrid[x,y] = false;
        for ( int i=0; i<4; i++ )
        {
            grid[newPos[i].X,newPos[i].Y] = (BlockTypes)currentBlockType;
            floatingGrid[newPos[i].X,newPos[i].Y] = true;
        } // for
        Sound.Play(Sound.Sounds.BlockMove);

        return true;
    } // else
} // MoveBlock(moveType)
#endregion
```

There are three kinds of moves you can do: Left, Right, and Down. Each of these moves is handled in a separate code block to see if the left, right, or down data is available and if it is possible to move there. Before going into the details of this method there are two things that should be mentioned. First of all there is a helper variable called movingDownWasBlocked defined above the method. The reason you have this variable is to speed up the process of checking if the current block reached the ground, and it is stored at the class level to let the Update method pick it up later (which can be several frames later) and make the gravity code you saw earlier update much faster than in the case when the user doesn't want to drop the block down right here. This is a very important part of the game because if each block were immediately fixed when reaching the ground the game would become very hard, and all the fun is lost when it gets faster and the grid gets more filled.

Then you use another trick to simplify the checking process by temporarily removing the current block from the grid. This way you can easily check if a new position is possible because your current position does not block you anymore. The code also uses several helper variables to store the new position and that code is simplified a bit to account for only four block parts. If you change the block types and the number of block parts, you should also change this method.

After setting everything up you check if the new virtual block position is possible in the three code blocks. Usually it is possible and you end up with four new values in the newPosNum array. If there are less than three values available you know that something was blocking you and the anythingBlocking variable is set to true anyway. In that case the old block position is restored and both the grid and the floatingGrid arrays stay the same way.

But in case the move attempt was successful the block position is updated and you clear the floatingGrid and finally add the block again to the new position by adding it both to the grid and the floatingGrid. The user also hears a very silent block move sound and you are done with this method.

Testing

With all that new code in the TetrisGrid class you can now test the unit tests in the TetrisGame class. In addition to the tests you saw before the two most important unit tests for the game logic are:

❑ TestRotatingBlock, which tests the RotateBlock method of the TetrisGrid class.

❑ TestFallingBlockAndKillLine, which is used to test the gravity and user input you just learned about.

It should be obvious that you often go back to older unit tests to update them according to the newest changes you require for your game. For example, the TestBackgroundBoxes unit test you saw earlier is very simple, but the layout and position of the background boxes changed quite a lot while implementing and testing the game components and it had to be updated accordingly to reflect the changes. One example for that would be the scoreboard, which is surrounded by the background box, but before you can know how big the scoreboard is going to be you have to know what the contents are and how much space they are going to consume. After writing the TestScoreboard method it became very obvious that the scoreboard has to be much smaller than the NextBlock background box, for example.

Another part of testing the game is constantly checking for bugs and improving the game code. The previous games were pretty simple and you only had to make minor improvements after the first initial runs, but the Tetris game is much more complex and you can spend many hours fixing and improving it.

One last thing you could test is running the game on the Xbox 360 — just select the Xbox 360 console platform in the project and try to run it on the Xbox 360. All the steps to do that were explained in Chapter 1, which also has a useful troubleshooting section in case something does not work on the Xbox 360. If you write new code you should make sure from time to time that it compiles on the Xbox 360 too. You are not allowed to write any interop code calling unmanaged assemblies, and some of the .NET 2.0 Framework classes and methods are missing on the Xbox 360.

Challenge: Create the NextBlock Game Component

This chapter did not really talk about the NextBlock game component and there is a reason for that. I want you to create it yourself. In the source code for this book the NextBlock class is empty and you have the task of filling it with life. The NextBlock game component is already added to the TetrisGrid class and you already saw all the available methods. If you are unsure about your solution you can check the complete source code with all the improvements and the full NextBlock class I made in the XNA Tetris full project source code, but I recommend you try coding the game component and maybe some other improvements to the game yourself to get more familiar with all the new classes.

The NextBlock component should show the next block type. Just use the BlockTypes enum from the TetrisGrid class and display the next block in a 5×5 grid and add a little text on top (see Figure 4-11).

Figure 4-11

A little tip: Don't waste too much time playing Tetris. It is a great game, but you have more to come in this book.

Summary

Your little game engine now has three new namespaces and you have many helper classes you can use for future projects. The new TextureFont class especially can be very useful for the next chapters. It is not only useful to display game data like the scoreboard, but it will also be used for unit tests; it is very useful to display help texts in unit tests to tell the user about all the available hotkeys and it is especially useful for displaying test data or debugging data in case you run into problems. For example, a camera class unit test can output the camera position and rotation values to see what is going on while the test is running.

I hope these last four chapters were fun to read and you enjoyed the sample games you developed here. Arcade games can be fun, but just writing simple 2D games is not state of the art and you will certainly not get much attention if you program another Pong clone. For learning purposes, to introduce all the helper classes and for learning more about the Agile Methodology and unit testing, it was very useful to have these real projects instead of just talking about some theoretical uses and some boring helper classes.

However, in the next part of this book you will dive into the world of 3D graphics and learn how to write your own 3D graphic engine in XNA. You don't really have to be a math professor to understand how to render a model on the screen. Thanks to XNA and the content pipeline it is possible to render 3D data on the screen without knowing much about the underlying math and 3D geometry involved. If you are serious about 3D graphic programming you should certainly know about vectors, matrices, and how to manipulate them in the right order. There are many tricks and knowing about all issues in the 3D game programming world not only requires a clever person, but you will also have to read constantly about new developments in this sector.

If you are a game programmer you might not care so much about the underlying graphic engine code and want to focus on the game itself. While most people just want to create cool games, it usually means that they also have to create the graphic engine because there is no perfect 3D engine available and every effect in the game might require another way to render the 3D data. The last part of this book talks more about game programming after your game engine is complete enough to handle more complex games.

Here's a final look at what you have learned in the previous chapters:

- ❑ It is important to write down your ideas and to develop a small concept, preferably limited to one page.
- ❑ To solve problems you use a top-down approach and you use unit testing.
- ❑ You learned about handling user input, playing sounds, and drawing sprites. All this can be done quite easily in XNA, but to avoid repeating the same code over and over again you put it in helper classes.
- ❑ A lot of helper classes were introduced to help you with rendering texture fonts, handling strings, going through enums, manipulating colors, writing log files, and much more.
- ❑ In every game you wrote some kind of collision testing was required. In the first two games you used the `BoundingBox` structure to check for collisions in 2D, and in this chapter you handled all the collisions in the Tetris grid yourself in the `MoveBlock` method.
- ❑ Unit testing rules, I can't repeat that often enough. Especially the static unit tests helped you out a lot and made creating the games in this chapter a lot more fun and productive than without using unit testing.

Part II: Basic Graphics Engine

5

Writing Your Own XNA Graphics Engine

In the first section of this book you learned all about the XNA Framework, rendering 2D graphics with the help of the `SpriteBatch` class, and you also made some fun games. Now it is time to explore the much more exciting world of 3D graphic programming. Creating 3D games is a lot more work than just putting together a 2D game, but many games would not be possible without the great advances in 3D graphic technology. Some games like strategy games are also possible in 2D, and the most successful strategy games of all times (StarCraft, WarCraft, Command & Conquer, Age of Empires) show that 2D games are still very popular. But if you take a look at shooter games, they would just not be possible without 3D graphics, and the better and more realistic the graphics get the more fun the games often are. Other game genres like beat-'em-ups, adventures, sport games, and so on have also benefited from the graphic advancements in recent years. Sure, Pong and the early tennis games were a lot of fun 10 or 20 years ago, but they don't compare in any way with today's sport games.

XNA is a great framework for quickly creating 2D games, and even if you are just an individual you will probably be able to quickly throw together a game idea, make some graphics or find someone to make some graphics for your game, and then program the whole game in a matter of weeks or months.

However, most game programmers are much more excited about creating 3D games, and a common mistake almost everyone makes is to compare their own game ideas with the most successful AAA titles that took big game studios many years to create. If you are an individual, you will probably not be able to compete with the next EA game, which will have had an experienced game studio with more than 100 people working on it, even if you think that their game will not be as good as it could be in your opinion.

But this does not matter; most of us got into the game development scene just because we like creating games and often because we think we can make it much better than all the other guys.

The good thing is that although it is hard to create a full-blown 3D game that can compete with AAA titles, you have to start somewhere, and getting into the world of 3D programming is getting easier and easier as we speak. Many great websites, tutorials, frameworks, and books are available to quickly guide even very inexperienced programmers through the first steps of creating 3D graphics for games.

Because there are already so many resources available I will not focus on the math basics, how to work with matrices, or other 3D graphic basics. It would just be boring for many programmers that already know about it and it would take away many pages for more interesting projects in this book. The same way I told you in the first chapter that you should start by reading a C# book first if you are inexperienced with C#, I suggest if you really want to know all the basics about 3D graphics, pick up a book for that. If you have worked with Direct3D or OpenGL before you are good to go and should know all the basics already (hopefully that covers most of the readers here).

This chapter takes the classic approach of first writing down the requirements and creating the unit test for that and then goes into detail for every required new class you need. As the chapter name says, your goal is to create your own graphics engine and the basic framework for all the projects and games for the rest of this book. The Tetris game from the last chapter already had many useful helper classes and some new graphic classes that will be refactored in this chapter, and you will add some new classes. Refactoring means that the classes will be rewritten to fit your new requirements.

What Should Your Engine be Able to Do?

Usually you would just write down the game idea here and then determine which classes you need to get the game and all components running. We still want to create a game at the end of this Part in Chapter 8, but for now we focus on creating a reusable graphics engine to make the creation process of future games easier. This and the next two chapters just focus on the graphics engine programming and how to get textures, models, fonts, shaders, effects, and so on working for your engine. Then in Chapter 7 advanced shaders are introduced and in Chapter 8 we learn more about post screen shaders and how to write a game with the graphics engine developed in this Part.

Thanks to the XNA Framework, which already gives you many helper classes and an easy way to manage the game window, game components, and content files (models, textures, shaders, and sound files), you don't have to worry that much about custom file formats, writing your own window management class, or how to get 3D models into your engine and then on the screen. If you have worked with DirectX or OpenGL before you probably know that the samples and tutorials were not that hard, but as soon as you wanted to get your own textures, 3D models, or sound files into the engine, you often ran into problems like unsupported file formats, no support for the 3D models, or no ability to play your sound files. Then you would either continue your search or write your own classes to support those features. Texture and model classes do exist, but that does not mean they are perfect. Sometimes you want to add more func-tionality or have an easier way to load and access textures and models. For this reason you are going to write new classes for texture and model management, which internally still use the XNA classes, but will make it easier for you to work with textures, models, and later, materials and shaders too.

Okay, first of all you want a cool 3D model displayed on your screen. It should not only have a texture, but also use an exciting shader effect on it. Just watching a static 3D model in the center of the screen is not very exciting and can also be accomplished by just showing a screenshot, so you have to create a camera class to move around a little in your 3D world.

To help you in your future unit tests and for the UI (user interface) you also need the ability to render 2D lines as well as 3D lines to help you find out if 3D positions are correct for unit tests and debugging. You might now say "Hey, rendering lines is nothing special, can't XNA do that already like OpenGL with a method like glLine?" Well, it would be nice, but the creators of XNA removed all the fixed function capabilities of DirectX, and though you can still render some lines with help of vertex buffers and then render line primitives, it is just way too complicated. Remember you are going to write your unit test first and that is not the way you think on how to render lines; you just want to draw a line from (0, 50) to (150, 150) or in 3D from (–100, 0, 0) to (+100, 0, 0). Besides that, the performance of your application will be really bad if you render each line by itself and create a new vertex buffer or vertex array for it and then get rid of it again, especially in the unit tests you will do at the end of this book with several thousand lines rendered every frame.

Then you also want the capabilities you had in the previous games to render text on the screen with the help of the TextureFont class. Your engine should also be able to render sprites, but you should stop thinking of sprites and just use textures. For example, if I load the background texture I don't want to think about the sprite class; I just put the background texture on the whole background or put a UI texture at the location I want it to be. This means you will hide the SpriteHelper class from the user and let the Texture class manage all this in the background for you, very similar to the TextureFont class, which also handles the entire sprite rendering in the background for you.

The Engine Unit Test

Before you go deeper into the implementation details and problems of the 3D graphics engine, write your unit test for the end of this chapter first and therefore specify what the engine should be capable of by then. Please note that the initial version of this unit test looked a little different; it is absolutely okay to change it a bit if you forgot something or if you have some dependencies that were not used in the unit test, but make sense in the engine and should be used. Generally you should try to make the unit test work without changing them; in the unit test I initially just wrote testModel.Render(); to render the test model, but it makes more sense to specify a matrix or vector to tell the model where it has to be rendered in the 3D world.

Enough talk; take a look at the code:

```
/// <summary>
/// Test render our new graphics engine
/// </summary>
public static void TestRenderOurNewGraphicEngine()
{
  Texture backgroundTexture = null;
  Model rocketModel = null;

  TestGame.Start("TestRenderOurNewGraphicEngine",
    delegate
    {
      // Load background and rocket
      backgroundTexture = new Texture("SpaceBackground");
      rocketModel = new Model("Rocket");
    },
    delegate
    {
      // Show background
```

```
        backgroundTexture.RenderOnScreen(
          BaseGame.ResolutionRect);
        SpriteHelper.DrawSprites(width, height);

        // Render model in center
        BaseGame.Device.RenderState.DepthBufferEnable = true;
        rocketModel.Render(Matrix.CreateScale(10));

        // Draw 3d line
        BaseGame.DrawLine(
          new Vector3(-100, 0, 0), new Vector3(+100, 0, 0), Color.Red);

        // Draw safe region box for the Xbox 360, support for old monitors
        Point upperLeft = new Point(width / 15, height / 15);
        Point upperRight = new Point(width * 14 / 15, height / 15);
        Point lowerRight = new Point(width * 14 / 15, height * 14 / 15);
        Point lowerLeft = new Point(width / 15, height * 14 / 15);
        BaseGame.DrawLine(upperLeft, upperRight);
        BaseGame.DrawLine(upperRight, lowerRight);
        BaseGame.DrawLine(lowerRight, lowerLeft);
        BaseGame.DrawLine(lowerLeft, upperLeft);

        // And finally some text
        TextureFont.WriteText(upperLeft.X + 15, upperLeft.Y + 15,
          "TestRenderOurNewGraphicEngine");
      });
  } // TestRenderOurNewGraphicEngine()
```

The test starts by initializing a background texture and a rocket model in the first delegate, and then another delegate is used to render everything on the screen each frame. In the previous chapters you only used very simple unit tests with just one render delegate; now you also allow data to be created in a special init delegate, which is required because you need the graphics engine to be started before you can load any content from the content manager in XNA.

You might wonder why I call a RenderOnScreen method of the Texture class or the Render method of the Model class, when these methods don't exist. The unit test also uses many properties and methods of the BaseGame that do not exist yet, but that does not mean you can't write it this way and want this to work out later. For example, you might say that the following line is too long and too complicated to write:

```
BaseGame.Device.RenderState.DepthBufferEnable = true;
```

Then just write it in a simpler way by using a new imaginary method BaseGame.EnableDepthBuffer and worry later about the implementation. The reason why I use a Texture and Model class and have methods like Render in this unit test is quite simple: That's the way I think about this problem. Sure, I know XNA does not have these methods for me, but nothing stops me from writing my own Texture and Model classes to do just that. If you'd like to simplify the unit test even more or have other additions you would like to make, feel free to edit the unit test and then implement the features as you read through this chapter.

As a little note before you get started, I like to mention that there are several additions to the BaseGame class and some new game components like the camera class, which are also used in this unit test, but are not visible in the form of code because they are executed automatically. You will learn more about these additions, new classes, and improvements as you go through this chapter.

3D Models

Before you can start rendering 3D models you need to have an idea first of what the 3D model should look like or, even better, have some working 3D models to use. If you are not really a professional in 3D Studio Max, Maya, or Softimage or don't have an artist that can throw some models at you quickly, don't start with that yourself. Instead use files that are freely available from samples and tutorials or files from previous projects. This chapter uses the Rocket model from the Rocket Commander game I wrote last year (see Figure 5-1).

Figure 5-1

The Rocket model consists of the 3D geometry data (vectors, normals, tangents, and texture coordinates), the `ParallaxMapping.fx` shader, and the textures for this shader:

❏ `Rocket.dds` for the rocket texture (red head, gray, all logos in the middle, and so on).

❏ `RocketNormal.dds` for the normal mapping effect discussed in Chapter 7.

❏ `RocketHeight.dds` for the parallax mapping effect used in the Rocket Commander game.

All this is created by the 3D model artist, who also specifies how the rocket should look by setting additional shader and material settings for the ambient, diffuse, and specular color and any other parameters defined in the shader or material that can be set in 3D Studio. This model file is saved as a .max file, which is a custom format just for 3D Studio Max (or in whatever modeling programs you or your artist use). To get this into your game you would need a .max importer, which does not exist for DirectX or XNA, and the .max files can get very big and it would not make sense to have a 100 MB file with all kinds of high polygon objects for your game if you just need the low polygon rocket model, which might fit into 100 KB. You need an exporter to just get the model data you need for your game. There are many formats available, so why do I even talk about this for so long? Well, none of the standard export formats in 3D Studio Max support the shader settings you need for your game. And XNA is also only able to import .x and .fbx files. That really sucks.

You probably could just export an .x file or use the .fbx format and live with the fact that there will be no exported shader settings, tangent data, and whatever else you need to perform normal mapping, parallax mapping, or whatever custom shader you want to use in your game. But then you would have a lot of work in your game engine to fix this for every single model. Or alternatively you could write your own custom exporter for 3D Studio Max, which many big game studios do, but they have a lot more time and money than you can ever have as an individual. Another way might be to have some custom xml files that store all the shader settings for each model and this is then imported and merged in your game engine, which again can lead to a lot of work, not only implementing the importing and merging, but also keeping the xml settings file up to date. I have seen all these approaches being used and you are free to do whatever you like, but I strongly suggest using a painless process if possible.

In this case the Rocket model can be exported to a custom .x file with help of the community-created Panda-Exporter for 3D Studio Max (see Figure 5-2), which then can be imported to the XNA Framework. It does not support all the features (tangent data is missing) and having more complex objects with bone and skinning data can be a pain, but you won't need that for your games yet. A good alternative is the new Collada format, which exports data from many 3D modeling programs in a very clear and easy-to-use xml data file, which can then be imported into your game more easily than writing your own custom exporter and importer for model data. For skinned models (that means your models use a bone skeleton and each vertex has several skinning factors to apply any bone movement to them, often used in shooter games and whenever your game has any character models running around), I would suggest the .fbx format (.x format works too in XNA) or just search for an .md3, .md5, or similar model format importer, which is the famous format used in the Quake and Doom series of games.

Figure 5-2

The exported `rocket.x` file can now be used in your XNA engine the same way you use textures or other content files. Just drop the content file into your project and it will automatically pick up all used shaders and textures and warn you if they are missing. You don't have to add the used textures and shaders yourself; the XNA .x Model processor will do that automatically for you. You just have to make sure the dependent files can be found in the same directory; in this case it would be the files `Rocket.dds`, `RocketNormal.dds`, `RocketHeight.dds`, and `ParallaxMapping.fx`. The implementation of the `Model` class and how to render the Rocket model on the screen is handled in the next part of this chapter.

Rendering of Textures

Until now you used the `Texture` class of the XNA Framework to load textures and then used the `SpriteHelper` class you wrote in Chapter 3 to render sprites on the screen with the help of the `SpriteBatch` class. This worked nice for your first couple of games, but it is not really useful for using textures in a 3D environment and it is still too complicated to use with all these sprite helper classes. As you just saw in the unit test for this chapter there should be a new method called `RenderOnScreen` to render the whole texture or just parts of it directly on the screen. In the background you still use the `SpriteHelper` class and all the code you wrote to render sprites, but this makes using textures much easier and you don't have to create instances of the `SpriteHelper` class anymore. Additionally, you could later improve the way sprites are rendered and maybe even implement your own shaders to accomplish that without having to change any UI code or any unit tests.

Figure 5-3 shows the layout of the new `Texture` class; the code is pretty straightforward and the previous chapters already covered most of the functionality. The only important thing to remember is that you now have two texture classes, the one from the XNA Framework and the one from your own engine. Sure, you could rename your own class to something crazy, but who wants to write `MyOwnTextureClass` all the time, when you can just write `Texture`? Instead you will just rename the use of the XNA `Texture` class, which is not required anymore except in your new `Texture` class, which internally still uses the XNA texture. To do that you write the following code in the using region:

```
using Texture = XnaGraphicEngine.Graphics.Texture;
```

Or this code when you need to access the XNA texture class:

```
using XnaTexture = Microsoft.Xna.Framework.Graphics.Texture;
```

Some of the properties and methods are not important yet and I just included them here to have the complete texture class working right now so you can use it later in this book without having to re-implement any missing features (for example, rendering rotated texture sprites).

Figure 5-3

Before you analyze the code in this class, you should first look at the unit test, which always gives a quick overview on how to use the class. Please note that I split up the static unit test into each class now instead of having them all in the main game class. It is more useful this way because there will be a lot of classes in your engine and it makes it easier to check out functionality and quickly test the capabilities of each class. The unit test just loads the texture with help of the texture constructor, which takes the content name, and then you can render it with the `RenderOnScreen` method:

```
/// <summary>
/// Test render textures
/// </summary>
public static void TestRenderTexture()
{
  Texture testTexture = null;
  TestGame.Start("TestTextures",
    delegate
    {
      testTexture = new Texture("SpaceBackground");
    },
    delegate
    {
      testTexture.RenderOnScreen(
        new Rectangle(100, 100, 256, 256),
        testTexture.GfxRectangle);
    });
} // TestTextures()
```

The most important method for you right now is the `RenderOnScreen` method. The `Valid` property indicates if the loading of the texture succeeded and if you can use the internal `XnaTexture` property. `Width` and `Height` and `GfxRectangle` give you the dimensions of the texture, and the other properties are not important to you right now. They will be used later when you render materials with shaders.

```
/// <summary>
/// Render on screen
/// </summary>
/// <param name="renderRect">Render rectangle</param>
public void RenderOnScreen(Rectangle renderRect)
{
  SpriteHelper.AddSpriteToRender(this,
    renderRect, GfxRectangle);
} // RenderOnScreen(renderRect)
```

Looks quite simple, doesn't it? There are several overloads that all add sprites to the `SpriteHelper` class, which uses code you already wrote in Chapter 3. Only the `AddSpriteToRender` method was changed to be static now and accept `GfxRectangles` instead of creating new instances of the `SpriteHelper` class:

```
/// <summary>
/// Add sprite to render
/// </summary>
/// <param name="texture">Texture</param>
/// <param name="rect">Rectangle</param>
/// <param name="gfxRect">Gfx rectangle</param>
```

```
public static void AddSpriteToRender(
   Texture texture, Rectangle rect, Rectangle gfxRect)
{
   sprites.Add(new SpriteToRender(texture, rect, gfxRect, Color.White));
} // AddSpriteToRender(texture, rect, gfxRect)
```

Finally, you also use the `TextureFont` class. It was moved to the graphics namespace, it uses the new `Texture` class now instead of the XNA `Texture` class, and it has a new unit test for text rendering. Other than that the class remains unchanged; you use it directly to write text on the screen with the help of the tatic `WriteText` methods (a few more overloads were added):

```
/// <summary>
/// Write text on the screen
/// </summary>
/// <param name="pos">Position</param>
/// <param name="text">Text</param>
public static void WriteText(Point pos, string text)
{
   remTexts.Add(new FontToRender(pos.X, pos.Y, text, Color.White));
} // WriteText(pos, text)
```

Line Rendering

To render lines in XNA you can't just use a built-in method, you have to do it your own way. As I said before there are several ways and the most efficient one is to create a big vertex list and render all lines at once after you've collected them throughout the frame (see Figure 5-4).

cam pos={X:-1,093441 Y:-11,36231 Z:2,097521}

Figure 5-4

Additionally, you use a very simple shader to draw the lines. You could also use the `BasicEffect` class of XNA, but it is much faster to use your own custom shader, which just spits out the vertex color for each line. Because rendering 2D and 3D lines is basically the same, just the vertex shader looks a tiny bit different; this section only talks about rendering 2D lines. The `LineManager3D` class works in almost the same manner (see Figure 5-5).

Figure 5-5

To learn how to use these classes, just take a look at the `TestRenderLines` unit test:

```
/// <summary>
/// Test render
/// </summary>
public static void TestRenderLines()
{
  TestGame.Start(delegate
    {
      BaseGame.DrawLine(new Point(-100, 0), new Point(50, 100),
        Color.White);
      BaseGame.DrawLine(new Point(0, 100), new Point(100, 0),
        Color.Gray);
      BaseGame.DrawLine(new Point(400, 0), new Point(100, 0),
        Color.Red);
      BaseGame.DrawLine(new Point(10, 50), new Point(100, +150),
        new Color(255, 0, 0, 64));
    });
} // TestRenderLines()
```

So all you have to do is to call the `BaseGame.DrawLine` method, which accepts both 2D points and 3D vectors to support 2D and 3D lines. Both `LineManager` classes work as shown in Figure 5-6, just call the `DrawLine` method of the `BaseGame` class a couple of times and let the `LineManager` class handle the rest.

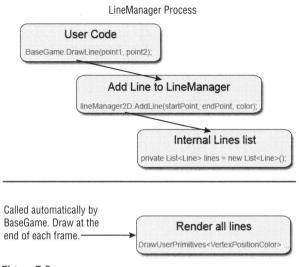

LineManager Process

User Code

BaseGame.DrawLine(point1, point2);

Add Line to LineManager

lineManager2D.AddLine(startPoint, endPoint, color);

Internal Lines list

private List<Line> lines = new List<Line>();

Called automatically by
BaseGame. Draw at the
end of each frame.

Render all lines

DrawUserPrimitives<VertexPositionColor> ...

Figure 5-6

The interesting code is in the Render method, which renders all the lines you have collected this frame. The collecting of the lines and adding them to your lines list is really not complicated code; check it out yourself if you want to take a close look. The Render method uses the VertexPositionColor structure for all the vertex elements and the vertex array is created in the UpdateVertexBuffer method. This is the main part of the method:

```
// Set all lines
for (int lineNum = 0; lineNum < numOfLines; lineNum++)
{
  Line line = (Line)lines[lineNum];
  lineVertices[lineNum * 2 + 0] = new VertexPositionColor(
    new Vector3(
    -1.0f + 2.0f * line.startPoint.X / BaseGame.Width,
    -(-1.0f + 2.0f * line.startPoint.Y / BaseGame.Height), 0),
    line.color);
  lineVertices[lineNum * 2 + 1] = new VertexPositionColor(
    new Vector3(
    -1.0f + 2.0f * line.endPoint.X / BaseGame.Width,
    -(-1.0f + 2.0f * line.endPoint.Y / BaseGame.Height), 0),
    line.color);
} // for (lineNum)
```

First you might wonder why each line start point and end point is divided through the width and height of your game and then multiplied by two and then subtracted by one. This formula is used to convert all 2D points from screen coordinates into your view space, which goes from –1 to +1 for both x and y. In the LineManager3D class this is not really required because you already have the correct 3D points. For each line you store two points (start and end) and each vertex gets the position and the color, hence the VertexPositionColor structure from the XNA Framework.

In the `Render` method you now just go through all primitives you have added (which are the lines; you got half as much as you have points) and render them with help of the `LineRendering.fx` shader:

```
// Render lines if we got any lines to render
if (numOfPrimitives > 0)
{
  BaseGame.AlphaBlending = true;
  BaseGame.WorldMatrix = Matrix.Identity;
  BaseGame.Device.VertexDeclaration = decl;
  ShaderEffect.lineRendering.Render(
    "LineRendering2D",
    delegate
    {
      BaseGame.Device.DrawUserPrimitives<VertexPositionColor>(
        PrimitiveType.LineList, lineVertices, 0, numOfPrimitives);
    });
} // if
```

The `AlphaBlending` property of `BaseGame` makes sure you can render lines with alpha blending to allow blending them in and out. `WorldMatrix` is discussed later; for now just make sure here that the world matrix is reset to use the original position values of the `lineVertices` list. This is especially important for the `LineManager3D`.

Then the vertex declaration is set, which just makes sure that you can render `VertexPositionColor` vertices now (this is just the way DirectX does this and XNA works very similar to that, but you still have the advantage of using generics and other cool .NET functionality):

```
decl = new VertexDeclaration(
  BaseGame.Device, VertexPositionColor.VertexElements);
```

That looks simple, doesn't it? Well, why even bother with the declaration; couldn't XNA do that for you automatically? Yes, it could, but remember you can also create your own custom vertex declaration if you need a custom format, which makes sense if you write your own custom shaders. See Chapter 7 on how to do that, in the discussion of the `TangentVertexFormat`.

The final thing you have to figure out to understand the rendering of the lines is to render data with shaders. Yeah, I know, it's a lot of work just to render a few lines, but you will need all the shader functionality for anything you do in 3D anyway. You cannot render anything in XNA without shaders; period! You might now say "What about the `SpriteBatch` class, you used it to render 2D graphics and you never talked about shaders yet?" That is correct; you don't have to know anything about shaders if you just want to create a simple 2D game. But that does not mean the `SpriteBatch` class does not use shaders internally. Another class that hides the shader capability is the `BasicEffect` class, which allows you to render 3D data without writing your custom shader effects first. It uses a basic shader internally to mimic the fixed function pipeline functionality, but it is similar to the fixed function pipeline, not as fast as writing your own custom shaders, and it does not support anything special.

The model class that is discussed in a little bit also uses shaders, but XNA allows you to hide all the shader management. You can just set the shader parameters for the matrices and then use the Draw method to let XNA render all mesh parts of the 3D model.

Shaders are discussed in great detail in Chapter 6. Before you take a look at the LineRendering.fx shader that brings the lines on the screen, you should first look at the ShaderEffect class that allows rendering of 3D data for the shader with help of a RenderDelegate:

```
/// <summary>
/// Render
/// </summary>
/// <param name="techniqueName">Technique name</param>
/// <param name="renderDelegate">Render delegate</param>
public void Render(string techniqueName,
   BaseGame.RenderDelegate renderDelegate)
{
   SetParameters();

   // Start shader
   effect.CurrentTechnique = effect.Techniques[techniqueName];
   effect.Begin(SaveStateMode.None);

   // Render all passes (usually just one)
   //foreach (EffectPass pass in effect.CurrentTechnique.Passes)
   for (int num = 0; num < effect.CurrentTechnique.Passes.Count; num++)
   {
      EffectPass pass = effect.CurrentTechnique.Passes[num];

      pass.Begin();
      renderDelegate();
      pass.End();
   } // foreach (pass)

   // End shader
   effect.End();
} // Render(passName, renderDelegate)
```

The ShaderEffect class uses the effect instance to load the shader from the content pipeline. You then can use the effect to render 3D data with it. This is done by first selecting the technique either by name or index, then the shader is started and you have to call Begin and End for each pass the shader has. Most shaders in this book and most shaders you will ever encounter will only have one pass, and that means you only have to call Begin and End once for the first pass. Usually only post screen shaders are more complex, but you can write shaders with many passes, which might be useful for fur shaders or things of this nature with multiple layers. In between Begin and End the 3D data is rendered with the help of the RenderDelegate you used earlier to call DrawUserPrimitives with the lineVertices array.

3D Programming

So how do you get the 3D data imported from a model file like `rocket.x` on your screen? Your screen can only display 2D data; this means you need a way to convert 3D data to your 2D screen. This is called projection, and there are many ways this can be done. In the early days of 3D games, techniques like ray-casting were used and done all on the CPU. For each pixel column of the screen the upper and lower bounds were calculated by a simple formula and this led to the first 3D games like Ultima Underground, Wolfenstein 3D, and later Doom, which was quite popular.

Not long after that more realistic games like Descent, Terminal Velocity, Quake, and so on were developed, which used a better way to convert 3D data to 2D. In the mid-nineties 3D hardware was becoming more popular and more and more gaming PCs suddenly had the ability to help rendering polygons in a very efficient matter.

Luckily, you don't have to worry about all the early problems of 3D games anymore. 3D graphics today are all done on the GPU (graphic processing unit on the graphic card). The GPU not only renders polygons on the screen and fills pixels, but it also performs all the transformations to project 3D data to 2D (see Figure 5-7). Vertex shaders are used to transform all 3D points to screen coordinates and pixel shaders are then used to fill all visible polygons on the screen with pixels. Pixel shaders are usually the most interesting and important part of shaders because they can greatly manipulate the way the output looks (changing colors, mixing textures, having lighting and shadows influence the final output, and so on). Older hardware that does not support vertex and pixel shaders is not even supported in XNA, so you don't have to worry about falling back to the fixed function pipeline or even doing software rendering. For XNA you need at least Shader Model 1.1, which means you need at least a GeForce 3 or ATI 8000 graphic card.

The code and images I'm going to explain in the next pages only cover the basics of 3D programming and how to work with matrices in XNA. If you want to know more I strongly recommend reading the XNA documentation and, even better, the original DirectX documentation, which has very good topics about getting started with 3D programming, matrices, and how everything is handled in the framework (which is very similar to XNA).

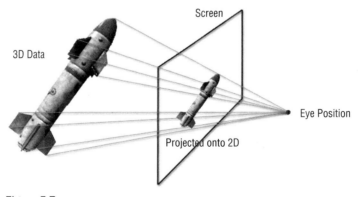

Figure 5-7

I won't have time to go into great detail about all these calculations and thanks to the many helper classes and methods in the XNA Framework, you can get along without knowing much about matrix transformations. Projecting 3D data usually consists of three steps:

❑ Bring the 3D data to the correct 3D position with help of the `WorldMatrix`. This means for the rocket, which was created in 3D Studio Max, to rotate it in the direction you want, scale it accordingly to fit correctly into your 3D scene, and then position it to wherever you want it to be. You can use the `Matrix` methods to help you do that; use `CreateRotation`, `CreateScale`, and `CreateTranslation` methods and combine them by multiplying the resulting matrixes:

```
BaseGame.WorldMatrix =
  Matrix.CreateRotationX(MathHelper.Pi / 2) *
  Matrix.CreateScale(2.5f) *
  Matrix.CreateTranslation(rocketPosition);
```

❑ Every single point of your 3D model is then transformed with this `WorldMatrix` to bring it to the correct position in your 3D world. In DirectX and the fixed function pipeline you didn't have to do that yourself, but as soon as you write shaders in XNA you have to transform all vertices yourself. And as you know everything in XNA is rendered with shaders, there is no support for the fixed function pipeline.

❑ What is visible on the screen depends on the location and orientation of your camera or eye (see Figure 5-7 earlier). Everything is projected to this camera location, but you can also rotate the world, tilt it, or do more crazy things with your camera matrix. You will probably just want to use the `Matrix.CreateLookAt` method in the beginning to create your camera matrix, which is then used in the vertex shader to transform the 3D world data to the camera space:

```
BaseGame.ViewMatrix =
  Matrix.CreateLookAt(cameraPosition, lookTarget, upVector);
```

❑ And finally the last step is to bring the projected camera space data to your screen. The reason why this operation is not already done in the `ViewMatrix` is to allow the view matrix to be calculated and changed more easily. The visible camera space goes from –1 to +1 for both x and y, and z contains the depth value for each point in relation to the camera position. The `ProjectionMatrix` converts these values to your screen resolution (for example, 1024×768) and it also specifies how deep you can look into the scene (near and far plane values). The depth is important in helping you find out which object is in front of which other object when you finally render the polygons in the pixel shaders (which are all 2D, because you can only render 2D data on your screen). The projection matrix is constructed this way:

```
/// <summary>
/// Field of view and near and far plane distances for the
/// ProjectionMatrix creation.
/// </summary>
private const float FieldOfView = (float)Math.PI / 2,
  NearPlane = 1.0f,
  FarPlane = 500.0f;
...
aspectRatio = (float)width / (float)height;
BaseGame.ProjectionMatrix = Matrix.CreatePerspectiveFieldOfView(
  FieldOfView, aspectRatio, NearPlane, FarPlane);
```

There is an important change in XNA that should be mentioned: In DirectX all the `Matrix` methods, tutorials, and samples used left-handed matrices, but in XNA everything is right handed; there are no methods to create any left-handed matrices. If you create a new game or if you are new to 3D programming this will probably not matter much to you, but if you have old code or old models, you might run into problems because of the way the 3D data is used. Using left-handed data in a right-handed environment means that everything looks turned inside out if you don't modify your matrices. Culling is also the other way around in XNA; it works counter-clockwise, which is the mathematical correct way. DirectX used clockwise culling by default. If your models are inside out and you switch from clockwise to counter-clockwise, they will look correct again; they are just mirrored now (the 3D data is still left-handed).

This is especially true if you import .x files, which use, by default, a left-handed system (see Figure 5-8). You can either convert all matrices or points yourself or just live with the fact that everything is mirrored. In this book you will use a lot of .x files and it does not matter if they are left-handed (like the Rocket model from Rocket Commander) or right-handed (like all new 3D content created here) because you do not care if left-handed data is mirrored. If you have to make sure all data in your game is correctly aligned, please make sure you have all the 3D data in an exportable format so you can later re-export any wrong data instead of having to fix it in your code yourself.

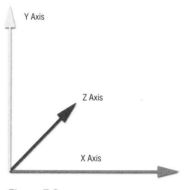

Figure 5-8

You probably remember from school that the left-handed coordinate system is named after the left hand, which can be used to show you the x (thumb), y (forefinger), and z (middle finger) axes. Just hold up your left hand and align these three fingers in 90 degrees to each other and you have your left-handed coordinate system. In school both math and physics used only the right-handed coordinate system and if you were writing with your right hand and held up your left hand to show you the axes, you got it all wrong and that was not cool if you just based your whole solution of an exam on that.

Anyway, the right-handed coordinate system is much cooler because almost all 3D modeling programs work with right-handed data, and most programs except games work with right-handed data too. Right-handed coordinate systems can be shown by using your right hand for the x (thumb), y (forefinger), z (middle finger) axes (see Figure 5-9).

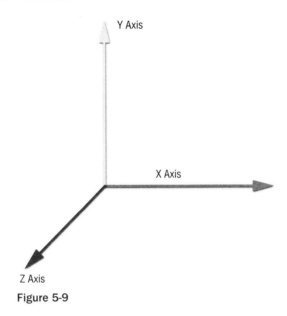

Figure 5-9

Looks almost the same, but having the z axis coming toward you is kind of unnatural if you worked with left-handed systems before. Another reason why it might be useful to rotate this system is to have it behave the same way as in 3D modeling programs where z points up. I also like x and y lying on the ground for positioning 3D data and building 3D landscapes (see Figure 5-10).

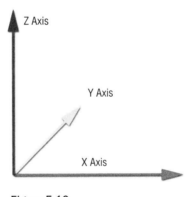

Figure 5-10

Enough talk about converting 3D to 2D and coordinate systems. You should now know enough about basic 3D calculations to render 3D models. If you are still unsure and want to learn more about 3D math and programming, please pick up a good book about that or read more on the Internet. Many great websites and tutorials are available there; just search for 3D programming.

Model Unit Test

You should now have the `Rocket.x` model file discussed earlier imported into your project (use the content directory to keep code and content data separated). Rendering the model data is not very complicated, but there is no `Render` method in the XNA `Model` class and you want to have such a method for your unit test. To accomplish this and to make it easier to later extend the model rendering, optimizing it and adding more cool features, you write your own `Model` class (similar to the `Texture` class you just wrote). It will just use the XNA model class internally and provide you with a `Render` method and handle all the scaling issues and set all required matrices automatically for you.

It is a good practice to write another unit test just for the class you are currently developing, even if another unit test already covers the basic functionality. In this class unit test you can make more special considerations and check more details. It is also useful to quickly check if new data is valid by just exchanging the content loaded in the unit test. Here is the very simple, but still very useful unit test for the `Model` class:

```
public static void TestRenderModel()
{
  Model testModel = null;
  TestGame.Start("TestRenderModel",
    delegate
    {
      testModel = new Model("Rocket");
    },
    delegate
    {
      testModel.Render(Matrix.CreateScale(10));
    });
} // TestRenderModel()
```

So you just load a test model named Rocket in the content system and then you render it every frame with a scaling of 10 directly in the 3D scene. All the other stuff is handled somewhere else and you don't have to worry about it. This includes setting shaders, updating matrices, making sure the render states are correct for rendering 3D data, and so on.

The only interesting method in the `Model` class (see Figure 5-11) is the `Render` method.

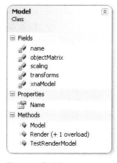

Figure 5-11

The constructor just loads the model from the content and sets the internal variables to make sure you got the correct object scaling and matrix to make it easier to fit it into your world:

```
/// <summary>
/// Create model
/// </summary>
/// <param name="setModelName">Set Model Filename</param>
public Model(string setModelName)
{
  name = setModelName;

  xnaModel = BaseGame.Content.Load<XnaModel>(
    @"Content\" + name);

  // Get matrices for each mesh part
  transforms = new Matrix[xnaModel.Bones.Count];
  xnaModel.CopyAbsoluteBoneTransformsTo(transforms);

  // Calculate scaling for this object, used for rendering.
  scaling = xnaModel.Meshes[0].BoundingSphere.Radius *
    transforms[0].Right.Length();
  if (scaling == 0)
    scaling = 0.0001f;

  // Apply scaling to objectMatrix to rescale object to size of 1.0
  objectMatrix *= Matrix.CreateScale(1.0f / scaling);
} // Model(setModelName)
```

After the `xnaModel` instance is loaded from the content directory, the transformations are pre-calculated because you don't support any animated data here (XNA does not really support it yet anyway). The transforms matrix list holds the render matrix for each model mesh part you have to render (the rocket consists just of one mesh part using only one effect). This transformation is set by the 3D Modeler in the 3D creation program and aligns your model the way the modeler wants it to be. Then you determine the scaling and make sure it is not zero because dividing by zero is not really fun. Finally, you calculate the object matrix, which will be used together with the transform matrices and the render matrix for rendering.

The `Render` method now just goes through all meshes of your model (for good performance always make sure you have as few meshes as possible) and calculates the world matrix for every mesh. Then each used effect is updated with the current world, view, and project matrix values as well any other dynamic data like the light direction, and then you are good to go. The `MeshPart.Draw` method calls the internal shader of the model the same way you did earlier for the line rendering. The next two chapters talk in more detail about this process and you re-implement it in your own way to be much more efficient when rendering many 3D models each frame.

```
/// <summary>
/// Render
/// </summary>
/// <param name="renderMatrix">Render matrix</param>
public void Render(Matrix renderMatrix)
{
  // Apply objectMatrix
  renderMatrix = objectMatrix * renderMatrix;
```

```
    // Go through all meshes in the model
    foreach (ModelMesh mesh in xnaModel.Meshes)
    {
        // Assign world matrix for each used effect
        BaseGame.WorldMatrix =
            transforms[mesh.ParentBone.Index] *
            renderMatrix;

        // And for each effect this mesh uses (usually just 1,multimaterials
        // are nice in 3ds max, but not efficiently for rendering stuff).
        foreach (Effect effect in mesh.Effects)
        {
            // Set technique (not done automatically by XNA framework).
            effect.CurrentTechnique = effect.Techniques["Specular20"];

            // Set matrices, we use world, viewProj and viewInverse in
            // the ParallaxMapping.fx shader
            effect.Parameters["world"].SetValue(
                BaseGame.WorldMatrix);
            // Note: these values should only be set once every frame!
            // to improve performance again, also we should access them
            // with EffectParameter and not via name (which is slower)!
            // For more information see Chapter 6 and 7.
            effect.Parameters["viewProj"].SetValue(
                BaseGame.ViewProjectionMatrix);
            effect.Parameters["viewInverse"].SetValue(
                BaseGame.InverseViewMatrix);

            // Also set light direction (not really used here, but later)
            effect.Parameters["lightDir"].SetValue(
                BaseGame.LightDirection);
        } // foreach (effect)

        // Render with help of the XNA ModelMesh Draw method, which goes
        // through all mesh parts and renders them (with vertex and index
        // buffers).
        mesh.Draw();
    } // foreach (mesh)
} // Render(renderMatrix)
```

As you can see there are quite a lot of comments in this code and you will see this in all methods written by me that are a little longer. I think it is very important to understand the code quickly later when you want to change something, refactor code to new requirements, or just for optimizing your code. For most programmers this is a hard step; we all are lazy and it takes a long time to understand how useful these comments can be, not only if other people read your code, but also if you come back to a part of code at a later point in time. Please also try to write your comments in English and use a language that simplifies the reading process and does not use code in the comments.

The render matrix you passed from the unit test (which was just a scaling matrix with the factor of 10) is now multiplied with the object matrix, which again scales the render matrix by the factor required to bring the object to the size 1, so in total your rocket now has a size of 10 units in your 3D world. Then you go through each model mesh (your rocket just has one mesh) and calculate the world matrix for this mesh by using the pre-calculated transforms matrix list and the render matrix. By using the world matrix in the vertex shader you can now be sure that every single 3D point of your rocket is transformed the way you want it to be. Before calling this method the view and projection matrices must obviously be set too because the vertex shader expects all these values to be able to convert the 3D data for the pixel shader to render it onto the screen.

XNA models store all the used effects for each model mesh and you can have multiple effects for one single mesh, but for most models you will ever use this is usually just one effect too. You will later see that the most efficient way to render a lot of 3D data is to render them in a bunch using the same shader for a long time and then flush everything to the screen at once. This allows you to render thousands of objects every frame with a very high frame rate. Please read Chapters 6 and 7 for more information about shaders and how to work with them in an efficient way.

But before you can render your mesh here you have to set the used technique first, which is not done automatically by XNA, even though it is set by the model artist. You will see in Chapter 7 how to get around this issue. Then you set the world, view, and project matrices the way the shader expects these values. For example, the view matrix is never directly required, you just use the view inverse matrix to figure out the camera position and use it for specular light calculations. All these shader parameters are set with the `Parameters` property of the effect class by using the names of these parameters. This is not a very efficient way to set effect parameters because using strings to access data is a huge performance penalty. You will later find ways to do this way better, but for now it works and you should be able to see your little rocket from the unit test after `mesh.Draw` is called (see Figure 5-12).

Figure 5-12

Testing Other Models

If you have other .x files on your disk or if you just want to test other .x files from the Rocket Commander game or one of its many game mods, you can quickly test that by dragging in the .x file to the content directory and changing the unit test to load the new model.

Let's do that with the `Apple.x` model from the Fruit Commander mod:

```
public static void TestRenderModel()
{
  Model testModel = null;
  TestGame.Start("TestRenderModel",
    delegate
    {
      testModel = new Model("Apple");
    },
    delegate
    {
      testModel.Render(Matrix.CreateScale(10));
    });
} // TestRenderModel()
```

This results in the screen shown in Figure 5-13. Please note that the specular color calculations are based on the normal mapping effect in the shader, which does not work correctly here because the tangent data of the apple is not correct (it was not even imported because XNA models don't support tangent data, and you have to implement it in your own way in Chapter 7).

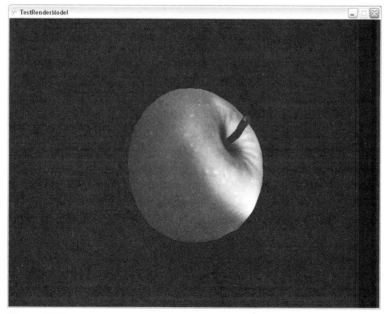

Figure 5-13

Plugging in More Game Components

Before you even noticed it your graphics engine has grown to a respectable size and you have a lot of useful classes right now, which help you to render both 2D and 3D data quite easily, as can be seen in the many unit tests available in most of the classes (see Figure 5-14).

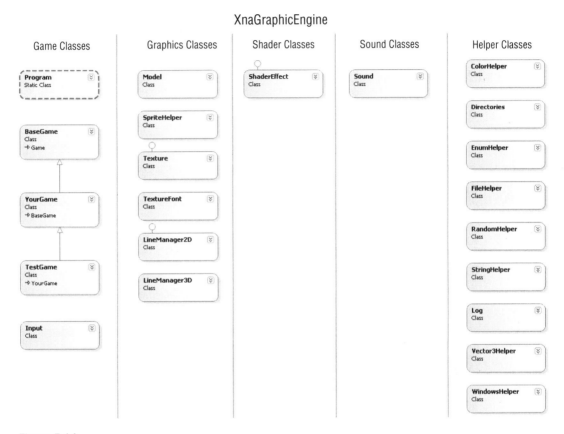

Figure 5-14

You haven't used many game components until now and in my opinion it does not make much sense to write the base graphics engine with components. You did not use any Update or Draw methods the way game components are used. Okay, the Model class uses a Render method and the Input class has an Update method, but other than that you did not have any functionality that is compatible with game components. The Render methods in the model and texture classes work quite differently because they expect the user to call them with different values and very often each frame. I guess the Input class could be changed to a game component, but I'm not quite excited about that idea.

Instead let's think of components, which fit perfectly into the game components model. It would make sense if you have a class that needs to be updated and drawn each frame. Examples for these kinds of classes would be frame per second counters or a camera class, which is still missing from your engine.

Simple Camera Class

You don't need a complex camera for your unit tests, but it would be nice to move around a little and to have a simple 3D look at the objects you render in your engine unit tests. With the help of the view matrix and the `Matrix.CreateLookAt` method you can easily create such functionality and set it wherever you need it. Even better would be the use of a game component class to do all this automatically; all you have to do is to create an instance of the camera class in the constructor of the `YourGame` class, which is derived from the `BaseGame` class, and suddenly all unit tests and other 3D code will use the new camera class without any extra code because `Update` is called automatically for each game component you have in the `YourGame` class.

```
public YourGame()
{
  // Init simple camera
  this.Components.Add(new SimpleCamera(this));
} // YourGame()
```

The `SimpleCamera` class has a constructor and an `Initialize` and `Update` method, which are both called automatically (see Figure 5-15). The class also has three fields for the x, y, and z position of the camera, which is initialized to (0, 0, 15). `Update` then changes x and y based on the mouse movement, or if you have a gamepad, based on the right thumb stick movement. Additionally you can zoom in and out with the left thumb stick.

Figure 5-15

The class is quite simple and it is easy to read through the code of the whole class:

```
/// <summary>
/// Simple camera class just to move around a little.
/// Always focuses on the center and uses the same height.
/// </summary>
class SimpleCamera : GameComponent
{
  #region Variables
  float x = 0, y = 0;
  float zHeight = 15.0f;
  #endregion

  #region Constructor
  public SimpleCamera(BaseGame game)
    : base(game)
```

```
    {
    } // SimpleCamera(game)
    #endregion

    #region Initialize
    public override void Initialize()
    {
      base.Initialize();
    } // Initialize
    #endregion

    #region Update
    public override void Update(GameTime gameTime)
    {
      base.Update(gameTime);
      // Update camera position (allow mouse and gamepad)
      x += Input.MouseXMovement / 10;
      y += Input.MouseYMovement / 10;
      x += Input.GamePad.ThumbSticks.Right.X;
      y += Input.GamePad.ThumbSticks.Right.Y;
      zHeight += Input.GamePad.ThumbSticks.Left.Y;
      BaseGame.ViewMatrix = Matrix.CreateLookAt(
        new Vector3(x, y, zHeight), Vector3.Zero, Vector3.Up);
    } // Update(gameTime)
    #endregion
  } // class SimpleCamera
```

The important thing here is the `ViewMatrix` from the `BaseGame` class, which is set at the end of the `Update` method. When rendering a shader in the model class or in any other class like the line managers, you will use this view matrix and make sure that all your 3D data is converted to your view space with this exact matrix until you change it again next frame.

You now have everything together for the `TestRenderOurNewGraphicEngine` test you wrote at the beginning of this chapter, and if you take a look at all the classes in the project you imported and wrote, it is quite a nice engine that is both easy to use and extensible, which you will explore in the next chapters.

ScreenshotCapturer Class

There is also another helper class in the engine called `ScreenshotCapturer`, which allows you to take screenshots with the Print-Screen key. It is implemented as a game component too and it is initialized in the `BaseGame` constructor. The `Update` method is called automatically and just calls `MakeScreenshot` if the user just pressed the Print-Screen key:

```
public override void Update(GameTime gameTime)
{
  if (Input.KeyboardKeyJustPressed(Keys.PrintScreen))
    MakeScreenshot();

  base.Update(gameTime);
} // Update(gameTime)
```

The `MakeScreenshot` method creates a temporary texture and stores the back buffer with the help of the `ResolveBackBuffer` method of the device. The result is then saved to disk with the help of some other helper methods in the class:

```
using (Texture2D dstTexture = new Texture2D(
  BaseGame.Device, BaseGame.Width, BaseGame.Height, 1,
  ResourceUsage.ResolveTarget,
  SurfaceFormat.Color,
  ResourceManagementMode.Manual))
{
  // Get data with help of the resolve method
  BaseGame.Device.ResolveBackBuffer(dstTexture);

  dstTexture.Save(
    ScreenshotNameBuilder(screenshotNum),
    ImageFileFormat.Jpg);
} // using (dstTexture)
```

Making Sure Games Run on the Xbox 360

The first two chapters already talked about the Xbox 360 and how to deploy some simple 2D games to it. This is the section in which I want to make sure that you have the XNA Game Launcher ready to work on your Xbox 360 console and you can test the graphics engine and games in each chapter as you go along. In the creation of my first XNA game I was not able to test it on the Xbox 360 first, and therefore, I only tested it on the Xbox 360 when it was almost done and I encountered many problems. 2D games ran fine and the only thing that I did wrong was to not respect the safe region on the Xbox 360 to support older TV sets. For 3D games and shaders, especially post screen shaders, so many things can go wrong. I just want to make sure that none of you have to go through the same troubles.

If you don't have an Xbox 360 or if you are not interested in Xbox 360 console development, you can probably skip this section. XNA is still a great platform for Windows only and superior to Managed DirectX because it supports .NET 2.0 and simplifies many processes, but having the ability to create console games is really a great feature.

Before you get started, take a quick look at the completed `TestRenderOurNewGraphicEngine` unit test, which shows some of the features of your new graphics engine (see Figure 5-16). It looks much cooler in real time, especially if you move around with the mouse or gamepad.

As you can see on the image, I have drawn a white rectangle at the border of the visible render area. This rectangle is not described in the XNA Framework and you will not find much information about that on the Internet because this safe region is not really documented well. It means that if you have a TV set the signal that is sent to it is usually overdrawn, even if it is a new HDTV set; that's just the way TVs work and accept signals. The older the TV set is the more pixels in the outer regions can be skipped. For this reason you should make sure that all the important game content is in the inner "safe region." On the PC you can put anything you want in the top-left corner or in the lower right and the user will still see it in the fullscreen mode because all pixels are rendered 1:1 onto the screen, but consoles and TV sets don't work this way. It is usually best to design your game in a way that the outer regions are not so important and only have some less important UI or 3D data on them, so it looks ok on the PC and still correct on the Xbox 360. Alternatively you could implement two modes: one for the PC, which uses the full resolution, and one mode for the Xbox 360, which cuts of 5%–10% of the borders to make the game fit on all TV sets.

Note: If you connect your Xbox 360 to a VGA monitor with a VGA cable, all this will not matter because then the Xbox 360 will render the full screen the same way the PC does; this applies only to TV sets.

Figure 5-16

Downloading the XNA Game Launcher

To get the XNA Framework on your Xbox 360 you have to download the XNA Game Launcher first. On the PC you can just install the XNA Framework Redistributables or you can install XNA Game Studio Express, which also installs the XNA Framework. Either way you will need .NET 2.0 to start any XNA application on the PC and in the same way you will need .NET 2.0 on the Xbox 360, which is obviously not installed by default (because none of the Xbox 360 components use .NET or any Managed code at all).

You can't just put a CD or DVD into your Xbox 360 and install XNA or .NET. The Xbox 360 does not allow any unauthorized data and it protects itself very well against any hacking attempts (just take a look at how long hackers have been trying to get around the Xbox 360 protection system; it is much more secure than the first Xbox). Though this is good for the Xbox 360 game developers because games can't be copied that easily and the Xbox 360 can't be used for anything other than the expected use by the manufacturers, it is not a good thing if you want to bring your custom content and game ideas to your Xbox 360.

For that reason and because Microsoft and especially the Xbox 360 team is very afraid of misuse and security risks, you have to join the so-called "XNA Creator's Club" first before you are allowed to download and install XNA on your console. Other than XNA it is not free to join the XNA Creator's Club; it will cost you a couple of bucks ($99 per year or just $49 for four months). To do that you can login with any Xbox Live account (create one first if you don't have one yet; make sure your console is connected to the Internet) and then go to All Games ➪ Memberships. There you can select the XNA Creator's Club memberships and subscribe to them.

143

After you have done that you can download the XNA Game Launcher, which will be installed to your Games ⇨ All Demos/Games section of your Xbox 360 Dashboard.

Xbox 360 Setup and Deploying Games

You can now start the XNA Game Launcher, which is the program to start all your XNA games, no matter if written by you or if you have downloaded them. The XNA Game Launcher can be found on your Games ⇨ All Demos/Games page if you are logged into an Xbox Live account that has the XNA Creator's Club membership. If you don't see it, go back to the Memberships page and make sure you are subscribed. After you start the XNA Game Launcher you can see the screen shown in Figure 5-17. Please make sure you are connected to the Internet at all times when the XNA Game Launcher is started, or else you will lose the connection to Xbox Live and the XNA Game Launcher will end itself.

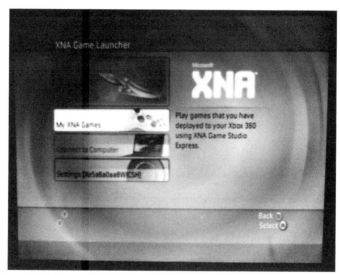

Figure 5-17

As already discussed in Chapter 1, you have to go into Settings first if this is your first time using the launcher and you want to deploy your games from your PC to the console. In Settings you can then generate a key, which you have to enter in XNA Game Studio Express under Tools ⇨ Options ⇨ XNA Game Studio ⇨ Add Console (see Chapter 1). You may have to repeat that step in case the connection to the PC does not work anymore or if you have reinstalled XNA Game Studio Express on your PC.

After the key is set you can connect the Xbox 360 to your computer and start deploying games from your PC. To deploy games, the PC and the Xbox 360 must be in the same network and because both have to be on the Internet, it makes sense to use a router or modem to connect all the devices together. You can deploy games by just opening an Xbox 360 project in XNA Game Studio Express and pressing F5 to start it. Alternatively you can just deploy the game without starting it in the Build menu. In any case the deployed games (if there were no build errors) are automatically stored on your Xbox 360 and can be accessed later with the "My XNA Games" menu entry of the XNA Game Launcher (see Figure 5-17). This is quite useful if you just want to play a game or show it to a friend without having to connect to the PC first.

Console Debugging and Tools

When you press F5 in XNA Game Studio a project will be debugged, no matter whether you start it on the PC or the Xbox 360. The cool thing is that debugging works great on the console too. This can be especially useful if you just have one PC monitor and then your Xbox 360 connected to a TV set. Then you can use your PC to do all the work and step through the code in the debugging mode while you can see the result on the Xbox 360 screen.

Additionally there are some tools to help you out with the Xbox 360 development. For example, XACT allows you to create and test sound projects for Windows and the Xbox 360. You learn all about that in Chapter 9. Professional Xbox 360 developers also have access to the XDK (Xbox Development Kit), which is not available to home users and it costs quite a lot of money to get such a kit, if your company is even accepted to be a certified Xbox 360 developer. There are many useful tools in the XDK, especially to find out about the performance of the console, get and log errors, and so on. All of this is not available to XNA developers. For this reason Microsoft created a special tool just for XNA to help you analyze the performance of your game project on the Xbox 360. The program is called "XNA Framework Remote Performance Monitor for Xbox 360" and you can find it at Start ➪ All Programs ➪ XNA Game Studio ➪ Tools. Check it out if you are serious about XNA console development.

Challenge: Write a Game Component

It is now your turn to write some code and test it on both the Windows and Xbox 360 platforms. To make it easy you just have to write a simple "frames per second" display in the upper-left corner of the screen. Remember the safe region on the Xbox 360; it would make sense to have different code for the Xbox 360 and the PC for the location of the frame per second number. Take a look at the following code to see how this can be done:

```
#if XBOX360
    Point fpsPos = new Point(2 + width / 15, 2 + height / 15);
#else
    Point fpsPos = new Point(2, 2);
#endif
```

You should plug the game component in the same way as the SimpleCamera class and you should put it in the game namespace too. For drawing the frames per second counter, use the last line of the BaseGame.Draw method before base.Draw is called. Then test a couple of unit tests (see the program class) and see if the frames per seconds counter is displayed correctly on Windows and the Xbox 360 if you have one.

To calculate the frames per seconds each frame you could use a frame counter variable and then find out how long the application runs and divide these two values to get the number of frames you have each second in average. A better way would be just to count the frames every second and then start over at 0 every time a second has passed.

If you are unsure about your implementation, skip a few chapters ahead and see the code that is used in the games there (they all have fps counters and the code for it in them). For example, the Rocket Commander game always uses an fps display in debug mode and for all unit tests to quickly help you to see any performance drops if you do anything wrong. For just the component code take a look at the FpsCounter class from the source code for this chapter.

Summary

In this chapter you learned a lot about the creation of a full-blown graphics engine and you have gone through quite a lot of new graphics classes. Most of them were quite simple, but they are all still very important for the upcoming projects in this book.

Besides the many unit tests you explored and that helped you to stay focused on the problems you had to solve to get your graphics engine running, you also learned about the process of converting 3D data to the 2D screen space and in which way to use right-handed matrices in XNA. To use these matrices in shaders, which are required to render anything in XNA, you took a quick look at vertex and pixel shaders, but you will dive much deeper into shaders in the next chapters.

If you take a look at the new classes (Figure 5-15) and the project overview (Figure 5-13) you can see that there are a lot more namespaces than in the previous projects and you also moved some classes around and refactored them to your new needs. This was important because the switch from 2D to 3D is not an easy one and you can always improve the way the classes work and make the unit tests simpler. When your engine becomes more and more complex it is even more important to have solid framework with many unit tests you can fall back on in case something does not work the way you want it to. Otherwise it would just not be possible to write a unit test at the end of the book that renders a complex car with many shaders and over 20,000 polygons into a scene with shadow mapping, post screen effects, and cool glass shaders in just a few lines of code.

BaseGame is now your main entry point for the application and all internal classes are somehow connected to this class. BaseGame not only stores the device or content manager, but it also allows you to get the width and height of the render area, all the matrices you need to render shaders, and it stores many more useful capabilities in the properties that allow you, for example, to quickly enable or disable alpha blending.

Finally you learned a little bit more about using the Xbox 360 to test your graphics engine and all the pitfalls that can happen if you don't test your game on the console early enough. In the next chapter you learn all about shaders and in Chapter 8 you will do some cool normal mapping, and you finally fix all these problems with the XNA models, tangent data, and so on. Then in Chapter 9 you learn about the powerful post screen shaders, which quickly give your whole game another look, and as an example game you can play the Rocket Commander game on the Xbox 360 with help of XNA.

6

Shader Management

With the basic graphics engine now up and running you can focus on shader development for a while. As mentioned in the last chapter everything that is rendered in XNA is done with the help of shaders, even if you don't interact with shaders directly when using the `SpriteBatch` class or the `SimpleEffect` class to simulate fixed function behavior. This chapter goes through the whole process of writing a shader from the ground up, and then you learn all about vertex buffers, the vertex shader process, and how pixel shaders finally bring the pixels on the screen. If you are already a shader expert you probably want to skip this chapter or just quickly fly over it. But because the next chapters all rely on a fundamental knowledge of shaders, I want to make sure everyone is on the same level.

Because shaders are so very important in XNA you should really try to follow all steps in this chapter if you don't have firm shader knowledge yet. The chapter is designed in a way to let you follow every single step by yourself, and by the end of the chapter you will have written your first shader and you should know everything from start to finish how it is done. Then you will be ready for the next chapters and you will be able to write your own shaders easily.

Before starting with cool normal mapping effects or post screen shaders in the next chapters you have to learn the basics first. Shaders are not just used for high-quality effects, but they also replace very simple rendering processes that were used in the days of the fixed function pipeline. After learning a little bit about the history of shaders and graphic card developments you will go through the process of creating a simple shader just to render an example 3D model with per-pixel specular lighting and then import the shader into your graphic engine. The main tool you are going to use to create shaders and test them out before you even start putting more code in your engine is FX Composer from Nvidia, which is a great tool to quickly create your own shaders.

Shader Overview

Fixed function means that the GPU developers have programmed a fixed way to transform vertices (in case the card is T&L able, which means it can transform and light vertices) and output pixels in a pre-programmed way directly on the GPU hardware. It is not possible to change this behavior; you can only enable and disable certain features. For early games this was quite nice because the GPU hardware did a lot of work and kept the CPU free for other tasks, and the GPU was a lot faster rendering 3D data than the CPU because the GPU is heavily optimized just for rendering polygons. If you hear of "Direct3D 7.0 capable graphic cards," this is exactly what they could do; earlier cards had a similar behavior, but in Direct3D 5.0 and before it was really hard to program directly on the hardware level of the GPU with execute buffers and things like that. Direct3D 7.0 simplified the rendering process when the Nvidia GeForce series of graphic cards were available around 1999. It was now possible to render polygons with multiple textures at once, use texture compression to fit more textures in video memory, and use vertex buffers directly in video memory for improved performance.

History

Even after these great advancements in Direct3D 7.0 the games did not look much different, they just ran faster, had maybe more polygons, and made use of texture compression and multi-texture effects to show more textures and mix them together a little. The real revolution came with DirectX 8 and DirectX 9. DirectX 8 did finally remove the `DirectDraw` component and introduced vertex shaders, pixel shaders, and many effects — bump mapping, custom texture mapping, and so on — but it only supports Shader Model 1.0 and it was not very user-friendly in the beginning because of the many API changes, and writing assembly shaders is no piece of cake.

DirectX 9 added support for HLSL (High Level Shader Language, which you learn about in this chapter) and new features with upcoming graphic cards like HDR (high dynamic range) rendering and multiple render targets, which allow techniques like deferred shading. DirectX 9 was very popular and many developers switched from OpenGL to DirectX just because OpenGL did not support shaders properly in the beginning and the OpenGL 2.0 Standard took way too long until it was approved. The extension model is also more inferior for shaders than using the Direct3D shader classes and it took a long time until better mechanisms were available in OpenGL. Direct3D 10 is also again much ahead of OpenGL, supporting Shader Model 4.0 and geometry shaders for more than a year now, and OpenGL has a lot of catching up to do. Direct3D 10 works currently only on Windows Vista, but you can still do some shader model 4.0 development with OpenGL extensions in XP. But most Windows game developers will switch to Vista just for Direct3D 10 in a few years. Contrary to the belief of some people there is no support for Shader Model 4.0 in DirectX 9, the so-called "DirectX 9.0L" is just a way to support DirectX 9.0 games and applications in Vista. In my opinion it is not good for game developers to have so many different versions of DirectX around, supporting DirectX 9 and falling back to older hardware, which can maybe only do DirectX 7 or 8, then having to implement Direct3D 10 for the newest effects in Vista and finally also make DirectX 9.0 an option for anyone running Windows XP. That does not sound like a joy ride. Luckily for you XNA does not have these problems; there is only one version available and it will just support Shader Models 1–3 (DirectX 8 and 9) and you don't have to worry about anything else. It will run fine on Windows XP, Vista, and even on the Xbox 360.

For more information about the history of DirectX and the relationship to the Windows versions and the available hardware technology, see Figure 6-1. It shows that DirectX versions were usually bound in some way to the newest operating system from Microsoft and you can expect this to be true in the future too. DirectX 1 and 2 were not really used. DirectX 3 did still have support for the retained (high level) mode, but that mode was not used much by game developers and it was depreciated in the next versions. DirectX 5 came out together with Windows 98 and was more widely used (the DirectX 4 Version number was skipped). DirectX advanced almost every year by a version until DirectX 7, which was more widely used and the graphic hardware was becoming faster and faster every year. Together with Windows XP, DirectX 8 was released and introduced shaders for the first time. Half a year later DirectX 9 was already available and there were many versions. In the first years (2002, 2003, 2004) Microsoft named each new version with a new letter (DirectX 9.0a, DirectX 9.0b, and so on) and each version allowed the use of a new shader model for the newest graphic hardware; after 9.0c they stopped renaming the version, but many DirectX 9.0c versions (11 by now) were released, often only a very few months apart. Direct3D 10 has been in beta since late 2005 and will finally be released with Windows Vista in early 2007. Graphic hardware for Shader Model 4.0 was already available by the end of 2006 (Nvidia GeForce 8800).

Figure 6-1

Shaders Everywhere in XNA

You already saw in the previous chapter that shaders are essential to render anything in XNA; you could not even put a line on the screen without having a shader to output the pixels on the screen. Sure, you can use the sprite classes for 2D interface graphics and maybe you will also use the SimpleEffect class to display some 3D data, but I don't like the SimpleEffect class and I will not use it in this book at all. I think it is too complicated to use and it really has no benefits when you are able to write your own shaders, which can be much simpler, faster, and more flexible. Using simple effects means you have to use the predefined features and if you need anything more you have to start over and write your own shader anyway. For the upcoming games in this book you will mainly use normal mapping shaders for displaying 3D data and then some cool post screen shader effects to manipulate the final screen data. Both of these shaders are not possible by just using the SimpleEffect class.

When you have worked with OpenGL or DirectX before and just used the fixed function pipeline, you might wonder why you put so much effort into shaders and why you can't just render some 3D data on the screen and be done with it. Well, writing is a little bit harder than that and though you could just render .x models in DirectX without even knowing much about matrices or how the GPU works internally, you could not really modify much if you never learned about the details. It may be harder to learn all about shaders, but at least you get a much closer look at the graphic hardware and you will be able to understand much better how polygons are rendered on the screen, why certain bugs can occur, and how to quickly fix them.

After the next two chapters this book doesn't talk about shaders anymore, and you will probably not spend too much time with shaders in your game after you have the important ones done at the beginning. Then you will just use the shaders and you won't even have to think about them anymore.

One final thing I want to mention is the increased amount of work connected with the use of shaders. Not only you as a programmer have to learn all about shaders and you will probably write most of them unless you have a "shader guy" in your team, but your graphic artists (hopefully not you again) have to know about shaders too. For example, using normal mapping shaders to achieve great looking effects like in the following games (for example, Doom 3) make sense only if your 3D data consists not only of the basic geometry, but also provides you with the normal maps to achieve those effects.

Not to take anything away from the next chapter, which discusses the normal mapping effect in great detail, you usually need a high-poly version (with up to several million polygons) of a 3D object and a low-poly version (just a couple of hundred or maybe few thousand polygons) for rendering. As you can see in Figure 6-2, the low-poly object can look quite bad without normal mapping applied, but once it is activated (see right side), the sphere looks suddenly much better.

As an alternative to creating high-detail models, which are usually a lot more work, you can also use a paint program to "paint" your own normal map by first drawing a height map and then converting it into a normal map. Usually such maps look much worse and you will never achieve the graphic quality of top games with this approach, but from time to time you can see games implementing normal maps this way to save money. In any case your 3D graphic artist should be aware of all the new techniques and you should think about the way content is created before you start writing your engine or game code.

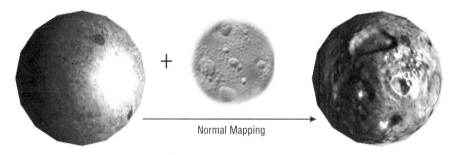

Normal Mapping

Figure 6-2

Example Games

If you want to see shaders in action just play any recent game — they almost all support shaders and even if you don't see heavy use of normal mapping and post screen effects, shaders might still be used for rendering the 3D models efficiently or executing shadow mapping techniques.

3D shooter games like Doom 3, Half-Life 2, Far Cry, and more recent games like Fear, Ghost Recon, and Gears of War show really top-notch graphics and make great use of shader effects. Shooters benefit greatly from most new graphic technologies because you see your surrounding world in so many detail levels. First you see yourself or at least your weapons, then you might be indoors and see walls and surrounding objects at a near distance, but there are also big rooms and even the outside world where you can see to great distances. This means levels are usually big and you are still able to look closely everywhere you want to because you can move wherever you want to. Obviously graphic cards, especially earlier ones, are not able to store that much detail in video memory and just mapping one big texture over the whole 3D level or just using the same wall texture all over the place is not really a good option. Instead the game developers have to think of many cool techniques to improve the visual quality by using detail maps, using normal mapping to make the player think geometry is much more detailed, and mixing in post screen effects to make the overall game appear more realistic.

Other games like strategy games or role playing games also benefit from shaders, but it took longer before strategy or role playing games even implemented shaders and these game focus more on the game play, how to render many units at once, and zooming in and out problems.

Anyway, you want probably cool shader effects in your game too and if you look at a screenshot of Rocket Commander (see Figure 6-3), you can see some normal mapping and post screen shaders at work. Without shaders enabled (left screen) the game looks really boring and asteroids don't really look very real because the lighting is just not right. Please note that the non-shader version was just provided as an option to support older graphics hardware; the game was designed with shaders in mind. It would be possible to create a better screenshot for the fixed function version, but in real time the game would look even more unrealistic if the lighting does not change and if you don't have any post screen effects.

For better examples between using shaders and the fixed function pipeline in games, take a look at water effects in 3D games. Water surfaces have evolved so much in the past few years that it is hard to keep up.

Figure 6-3

If you want to see more examples in games or have a little longer instruction I recommend that you watch my Rocket Commander Video Tutorials, which you can find on www.RocketCommander.com. Or you can watch my XNA Racing Game Video Tutorials on www.XnaRacingGame.com. There are also more links to useful shader resource sites, more screenshots, and so on.

Step-by-Step Shader Tutorial

This section goes through the whole process of creating your own shader. It will not be the most useful shader in the world, but it shows how to get shaders done, which tools can be used, and prepares you for future shaders, which might be more exciting.

To see where you are heading take a look at Figure 6-4, which shows the apple model from the last chapter, but this time your new shader `SimpleShader.fx` is applied onto it and another texture is used with some text on it.

Figure 6-4

The `SimpleShader.fx` uses a normal vertex shader, which just transforms the 3D data and a simple specular per-pixel technique for the pixel shader, which processes every pixel and calculates the ambient, diffuse, and specular components for it. This kind of calculation is not possible with a fixed function shader because you cannot program any special formulas for the pixel shader and the only way to show specular light effects is to do them in the vertex shader. You might ask why it is that bad to calculate the specular color component in the vertex shader. Well, if you have a low-polygon object like the apple here or the sphere from the normal mapping example earlier, just calculating color components in the vertex shader will look very bad because you can only calculate the resulting colors for every vertex. If you take a look at the wireframe for the apple (see Figure 6.5) you can see that there are only a bunch of vertices, but you have many more pixels to fill in between. If you only calculate the vertices (the points that connect the wires), all data in between is not calculated the right way and can only be interpolated. But if such a highlight as in Figure 6-4 is between two vertices, it will not be visible at all. By the way, if you want to render in wireframe mode just add the following line before you render any 3D data:

```
BaseGame.Device.RenderState.FillMode = FillMode.WireFrame;
```

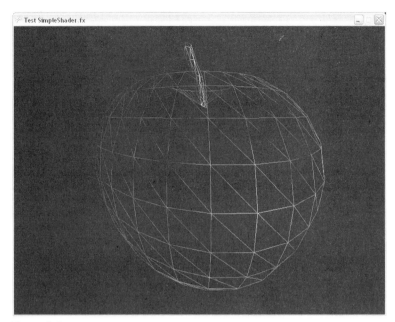

Figure 6-5

FX Composer

To get started with the little `SimpleShader.fx` shader you are going to use the freely available FX Composer tool, which you can download at the Nvidia home page (`www.Nvidia.com`) in the developers section (or just Google for it).

After you have installed and started FX Composer you will see the screen shown in Figure 6-6. It shows you several panels and can even be used by artists to test out textures, shader techniques, and to modify shader parameters like color values, effect strengths, and more. For you as the developer the most important panel is in the center, which shows the source code of the currently selected .fx file (similar to Visual Studio). As you can see the .fx file looks very similar to C# or CPP and it has syntax highlighting and many keywords, which look similar to C#. For example, string is just a text string; float is just a floating-point number, and so on, just like in C#. But there are also other types like `float3` or `float4x4`. These numbers behind the float name just indicate the dimensions; `float3` is the same structure as a `Vector3` in XNA, which contains three floats too (x, y, and z). `Float4x4` describes a matrix and contains 16 `float` values (4x4); it is also in the same format as the XNA Matrix structure. The last variable types you have to know are for textures. Textures are defined with the texture type and you also have to specify a sampler to tell the shader how to use this shader (which filtering to use, which dimensions the texture has, and so on).

Last but not least you see the optional semantics values (`WorldViewProjection`, `Diffuse`, `Direction`, and so on) behind variables indicated by a column. They tell FX Composer how to fill in this value and how to use it. For your XNA program these values do not matter, but it is very common to always specify these semantics. It allows you to use the shader in other programs like FX Composer,

3D Studio Max, and it is also helpful when you read through the shader later. The semantics tell you exactly which variable was intended for what use. In XNA you are not limited to the use; you can set the `world` matrix to the `viewInverse`, for example, but that would be very confusing after a while, wouldn't it?

Figure 6-6

The other panels are not so important to you right now, but here's an explanation of what each of them does:

❑ Use the toolbar on the top to quickly load a shader and save your current file. The last button in the toolbar builds your shader and shows you any compiler errors in the log panel below (very similar to Visual Studio). Every time you build a shader it gets saved automatically and you should use this button (or the Ctrl+F7 hotkey) as often as possible to make sure your shader always compiles and is saved.

❑ The Materials panel on the left side shows you a list of all shaders you have currently loaded into FX Composer with a little preview sphere, which changes as soon as you change any shader. The most important button here is the "Assign to Selection" button to set this material to the currently selected Scene panel object.

❏ Textures show the textures used in the current shader. If you load external shaders, texture files are often not found because they reside in another directory or were not shipped with the .fx shader file. Textures that could not be loaded are shown as all blue bitmaps and you should make sure to load a texture first, otherwise the shader output is usually black and useless.

❏ The Properties panel on the right side shows all the parameters in the shader you can set (or not, because they are already filled in by FX Composer, like world, viewInverse, and so on). To make the shader work the same way in your XNA engine you have to set all these values in your game engine too, especially the matrices, which are dependent on the current camera position, viewport, and object in the 3D world. If you don't set a parameter the default value is used, which can be set directly in the source code of the .fx file. To make sure all parameters always have valid values, even if the user or engine does not set any of the color parameters, for example, you should always make sure the parameters have useful default settings like setting the diffuse color to white:

```
float4 diffuseColor : Diffuse = {1.0f, 1.0f, 1.0f, 1.0f};
```

❏ And finally, the Scene panel shows a simple example object to test your shader like the standard sphere. You can also change it to a cube, cylinder, or something else. Alternatively you can even import model files and play around with them, but most files do not work very well and the camera in FX Composer always gets messed up when you import scenes. I would just stick with the standard sphere object and do all advanced tests in your XNA engine. FX Composer 2.0 will be much better for loading and handling custom 3D data and model files. You can use Collada files and even manage all the shaders that are used by every mesh in your model. Use FX Composer 2.0 if it is available by the time you read this.

FX File Layout

If you have worked with OpenGL before and had to write your vertex and fragment shaders (which just means vertex and pixel shaders in DirectX) yourself, you will be happy to hear that .fx files have all the shader code in one place and you can have many different pixel shader blocks in your .fx files to support multiple target configurations like pixel shader 1.1 for the GeForce 3 and pixel shader 2.0 support for the Nvidia GeForce FX or the ATI Radeon 9x series. Another useful side effect of having the ability to support multiple vertex and pixel shaders in one .fx file is to put similar shaders together and have them all use some common methods and the same shader parameters, which makes shader development much easier. For example, if you have a normal mapping shader for shiny metal surfaces, which looks really good on metal, you maybe want another more diffuse looking shader for stones, and you can put another shader technique in the same shader file and then select the used technique in your engine based on the material you want to display.

Figure 6-7 shows the SimpleShader.fx file layout as an example of a typical .fx file. More complex shaders will have more vertex and pixel shaders and more techniques. You don't have to create new vertex shaders or pixel shaders for each technique; you can combine them in any way you want to. Some shaders might also use multiple passes, which means they render everything with the first pass, and then the second pass is rendered with the exact same data again to add more effects or layers to a material. Using multiple passes is usually too slow for real-time applications because rendering with 10 passes means your rendering time will be 10 times higher than just rendering one pass with the same shader. In some cases it can be useful to use multiple passes to achieve effects that would otherwise not fit into the shader instruction limit or for post screen shaders where you can use the results from the first pass and modify them in the second pass to achieve much better effects. For example, blurring takes a lot of instructions because to get a good blurred result you have to mix many pixels to calculate every blurred point.

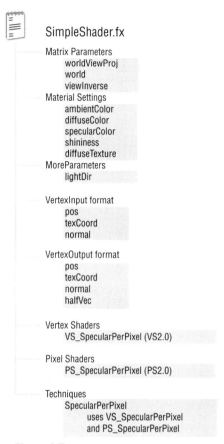

SimpleShader.fx

Matrix Parameters
    worldViewProj
    world
    viewInverse
Material Settings
    ambientColor
    diffuseColor
    specularColor
    shininess
    diffuseTexture
MoreParameters
    lightDir

VertexInput format
    pos
    texCoord
    normal

VertexOutput format
    pos
    texCoord
    normal
    halfVec

Vertex Shaders
    VS_SpecularPerPixel (VS2.0)

Pixel Shaders
    PS_SpecularPerPixel (PS2.0)

Techniques
    SpecularPerPixel
        uses VS_SpecularPerPixel
        and PS_SpecularPerPixel

Figure 6-7

As an example, blurring with the range of 10×10 pixels would take 100 pixel read instructions and that does not sound good if you have one or two million pixels you want to blur the whole screen. It is much better in this case just to blur in the x direction (10 pixel read instructions) and then take the result and blur it in the y direction in the second pass with another set of 10 pixel read instructions. Now your shader runs five times faster and looks pretty much the same. You can even achieve much better performance results by first sampling down the background image from 1600×1200 to 400×300 and then perform the blurring, which gives you another performance improvement by the factor of 16 (now that is amazing).

Chapter 8 talks about post screen shaders; but first, write the `SimpleShader.fx` file. As you see in Figure 6-7 the shader file uses quite a lot of shader parameters. Some of them are not so important because you could also hard-code the material settings directly into the shader, but this way you have the ability to change the color and appearance of the material in your engine and you can use the shader for many different materials. Other parameters like the matrices and the texture are very important and you cannot use the shader if these parameters are not set by the engine. Material data like the color values and the texture should be loaded at the time you create the shader in your engine and the world matrices, light direction, and so on should be set each frame because this data can change every frame.

Parameters

If you want to follow the creation steps of this shader closely you might want to open up FX Composer now and start with an empty .fx file. Select File ➪ New to create a new empty .fx file and delete all content. You will start with a completely empty file.

The first thing you might want to do to quickly remember what this file is about when you open it up later is to add a description or comment at the top of the file:

```
// Chapter 6: Writing a simple shader for XNA
```

As you saw in the `SimpleShader.fx` overview you need several matrices first to be able to transform the 3D data in the vertex shader. This would be the `worldViewProj` matrix, the `world` matrix, and the `viewInverse` matrix. The `worldViewProj` matrix combines the world matrix, which puts the object you want to render at the correct position in the world; the view matrix, which transforms the 3D data to your camera view space (see Figure 5-7 from the previous chapter); and finally, the projection matrix, which puts the view space point to the correct screen position. This matrix allows you to quickly transform the input position with just one matrix multiply operation to get the final output position. The `world` matrix is then used to perform operations in the 3D world like calculating the world normal, lighting calculations, and more. The `viewInverse` is usually just used to get more information about the camera position, which can be extracted from this matrix by getting the 4th row:

```
float4x4 worldViewProj : WorldViewProjection;
float4x4 world : World;
float4x4 viewInverse : ViewInverse;
```

Each of these matrix values is a float 4×4 type (which is the same data type as Matrix in XNA) and you use the shader semantics to describe these values better and to have support in applications like FX Composer or 3D Studio Max, which is important when the modeler wants to see how his 3D model looks with your shader. The cool thing is that it will look absolutely the same no matter whether it is displayed in FX Composer, 3D Studio, or in your engine. This fact can save you a lot of game development time; it especially shortens the testing process to get the appearance of all 3D objects right.

Time to save your file now. Just press the Build button or Ctrl+F7 and you are prompted to enter a name for the new shader. Just name it SimpleShader.fx and put it into your XnaGraphicEngine content directory so you can quickly use it in XNA later. After saving FX Composer will tell you that "There were no techniques" and "Compilation failed" in the Tasks panel below the source code. That's ok; you will implement the techniques soon, but first implement the rest of the parameters. Because your shader uses a light to lighten up your apple (see Figure 6-4) you need a light, which can be either a point light or a directional light. Using point lights is a little bit more complicated because you have to calculate the light direction for every single vertex (or even for every single pixel if you like). The calculation becomes even more complex if you use a spot light. Another problem with point lights is that they usually become weaker over the distance and you will need a lot of lights if your 3D world is big. Directional lights are much easier and are very useful to quickly simulate the sun in an outside environment, like for the game you will create in the next chapters.

```
float3 lightDir : Direction
<
  string Object = "DirectionalLight";
  string Space = "World";
> = { 1, 0, 0 };
```

In addition to ambient lighting, which just adds a general brightness to all materials, the following light types are commonly used in games:

❑ **Directional Lights:** Simplest light type, very easy to implement. You can directly use the light direction for the internal lighting calculations in shaders. In the real world no directional lighting exists; even the sun is just a big distant point light, but it is much easier to implement it for outdoor lighting scenes.

❑ **Point Lights:** Calculating a single point light is not much harder, but you have to calculate the falloff to make the light weaker over distance, and in case you need the light direction it needs to be calculated in the shader too, which slows things down. But the main problem for point lights is that you need more than one light for any scene bigger than just a room. 3D shooters usually use tricks to limit the amount of point lights that can be seen at the same time, but for outdoor games like strategy games it is much easier to use a directional light and just adding maybe a few light effects and simple point lights for special effects.

❑ **Spot Lights:** These are the same thing as point lights, but they point in just one direction and only lighten up a small spot with help of a light cone calculation. Spot lights are a little bit more difficult to calculate, but if you are able to skip the hard part of the lighting calculation (for example, when using a complex normal mapping shader with multiple spot lights), it can even be a lot faster than using point lights. Currently you can only do conditional statements like "if" in Shader Model 3.0, previous Shader versions support these statements too, but all "if" statements and "for" loops will just be unrolled and expanded, you will not gain a great performance benefit like on Shader Model 3.0.

Now the preceding code does look a little bit more complicated; the first line is pretty much the same as for the matrices. `float3` specifies that you use a `Vector3` and `Direction` tells you that `lightDir` is used as a directional light. Then inside the brackets an `Object` and a `Space` variable is defined. These variables are called *annotations* and they specify the use of the parameter for FX Composer or other external programs like 3D Studio Max. These programs now know how to use this value and they will automatically assign it to the light object that may already exist in the scene. This way you can just load the shader file in a 3D program and it will work immediately without having to link up all light, material settings, or textures by hand.

Next you are going to define the material settings; you are going to use the same material settings that a standard DirectX material uses. This way you can use similar shaders or older DirectX materials in programs like 3D Studio Max and all color values are automatically used correctly. In the engine you usually will just set the ambient and diffuse colors and sometimes you also specify another shininess value for the specular color calculation. You might notice that you did not use any annotations here — you can specify them too here, but material settings work fine in both FX Composer and 3D Studio Max even if you don't define annotations. The engine can also just use the default values in case you don't want to overwrite the default values for your unit test later.

```
float4 ambientColor : Ambient = { 0.2f, 0.2f, 0.2f, 1.0f };
float4 diffuseColor : Diffuse = { 0.5f, 0.5f, 0.5f, 1.0f };
float4 specularColor : Specular = { 1.0, 1.0, 1.0f, 1.0f };
float shininess : SpecularPower = 24.0f;
```

Last but not least your shader needs a texture to look a little bit more interesting than just showing a boring gray sphere or apple. Instead of using the apple texture from the original apple like in the last chapter, you are going to use a new test texture, which will become more interesting in the next chapter when you add normal mapping. The texture is called `marble.dds` (see Figure 6-8):

```
texture diffuseTexture : Diffuse
<
  string ResourceName = "marble.dds";
>;
sampler DiffuseTextureSampler = sampler_state
{
  Texture = <diffuseTexture>;
  MinFilter=linear;
  MagFilter=linear;
  MipFilter=linear;
};
```

The `ResourceName` annotation is only used in FX Composer and it automatically loads the `marble.dds` file from the same directory the shader is in (make sure the `marble.dds` file is in the XnaGraphicEngine content directory too). The sampler just specifies that you want to use linear filtering for the texture.

Figure 6-8

Vertex Input Format

Before you can finally write your vertex and pixel shader you have to specify the way vertex data is passed between your game and the vertex shader, which is done with the `VertexInput` structure. It uses the same data as the XNA structure `VertexPositionNormalTexture`, which is used for the apple model. The position is transformed with the `worldViewProj` matrix defined earlier in the vertex shader later. The texture coordinate is just used to get the texture coordinate for every pixel you are going to render in the pixel shader later and the normal value is required for the lighting computation.

You should always make sure that your game code and your shaders are using the exact same vertex input format. If you don't do that the wrong data might be used for the texture coordinates or vertex data might be missing and mess up the rendering. The best practice is to define your own vertex structure in both the application (see TangentVertex in the next chapter) and then define that same vertex structure in the shader. Also set the used vertex declaration, which describes the vertex structure layout, in your game code before calling the shader. You can find more details about that in the next chapter.

```
struct VertexInput
{
    float3 pos : POSITION;
    float2 texCoord : TEXCOORD0;
    float3 normal : NORMAL;
};
```

In a similar way you have also to define the data that is passed from the vertex shader to the pixel shader. This may sound unfamiliar at first and I promise you this is the last thing you have to do to finally get to the shader code. If you take a look at Figure 6-9 you can see the way 3D geometry is traveling from your application content data to the shader, which uses the graphic hardware to finally end up on the screen in the way you want it to be. Though this whole process is more complicated than just using a fixed function pipeline like in the old DirectX days, it allows you to optimize code at every point, and you can modify data in every single step (either at the application level, or dynamically when the vertices are processed in the vertex shader or you can modify the color of the final pixel when it is rendered on the screen).

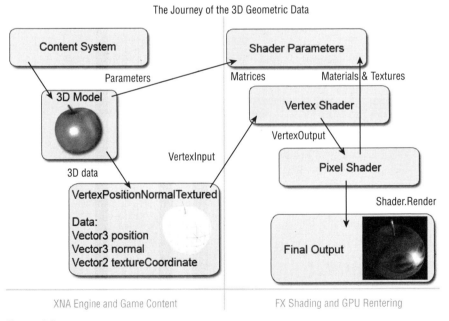

Figure 6-9

The `VertexOutput` structure of your shader passes the transformed vertex position, the texture coordinate for the used texture, and a `normal` and `halfVec` vector to perform the specular color calculation directly in the pixel shader. Both vectors have to be passed as texture coordinates because passing data from the vertex to the pixel shader can only be position, color, or texture coordinate data. But that does not matter; you can still use the data the same way as in the `VertexInput` structure. It is very important to use the correct semantics (`Position`, `TexCoord0`, and `Normal`) in the `VertexInput` structure to tell FX Composer, your application, or any other program that uses the shader.

Because you define the `VertexOutput` structure yourself and it is only used inside the shader, you can put anything you want in here, but you should keep it as short as possible and you are also limited by the number of texture coordinates you can pass over to the pixel shader (four in pixel shader 1.1, eight in pixel shader 2.0).

```
struct VertexOutput
{
  float4 pos : POSITION;
  float2 texCoord : TEXCOORD0;
  float3 normal : TEXCOORD1;
  float3 halfVec : TEXCOORD2;
};
```

Vertex Shader

The vertex shader now takes the `VertexInput` data and transforms it to the screen position for the pixel shader, which finally renders the output pixel for every visible polygon point. The first lines of the vertex shader usually look very much the same as for every other vertex shader, but you often pre-calculate values at the end of the vertex shader for use in the pixel shader. If you are using pixel shader 1.1 you cannot do certain things like normalizing vectors or execute complex mathematical functions like power. But even if you use pixel shader 2.0 (like you are for this shader) you might want to pre-calculate certain values to speed up the pixel shader, which is executed for every single visible pixel. Usually you will have far fewer vertices than pixels, and every complex calculation you make in the vertex shader can speed up the performance of the pixel shader several times.

```
// Vertex shader
VertexOutput VS_SpecularPerPixel(VertexInput In)
{
  VertexOutput Out = (VertexOutput)0;
  float4 pos = float4(In.pos, 1);
  Out.pos = mul(pos, worldViewProj);
  Out.texCoord = In.texCoord;
  Out.normal = mul(In.normal, world);
  // Eye pos
  float3 eyePos = viewInverse[3];
  // World pos
  float3 worldPos = mul(pos, world);
  // Eye vector
  float3 eyeVector = normalize(eyePos-worldPos);
  // Half vector
  Out.halfVec = normalize(eyeVector+lightDir);

  return Out;
} // VS_SpecularPerPixel(In)
```

The vertex shader takes the VertexInput structure as a parameter, which is automatically filled in and passed from the 3D application data by the shader technique you will define later at the end of the .fx file. The important part here is the VertexOutput structure, which is returned from the vertex shader and then passed to the pixel shader. The data is not just passed 1:1 to the pixel shader, but all values are interpolated between every single polygon point (see Figure 6-10).

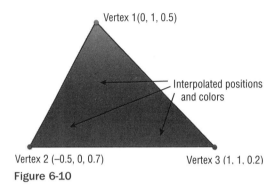

Figure 6-10

This is of course a good thing for any position and color values because the output looks much better when values are interpolated correctly. But in case you use normalized vectors they can get messed up in the process of the interpolation that the GPU does automatically. To fix this you have to re-normalize vectors in the pixel shader (see Figure 6-11). Sometimes this can be ignored because the artifacts are not visible, but for your specular per pixel calculation it will be visible on every object with a low polygon count. If you are using pixel shader 1.1 you can't use the normalize method in the pixel shader. Instead you can use a helper cube map, which contains pre-calculated normalized values for every possible input value. For more details please take a look at the NormalMapping and ParallaxMapping shader effects of the next chapters.

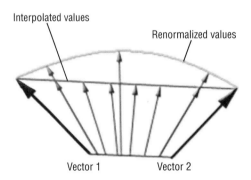

Figure 6-11

If you take a quick look at the source code again (or if you are typing it in yourself to write your first shader), you can see that you start by calculating the screen output position. Because all matrix operations expect a Vector4 you have to convert your input Vector3 value to Vector4 and set the w component to

1 to get the default behavior of the translation part of the `worldViewProj` matrix (translation means movement for matrices).

Next the texture coordinate is just passed over to the pixel shader; you are not interested in manipulating it. You can, for example, multiply the texture coordinates here or add an offset. Sometimes it can even be useful to duplicate the texture coordinate and then use it several times in the pixel shader with different multiplication factors and offsets for detail mapping or water shaders.

Each normal vector from the apple model is then transformed to the world space, which is important when you rotate the apple model around. All normals are rotated then as well, otherwise the lighting will not look correct because the `lightDir` value does not know how each model is rotated, and the `lightDir` values are just stored in the world space. Before applying the world matrix your vertex data is still in the so-called object space, which can be used for several effects too, if you like to do that (for example, wobble the object around or scale it in one of the object directions).

The last thing you do in the vertex shader is to calculate the half vector between the light direction and the eye vector, which helps you with calculating the specular color in the pixel shader. As I said before it is much more effective to calculate this here in the vertex shader instead of re-calculating this value for every single point over and over again. The half vector is used for phong shading and it generates specular highlights when looking at objects from a direction close to the light direction (see Figure 6-12).

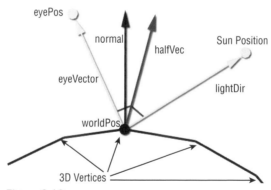

Figure 6-12

Pixel Shader

The pixel shader is responsible for finally outputting some pixels on the screen. To test this you can just output any color you like; for example, the following code outputs just a red color for every pixel that is rendered on the screen:

```
// Pixel shader
float4 PS_SpecularPerPixel(VertexOutput In) : COLOR
{
  return float4(1, 0, 0, 1);
} // PS_SpecularPerPixel(In)
```

If you press Build now the shader still does not compile because you have not defined a technique yet. Just define the following technique to get the shader to work. The syntax of techniques is always similar; usually you just need one pass (called P0 here) and then you define the used vertex and pixel shaders by specifying the used vertex and pixel shader versions:

```
technique SpecularPerPixel
{
  pass P0
  {
    VertexShader = compile vs_2_0 VS_SpecularPerPixel();
    PixelShader = compile ps_2_0 PS_SpecularPerPixel();
  } // pass P0
} // SpecularPerPixel
```

Now you are finally able to compile the shader in FX Composer and you should see the output shown in Figure 6-13. Make sure you have the shader assigned to the selection in the Scene panel in FX Composer (click the sphere, then click the SimpleShader.fx material in the Materials panel and click the "Apply Material" button).

Figure 6-13

The next step you should take is to put the marble.dds texture onto the sphere. This is done with the help of the tex2D method in the pixel shader, which expects a texture sampler as the first parameter and the texture coordinates as the second parameter. Replace the return float4 line from the previous code with the following code to texture your 3D object:

```
float4 textureColor = tex2D(DiffuseTextureSampler, In.texCoord);
return textureColor;
```

After compiling the shader you should now see the result shown in Figure 6-14. If you just see a black sphere or no sphere at all you probably don't have the marble.dds texture loaded (see the Textures panel and make sure the texture is loaded as described previously; you can click the `diffuseTexture` in properties and load it yourself).

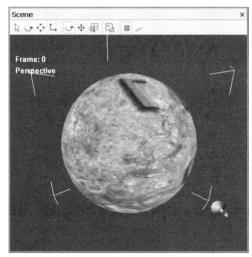

Figure 6-14

The last thing you have to do is to calculate the diffuse and specular color components based on the `lightDir` and `halfVec` values. As mentioned, you also want to make sure the normals are re-normalized in the pixel shader to get rid of any artifacts.

```
// Pixel shader
float4 PS_SpecularPerPixel(VertexOutput In) : COLOR
{
  float4 textureColor = tex2D(DiffuseTextureSampler, In.texCoord);
  float3 normal = normalize(In.normal);
  float brightness = dot(normal, lightDir);
  float specular = pow(dot(normal, In.halfVec), shininess);
  return textureColor *
    (ambientColor +
    brightness * diffuseColor) +
    specular * specularColor;
} // PS_SpecularPerPixel(In)
```

The diffuse color is calculated by taking the dot product of the re-normalized normal (in world space, see the vertex shader discussion earlier in this chapter) and the `lightDir`, which is also in world space. It is always important that you are in the same space if you do any matrix, dot, or cross product calculations, otherwise the results will be very wrong. The dot product behaves just the way you need for the diffuse color calculation. If the `lightDir` and the normal point in the same direction it means that the normal is pointing right at the sun and the diffuse color should be at the maximum value (1.0); if the normal is at a 90 degree angle, the dot product will return 0 and the diffuse component is zero. To even see the sphere from the dark side the ambient color is added, which lights up the sphere even when no diffuse or specular light is visible.

Then the specular color is calculated with the Phong formula to take the dot product of the normal and the half vector you calculated in the vertex shader. Then you take the power of the result by the shininess factor to make the area much smaller that is affected by the specular highlight. The higher the shininess value, the smaller the highlight gets (play around with the shininess value if you want to see it). At the end of the pixel shader you can finally add all color values together and you multiply the result by the texture color and return everything to be painted on the screen (see Figure 6-15).

Figure 6-15

You are now finished with working on the shader. The saved shader file can now even be used in other programs like 3D Studio Max to help artists to see how the 3D models will look in the game engine. Next you are going to implement the shader into your XNA engine.

Importing the Shader into Your Engine

To get the shader you just wrote into your graphic engine you basically do the same thing FX Composer does to display the shader. Thanks to DirectX or XNA it is easy to load a shader effect file and set all required parameters (you already did that in the last chapter for the line rendering shader). In the next chapter you are going to use a more general class that accepts many different shaders and uses a more optimized way to set all required shader parameters, but for this chapter you just want to get the `SimpleShader.fx` file to work in your engine.

As usual you start by defining the unit test. Create a new file called `SimpleShader.cs` in the `Shaders` namespace and write the following code:

```
#region Unit Testing
public static void TestSimpleShader()
{
    SimpleShader shader = null;
    Model testModel = null;
    Texture testTexture = null;
```

```
    TestGame.Start("Test SimpleShader.fx",
      delegate
      {
        shader = new SimpleShader();
        testModel = new Model("Apple");
        testTexture = new Texture("Marble");
      },
      delegate
      {
        // Render model
        shader.RenderModel(testModel.XnaModel, testTexture);
      });
  } // TestSimpleShader
#endregion
```

The unit test should compile except for the RenderModel method of the new SimpleShader class, which has not been defined. Let's quickly define that method:

```
public void RenderModel(XnaModel someModel, Texture texture)
{
} // RenderModel(someModel, texture)
```

The unit test compiles now and you can start it just to see a blank screen.

Compiling Shaders

To get anything useful on the screen for your little unit test, you have to load and compile the shader first. To do that you use the content pipeline of XNA as you did for models and textures before. Just drop the .fx file into your project (put it into the content directory together with the rest of the textures and models) and it will get compiled automatically when the project is built. You will even get a shader compilation error in case the shader does not compile. This way you don't have to start your game and then have to track down an exception thrown by the shader compiler at runtime; you can already make sure the shader is correct before the game is run. While you are at it, make sure the marble.dds texture is also in the content directory and gets compiled by XNA; you use this texture in your unit test.

Loading the compiled effect is as simple as loading a texture. Just define an effect variable and then load it in the SimpleShader constructor:

```
#region Variables
Effect effect = null;
#endregion

#region Constructor
public SimpleShader()
{
  effect = BaseGame.Content.Load<Effect>(
    Path.Combine(Directories.ContentDirectory, "SimpleShader"));
} // SimpleShader()
#endregion
```

If you are on the Windows platform you can also dynamically load shaders (not precompiled already by the XNA Framework), which can be useful to test and change shaders while your game is running. I usually use un-compiled shader files for most of the shader development time and then I put them into the content pipeline when the game is done or I don't want to change the shaders anymore. The following code is used to compile and load shaders yourself.

Please note that these classes and methods are only available on the Windows platform. Use #if !XBOX360 #endif around these lines if you want the code to get compiled on the Xbox 360 (where dynamically reloading shaders is not supported and does not make so much sense anyway):

```
CompiledEffect compiledEffect = Effect.CompileEffectFromFile(
    Path.Combine("Shaders", shaderContentName + ".fx"),
    null, null, CompilerOptions.None,
    TargetPlatform.Windows);

effect = new Effect(BaseGame.Device,
    compiledEffect.GetEffectCode(), CompilerOptions.None, null);
```

Using Parameters

As you learned in the process of creating your shader, the world, view, and projection matrices are really important to transform your 3D data and get everything correctly on the screen. To set all these shader parameters you just use the RenderModel method, which is called by your unit test:

```
BaseGame.WorldMatrix =
    Matrix.CreateScale(0.25f, 0.25f, 0.25f);

effect.Parameters["worldViewProj"].SetValue(
    BaseGame.WorldMatrix *
    BaseGame.ViewMatrix *
    BaseGame.ProjectionMatrix);
effect.Parameters["world"].SetValue(
    BaseGame.WorldMatrix);
effect.Parameters["viewInverse"].SetValue(
    BaseGame.InverseViewMatrix);
effect.Parameters["lightDir"].SetValue(
    BaseGame.LightDirection);
effect.Parameters["diffuseTexture"].SetValue(
    texture.XnaTexture);
```

The first thing that happens in this code is setting the world matrix. This is very important because if the world matrix is not set and maybe has some crazy values from any previous operation, the 3D model is rendered at some random location you don't want it to be. Because your apple model is pretty big, you scale it down a little to fit on the screen with your default SimpleCamera class from the last chapter.

Then the worldViewProj matrix is calculated and you also set all the other matrices, the lightDir value, and even the diffuseTexture, which is important because by just loading the shader effect none of the textures are loaded automatically like in FX Composer; you still have to set these values yourself. If you load Models from the XNA content pipeline, XNA does help you out a little and will automatically load all used textures from the Model data. In your case you just set the texture you have loaded in the unit test to display the `marble.dds` texture like in FX Composer.

Vertex Formats

Before you can render the data used in your 3D apple model you have to make sure that your application and the shader know which vertex format to use. In DirectX it was possible to just set one of the prede-fined fixed function vertex formats, but these formats do not exist anymore and you can't just set them. Instead you have to define the full vertex declaration in a similar way as you did in the shader for the `VertexInput` structure. Because you are just using the built-in `VertexPositionNormalTexture` structure you don't have to define everything yourself, but in the next chapter you will learn how to do that with your custom `TangentVertex` format.

```
// Use the VertexPositionNormalTexture vertex format in SimpleShader.fx
BaseGame.Device.VertexDeclaration =
  new VertexDeclaration(BaseGame.Device,
    VertexPositionNormalTexture.VertexElements);
```

You don't really have to create a new vertex declaration every time you call `RenderModel`, but just to keep things simple you build a new vertex declaration every call. It takes the graphics device as the first parameter and the vertex elements array from the XNA `VertexPositionNormalTexture` structure as the second parameter. For more information refer to Chapter 7.

Rendering with Shaders

To render the apple with your shader now you first specify the technique you want to use (which is by default set to the first technique anyway, but it is good to know how to set techniques). For rendering a shader you will always use the `CurrentTechnique` property of the `effect` class. Then you go through the technique the same way FX Composer does — you draw all 3D data for every pass you have in the technique (as I said before usually you just have one pass). Rendering the apple itself is not that easy because the only method XNA gives you to render it is to call `mesh.Draw` for every mesh that is in the model after setting the required shader parameters first like you saw in the last chapter when you wrote the `Model` class.

Another thing missing from the XNA Framework are the mesh helper methods to create boxes, spheres, or teapots. You will also notice that most of the Direct3DX namespace functionality is just non-existent in XNA. You can only access some of the methods when writing your own content processor, but that does not help you when writing your engine or wanting to test models, meshes, or shaders. You also can't access any of the vertices or the index data of the loaded models because all the vertex and index buffers are write-only, which is good for fast hardware access, but bad if you just want to modify anything. In your little code part here you are just mimicking the behavior of the `mesh.Draw` method, just without the effect code that is used there because you have your own effect class here.

```
effect.CurrentTechnique = effect.Techniques["SpecularPerPixel"];

effect.Begin();
foreach (EffectPass pass in effect.CurrentTechnique.Passes)
{
  pass.Begin();
```

```
      // Render all meshes
      foreach (ModelMesh mesh in someModel.Meshes)
      {
        // Render all mesh parts
        foreach (ModelMeshPart part in mesh.MeshParts)
        {
          // Render data our own way
          BaseGame.Device.Vertices[0].SetSource(
            mesh.VertexBuffer, part.StreamOffset, part.VertexStride);
          BaseGame.Device.Indices = mesh.IndexBuffer;

          // And render
          BaseGame.Device.DrawIndexedPrimitives(
            PrimitiveType.TriangleList,
            part.BaseVertex, 0, part.NumVertices,
            part.StartIndex, part.PrimitiveCount);
        } // foreach
      } // foreach
      pass.End();
    } // for
    effect.End();
```

In detail this means you go through every pass (again, you just have one) and draw all meshes (also just one for your apple) and then you draw all mesh parts (guess what, again only one) by setting the vertex and index buffers with help of the XNA properties of the `Device` class. Finally you call `DrawIndexedPrimitives` to render all the vertices inside the shader. Then the pass and the shader are closed and you can finally see your apple with the `marble.dds` texture on the screen (see Figure 6-16).

Figure 6-16

Testing the Shader

Just because everything works now, it does not mean you can't play around a little bit with your shader and test other material settings, textures, or render modes.

To achieve the wireframe effect that you saw in Figure 6-5 previously, you can just change the `FillMode` before starting the shader:

```
BaseGame.Device.RenderState.FillMode = FillMode.WireFrame;
```

Or you can manipulate the shader material a little bit; if you want you can load another texture or even another model. The shader class is written in a way that allows you to load any XNA model and texture and test it out. One simple way to modify the output of the shader would be to change the ambient, diffuse, and specular values to make an evil alien apple (see Figure 6-17).

```
effect.Parameters["ambientColor"].SetValue(
    Color.Blue.ToVector4());
effect.Parameters["diffuseColor"].SetValue(
    Color.Orange.ToVector4());
effect.Parameters["specularColor"].SetValue(
    Color.Orchid.ToVector4());
```

Figure 6-17

Please note that you have to convert the colors to `Vector4` because `SetValue` does not have an overload for color values (seems like there was someone really lazy). When you set any effect parameters between a shader `Begin` and `End` call you should also call the `Effect CommitChanges` method to make sure that all your changes are sent to the GPU. If you call `Begin` after setting the parameters like in the `SimpleShader` class you don't have to worry about that.

In the next chapter you are going to use effect parameters much more effectively because setting them by name is not really performant and it is also error prone. If you mistype one of the parameters an exception will occur and that's never good.

Challenge

As a little challenge to get more familiar with shaders you should now write a simple `DiffusePerPixel` shader, which works the same way as the `SpecularPerPixel` shader except for the specular color component, which is cut out. `DiffusePerPixel` will be more useful for non-shiny materials, and to switch between `SpecularPerPixel` and `DiffusePerPixel` you should have two techniques in the `SimpleShader.fx` file.

With the following code you can then dynamically choose between the two techniques based on whether or not the user currently pressed space:

```
if (Input.Keyboard.IsKeyDown(Keys.Space))
   effect.CurrentTechnique = effect.Techniques["DiffusePerPixel"];
else
   effect.CurrentTechnique = effect.Techniques["SpecularPerPixel"];
```

If you are still very excited about the whole shader idea you also might want to check out the shaders included with FX Composer in the HLSL directory of the program. Maybe you can play around with them a little or even try to implement them into `SimpleShader.fx`.

Have fun!

Summary

In this chapter I tried to make sure that you finally understand how shaders work, why you have to do certain things like declaring vertex formats, and how vertex data is processed through the shaders. Most of the time when I talk to other developers who have not worked with shaders before they are afraid of shaders and do not have a clear concept of what they are all about. If you have worked with shaders before, this chapter might not be the most exciting one, but maybe you learned some details you didn't know about yet.

The following steps describe how 3D data is processed in XNA:

❑   Get the 3D geometry data from the `Model` class (or define it yourself with vertex buffers).

❑   Make sure your shader and your XNA code use the same vertex formats.

❑ Call the shader technique and execute each pass by rendering your 3D data.

❑ The vertex shader processes the input data and passes it to the pixel shader with the `VertexOutput` structure. The positions get transformed from world coordinates to the screen position.

❑ The pixel shader finally brings each pixel of every rendered visible polygon on the screen. Always try to make the pixel shader as short and fast as possible.

In the next chapter you are going to use the acquired knowledge and create great looking `NormalMapping` shader effects. Then you will be ready to create your next game in Chapter 8, where you also add cool post screen shader effects.

7

Realism through Normal Mapping

The really cool advantage of using shaders is that every step of the rendering pipeline can be customized. For Pixel Shader version 1.1 (GeForce 3) you have just eight instructions available and in reality the programmable pipeline is not really so great because all it does is emulate the Pixel Shader instructions with preprogrammed hardware. Pixel Shader 2.0 is much more flexible by allowing many more functions (as you saw in the previous chapter the `normalize` and `pow` methods are only available for Pixel Shader 2.0 and up) and the ability to write more instructions (the limit is 96 here, but some methods require more than one instruction).

Pixel Shader version 3.0 is even better by allowing better flow control, which means you can exit the shader code based on programmed conditions to optimize the performance. Complex shaders in Pixel Shader 3.0 can have up to 512 instructions and even with very fast graphics hardware this is a lot. When rendering many million of pixels it takes a lot of time to execute that many instructions for every single pixel, even when you have 16, 24, or even 32 pixel shader units working in parallel; the new NVidia 8800 GTX graphic card has even 128 shader units working in parallel. Sometimes you might want to skip complex calculations if a pixel is not affected by several lights or doesn't lie in the shadow. This way you can still achieve great looking and expensive Pixel shader effects, but you limit them to where they are required. Sounds great, but in reality most new games just use Pixel Shader 2.0 because it is supported by many graphics cards; most typical games don't support the more expensive graphics hardware.

Shader Model 4.0 was introduced with Direct3D 10 (early 2006) and the first graphics hardware (GeForce 8800) to support it was available by the end of 2006, but Direct3D 10 only works on Vista and the hardware is quite expensive. It will take a while until game developers can fully utilize shader model 4.0. XNA currently only supports shader models 1.1 up to 3.0. Shader Model 4.0 allows even more instructions and introduces geometry shaders that manipulate and even add geometry data before your vertex and pixel shaders are executed. All shader units are also unified in Shader Model 4.0, which means you can use them for whatever you want. There are no longer just

8 vertex and 16 pixel units, you just have 128 shader units and they all can be used for geometry, vertex and pixels shaders. This is great for level-of-detail effects and amazing effects like displacement mapping. In 2007 you can hopefully expect some cool demos, but games will probably not use geometry shaders until 2008 or later.

Adding Detail to Objects

For your next couple of games in this book you just want to use Normal Mapping shaders, which also greatly improve the realism of many 3D objects, especially if they have a lot of structure on the surface and many little details, riffs, tubes, cables, and so on that would normally cost many million of polygons to display all those details correctly (see Figure 7-1). You will often see Normal Mapping examples on Internet sites that compare totally ridiculous looking objects and bad textures with a super high resolution Normal Mapped object. I tried to use a real object from a real game here (it is used in the racer game later in this book) and you can see that the version without Normal Mapping looks ok too because the diffuse texture is already shaded a little bit. This way you can render without using the Normal Map and the object still looks ok. With Normal Mapping enabled the object looks even better and even though it only has 1000 polygons, it looks very smooth (see right side of Figure 7-1).

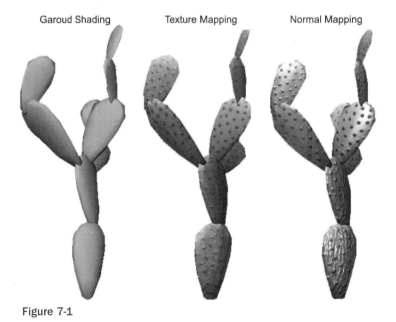

Garoud Shading   Texture Mapping   Normal Mapping

Figure 7-1

Even better effects can be achieved through Parallax Mapping (faking the height), Offset Mapping (multiple layers to fake the height even better), or Displacement Mapping (really moving vertices around, possible with Shader Model 4, but very expensive and slow computation). These techniques are a bit more complex and they also require a height map in addition to the diffuse and Normal Map textures. But just using Normal Mapping looks fine too.

The good thing about Normal Mapping is that it is not that hard to implement it if you have a shader-enabled graphics card. It even works with the very old GeForce 3 (Pixel Shader version 1.1), but can also be improved for Pixel Shader 2.0 support to enable better specular lighting effects on today's hardware. With the knowledge from the previous chapter you already have the basic foundation for creating shaders and you know how the vertices are transformed and the pixel finally is displayed on the screen.

Normal Mapping uses an additional texture. The diffuse texture is used to display the basic material structure, color, and so on. The Normal Map then adds additional 3D detail by supplying an additional normal vector for every single pixel you are going to render in the Pixel Shader (see Figure 7-2).

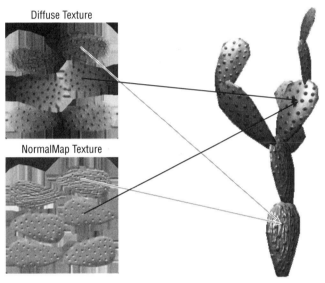

Figure 7-2

Please note that if you open up the `KaktusSeg.dds` and `KaktusSegNormal.dds` textures of the cactus 3D model, the Normal Map bitmap will look different. The Normal Map is compressed and has the alpha and red channels reversed. This trick is used to allow compressing the normal texture by a factor of 1:4 without losing much detail, and the result still looks great. More details about this technique in a second — just remember that internally the Normal Map texture looks like the texture in Figure 7-2; the compressed version just stores the data differently.

To compute the light for every pixel in the Pixel Shader of your Normal Mapping shader the Normal Map texture data is used. Every pixel in the Normal Map texture represents a normal vector for the surface of the polygon. This data is stored in tangent space, which is discussed in Figure 7-4 in a bit. To get a normal vector from the color data in the texture the formula `(each r, g and b value-0.5)/0.5` is used (see Figure 7-3). The RGB data in the Normal Map viewed as floats lets you use this formula. To convert from RGB to floats just divide by the floating value 255. This is done automatically in your pixel shader. It is always easier to work with these floating-point values instead of the byte data stored in the bitmap file.

Figure 7-3

Most pixels in the Normal Map are light blue (RGB 128, 128, 255) and this means that most resulting vectors just point up like `Vector3 (0, 0, 1)`. If the complete texture is just light blue it means every vector is `(0, 0, 1)` and the Normal Map will have no effect because this is the behavior you got anyway with normal diffuse lighting calculations.

These Normal Mapping pixels are usually stored in the tangent space, which means that each normal is stored relative to the polygon surface. It is called tangent space because you can construct the tangent matrix with the help of the tangent and binormal vectors of each vertex point. If you don't have a binormal it can easily be created with the help of the cross product of the normal and tangent vectors (see Figure 7-4). In the previous chapter you only had the position, normal, and texture coordinate for each point. This data is not sufficient for Normal Mapping; you need at least the tangent vector for each vertex to build this very important tangent matrix. Without it Normal Mapping will not look correct and you should not even bother to implement it if you don't have these tangents.

You can think of the tangent and binormal vectors as being the vectors that point to the next vertex in the x and y direction, but they are still octagonal (in a 90 degree angle) to the normal vector. This means even if your 3D geometry does not have any tangent data, you can construct it yourself by going through all vertices (not easy, but possible).

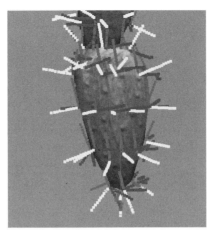

Figure 7-4

Problems

The problem with that is that often vertices are used for more than one polygon and sometimes the texture coordinates do not merge well. For just diffuse mapping this does not matter because you only use the normal vectors for lighting calculations, but if you rely on the tangent space to transform your normals for each pixel, the data must fit. This means it is much better to have the tangent data generated in the 3D program, which was used to create the 3D geometry. It knows which tangents are used and the exported normals are much better for the Normal Mapping shader. Inside the vertex shader you only have access to the current vertex you are processing; you can't just get the next vertex or build a new vector pointing to the next vertex. This means it is very important to pass valid tangent data to the vertex shader. If you just define the vertex input structure to support tangents in the shader, it does not mean the application is able to pass valid tangent data. By default if you have an .x or .fbx file in your content pipeline, it does not have any tangent data (see Figure 7-5).

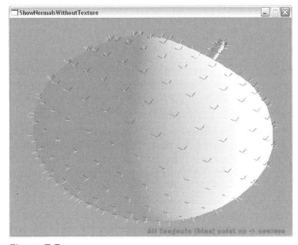

Figure 7-5

This means that you only have the valid normals, but the missing tangents will not allow you to construct the tangent space for the Normal Mapping. For simple objects like this apple it does not mater so much, but the more curves and texture coordinates you have in a model that do not fit together, the worse this problem gets. Figure 7-6 shows the tangent errors of the apple model; you can check it out by starting the demo application from the previous chapter.

Figure 7-6

After having knowledge about all these issues you can get to the 3D models and shaders now.

Asteroids! Wrong Game or What?

It is hard to create good looking 3D objects like the ones you saw in Figure 7-1; your modeler usually will spend most of the time creating the high-poly version, which can have several million polygons. You will probably spend a lot of time fine-tuning shaders and optimize them to allow your engine to display many objects at the same time with high frame rates. To keeps things simple you will just use some cool looking asteroid objects, which have several million polygons in the high-poly versions, but they were not that hard to create and the low-poly version has just around 1000 polygons. These models will be used in the next chapter for the Rocket Commander XNA game.

To optimize the performance even further, more versions with 500, 200, and even 50 polygons were created of the same asteroids, which was not very hard because the same high-poly object could be used and even the Normal Maps from the higher polygon objects look ok with the low-poly versions. In performance tests the 200 polygon version was the most efficient. It renders almost as fast as the 50 polygon version, but it looks much nicer. The 500 polygon version did not look much better, but took longer to render, especially on low-end computers. Thus the final game ended up with just the 1000 polygon and 200 polygon versions of all asteroids (see Figure 7-7).

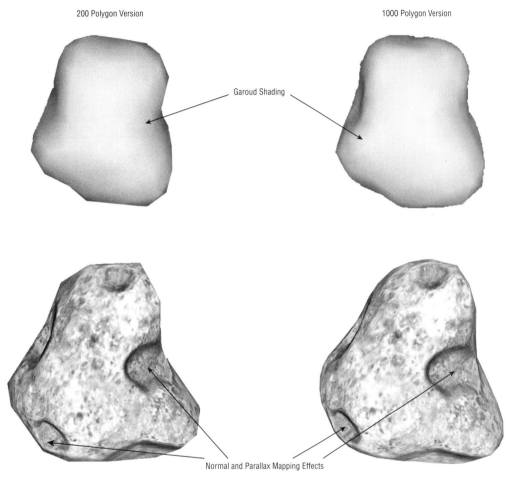

Figure 7-7

Figure 7-8 shows the three textures used for this asteroid. Because all asteroid models of Rocket Commander use a parallax mapping shader, you need a diffuse, normal, and height map for each object. As mentioned before the Normal Maps are compressed and this means they will look reddish instead of the default bluish look of Normal Maps. The compressed Normal Map is red because the red color channel is completely white and the alpha channel, which stores the original red channel, is not visible. For more details check out the `ParallaxMapping.fx` shader in the next chapter and open up the Normal Mapping textures.

Asteroid Diffuse Texture   Compressed Normal Map Texture   Height Map for Parallax Mapping

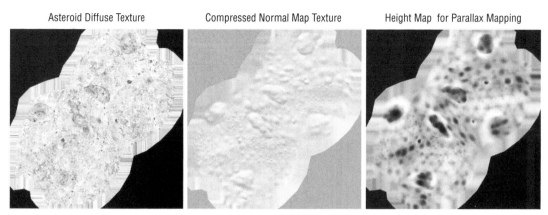

Figure 7-8

I wrote a little tool in 2005 named NormalMapCompressor (see Figure 7-9), which is available from my blog at `http://abi.exdream.com`. It can be used to convert Normal Maps to compressed Normal Maps and you will save 75% of the disk and texture space these textures use without losing much quality. That is really cool because if you think about texture sizes for a second, you can get into a lot of video memory problems just by using Normal Mapping or parallax mapping. In the past you had only a diffuse texture and small resolutions like 128×128, 256×256, and sometimes 512×512 were common.

The 128×128 textures stored as uncompressed bitmaps with 32 bits per channel (RGBA) take 128*128*4 bytes = 64 KB. Compressed as a DXT1 dds file it is only 8 KB in size. As a jpg file it is only around 5–10 KB. For 256×256 these sizes are four times as big (256 KB uncompressed, 32 KB for DXT1, around 20 KB for Jpeg), and for 512×512 it is again four times bigger. Even here you only have 1 MB even if you use no compression at all.

But today texture sizes of 1024×1024, 2048×2048, and even 4096×4096 are more common. Even if you just take 1024×1024 textures, you already have 4 MB of texture space for the diffuse map if you don't use compression. Because you also need the Normal Map and the height map now for cool shader effects, you have suddenly up to 12 MB just for one single texture. If your game uses a few hundred different textures, this is completely impractical. You just have to use compression and think about loading only the data you really need. This is why console games often reload level data and generally don't use very high texture resolution; it just costs too much memory, especially on the Xbox 360 and older consoles.

Diffuse textures can be compressed quite easily with DXT1, which uses eight times less space than RGBA or six times less for RGB. If you still need alpha data for transparent objects, you can use DXT5, which still is four times smaller than uncompressed RGBA data. You might say "Why not use .jpg or .png files?" Well, you could save disk space by using .jpg files, but in video memory you would still need to uncompress the files and store them in video memory. The great thing about dds files is that the DXT format is compatible with today's graphics hardware and saves video memory too.

For Normal Maps the major problem here is that the DXT compression algorithms were designed for color data; the green channel eats up most of the compression because green colors are more visible. The blue channel is not that important in Normal Maps because it is usually very bright anyway (see Figure 7-3), but the red channel will look like crap after the DXT1 compression. Especially in Pixel Shader 1.1 you can't normalize the normals again, and the vector length will be completely wrong in many cases and the Normal Map lighting will look very wrong and weak (see Figure 7-10).

Figure 7-9

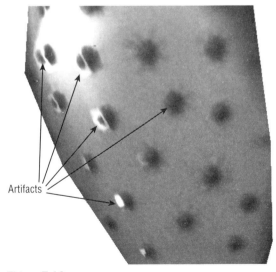

Artifacts

Figure 7-10

It is really hard to explain without switching the compression on and off. On the screen the visual difference is clearly visible. The NormalMapCompressor solves this problem by using the DXT5 compression format and storing the red channel in the alpha channel, which gets compressed separately in DXT5. This gives the green and blue a little better compression ratio because the red channel is all white now. In the shader you just have to switch the red and alpha channel and you are good to go. If you look closely at the NormalMapCompressor (Figure 7-9) you can see that the red channel has the highest variation (information panel on the left side), which means that the red channel has the most different color values and variations. The blue channel is usually very low. Try out several Normal Maps to see the different variance values.

For the diffuse and height map you can use DXT1. If you just use Normal Mapping, you don't need a height map and can save even more video memory. Now a 1024x1024 texture only takes 512 KB for the diffuse map, 1 MB for the Normal Map (DXT5 takes twice as much space), and another 512 KB for the optional height map, if needed. If you use mip-mapping you can add another 25% to that. With 2–2.5 MB you are good to go and it looks almost as good as the uncompressed 12 MB of textures for 1024×1024. I should also mention that through the cool looking Normal Mapping or parallax mapping effects textures often look a lot sharper and you can get away with 512×512 textures instead of using 1024×1024 textures like I did in Rocket Commander. The amazing thing is that the complete Rocket Commander game is under 10 MB including two sound tracks, many sound effects, five asteroid types, five item models, the rocket model and many more models, textures, and effects and four cool-looking levels. On the Xbox 360 it takes a little bit more because playing .mp3s is not possible, but it is amazing to display a 3D game with less than 15 MB to a screen with a resolution of 1920×1080 pixels (HDTV), which looks sharper than most commercial games for the Xbox 360.

The later chapters of this book also discuss the option of how to use Normal Mapping for your own custom 3D data like the track and other vertex buffer generated 3D data, which looks great with Normal Maps and does not take much texture space thanks to the compression technique discussed here.

So How Do Shaders Work?

Enough pictures, let's do some coding. For the shader, you are going to write in FX Composer (see Chapter 6 for an introduction). You'll use the asteroid textures you saw in Figure 7-8 previously.

If you like you can try to follow the steps described here and program your own Normal Map shader like the simple shader in the last chapter, but you don't have to. You can just follow the shader code and play around with the complete vertex and Pixel Shader once you get through everything here. Normal Mapping is quite a cool effect, but fine-tuning can take a lot of time and it can be a lot of fun to tweak. Leave some tweaking options to the model artist and write some different shaders for Normal Mapping so he can choose which effect to use for which material. For example, metal should look different from stone or wood materials.

Start FX Composer and open the `NormalMapping.fx` shader file. The layout for the shader file is similar to the `SimpleShader.fx` file, but you use more annotations and you will see that future shaders in this book all use a similar file structure. This way it is easier to work with shaders from the C# code.

The basic file layout is:

- ❑ Header comment and description of the shader
- ❑ Matrices (`world`, `worldViewProj`, `viewInverse`, and whatever else is required)
- ❑ Other global variables like time, factors, or testing values
- ❑ Material data, first the material colors, then all used textures and samplers
- ❑ Vertex structures, most importantly the `VertexInput` structure, which is always the same and uses the `TangentVertex` format you have also defined in your engine.

Then for each technique in the shader you have a code block usually separated by a comment line like `//————————————`.

- ❑ Vertex Shader
- ❑ Pixel Shader
- ❑ Technique that puts these shaders together, often using the same vertex shaders for different shader models over and over again.

To keep things simple I am just going to explain the vertex and Pixel Shader for the default Normal Mapping effect used for all the upcoming games in this book called `Specular20`. There is also a technique called `Specular`, which works the same way on shader model 1.1, but has some features turned off or reduced because of the eight instruction limit in Pixel Shader 1.1.

Please go through the shader file header and parameters after you open the file; they are basically in the same form as for `SimpleShader.fx` from the last chapter. What has changed since last chapter is the `VertexInput` format, which looks similar, but it expects a tangent input now. You already learned about the problems with .x and .fbx content files before and this will be solved later in this chapter. Assume for now that you have valid tangent data, which can be used in the shader. Luckily for you FX Composer always gives you valid tangent data for the standard test objects (sphere, teapot, cube, and so on).

```
// Vertex input structure (used for ALL techniques here!)
struct VertexInput
{
   float3 pos      : POSITION;
   float2 texCoord : TEXCOORD0;
   float3 normal   : NORMAL;
   float3 tangent  : TANGENT;
};
```

In `SimpleShader.fx` you simply started coding and once it worked you did not refactor the shader code anymore. This is totally fine, but the more shaders you write, the more you will think about reusing components. One way to do that is to define the most commonly used methods directly in the shader file:

```
// Common functions
float4 TransformPosition(float3 pos)//float4 pos)
{
   return mul(mul(float4(pos.xyz, 1), world), viewProj);
} // TransformPosition(.)
```

```
float3 GetWorldPos(float3 pos)
{
  return mul(float4(pos, 1), world).xyz;
} // GetWorldPos(.)

float3 GetCameraPos()
{
  return viewInverse[3].xyz;
} // GetCameraPos()

float3 CalcNormalVector(float3 nor)
{
  return normalize(mul(nor, (float3x3)world));
} // CalcNormalVector(.)

// Get light direction
float3 GetLightDir()
{
  return lightDir;
} // GetLightDir()

float3x3 ComputeTangentMatrix(float3 tangent, float3 normal)
{
  // Compute the 3x3 tranform from tangent space to object space
  float3x3 worldToTangentSpace;
  worldToTangentSpace[0] =
    mul(cross(normal, tangent), world);
  worldToTangentSpace[1] = mul(tangent, world);
  worldToTangentSpace[2] = mul(normal, world);
  return worldToTangentSpace;
} // ComputeTangentMatrix(..)
```

Another way would be to store methods or even parameters and constants in separate .fxh files, similar to C++ header files. I don't like that approach because FX Composer can only show one source file at a time and you will most likely still change a lot of code at this stage.

The first common function is TransformPosition, which just converts the 3D vertex position in the vertex shader to the screen space. It works exactly the same way as in the last chapter except that you don't have a combined worldViewProj matrix anymore. Instead you have a world matrix, which you had in SimpleShader.fx too, but the viewProj matrix is new. After multiplying world with viewProj you would have worldViewProj again, but there is a reason why this is not done in the code, but in the shader instead, which costs you one additional vertex shader instruction.

By separating the world matrix from the worldViewProj matrix you only have to worry about one single matrix that changes for every object, mesh, or custom 3D data you are going to render. The more data you have to pass from the program to the shader, the longer it takes and it can significantly slow down your rendering code if you set parameters over and over again and even start shaders too often per frame. It is much better to just set up the shader once and then render thousands of objects in a bunch by just changing the world matrix for each of them. You can take this idea even further by using an array of world matrices to store 20 or more matrices at once and then go through all of them. This technique is called *instancing* and is sometimes used by shooter games to optimize the performance even more if many objects of the same kind with the same shader are used. In earlier versions of Rocket Commander I had instancing implemented too, but it was too much work to get it to work in all shader models (1.1, 2.0, and 3.0) and also to support the fixed function pipeline. It did not matter anyway because the performance was quite good after all the other shader optimizations.

The other helper methods are pretty simple and you should understand them quickly just by looking at them, except for the last one, which is used to build the tangent space matrix I talked about. Check out Figures 7-4 and 7-5 again to see which vector is which. CalculateTangentMatrix is used in the vertex shader (like all the other helper methods) and it expects the tangent and the normal vector for each vertex point. Good thing you got these from the VertexInput structure. The binormal vector is generated by calculating the cross product between the normal and tangent vectors. You can reconstruct this matrix with your right hand (remember Chapter 5?) — the middle finger is the normal vector, the forefinger is the tangent, and the thumb represents the binormal, which is the cross product of the middle and forefinger and is in a 90 degree relationship with them because of that.

This tangent space matrix is very useful to quickly transform normals and the light direction from the world space to the tangent space, which is required for the Pixel Shader Normal Mapping calculation. The reason you need this tangent space matrix is to make sure all vectors are in the same space. This space lies directly on top of the polygon and points up (z) like the normal vectors do while x and y describe the tangent and binormal. Using this tangent space is the easiest and fastest way in the Pixel Shader and all you have to do to get to the correct order of the binormal and tangent that are used to construct this tangent space matrix. The order and even the cross product for the binormal might have to be reversed for a left-handed engine. Use unit testing to figure out which way is the correct one; you can also take a look at the shaders from the original Rocket Commander game (left-handed) to see the differences that were made in the XNA port (right-handed).

Vertex Shaders and Matrices

With all these helper methods it should be easy to write the vertex shader now. Before you do that you should define the VertexOutput structure first. I'm only going to explain the Pixel Shader 2.0 version here because the Pixel Shader 1.1 version is really complicated and uses a lot of assembly shader code, which is outside the scope of this book. Please pick up a good shader book to learn more about shader details and the shader assembly language if you really want to support Pixel Shader 1.1. I recommend the Programming Vertex and Pixel Shader, GPU Gems, or Shader X series books. Wolfgang Engel, a hardcore shader expert, is involved in most of them and you can learn a lot of shader tricks that were developed in the last few years by many professionals. This topic is even so big that a new programmer job is born: Shader Programmer.

If you are in a small team or even have to do all the programming yourself, this can be a hassle because you have to learn so much and you have very little time because the technology is advancing so fast. Try to keep it simple and only use the easiest shader model for you. It may be bad for some gamers that XNA does not support the fixed function pipeline and it also does not support Direct3D 10 shader model 4.0, but this way you can concentrate on just creating Pixel Shader 2.0 shaders (or maybe use Pixel Shader 3.0 too) and getting a game done.

Your vertex structure needs the screen space position, as always, and you have to pass the texture coordinates over to the Pixel Shader too so the diffuse and Normal Maps can be used correctly. Please note that you have to duplicate the texture coordinates in Pixel Shader 1.1 because each texture vertex input in the Pixel Shader can only be used once. This is one of the many problems with Pixel Shader 1.1; you also can't do `normalize` there or even use the `pow` function. It is also harder to uncompress the compressed Normal Map back to a useful format. Good thing you don't have to think about it here anymore.

```
// vertex shader output structure
struct VertexOutput_Specular20
{
   float4 pos          : POSITION;
   float2 texCoord     : TEXCOORD0;
   float3 lightVec     : TEXCOORD1;
   float3 viewVec      : TEXCOORD2;
};
```

The `lightVec` and `viewVec` variables are just helpers to make the Pixel Shader computation a little bit easier. The lighting calculation is basically the same as in the previous chapter, but this time you have to calculate all vectors in the tangent space because it is easier to work in the tangent space than to convert all tangent space vectors to the world space. That makes sense because you have a lot more pixels than vertices. Converting every pixel with a complex matrix operation in the Pixel Shader would be too slow and just converting the light direction and the view vector in the vertex shader does not cost much time.

Take a look at the whole vertex shader code. The important part here is the use of the `worldToTangentSpace` matrix, which is calculated by the `ComputeTangentMatrix` method you saw before:

```
// Vertex shader function
VertexOutput_Specular20 VS_Specular20(VertexInput In)
{
   VertexOutput_Specular20 Out = (VertexOutput_Specular20) 0;
   Out.pos = TransformPosition(In.pos);
   // We can duplicate texture coordinates for diffuse and Normal Map
   // in the Pixel Shader 2.0.
   Out.texCoord = In.texCoord;

   // Compute the 3x3 tranform from tangent space to object space
   float3x3 worldToTangentSpace =
      ComputeTangentMatrix(In.tangent, In.normal);

   float3 worldEyePos = GetCameraPos();
   float3 worldVertPos = GetWorldPos(In.pos);

   // Transform light vector and pass it as a color (clamped from 0 to 1)
   // For ps_2_0 we don't need to clamp from 0 to 1
   Out.lightVec = normalize(mul(worldToTangentSpace, GetLightDir()));
   Out.viewVec = mul(worldToTangentSpace, worldEyePos - worldVertPos);

   // And pass everything to the pixel shader
   return Out;
} // VS_Specular20(.)
```

Pixel Shader and Optimizations

The Pixel Shader now takes the vertex output and computes the light influence for each pixel. The first thing you have to do is to get the diffuse and Normal Map colors. The diffuse map just has the RGB values and maybe an alpha value if you use alpha blending (not really right now, but it is supported by this shader). The more complicated call is getting the normal vector from the compressed Normal Map. If you remember the way the compressed Normal Maps were built earlier with the NormalMapCompressor tool you can probably guess that you have to exchange the red and alpha channels again to make the RGB data valid and usable as an XYZ vector again. The first step to do this is to use a so-called swizzle, which takes the RGBA or XYZW data from a texture or a shader register and changes the order. For example, ABGR reverses the order of RGBA. In your case you just need the alpha channel (x) and the green (y) and blue (z) channels, so you use the .agb swizzle.

Then you use the formula described earlier to get the floating-point color values to vector values by subtracting 0.5 and dividing by 0.5, which is the same as multiplying by 2 and subtracting 1 (because 0.5 * 2 is 1). To fix any remaining compression errors you normalize the vector again, which takes one extra Pixel Shader instruction, but it is definitely worth it.

```
// Pixel Shader function
float4 PS_Specular20(VertexOutput_Specular20 In) : COLOR
{
  // Grab texture data
  float4 diffuseTexture = tex2D(diffuseTextureSampler, In.texCoord);
  float3 normalVector = (2.0 * tex2D(normalTextureSampler,
    In.texCoord).agb) - 1.0;
  // Normalize normal to fix blocky errors
  normalVector = normalize(normalVector);

  // Additionally normalize the vectors
  float3 lightVector = In.lightVec;//not needed: normalize(In.lightVec);
  float3 viewVector = normalize(In.viewVec);
  // For ps_2_0 we don't need to unpack the vectors to -1 - 1

  // Compute the angle to the light
  float bump = saturate(dot(normalVector, lightVector));
  // Specular factor
  float3 reflect = normalize(2 * bump * normalVector - lightVector);
  float spec = pow(saturate(dot(reflect, viewVector)), shininess);
  //return spec;

  float4 ambDiffColor = ambientColor + bump * diffuseColor;
  return diffuseTexture * ambDiffColor +
    bump * spec * specularColor * diffuseTexture.a;
} // PS_Specular20(.)
```

With this normalVector (still in tangent space) you can now do all the lighting calculations. The light vector and view vector are extracted from the VertexOutput_Specular20 structure. The light vector is the same for every vertex and pixel because you just use a directional light source, but the view vector can be very different if you are close to the object you are rendering. Figure 7-11 again shows why it is important to re-normalize this view vector like in the previous chapter. For Normal Mapping it is even more important because you calculate the light for every single pixel and the vectors can vary a lot from pixel to pixel through the variation in the Normal Map.

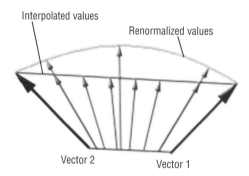

Figure 7-11

The bump value is calculated the same way you calculated the diffuse color in the previous chapter. For every normal pointing toward the light you use a bright color, and if it points away, it gets darker. Both the normal vector and the light vector are in tangent space and this way the basic formula stays the same. You can test out simple lighting effects in the SimpleShader.fx file and then re-implement them here together with Normal Mapping, which is cool because even though this shader is a lot more complex, the basic lighting calculation is still simple and exchangeable. If you take a look at the Normal Mapping and parallax mapping shaders of the next chapters you will see that this is the only place you make modifications; the rest of the Normal Mapping shader stays the same.

The last thing you have to calculate is the specular color component before putting the final color together. You don't have a half vector yet, but you have the view vector in tangent space and you know in which way the normal points. The code uses a little bit simplified formula by just subtracting the light vector from two times the normal vector to generate a pseudo normalized half vector. Doing the same computation as in the SimpleShader.fx vertex shader would be too expensive in a Pixel Shader and the Normal Mapping shader looks fine with this calculation too, it does not really matter how exact the half vector is. The important thing is the pow method that makes the shiny effect small and you should fine-tune the shininess and specularColor values for each material because they greatly influence the way the final output looks like (see Figure 7-12).

Putting together the final color may look a little bit strange to you. The first two lines are pretty easy to understand. First you mix together the ambient color with the result of the bump value with the diffuse color. This operation is actually just one instruction in the shader and that's the reason why it is written that way (it is easier to read the assembly output and use the same code for Pixel Shader 1.1 this way).

Then the specular color is multiplied by the spec value, which shows the highlights, but then again by the bump value and finally by the diffuseColor alpha value. The bump value makes sure that the specular value gets darker when you point away from the light and the diffuseColor alpha value helps you to fade out the specular highlights in case the texture is transparent here (alpha blending feature, not used in Rocket Commander).

Figure 7-12

That's everything you have to know for now to get the Normal Mapping shader to work in FX Composer. Feel free to play around with it a little bit — change color values and use different textures and parameters. Now you have to worry about getting the correct tangent data in the application and the ability to easily import model files a model artist might have created for you.

ShaderEffect Class

To render the shader you will use the `ShaderEffect` class introduced two chapters ago. All the basics were covered in the last chapter; the only thing you are going to add here is more shader parameters, and the rest of the functionality stays the same (see Figure 7-13). You also use the `Render` method to render 3D data with the shader like in the line manager class in Chapter 5.

Figure 7-13

To render 3D data you do not only need the 3D geometry or the 3D render code, but also the material parameters, which include the material color values and textures, just like in FX Composer. To manage this data a little new helper class is introduced just to store all this material data in one place: `Material.cs` (see Figure 7-14).

The `ShaderEffect` `SetParameters` method accepts the `Material` class as a parameter, which can also be passed in the `Render` method. This way you can easily assign materials without having to set all the effect parameters yourself.

Figure 7-14

With the new classes you can now easily write a new unit test to change the apple model from the previous chapter to support your new `NormalMapping.fx` shader. Additionally you change the material to the asteroid material by loading the asteroid diffuse and Normal Map to test out your new `Material` class.

TangentVertex Format

Before you can write the unit test to test out the Normal Mapping shader you need the same `VertexInput` structure from the .fx file in your code too. Unlike the `VertexPositionNormalTexture` structure from Chapter 6 there is no predefined structure that contains tangent data. You have to define it yourself. The following `TangentVertex` class (see Figure 7-15) is used to define the `VertexInput` structure used by `NormalMapping.fx` and all the shaders that you will write in this book from this point on.

Figure 7-15

Defining the fields of this structure is nothing special; just define the four types you need: pos, normal, tangent, and UV texture coordinates:

```
/// <summary>
/// Position
/// </summary>
public Vector3 pos;
/// <summary>
/// Texture coordinates
/// </summary>
public Vector2 uv;
/// <summary>
/// Normal
/// </summary>
public Vector3 normal;
/// <summary>
/// Tangent
/// </summary>
public Vector3 tangent;
```

Some methods for vertex buffers require that you specify the size of this structure. In MDX you could use a Direct3DX method or you could use unsafe code to use the `sizeof` method. In XNA it is not that easy; just define the size yourself.

```
/// <summary>
/// Stride size, in XNA called SizeInBytes.
/// </summary>
public static int SizeInBytes
{
  get
  {
    // 4 bytes per float:
    // 3 floats pos, 2 floats uv, 3 floats normal and 3 float tangent.
    return 4 * (3 + 2 + 3 + 3);
  } // get
} // StrideSize
```

The rest of the structure is pretty straightforward; the only other field that you need externally is the Vertex Declaration, which has to be generated by custom code:

```
#region Generate vertex declaration
/// <summary>
/// Vertex elements for Mesh.Clone
/// </summary>
public static readonly VertexElement[] VertexElements =
  GenerateVertexElements();

/// <summary>
/// Vertex declaration for vertex buffers.
/// </summary>
public static VertexDeclaration VertexDeclaration =
  new VertexDeclaration(BaseGame.Device, VertexElements);

/// <summary>
/// Generate vertex declaration
/// </summary>
private static VertexElement[] GenerateVertexElements()
{
  VertexElement[] decl = new VertexElement[]
    {
      // Construct new vertex declaration with tangent info
      // First the normal stuff (we should already have that)
      new VertexElement(0, 0, VertexElementFormat.Vector3,
        VertexElementMethod.Default,
        VertexElementUsage.Position, 0),
      new VertexElement(0, 12, VertexElementFormat.Vector2,
        VertexElementMethod.Default,
        VertexElementUsage.TextureCoordinate, 0),
      new VertexElement(0, 20, VertexElementFormat.Vector3,
        VertexElementMethod.Default,
        VertexElementUsage.Normal, 0),
```

```
      // And now the tangent
      new VertexElement(0, 32, VertexElementFormat.Vector3,
        VertexElementMethod.Default,
        VertexElementUsage.Tangent, 0),
    };
  return decl;
} // GenerateVertexElements()
#endregion
```

`VertexElement` takes the following parameters to define in which order the 3D data is declared:

❑ Stream (first parameter): Usually just 0, use it only if you have multiple vertex buffer streams, which is complicated stuff.

❑ Offset (second parameter): Offset from the start of the stream in bytes. Just calculate how far you are in the structure in bytes. Floats and integers and dwords take 4 bytes.

❑ Vertex element format (third parameter): Defines which type of data is used; this is the same name as defined in the `VertexInput` format in the shader. Usually you will use `Vector2`, `Vector3`, and `Vector4` here. Integer numbers or other floating-point values are usually only used for skinning and skeletal animation.

❑ Vertex element method: Just use default. Allows also UV and Lookup, but that's not really required often.

❑ Vertex element usage: How should this data type be used? This is similar to the semantics value you defined in the shader. You should always set this to the data type that is used because even if the order is not the same as in the shader, the data will be reordered based on this usage type. If you don't specify tangent here, the `VertexInput` data might be completely messed up and XNA usually complains if the format does not fit.

❑ Finally you can also specify the usage index, but again you probably will never need this value; just leave it to 0.

Normal Mapping Unit Test

Normally you would write the unit test first, but you already have a unit test for shaders from the previous chapter and you need to define how your new shader works first to figure out which classes are required. Now it is much easier to write shader unit tests again. Please note that you should not write any unit tests in the `ShaderEffect` class because once `ShaderEffect` gets called all shaders get initialized, which should not happen before the device is initialized!

Take a look at the Normal Mapping shader unit test:

```
public static void TestNormalMappingShader()
{
  Model testModel = null;
  Material testMaterial = null;

  TestGame.Start("TestNormalMappingShader",
    delegate
    {
      testModel = new Model("apple");
```

```
        testMaterial = new Material(
          Material.DefaultAmbientColor,
          Material.DefaultDiffuseColor,
          Material.DefaultSpecularColor,
          "asteroid4~0", "asteroid4Normal~0", "", "");
      },
      delegate
      {
        // Render model
        BaseGame.WorldMatrix = Matrix.CreateScale(0.25f, 0.25f, 0.25f);
        BaseGame.Device.VertexDeclaration =
          TangentVertex.VertexDeclaration;

        ShaderEffect.normalMapping.Render(testMaterial, "Specular20",
          delegate
          {
            // Render all meshes
            foreach (ModelMesh mesh in testModel.XnaModel.Meshes)
            {
              // Render all mesh parts
              foreach (ModelMeshPart part in mesh.MeshParts)
              {
                // Render data our own way
                BaseGame.Device.Vertices[0].SetSource(
                  mesh.VertexBuffer, part.StreamOffset, part.VertexStride);
                BaseGame.Device.Indices = mesh.IndexBuffer;

                // And render
                BaseGame.Device.DrawIndexedPrimitives(
                  PrimitiveType.TriangleList,
                  part.BaseVertex, 0, part.NumVertices,
                  part.StartIndex, part.PrimitiveCount);
              } // foreach
            } // foreach
          });
      });
    } // TestNormalMappingShader()
```

The model is loaded like in the unit test from the previous chapter, but instead of loading a texture you now load a complete material with several color values and the diffuse and Normal Maps of your asteroid4 model. In the render loop you just make sure that the world matrix is set like before and then you set your new `TangentVertex` structure. The render code itself is the same as in `SimpleShader RenderModel` and just goes through all the meshes and renders everything with the new asteroid material. Figure 7-16 shows the result of this unit test.

The apple is still there, but it is very dark and the Normal Map does not look good yet and certainly not the way it looked in FX Composer. Well, it is the tangent issue again. You are telling XNA how to use the input data, but the tangent data is still missing and has to be generated before the model lands in your content pipeline.

Figure 7-16

Adding Tangent Data with a Custom Processor

It is not easy to get this tangent problem right, and writing a custom processor is also not an easy task. The basic steps are described here. If you want to know more about writing custom processors or how to write a whole new content importer class, you should refer to the XNA documentation and additional samples on the Web.

First you have to create a new DLL project; just add it to the existing solution and choose XNA DLL or C# DLL as the type. Now make sure that the XNA Framework and XNA pipeline DLLs are added in the references section of this new project (see Figure 7-17).

Figure 7-17

Now write the following code into the main class of the DLL. You are deriving from the `ModelProcessor` class and extending the default behavior of XNA models. The code just calls `CalculateTangentFrames` for each mesh in the model. The code in the project for this chapter is much more complex and also fixes several other things and prepares the model for complex highly optimized rendering.

```
/// <summary>
/// XnaGraphicEngine model processor for x files. Loads models the same
/// way as the ModelProcessor class, but generates tangents and some
/// additional data too.
/// </summary>
[ContentProcessor(DisplayName = "XnaGraphicEngine Model (Tangent support)")]
public class XnaGraphicEngineModelProcessor : ModelProcessor
{
    #region Process
    /// <summary>
    /// Process the model
    /// </summary>
    /// <param name="input">Input data</param>
    /// <param name="context">Context for logging</param>
    /// <returns>Model content</returns>
    public override ModelContent Process(
        NodeContent input, ContentProcessorContext context)
    {
        // First generate tangent data because x files don't store them
        GenerateTangents(input, context);

        // And let the rest be processed by the default model processor
        return base.Process(input, context);
    } // Process
    #endregion

    #region Generate tangents
    /// <summary>
    /// Generate tangents helper method, x files do not have tangents
    /// exported, we have to generate them ourselfs.
    /// </summary>
    /// <param name="input">Input data</param>
    /// <param name="context">Context for logging</param>
    private void GenerateTangents(
        NodeContent input, ContentProcessorContext context)
    {
        MeshContent mesh = input as MeshContent;
        if (mesh != null)
        {
            // Generate trangents for the mesh. We don't want binormals,
            // so null is passed in for the last parameter.
            MeshHelper.CalculateTangentFrames(mesh,
                VertexChannelNames.TextureCoordinate(0),
                VertexChannelNames.Tangent(0), null);
        } // if
```

```
      // Go through all childs
      foreach (NodeContent child in input.Children)
      {
        GenerateTangents(child, context);
      } // foreach
    } // GenerateTangents(input, context)
    #endregion
  } // class
```

The `MeshHelper` class is only available in the content pipeline here; there are several methods that help you out if you want to modify the incoming data. The method `GenerateTangents` generates the tangent frames from the first set of texture coordinates and it ignores the creation of binormal values. Though it is nice to finally have some generated tangents, they will often look wrong, especially if the model was created a while ago. Newer versions of 3D Studio Max (8 and 9) use the so-called Rocket Mode (named after the Rocket model in Rocket Commander) for Normal Map creation, but older versions and other tools might generate rounded Normal Maps, which will be messed up by the auto-tangent creation of XNA (or MDX for that matter). In the original XNA game I implemented my own tangent processor and generator, but in XNA this is not that easy. You don't have direct access to the vertex data of the model, but there are some helper methods. It still would be a lot of work to extract all data and put it back together.

It would probably be easier to write a completely new content importer than to mess with an existing format if you really need a lot of changes and additional features for your 3D model data. For example, many 3D models exist in many different formats; md3 or md5 are quite popular in the Quake/Doom world and often people write their own importers just to get some cool looking models from other games to be shown in their own graphics engine. Please refer to the XNA documentation for how to write your own custom content importer. Additionally there will hopefully be a lot of user-written custom content importers on the Web in the future. The easiest format to import in my opinion is the Collada format if you don't want to mess with .x or .fbx files. It requires some custom code, but once you have done that it is quite easy to extend your importer, add new features, and change the behavior completely in whatever way you like.

But you are happy with your custom model processor for now. It generates tangent data and that is all you need for your Normal Mapping shaders. To get a custom processor working in your XNA project you have to select it yourself by opening each content file properties. Before you can even select your own custom model processor you have to make sure the content pipeline knows it exists; for now you just created a DLL file somewhere on the disk. To include your processor open up your project properties (right-click in the Solution Explorer on the XnaGraphicEngine .csproj file on the top, right below the XnaGraphicEngine solution, and select `Properties` here). The last option in the project properties is called `Content Pipeline` and this is where you can select additional content importers and processors (see Figure 7-18). If you click Add… you can select the `XnaGraphicEngineContentProcessors.dll` file by browsing two levels up and then selecting its `bin\Debug\` directory. For release mode you probably want to select `bin\Release\`.

After the new content pipeline assembly is loaded you should now be able to select "XnaGraphicEngine Model (Tangent support)" for each .x file model you have in your project. You can also select multiple .x files in the Solution Explorer and then change the model content processor for all of them (see Figure 7-19).

Figure 7-18

Figure 7-19

With all that heavy lifting behind you, you can now start your last unit test again and check out what has changed. Please note that you did not change a single line of code in your project for the new content processor support; it is all done in the processor DLL. If you made any mistake in the content processor or one of the content files does not contain valid data, you will get a warning or error before the project is started because the content pipeline builds all the content before you start the project. Once the content is built with your new processor it does not change anymore and it does not have to be rebuilt again. XNA will skip that automatically for you.

As you can see in Figure 7-20, your apple with the asteroid material now looks much better and you can even assign different materials on it (just for fun). Please note that the internal structure of the apple is different from your own `TangentVertex` format. If you set the apple material directly on it, make sure the correct vertex declaration from the mesh is used and not your own, or else the texture coordinates will not match (but that does not matter for your testing; none of the textures fit).

Apple with Asteroid4 Material

Apple with Rocket Material

Apple with Marble Test Material

Figure 7-20

You might notice that both the rocket and the marble test textures seem to be mirrored. This is normal because the apple model was generated for DirectX and uses a left-handed matrix. You could export all models again with a right-handed mode (which the Panda DirectX Exporter in 3D Studio Max luckily supports) or you could just ignore this issue because it does not matter so much in Rocket Commander. If you have text on textures in your game or you want the textures to fit and not to be mirrored, make sure that everything is aligned the correct way from day one. It is always important to use the same format in the modeling program your artists use and in your graphics engine. If it does not fit, either adjust your engine or convert the content the way you need it to be.

Final Asteroid Unit Test

You did not need all this knowledge just to display a simple asteroid model, because the following unit test shows it is possible to just load the model and use the shader that was selected in 3D Studio automatically. The problem with this approach becomes apparent when you try to render 1000 asteroids per frame. It is just way too slow and impractical to start a new shader for every single asteroid, set all the parameters all over again, and then use the unoptimized mesh draw method.

Instead you are going to start your own shader class in the future and then initialize the material and shader settings only once and render a lot of models as fast as possible. In this way you can achieve great performance in the Rocket Commander game.

```
public static void TestAsteroidModel()
{
  Model testModel = null;

  TestGame.Start("TestNormalMappingShader",
    delegate
    {
      testModel = new Model("asteroid4");
    },
```

```
        delegate
        {
          // Render model
          testModel.Render(Matrix.CreateScale(10.25f, 10.25f, 10.25f));
        });
    } // TestAsteroidModel()
```

If the asteroid4 model (by the way, you can also use asteroid4Low for testing here) uses the correct model processor with tangent support you should be able to see it correctly in 3D (see Figure 7-21) with the parallax mapping effect on it (which is the same as Normal Mapping, it just uses an additional height texture to move the output texture around a little bit for a fake displacement effect). One problem with the asteroid model is that there are visible raw edges on it. It seems like the texture mapping does not match, but if you disable the Normal Mapping effect, it looks ok. So the problem comes from the tangent data. The Normal Map is correct as you can see in the DirectX version of Rocket Commander (fits perfectly thanks to the custom way tangent data is re-generated, which is sadly not possible in XNA for .x files). Other models like the rocket and future models created for XNA games look fine, but this is still an un-fixable problem with older models and a limitation of XNA. You have to live with it.

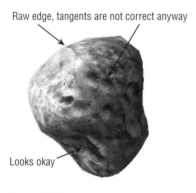

Raw edge, tangents are not correct anyway

Looks okay

Figure 7-21

It probably would be possible to somehow fix all asteroids, re-export them, make sure all data is correct, and maybe even re-generate the Normal Map to fit correctly. But that is a lot of work and the asteroid looks good enough now. The original Rocket Commander game still exists and shows how it is done; for the XNA port you can live with some minor glitches.

For a native XNA game this should not happen, and in the next games for this book you will make sure that all models are exported and displayed correctly. Please note that it can be a lot of work working with 3D models, exporting them correctly, importing them again into your engine, writing all the shaders required to make them look the way the artist intended them to look, and so on. Sometimes you will be better off by just using an existing engine (like the one you develop in this book) and use it for a while until you see your custom needs and start writing your own 3D code anyway. But don't spend all your time just developing a 3D engine without writing a game. XNA is about game development and a common mistake in the DirectX world was that everyone wrote his own engine, but only very few people made games out of their engines. Be smarter than them.

More Shaders

Normal Maps are great, but there are many more ways to improve the visual quality of 3D objects. For the Rocket Commander game we are happy with a little parallax mapping and some cool post screen shaders. If you are more ambitious about your game you probably want to implement glass shaders, reflection effects, cool water shaders, and more. This section gives a small overview about possible shaders you could write for your XNA graphics engine. There are many more examples available online or in the many shader books out there. Good examples are the Nvidia homepage, www.shadertech.com, the GPU Gems (by Nvidia), or Game Programming Gems books (by Charles River Media), or Shader X book series (by Charles River Media, edited by Wolfgang Engel). There is a lot that can be learned from these books, but in the end you will probably end up writing your shader code unless you find someone that does it for you.

Offset Mapping

Parallax mapping is sometimes also called offset mapping because the points are remapped, but usually offset mapping means that the original parallax mapping effect is taken to another level by going through several height layers in the pixel shader. Another popular name for offset mapping is steep parallax mapping, which was shown in a paper from Morgan McGuire and Max McGuire in April, 2005. The game F.E.A.R. is a prominent example of this technique. It uses parallax mapping with maybe two or three height layers, but the results are fine-tuned and look pretty good.

The steep parallax mapping approach is a little more complex and usually takes 20 or more height steps until it looks really good. The advantage is that you can also calculate self-shadowing (see Figure 7-22), which looks really amazing if you consider that all of this happens in the pixel shader, there is no actual 3D geometry, and it is all faked.

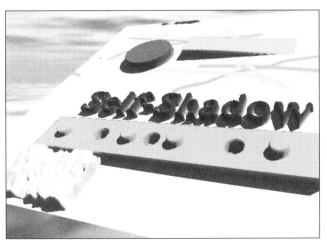

Figure 7-22

The major problem with this technique is the high cost associated with it. Not only will you spend a lot of time implementing this technique and trying to get it right, but more importantly it will cost an insane amount of Pixel Shader power to execute. The shader is about 20 times slower than a normal parallax mapping shader, and though it is possible to create cool looking scenes in demos with very few polygons, in a real game you will need a lot more than just one cool effect. Maybe it will be an option in the future to improve existing games or allow really high-end graphics hardware to make the game look even better.

Glass Shader

Simulating glass is not that easy, at least if you try to get it right. The main problem with glass is that it does two things: it reflects the side of the world you are on and it refracts the world behind the glass. Reflection means that light from the viewer side of the glass is reflected like on a mirror and will be seen by the viewer, including himself if he stands in front of the glass and the lighting conditions are correct. Refraction means that the world behind the glass (for example, if you are looking outside through a window) is distorted a bit depending on the glass thickness, the structure, and even the color of the glass. This is especially true if you have a glass surface with a structure on it (like glass on the bathroom window).

To make things even more complicated glass does not always behave the same way. Viewing it from the top gives you other reflection values for reflection than viewing the glass from the side, which usually gives you a better reflection. If the lighting conditions are poor or the glass is dirty it might not be so reflective at all, and so on. There are many more options that could be considered.

Because you don't have a lifetime to get it right and you just want it to work you usually leave out everything that is not really important and are still left with some cool looking effects (see Figure 7-23). You can find more information about the cars and the shaders in the last part of this book.

Figure 7-23

Reflection and Water

For glass you can get away with implementing a simple reflection shader, which reflects the sky cube box (see the next chapter for more information about the sky) on the glass. For more shiny metal surfaces or mirrors, just reflecting the sky might not be sufficient. You may have to think about reflecting the world around certain objects for more realistic effects. This is neither easy nor fast because for a complete reflection around a simple 3D object you would have to render a reflection cube map to show the world in every direction from that reflective material. In Direct3D 10 it is possible to render this in one step, but you still need a fast graphics card for this kind of dynamic update for materials in your engine. In DirectX 9 or XNA it will probably be too slow in most cases because you have to render the scene six times for every cube direction just for one materials reflective cube map.

Reflection can be a little bit simpler when you just reflect the world on a planar surface like a mirror. Now you only have to render the world mirrored on this surface once and you are good to go for your reflection effects. This technique is also used for many water shaders and it can look really cool, especially if you don't just reflect the sky, but also the objects and effects of the world. Additionally, water has many effects (reflection, refraction, water color, water animation, waves, and so on), which can take a lot of time to fine-tune, but it can also be a lot of fun playing around with water shaders (see Figure 7-24).

Figure 7-24

Challenge: Add Parallax Mapping

Phew, that was a lot of reading. I hope you still have some energy left for your little task here. This chapter talked a lot about Normal Mapping and parallax mapping, but you only saw how Normal Maps were implemented. It is now your turn to implement parallax mapping. Don't worry; it is not very hard once you get the basic idea.

First of all you have to understand that each pixel produced by the Pixel Shader shows the interpolated texture coordinates you passed in through the vertices. But if you are able to interpolate and scale the texture coordinates, you should also be able to move them around depending on the location you are looking from. This is already the basic idea of parallax mapping, as shown in Figure 7-25.

Figure 7-25

To get this effect in your shader you have to define a height-texture first (the black curvy line in the figure represents the height for each pixel). Just add it after the Normal Map and use the default sampler values (linear interpolation). Now you can access the height map data in the Pixel Shader with the following code:

```
float height = tex2D(heightTextureSampler, In.texCoord);
```

Only a float value is used because you only need the height value, not the real color in the height map (which is gray anyway). Now you have to calculate the offset this height value produces. Then use very small values here, or else parallax mapping will look very bad if the effect is too strong. This is the basic code for that:

```
// Calculate parallax offset, parallaxAmount should be 0.05 or less.
float2 offsetTexCoord = In.texCoord +
    (height*parallaxAmount - parallaxAmount*0.6f) * normalize(In.viewVec);
```

The last thing you have to do now is to use this offsetTexCoord for the diffuse and Normal Map instead of In.texCoord and your parallax mapping effect should work. Fine-tune it a little and use a variable in FX Composer for the parallaxAmount for easier testing. Good luck. If you don't get it to work right away or run into troubles please take a look at the ParallaxMapping.fx shader in the content directory for additional assistance.

Summary

You learned a lot about advanced shader effects in this chapter and you should be ready now to create your own shaders and play around with some ideas you might have. Because shaders are completely programmable today it is impossible to explain all the possibilities and ways shaders can be used. In the future many more new techniques might appear and make games look even better. But shaders are not only used for games; certain applications try to use the GPU power for other uses too and there are several experiments that show how to use the GPU for math calculations or physics. It may sound crazy, but for some of these tasks the GPU is a far better processing unit than the CPU because it works so well for just processing pixels and it works in parallel with 24-pixel processing units or even more.

Here's the list of shaders and problems you encountered in this chapter:

- ❑ You saw that Normal Mapping can greatly improve 3D models. Objects with just few hundred polygons can look almost as good as 3D objects with millions of polygons. But in order to get them to work correctly you need valid tangent data in the 3D geometry.

- ❑ By compressing Normal Maps you can save a lot of video memory while still having great visual quality. Use the NormalMapCompressor tool to quickly generate compressed Normal Maps.

- ❑ FX Composer is still the program to do all the heavy lifting for your shader code. Visual Studio is nice for code, but FX Composer is clearly the better IDE for shaders. The preview scene is especially useful.

- ❑ To work painlessly with shaders in the future several new classes were introduced into the graphics engine that allow you to load and render shaders (`ShaderEffect` class), assign and set materials (`Materials` class), and to use 3D geometry data with tangent support (`TangentVertex` structure).

- ❑ Finally, you saw several other shaders including offset mapping/steep parallax mapping, glass shaders, reflection and water shaders, and the parallax mapping shader in the Challenge (I hope you got it right).

- ❑ Playing around with shaders can be fun.

With all this new code you can now get ready for a new game in the next chapter, where you also learn about post screen shaders to greatly improve the visual quality and overall look of your upcoming games.

8

Post-Screen Shaders and the Rocket Commander Game

Well, it was fun to write the graphics engine the last couple of chapters, but where is the next game? Don't worry, now you get to a really cool game: Rocket Commander. The original version was released in March 2006 at the time the German www.Coding4Fun.de site went offline and Visual Studio 2005 came out in Germany. One month and many thousand played games later, the English Rocket Commander Tutorial Videos were created and two additional mods were released with it. Half a year later, 100,000 games were played online; even more if people were playing offline. Many other mods were also created and the engine proved to be reliable enough, even for two commercial games that were released with the Rocket Commander engine: Pizza Commander and Rocket Racer.

The Rocket Commander game and the complete source code are free to download and you are encouraged to play around with it or even use it to create your own games. I received many nice stories via email of people learning C# for the first time, and they were able to create their own engines and games in a short time thanks to the Rocket Commander and the video tutorials on the German and English Coding4Fun sites.

Let's just say the Rocket Commander game was a success. I didn't get rich or anything, just famous. In December 2006 the final version the of XNA Framework and XNA Game Studio Express were finally released and I was working hard on the release of Rocket Commander XNA, a complete port of the Rocket Commander engine to XNA to make it possible to play the Rocket Commander game on the Xbox 360. The performance of the XNA port is great; it runs even better than the old version and the game has no problems with thousands of asteroids rendered at the highest detail level with anti-aliasing in the highest HDTV resolution (1920×1080, I wish I had such a monitor or TV) on the Xbox 360. One major improvement of the new version is the support for multiple cores, which is both important for the Xbox 360 and today's PCs. The game now calculates all the physics, collision testing, and other game data in an extra thread that is executed on another CPU core (if available like on the Xbox 360) than the rendering thread, which is always busy pushing data to the GPU.

Before you get into the Rocket Commander game you are going to learn all about post-screen shaders first, which is also a major part of Rocket Commander in addition to the powerful rendering engine and the physics. For more information about physics please read Chapter 13. Most information about the shaders for the 3D objects were already discussed in the previous chapters and if you are interested in the game logic, take a look at the source code or watch the Rocket Commander Video Tutorials.

For the rest of the book you will of course still use the XnaGraphicEngine, but any improvements like the heavily optimized render system in Rocket Commander XNA or the physics system can still be used for future projects. Most importantly for the look of all upcoming games, including Rocket Commander, will be the many pre- and post-screen shaders that are introduced in this chapter. Pre-screen shaders are executed before the 3D scene is rendered and allow you to render textures, sky cubes, and other effects in the background. Writing such a shader is quite easy.

Post-screen shaders, on the other hand, are much more complex and they are executed at the very end of the frame rendering process. They take the fully rendered scene as a texture on a render target and modify it in several steps to output the post-screen shader result on the screen, which the user then finally sees. Getting this render target right is not a piece of cake, but once you've got the system up you can easily plug in more post-screen shaders and play around with effects. Don't overuse bloom and motion blur effects; it is cool to use those kinds of shader effects, but overusing them will not make your game better. Try also to make sure that the post-screen shaders run as fast as possible because they can heavily reduce performance on high resolutions, especially if you have five or more passes and modify every single pixel on the screen.

Handling Post-Screen Shaders

The first thing you have to get for any post-screen shader is the rendered scene and put it into a render target (see Figure 8-1). The image illustrates some example post-screen shaders in FX Composer, which can be used to test out the post-screen effects before you include them into your graphics engine.

Before getting into the more complex post-screen shaders and how you can get the scene render target with help of the new `RenderToTexture` helper class, you will first test out the Pre-Screen Sky Cube Mapping shader and get it to work in your engine the same way it works in FX Composer.

Pre-Screen Sky Cube Mapping

First of all you need a sky cube map, which consists of six faces like a cube. Each of these faces should be in high resolution because in the game you only look in one direction. It's okay to use 512×512 for each face if you use a lot of post-screen shaders; 1024×1024 is even better, because the sky on high-resolution screens will look much better this way.

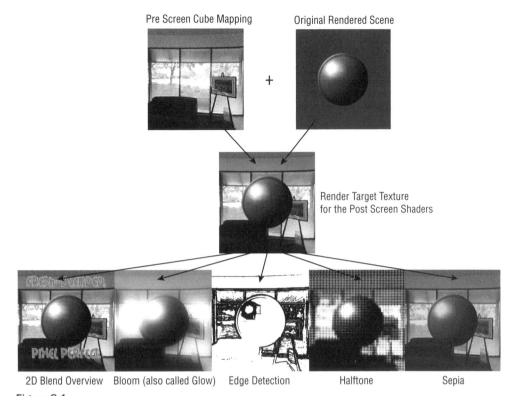

Figure 8-1

It is not easy to create such a sky cube texture. You can either use the DirectX DxTexture tool and put together the cube map with six separate faces yourself (or do the same thing in your code, but it is much easier to load one single cube map file that contains all six faces instead of loading six separate textures and putting them together yourself). Alternatively a program like Photoshop can be used to store a big 6*512×512 texture and save it as a cube map dds with help of the Nvidia DDS Exporter plug-in for Photoshop (see Figure 8-2).

Figure 8-2

If you don't have a good looking cube map, search the Web for one; there are some example textures available. Most of them have bad resolutions, but for testing they are fine. Or just use the cube map from this book if you like it. For the Rocket Commander game you use a space cube map that looks a little different on each of the six sides to help you with navigating through the 3D space levels of the game (see Figure 8-3).

Figure 8-3

Take a look at the shader to put this cube texture on the screen. You call this shader even before rendering the scene, and because it will fill all background buffer pixels you don't have to clear the background color target anymore (but you probably still want to clear the z-buffer). To render this shader you should also disable depth comparing because you don't care how far away the sky is, so it should always be rendered.

The following code is from the PreScreenSkyCubeMapping.fx shader:

```
struct VertexInput
{
    // We only need 2d screen position, that's all.
    float2 pos      : POSITION;
};
```

```
struct VB_OutputPos3DTexCoord
{
  float4 pos      : POSITION;
  float3 texCoord : TEXCOORD0;
};

VB_OutputPos3DTexCoord VS_SkyCubeMap(VertexInput In)
{
  VB_OutputPos3DTexCoord Out;
  Out.pos = float4(In.pos.xy, 0, 1);
  // Also negate xy because the cube map is for MDX (left handed)
  // and is upside down
  Out.texCoord = mul(float4(-In.pos, scale, 0), viewInverse).xyz;

  // And fix rotation too (we use better x, y ground plane system)
  Out.texCoord = float3(
    -Out.texCoord.x*1.0f,
    -Out.texCoord.z*0.815f,
    -Out.texCoord.y*1.0f);

  return Out;
} // VS_SkyCubeMap(..)

float4 PS_SkyCubeMap(VB_OutputPos3DTexCoord In) : COLOR
{
  float4 texCol = ambientColor *
    texCUBE(diffuseTextureSampler, In.texCoord);
  return texCol;
} // PS_SkyCubeMap(.)

technique SkyCubeMap < string Script = "Pass=P0;"; >
{
  pass P0 < string Script = "Draw=Buffer;"; >
  {
    ZEnable = false;
    VertexShader = compile vs_1_1 VS_SkyCubeMap();
    PixelShader  = compile ps_1_1 PS_SkyCubeMap();
  } // pass P0
} // technique SkyCubeMap
```

For rendering the shader you only need a `Vector2` screen position, which can be converted to the sky cube position by multiplying it with the inverse view matrix. The scale variable can be used to tweak the zooming a little bit, but usually this value should be 1.0. After getting the texture coordinate for the sky cube map, you need to convert it from the standard left-handed system cube that maps are usually stored in. To do that you have to swap the y and z coordinates and you also invert the direction the cube map texture coordinate is pointing to. And finally you multiply the y value by a custom value of 0.815 to make the sky rendered in a 1:1 aspect ratio mode look correct on a 4:3 aspect ratio of the screen. All these tweaking variables were tested with the unit test presented next until the background sky just looked correct.

If you want to build your own sky cube map, you can use the DirectX Texture Tool from the DirectX SDK to load normal 2D images on each of the six cube map faces of a cube texture. Additionally, many tools are available to directly render 3D scenes into cube maps such as Bryce, 3D Studio Max, and many other 3D content creation applications.

Then you rotate the sky cube map for XNA compatibility because it was created for MDX and uses a left-handed system. Rendering the sky cube map is pretty easy — just grab the cube texture color value and multiply it with the optional ambient color value, which is usually white. The shader is not using any advanced Shader Model 2.0 functionality and it is absolutely no problem to compile it to Shader Model 1.1.

To get it to work in your XNA graphic engine you use the following unit test:

```
public static void TestSkyCubeMapping()
{
  PreScreenSkyCubeMapping skyCube = null;

  TestGame.Start("TestSkyCubeMapping",
    delegate
    {
      skyCube = new PreScreenSkyCubeMapping();
    },
    delegate
    {
      skyCube.RenderSky();
    });
} // TestSkyCubeMapping()
```

The class is derived from the ShaderEffect class from the previous chapters and it just loads the PreScreenSkyCubeMapping.fx shader in the constructor; all other shader effect parameters are already defined in the ShaderEffect class. The important new method in this class is RenderSky, which basically executes the following code:

```
AmbientColor = setSkyColor;
InverseViewMatrix = BaseGame.InverseViewMatrix;

// Start shader
// Remember old state because we will use clamp texturing here
effect.Begin(SaveStateMode.SaveState);

for (int num = 0; num < effect.CurrentTechnique.Passes.Count; num++)
{
  EffectPass pass = effect.CurrentTechnique.Passes[num];

  // Render each pass
  pass.Begin();
  VBScreenHelper.Render();
  pass.End();
} // foreach (pass)

// End shader
effect.End();
```

Like in any other shader you wrote before you set the effect parameters first, which is only the ambient color and the inverse view matrix because the shader does not use anything else. Then the shader is started and you render all passes (well, you only have one pass) with the help of the VBScreenHelper Render method, which is also used for all post-screen shaders.

`VBScreenHelper` generates a very simple screen quad for you and handles all the vertex buffer initialization and rendering. The following code initializes the vertex buffer with just `VertexPositionTexture` vertices. You only have one static instance of the helper class and it is used only in pre and post-screen shaders.

```
public VBScreen()
{
   VertexPositionTexture[] vertices = new VertexPositionTexture[]
      {
         new VertexPositionTexture(
            new Vector3(-1.0f, -1.0f, 0.5f),
            new Vector2(0, 1)),
         new VertexPositionTexture(
            new Vector3(-1.0f, 1.0f, 0.5f),
            new Vector2(0, 0)),
         new VertexPositionTexture(
            new Vector3(1.0f, -1.0f, 0.5f),
            new Vector2(1, 1)),
         new VertexPositionTexture(
            new Vector3(1.0f, 1.0f, 0.5f),
            new Vector2(1, 0)),
      };
   vbScreen = new VertexBuffer(
      BaseGame.Device,
      typeof(VertexPositionTexture),
      vertices.Length,
      ResourceUsage.WriteOnly,
      ResourceManagementMode.Automatic);
   vbScreen.SetData(vertices);

   decl = new VertexDeclaration(BaseGame.Device,
      VertexPositionTexture.VertexElements);
} // VBScreen()
```

As discussed in Chapters 5 and 6 the view space uses –1 to +1 as the minimum and maximum values for the screen borders. Everything above these values will not be on the screen. The projection matrix then puts the pixels at the real screen positions. You use simple `VertexPositionTexture` vertices here. For the sky cube mapping shader you don't even need the texture coordinates, but they will be used for the post-screen shaders later. Please note that the position in screen coordinates of +1, +1 is the lower-left corner of the screen and –1, –1 is the upper-right corner. If you want the top-left corner of a screen texture to be displayed on the top left, the texture coordinates of 0, 0 should be in the –1, +1 corner.

You should always specify `WriteOnly` and `Automatic` when creating `VertexBuffers`; this way the hardware can access them much faster without having to worry about read access from the CPU, and `Automatic` makes it easier to get rid of the vertex buffer and let XNA handle re-creation issues when the vertex buffer gets lost and has to be re-created (which can happen when the user presses Alt+Tab in a fullscreen application and then returns).

With all these new classes up and ready you should now be able to execute your `TestSkyCubeMapping` unit test and see the result shown in Figure 8-4.

Figure 8-4

Writing a Simple Post-Screen Shader

Writing post-screen shaders is no picnic. It involves a lot of testing, handling render targets correctly, and it is not always easy to get the shader to work in both FX Composer and your engine and behave the same way. To make it a little simpler for the first post-screen shader you are just going to add a very simple effect to your scene. Instead of really modifying the rendered scene you are just going to darken down the screen borders to give the game a TV-like look. To change something that would not be possible without a post-screen shader, you also turn the whole screen to black and white.

Start with the `PostScreenDarkenBorder.fx` shader file in FX Composer. After the header comment and the description of the shader you define a script, which is only used for FX Composer to indicate that this shader is a post-screen shader and should be rendered a certain way. All variables starting with an uppercase letter are considered to be constant for your purposes.

Neither your engine nor FX Composer care about the casing, but this way you can easily spot which variables should be constant and not be changed in the app and which ones have to be set from the application. `ClearColor` and `ClearDepth` are both used only in the FX Composer. In your application you don't have to worry about that because you handle your own clearing. For testing you can set other colors as black for `ClearColor` or 1.0 for depth if you like, but most of the time, these values will always be the same and they default to the same values for all upcoming post-screen shaders.

```
// This script is only used for FX Composer, most values here
// are treated as constants by the application anyway.
// Values starting with an upper letter are constants.
float Script : STANDARDSGLOBAL
<
```

```
    string ScriptClass = "scene";
    string ScriptOrder = "postprocess";
    string ScriptOutput = "color";
    // We just call a script in the main technique.
    string Script = "Technique=ScreenDarkenBorder;";
> = 0.5;
const float4 ClearColor : DIFFUSE = { 0.0f, 0.0f, 0.0f, 1.0f};
const float ClearDepth = 1.0f;
```

Post-screen shaders need to know about the screen resolution and you need access to the scene map render target. The following code is used to allow you to assign the window size and the scene map. The window size is the resolution you render into and the scene map render target contains the fully rendered scene as a texture. Please note the semantics like VIEWPORTPIXELSIZE used here to help FX Composer to assign the correct values for the preview rendering automatically. If you don't use them FX Composer will not be able to use the correct window size and you would have to set it yourself in the properties panel.

```
// Render-to-Texture stuff
float2 windowSize : VIEWPORTPIXELSIZE;

texture sceneMap : RENDERCOLORTARGET
<
  float2 ViewportRatio = { 1.0, 1.0 };
  int MIPLEVELS = 1;
>;
sampler sceneMapSampler = sampler_state
{
  texture = <sceneMap>;
  AddressU  = CLAMP;
  AddressV  = CLAMP;
  AddressW  = CLAMP;
  MIPFILTER = NONE;
  MINFILTER = LINEAR;
  MAGFILTER = LINEAR;
};
```

For darkening down the screen border you also use a little helper texture with the name ScreenBorderFadeout.dds (see Figure 8-5):

```
// For the last pass we add this screen border fadeout map to darken the borders
texture screenBorderFadeoutMap : Diffuse
<
  string UIName = "Screen border texture";
  string ResourceName = "ScreenBorderFadeout.dds";
>;
sampler screenBorderFadeoutMapSampler = sampler_state
{
    texture = <screenBorderFadeoutMap>;
    AddressU  = CLAMP;
    AddressV  = CLAMP;
    AddressW  = CLAMP;
    MIPFILTER = NONE;
    MINFILTER = LINEAR;
    MAGFILTER = LINEAR;
};
```

Figure 8-5

This texture has to be added to your content directory as well as the .fx shader file. XNA will not automatically add this texture like for models that contain materials and textures.

To achieve the darkening effect every pixel from the scene map is simply multiplied by the color value in the screen border fadeout texture. This way most pixels stay the same (white middle); pixels at the screen border will get darker and darker, but not completely black (or else the border would be black), so you just want to make it a little darker.

Take a look at the very simple vertex shader, which just passes the texture coordinates to the Pixel Shader. To make the shader compatible to Pixel Shader 1.1 you have to duplicate the texture coordinates because you need to access them twice, once for the scene map and once for the screen border fadeout texture. Please also note that you are adding half a pixel to the texture coordinates to fix a very common problem of rendering textures on the screen. In DirectX (and XNA) all the pixels have an offset of 0.5 pixels; you just fix this by moving the pixel to the correct location.

You can read more about this issue online. You don't have to worry about it normally because all the helper classes (for example, `SpriteBatch`) take care of this issue for you, but if you render your own post-screen shader you might want to fix this. For this shader it does not matter so much, but if you have a very precise shader that shadows certain pixels you want to make sure to completely hit the pixel position and not draw somewhere else.

```
struct VB_OutputPos2TexCoords
{
    float4 pos       : POSITION;
    float2 texCoord[2] : TEXCOORD0;
};

VB_OutputPos2TexCoords VS_ScreenQuad(
    float4 pos       : POSITION,
    float2 texCoord : TEXCOORD0)
{
    VB_OutputPos2TexCoords Out;
    float2 texelSize = 1.0 / windowSize;
    Out.pos = pos;
    // Don't use bilinear filtering
    Out.texCoord[0] = texCoord + texelSize*0.5;
    Out.texCoord[1] = texCoord + texelSize*0.5;
    return Out;
} // VS_ScreenQuad(..)
```

The position is already in the correct space and will just be passed over. The Pixel Shader now accesses the scene map, and for testing if everything is set up correctly you can just return the scene map colors here:

```
float4 PS_ComposeFinalImage(VB_OutputPos2TexCoords In) : COLOR
{
    float4 orig = tex2D(sceneMapSampler, In.texCoord[0]);
    return orig;
} // PS_ComposeFinalImage(...)
```

After adding the ScreenDarkenBorder technique you should see the normal scene as always in FX Composer (see Figure 8-6). Please note that all the annotations here are required for FX Composer only! For rendering you use the pre-screen sky cube mapping shader described earlier and the standard sphere.

```
// ScreenDarkenBorder technique for ps_1_1
technique ScreenDarkenBorder
<
    // Script stuff is just for FX Composer
    string Script = "RenderColorTarget=sceneMap;"
        "ClearSetColor=ClearColor; Clear=Color;"
        "ClearSetDepth=ClearDepth; Clear=Depth;"
        "ScriptSignature=color; ScriptExternal=;"
        "Pass=DarkenBorder;";
>
{
    pass DarkenBorder
    <
        string Script = "RenderColorTarget0=; Draw=Buffer;";
    >
    {
        VertexShader = compile vs_1_1 VS_ScreenQuad();
        PixelShader  = compile ps_1_1 PS_ComposeFinalImage(sceneMapSampler);
    } // pass DarkenBorder
} // technique ScreenDarkenBorder
```

Figure 8-6

Improvements

Just to test if the shader is activated (which can be done in FX Composer by clicking the shader in the materials panel and selecting "Apply to Scene"), you can now easily modify the output. Just change the last line in the Pixel Shader:

```
return 1.0f - orig;
```

This will subtract the color value from 1.0 for each component (shaders will automatically convert from `float` to `float3` or `float4` if required; you don't have to specify `float4 (1, 1, 1, 1)`). You can probably guess that this formula will invert the whole image (see Figure 8-7), which looks funny, but is not really useful.

Figure 8-7

Okay, back to your initial mission: Apply the screen border texture. To darken down the edges you first load the screen border texture and then multiply the original scene map color value with it, that's it. You just have to return the result of that and you are almost done (see Figure 8-8):

```
float4 orig = tex2D(sceneSampler, In.texCoord[0]);
float4 screenBorderFadeout =
  tex2D(screenBorderFadeoutMapSampler, In.texCoord[1]);
float4 ret = orig;
ret.rgb *= screenBorderFadeout;
return ret;
```

Figure 8-8

You could now also convert the image to black and white by applying the Luminance formula, which just tells you which component to weight how much (green is always the most visible color):

```
// Returns luminance value of col to convert color to grayscale
float Luminance(float3 col)
{
  return dot(col, float3(0.3, 0.59, 0.11));
} // Luminance(.)
```

This method can be applied to the original scene map by just modifying one line in your Pixel Shader to finally achieve the expected post-screen shader effect: Darken down the screen borders and apply a black and white effect (see Figure 8-9):

```
float4 ret = Luminance(orig);
```

Figure 8-9

Writing post-screen shaders can be a lot of fun once you have your basic setup, but you should try to implement the shader first into your engine before moving on to even more cool post-screen shaders and possibilities.

Implementing Post-Screen Shaders

A few helper classes like `VBScreenHelper` and `PreScreenSkyCubeMapping` were already introduced, but for post-screen shaders you really need render targets, which can be accessed and handled through the `RenderTarget` class in XNA. The problem with that class is that you still have to call a lot of methods and handle a lot of things yourself. This is especially true if you also want to use the depth buffer for render targets and restore them after they have been modified, which is useful for shadow mapping shaders.

RenderToTexture Class

For that reason a new helper class is introduced: RenderToTexture, which provides important methods to make post-screen shaders easy to handle (see Figure 8-10). The most important methods for you are the constructor, which takes SizeType as a parameter, Resolve, and SetRenderTarget. Getting the XnaTexture and the RenderTarget via the properties is also very useful. Please note that this class also inherits all the features from the Texture class.

Figure 8-10

For example, if you want to create a fullscreen scene map for the PostScreenDarkenBorder.fx shader you would use the following line:

```
sceneMapTexture = new RenderToTexture(
  RenderToTexture.SizeType.FullScreen);
```

The constructor does the following:

```
/// <summary>
/// Creates an offscreen texture with the specified size which
/// can be used for render to texture.
/// </summary>
public RenderToTexture(SizeType setSizeType)
{
  sizeType = setSizeType;
  CalcSize();

  texFilename = "RenderToTexture instance " +
    RenderToTextureGlobalInstanceId++;
```

```
[...]

    SurfaceFormat format = SurfaceFormat.Color;
    // Create render target of specified size.
    renderTarget = new RenderTarget2D(
      BaseGame.Device,
      texWidth, texHeight, 1,
      format);
} // RenderToTexture(setSizeType)
```

To use this render target and let everything be rendered into it you just have to call `SetRenderTarget` now, which uses some new helper methods in the `BaseGame` class to take care of multiple stacked render targets (required for more complex post-screen shaders):

```
    sceneMapTexture.SetRenderTarget();
```

After all the rendering is done you can call `Resolve` to copy the render target results to the internal texture (which can be accessed through the `XnaTexture` property). This step is new in XNA; it was not required in DirectX and the reason for it is to support the Xbox 360 hardware, which works quite differently than PC graphics cards. On the PC you can directly access the render target and use it for post-screen shaders, but on the Xbox 360 the render target results reside in a write-only hardware location and cannot be accessed. Instead you have to copy the render target over to the internal texture. This call takes some time but it is still very fast, so don't worry about it.

After resolving the render target you have to reset the render target back to the default background buffer, or else you are still rendering into the render target and will see nothing on the screen. To do that just call the `BaseGame ResetRenderTarget` method and pass in true to get rid of any started render targets. The method will also work if you don't have any render targets started. In that case it just returns and does nothing.

```
    // Get the sceneMap texture content
    sceneMapTexture.Resolve();
    // Do a full reset back to the back buffer
    BaseGame.ResetRenderTarget(true);
```

That is almost everything you have to know to work with the `RenderToTexture` class. Additional functionality will not be required for a while (until the last chapters of this book). Check out the unit tests of the `RenderToTexture` class to learn more about it.

PostScreenDarkenBorder Class

Before even thinking about writing the `PostScreenDarkenBorder` class you should define a unit test and specify the entire feature set you want to have in your post-screen class. Please note that you derive this class from `ShaderEffect` like for the pre-screen shader and have easier access to the effect class and the effect parameters. But you still have to specify the new effect parameters used in `PostScreenDarkenBorder.fx`.

Take a look at the unit test for this post-screen shader:

```
public static void TestPostScreenDarkenBorder()
{
  PreScreenSkyCubeMapping skyCube = null;
  Model testModel = null;
  PostScreenDarkenBorder postScreenShader = null;

  TestGame.Start("TestPostScreenDarkenBorder",
    delegate
    {
      skyCube = new PreScreenSkyCubeMapping();
      testModel = new Model("Asteroid4");
      postScreenShader = new PostScreenDarkenBorder();
    },
    delegate
    {
      // Start post screen shader to render to our sceneMap
      postScreenShader.Start();

      // Draw background sky cube
      skyCube.RenderSky();
      // And our testModel (the asteroid)
      testModel.Render(Matrix.CreateScale(10));

      // And finally show post screen shader
      postScreenShader.Show();
    });
} // TestPostScreenDarkenBorder()
```

By the way, always try to name your shader and source code files the same way; it will make it much easier when looking for bugs. Another nice thing you can sometimes do if shaders use similar features is to derive from one post-screen shader class when writing a new one. This trick is used for most of the following games to save coding the same effect parameters and render target code over and over again.

You use three variables in the unit test:

❑   skyCube initializes and renders the sky cube mapping shader like in FX Composer.

❑   testModel loads the asteroid4 model and displays it with a scaling factor of 10 after rendering the sky cube map background.

❑   And finally, postScreenShader holds an instance of the PostScreenDarkenBorder class. Because this shader needs a valid scene map you have to call it twice, first with the Start method to set up the scene map render target and then at the end of the frame rendering. Show is then called to bring everything to the screen.

If you take a look at the final unit test in the PostScreenDarkenBorder.cs file you may notice some additional code to toggle the post-screen shader and show some help on the screen. This was added later and only improves the usability of the shader; the basic layout is the same.

The layout of post-screen shader classes is very similar to the one you already saw in PreScreenSkyCube-Mapping. You just need a new Start and Show method and some internal variables to hold the new effect parameters and check whether or not the post-screen shader was started (see Figure 8-11).

Figure 8-11

The Start method just calls SetRenderTarget for the scene map texture; the important code is in the Show method:

```
/// <summary>
/// Execute shaders and show result on screen, Start(..) must have been
/// called before and the scene should be rendered to sceneMapTexture.
/// </summary>
public virtual void Show()
{
  // Only apply post screen glow if texture and effect are valid
  if (sceneMapTexture == null || Valid == false || started == false)
    return;

  started = false;
  // Resolve sceneMapTexture render target for Xbox360 support
  sceneMapTexture.Resolve();

  // Don't use or write to the z buffer
  BaseGame.Device.RenderState.DepthBufferEnable = false;
  BaseGame.Device.RenderState.DepthBufferWriteEnable = false;
  // Also don't use any kind of blending.
  BaseGame.Device.RenderState.AlphaBlendEnable = false;

  if (windowSize != null)
    windowSize.SetValue(new float[]
      { sceneMapTexture.Width, sceneMapTexture.Height });
  if (sceneMap != null)
    sceneMap.SetValue(sceneMapTexture.XnaTexture);

  effect.CurrentTechnique = effect.Techniques["ScreenDarkenBorder"];

  // We must have exactly 1 pass!
  if (effect.CurrentTechnique.Passes.Count != 1)
    throw new Exception("This shader should have exactly 1 pass!");
```

```
    effect.Begin();
    for (int pass= 0; pass < effect.CurrentTechnique.Passes.Count; pass++)
    {
      if (pass == 0)
        // Do a full reset back to the back buffer
        BaseGame.ResetRenderTarget(true);

      EffectPass effectPass = effect.CurrentTechnique.Passes[pass];
      effectPass.Begin();
      VBScreenHelper.Render();
      effectPass.End();
    } // for (pass, <, ++)
    effect.End();

    // Restore z buffer state
    BaseGame.Device.RenderState.DepthBufferEnable = true;
    BaseGame.Device.RenderState.DepthBufferWriteEnable = true;
  } // Show()
```

First you are checking if Start was called properly and if you still have the shader started, otherwise the content in the scene map render target will not contain any useful data. Then you resolve the render target for full Xbox 360 support and you can start setting up all required effect parameters and the technique. You might ask why the technique is added by name here and you are right, it would be faster to do this by a reference to the technique, which could be initialized in the constructor. But it does not matter so much; you only call this shader once per frame and this performance difference will never show up in any profiler tool (because one line for a frame that goes through many thousand lines of code is not affecting performance that much). If you will call a shader more often you should definitely cache this technique reference and maybe not even set it again and again every frame (it is still set from the last frame). See the ShaderEffect class for more information about this kind of optimization.

Now the shader is started and you render the screen quad with the VBScreenHelper class as usual, but you have to make sure that the correct render target is set for each pass. In your case you just have one pass and all you have to do is to reset it to the back buffer (you will always have to do that for the last pass in post-screen shaders, or else you will not see anything on the screen). For a more complex example you can check out the PostScreenGlow class.

Unit Test Result

After you are done with rendering the device, render states are restored (maybe you still want to render some 3D data after showing the shader). If you look at the code in the project you can also see some additional try and catch blocks to make sure that the render engine stays stable even if a shader crashes. The shader will just set to an invalid state and not be used anymore. An error is logged and the user will no longer see the post-screen shader, but the rest of the game still runs.

You should always provide alternatives if some code does not work or crashes. Most of the time the code is only providing visual elements to your game like this post-screen shader. The game is still the same even if you don't use this shader; it will just not look as pretty. In practice a shader will never crash and you don't have to worry about this for your final game, but during development you can easily mess up an effect parameter or try new things in the Pixel Shader, and you don't want your whole game or unit test to crash; it should still continue to run.

You should now see the result shown in Figure 8-12 when running the `TestPostScreenDarkenBorder` unit test. Feel free to play around with the shader and change code in your application. For example, you could try to render into a smaller render target like using only one quarter of the screen and see how this affects the final output (big blocky pixels).

You should also test out all post-screen shaders as early as possible on your Xbox 360 if you have one. This is very important because shaders can sometimes behave differently and you have to make sure that all render targets fit in the Xbox 360 memory and still perform well. The `PostScreenDarkenBorder` and the `RenderToTexture` classes are fully compatible with the Xbox 360; and they work great on Xbox 360 too.

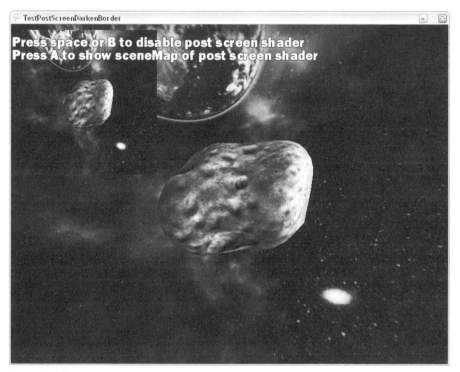

Figure 8-12

More Post-Screen Shaders

Changing the screen border, adding the sky in the background, and inverting or gray-scaling your scene map is nice, but there are many more possibilities and way more powerful post-screen shaders possible. The Rocket Commander game uses a pretty complex glow shader by faking HDR lighting in the alpha channel and performing several passes, adding radial motion blur by mixing the result with the scene map result from the last frame and doing a lot of glow effects.

The shader is called `PostScreenGlow` and it can be found in the Rocket Commander game (both the DirectX and the XNA version). Figure 8-13 shows the basic functionality; the shader is even more complex than that because it supports multiple Shader Models (1.1 and 2.0) and there are some optimizations built in to improve the performance for slow computers. In the Rocket Commander game the Shader Model can be chosen or you can disable the post-screen shader for very slow computers, but the game is only half the fun without the cool effects.

Well, that does look a little bit complicated and it is quite a lot of work to get it right, but there are many good shader books available and you can often achieve something quickly by taking a shader from someone else and playing around with it.

Figure 8-13

Before   After PostScreenGlow

Figure 8-14

The effect of this shader becomes most apparent if you hold two images right beside each other with and without the post-screen glow shader (see Figure 8-14).

Motion Blur

You already saw a simple way to do motion blur with post-screen shaders in the `PostScreenGlow` example. It may not seem simple to you, but the motion blur effect is the easiest part of the glow and it can be extended quite a bit by using the so-called "Per Pixel Motion Blur" effect. To do per pixel motion blur you have to save the velocity for every pixel in the scene with the help of a special shader. You don't have to render the full geometry with all the shaders; just render the objects that are moving and leave the rest of this special texture black (unused).

Then in the motion blur post-screen shader you take each pixel and determine how far it should be blurred based on the current direction the player is looking and overall velocity as well as the per pixel velocity and direction. Several newer racing games implemented this technique and also some upcoming game engines are able to do such effects, but it is not easy to implement and it also costs a lot of performance to render the special texture and then a lot of shader instructions to get it to work in the post-screen shader.

The way motion blur was implemented earlier this chapter works only with such big motion blur values because you always reuse the last screen. This means you only have to add 10% new motion blur and reuse 90% of the motion blur from the last screen. Per pixel motion blur could do that too, but it will be a lot harder to track if everything is moving (you, many objects in the scene, and so on) and therefore it is probably best to calculate the whole motion blur with many pixels trailing after each object in the per pixel motion blur shader.

One relatively simple trick is to divide the screen quad you are going to render for the post-screen shader into 10×10 grid pieces and then render them like the big quad, but allow the vertex shader to use different weights depending on how strong the motion blur should be for each vertex. See Figure 8-15 for a comparison between rendering motion blur with just a screen quad and using a 5×5 grid as an example. Using a 10×10 grid looks even a little bit better.

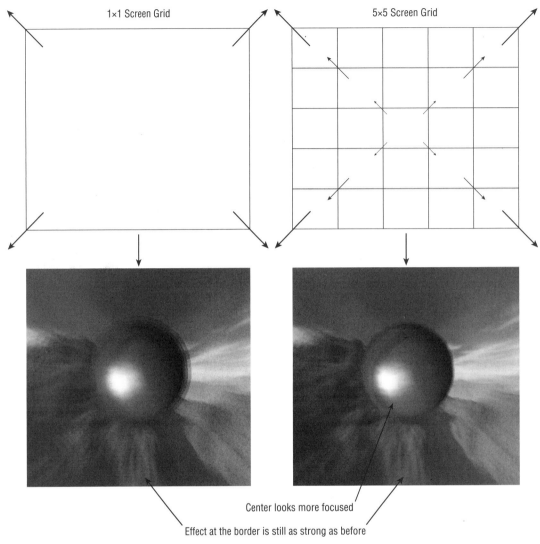

Figure 8-15

Color Correction

I often use color correction in my post-screen shaders because they are easy to use and can greatly influence the way the final output looks. It also helps you to make all textures look more equal and more realistic because the color correction affects all pixels, like real lighting situations in the outside world. For example, if you stay in a cave it is probably dark inside and only a little light comes from the outside world. But if you have some bright stone material it might look a lot brighter than the rest of materials in the cave. Using color correction shaders on the rendered scene will not fix this problem (because you should really put better objects in your cave that fit together in a better way), but it makes the scene a little bit better by changing all the color values a bit. For example, if you give the whole scene a dark look (brightness down), and add a little blue color to each pixel, then all materials will fit together better because the color values are more similar (see Figure 8-16). The scene in the figure is from a prototype game I coded one year ago. It was developed without any color correction shader and one day I said hey, why not do it like in the movies, where everyone uses a lot of color correction and contrast adjustment shaders. The result was pretty good and all new games I do will always have a color correction shader.

Figure 8-16

The basic code to do brightness effects is to just multiply the color with a constant (or variable if you want to change it dynamically). For example, 0.5 makes the whole image half dark, 2.0 makes it two times brighter, 0.0 makes it completely black, and so on. The following line costs only one shader instruction and you could even combine it with the color correction shader we will do later in this chapter and it will still only cost one shader instruction. Figure 8-17 shows the brightness effect in action.

```
return brightness * originalColorValue;
```

Figure 8-17

Changing the contrast is a little bit trickier. A value of 1.0 should let everything stay the same way, 0.0 should make the image completely gray (no more contrast left), and higher values should make the image a lot sharper. To achieve this effect you have to subtract 0.5 from each color channel first and then multiply the result with the contrast value and finally add 0.5 to each color channel again.

This way values below 1.0 make the image lose a lot of color and 0.0 makes it completely gray (because only the 0.5 you add at the end is used; the rest is canceled out). Higher values give the image more contrast by darkening dark values down and bright light color values up (see Figure 8-18).

```
return (originalColorValue-float3(0.5, 0.5, 0.5)) * contrast +
    float3(0.5, 0.5, 0.5);
```

Figure 8-18

To achieve the effect in Figure 8-16 use only very dense values close to 1 for the brightness and contrast. I used values like 0.96 for brightness and 1.2 for contrast. Additionally you can change the color by adding a little color to each resulting pixel.

Be aware that the green color is more visible than blue or red and as soon as you add or subtract more than 0.1 to any color channel, the final output will look way too colorful; use very small values between 0.01 and 0.05. The following code makes the output image more bluish and removes a little bit of the red color. It was used for an arctic world. In the desert you want probably orange tones, for a Vulcan world you might use more red colors, and so on.

```
inputColor = float3(
    inputColor.r-0.04f,
    inputColor.g,
    inputColor.b+0.05f);
```

This is only a very easy way to change the colors; if you want to do more complex operations or even optimize the color correction part of your shader you can use a matrix for each operation and then pre-calculate the result of all these matrices combined, and then you would only have to modify each pixel once. Here are some example matrices:

```
brightnessMatrix = float4x4(
    brightness, 0, 0, 0,
    0, brightness, 0, 0,
    0, 0, brightness, 0,
    0, 0, 0, 1);
```

```
contrastMatrix = float4x4(
  1, 0, 0, 0,
  0, 1, 0, 0,
  0, 0, 1, 0,
  -0.5, -0.5, -0.5, 1);
contrastMatrix *= float4x4(
  contrast, 0, 0, 0,
  0, contrast, 0, 0,
  0, 0, contrast, 0,
  0, 0, 0, 1);
contrastMatrix *= float4x4(
  1, 0, 0, 0,
  0, 1, 0, 0,
  0, 0, 1, 0,
  +0.5, +0.5, +0.5, 1);

addColorMatrix = float4x4(
  1, 0, 0, 0,
  0, 1, 0, 0,
  0, 0, 1, 0,
  -0.04, 0.0, +0.05, 1);
```

You can obviously do a lot more things with matrices like rotations or only scaling one row, and so on. Rotations can be useful to change the colors completely and switch color channels; scaling rows differently can be used to do a luminance effect you saw earlier. Feel free to play around.

Menu Effects

In the last game of this book you will also use a menu post-screen effect, which is pretty similar to the PostScreenGlow shader you saw earlier. It does not glow as strong, but the glow effect is still visible. More importantly it adds a film-like effect like in old movies, which looks funny when you see it animated. It might not fit into every game, but it was quite cool for the racing game and it fits to the menu music.

The basic idea here is to take a noise texture and go through it very slowly and power up the values so much that only the brightest points get used. Then the whole effect is stretched from the top to the bottom and several other effects are added on top of it (see Figure 8-19).

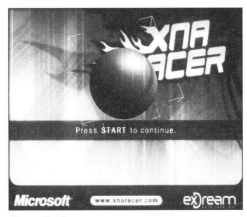

Figure 8-19

There are many more possibilities with post-screen shaders and sometimes you don't even want to do anything in the post-screen space, but it is just easier to remember and mark some pixel data in the rendering process and then later use it in a post-screen shader to show some effects with it. Not only can this be a lot faster than doing complicated calculations for each pixel, but in the post-screen space it is easier to do things like mixing neighboring pixels together, moving around a few pixels, and changing colors. For example, for shadow mapping shaders you first render the scene into a special shadow map rendered from the lights perspective and then you render the scene again and use the shadow map for comparisons. It works great, but if you have a lot of different shaders you need to modify all of them and often the shaders, especially for Pixel Shader 1.1, are at the instruction limit and you can't just add more instructions. Then you have to add another pass and render the geometry again.

Another approach is to render the shadowed scene again, but this time just for a scene shadow map, which is later used in a post-screen shader to mix in the normally rendered scene without any special shadow shaders with the shadows. Thanks to the screen space you can then also easily blur the shadow or change the intensity of the shadow without much trouble.

For more information about shaders, post-screen shaders, shadow mapping, and rendering techniques for today's hardware I recommend that you read one of the many good advanced books about shaders (yes, you are an advanced shader guy now if you read through all this) such as *Shader X*, *GPU Gems*, *Game Programming Gems*, and many vertex and Pixel Shader books you can easily find on sites like Amazon. I also recommend downloading the Nvidia SDK and checking out the many sample shaders.

Rocket Commander Game

We already talked so much about post-screen shaders, there is barely space left to talk about the Rocket Commander game. Well, that doesn't matter so much because the Rocket Commander game has already been out for a year now and there are many tutorials available about it, including the very popular video tutorials series on Coding4Fun (which you can find on www.msdn.com or in any search engine).

It would not make sense to repeat all that again here. The Rocket Commander game is also written in Managed DirectX for .NET 1.1; the game itself runs in .NET 2. Managed DirectX is quite different from XNA — a lot of things could be ported easily, but all the font rendering, sprite handling, and so on is completely different code in DirectX and several features like animated models are not supported yet in XNA (or at least they are not easy to import).

For that reason Rocket Commander XNA only shows the basic engine, but it is still a great game and a lot of fun, even on the Xbox 360 with the Xbox 360 controller, for which the game was never intended. This section only talks about the transition problems from MDX to XNA. If you want to know more about Rocket Commander please visit its website at www.RocketCommander.com and check out the video tutorials. Read the source code and documentation and play one of the many game modifications that exist today.

Performance in XNA

No one believes how well XNA performs. The main reason for that is that most of the XNA games that exist today are just simple 2D games, which do not care much about performance and 3D hardware effects and shaders. The other reason is that many people think it is bad for performance to wrap

DirectX to Managed DirectX or XNA, which just redirects the calls to the DirectX base framework. The important part here is how much code you can save and how much easier it is to write games in XNA, especially if you want to do a cross-platform game for both the Windows and Xbox 360 platforms. It would be a lot more work to get all these features by just using C++. You would probably need at least twice as many programmers to get everything to work as fast as an experienced XNA team could create a game. More likely you will also run into more problems with memory issues, pointer management, and overall manageability in an unmanaged environment.

I have proven in the past that most programmers are just plain wrong assuming Managed DirectX is a lot slower than DirectX; it does not really matter. If your code uses 100% of the GPU and 100% CPU you probably don't have a game, but just a benchmark to stress test or play around. Even in these situations Managed DirectX reaches almost the same performance (98%–99%), but for a real game it does not matter anyway because you will not have time to optimize every single line of your code. Instead you will focus on the important parts and try to get 10%–20% of the code, which is called the most often, to work as fast as possible. Adding performance improvements to the other 80%–90% takes five times longer and the improvements would only bring you a very few percent better frame rate.

Instead, you should focus on the game itself. The gamer does not care if the game runs at 59 or 58 frames; he wants a fun game and if you allow different settings he can even minimize the resolution and disable effects to get to a higher frame rate. Too many games today only focus on the graphics (like I do in this book, but at least I try also to show many cool game ideas, and hopefully you can use the base code and make your own games without writing graphics engines for a long time without writing any new game).

Anyway, the Rocket Commander code was heavily optimized and I did a lot of performance tests back when I developed the first version. The whole game was also coded in just four weeks and it is not always easy to get the most out of the shaders if you have such little time. I still managed to get over 100 frames per second on a medium PC with a Shader Model 2.0 card and a high screen resolution while showing up to 5000 asteroids (in some cases over 30 million polygons were rendered each second) at the same time each frame including collision testing and some other effects. Lower-end PCs, even ones completely without shader support, were still able to run the game. It did not look as pretty, but it ran very nicely.

Today computers are even faster and CPUs have multiple cores, which can be used to execute several tasks at the same time. The Xbox 360 has three cores too and it uses six threads, which execute all the game code you need. I don't know of any game today that really needs this immense CPU power on the Xbox 360; the GPU is pretty fast too, but especially on high resolutions it is still the GPU that will prevent you from getting better frame rates.

The Rocket Commander game is actually a nice example of how to split the work into two cores. The physics calculations and the pre-testing if asteroids and sectors are even visible take up half of the CPU time (sometimes even more). The rendering plus additional effects take the other half of the CPU time each frame. The physics can be done in parallel to the rendering because all the physics calculation checks is whether two asteroids intersect with each other and in that case, it bounces both of them off (see Figure 8-20) and makes sure they don't intersect anymore.

The next frame the newly updated physics positions, movement vectors, and so on can be used, which is only a slight disadvantage because the physics is now calculated for the next frame and not for the current frame (it would be too late trying to render the new physics positions because most of the asteroids will already be rendered when the physics update is complete). As you can see in the image you don't have to check every asteroid, only the ones near to each other, and this can even be optimized further by putting them into sectors, which helped to improve the physics performance by a factor of 10 in the original Rocket Commander.

The important thing here is that Rocket Commander XNA performs even better than the original. It is possible to play the game in HDTV 1080p resolution on the Xbox (or the PC) and still use all the graphics effects, use full anti-aliasing, and show several thousand asteroids at the same time at very high frame rates.

Figure 8-20

Moving from MDX to XNA

The base engine of Rocket Commander has quite similar concepts to the XnaGraphicEngine. In some places there are more features in the Rocket Commander engine like animated models or better handling and rendering of many asteroids. For example asteroids all use the same shaders and materials and allow the game to render them in a very efficient way. But some other features are implemented in an easier and better way in XnaGraphicEngine than in Rocket Commander like the font and sprite management in XNA. You also can take advantage of the new shader classes you wrote and you can even plug in new shaders if you want to play around with the visual appearance of Rocket Commander XNA a bit.

Please also note that some features like the animated model support or the occlusion testing for the lens flare effects in the original Rocket Commander are not possible in XNA yet. The occlusion testing is something that is just missing from the XNA Framework. I would guess it was too hard to get it to work on both the PC and the Xbox 360 the same way, but it is still bad for the lens flare effect because it will no longer disappear and blend in and out when an asteroid moves in front of the sun. The animated model can still be done by doing custom model processing or even introducing a new format for all the models, but you want to keep the port as simple as possible and you certainly don't want to re-export every single model and re-test it all over again.

The network code of the game was also ripped out in the Xbox 360 version because there isn't any access to the System.Net namespace on the Xbox 360. On the Windows platform the game still sends and receives high-scores to and from the Internet server via web services. All the levels and other game data is 100% compatible and even porting the mods to XNA would be possible, but I have other things to do. Feel free to write more Rocket Commander mods, especially on the XNA Framework. I'm always happy to receive emails from people all over the world using the code, writing mods, and telling me success stories by learning from the tutorials and the source code.

At the end of 2006 I wrote a long blog post on my website comparing MDX with XNA and talking all about the advantages and disadvantages of using XNA. If you worked with MDX before and are still wondering if XNA is worth the effort, read this article. In Rocket Commander XNA some new features were added, especially more unit tests and the multithreading that I will talk about in a second, but the overall number of source code lines decreased by more than 10%, which shows you that even porting a project makes it simpler. This effect is obviously even greater if you start fresh with an XNA project.

Using Threads to Improve Performance

The overall performance of Rocket Commander XNA is great on both Windows and the Xbox 360, especially when just doing some benchmarks and performance is absolutely perfect. The GPU is pushed to its limits and there is no reason why you should be afraid of Managed code. Windows performance is especially great; all my programs and games are completely GPU bound even in low resolutions and even when they only have one thread.

On the Xbox 360 the performance is a little bit worse and you have to take many things into consideration, which is hard because there is again not much documentation around. For example, the worst thing you can do on the Xbox 360 is to generate new data each frame, and even if you just create an enumerator by executing a foreach loop, it will affect your performance. The good thing is that you have three cores (and six hardware threads) at your fingertips, which allow you to optimize performance. It was possible for the Rocket Commander game to optimize the game loop a lot because the physics and update threads eat up almost 50% of the CPU time. On the PC it does not matter much because my GPU is slowing everything down (see Figure 8-21), but on the Xbox 360 I was able to almost double the frame rate using multiple threads. Nice.

Result and Screenshots

Rocket Commander XNA is a great game and it runs even better than the original, and it has now support for the Xbox 360 and the XNA Framework on the PC. Thanks to the new multithreading ability of the game and the fact that you can split up the physics and the rendering engine so easily, the game performs a lot better than before, the physics are now more precise, and the rendering engine has more time to render more asteroids if you like or add other cool effects.

Both games look so similar that it is hard to tell the difference between the original game and the XNA port. You will probably detect it only through the missing features (like animated models and occlusion checking for lens flares) or by just looking at the new game font. I added the XNA logo in the main menu to tell the difference between running the original game and the XNA version (see Figure 8-22).

I hope you have fun with the game. It is freely available like the original Rocket Commander game and you can use it for your own game ideas or just play around with it a little. Check out Figure 8-23 for a screenshot of Rocket Commander XNA in action.

Rocket Commander, Single-threaded (simplified):

OneGameLoop	⊗

AsteroidManagerUpdate	⊗	GameLogicAndUI	⊗	RenderModels	⊗	WaitForGPU	⊗

SectorUpdate	⊗	Physics	⊗	RenderAsteroids	⊗	RenderRest	⊗

...

Time for 1 Frame: 20ms → 50 fps

Rocket Commander XNA, Multi-threaded (simplified):

OneGameLoop	⊗

Thread1:

AsteroidManagerUpdate	⊗	GameLogicAndUI	⊗	RenderModels	⊗	WaitForGPU	⊗

RenderAsteroids	⊗	RenderRest	⊗

Thread2:

SectorUpdate	⊗	Physics	⊗	OtherUpdatesAndSleeping	⊗

Time for 1 Frame: 12ms → 80–90 fps

Figure 8-21

Figure 8-22

Figure 8-23

Challenge: Write an Edge Detection Shader

This chapter talked about a lot of post-screen shaders and covered almost every basic post-screen shader that exists, and you learned about the basic components to write similar shaders. For example, the color correction shader can be used to achieve sepia effects like in Figure 8-1. One shader I left out intentionally is the edge detection shader. It may not be useful for every single game, but there are a lot of other shaders that use the basic functionality of an edge detection shader. Here are some examples:

❑ Edge detection shaders for an evil alien-like look or for a high-tech special ops view mode that allows you to see much sharper in the night.

❑ Comic and toon shaders, which just take the input color and reduce it to very few colors, for example from a color table or simple image that maps each color value to certain predefined colors. Then the thick border lines are drawn for every 3D surface, which can be done via an edge detection shader quite easily. You could also improve it a bit by drawing the lines in 3D and then adding the solid geometry on top of it, leaving you with the outlines for each 3D object, which the edge detection shader can pick up more easily.

❑ Edge detection shaders can be used to add contrast to the scene or to find lines or contours. Edge detection is often the opposite of a blur effect, which mixes everything together making the final result sometimes washed out too much. An edge detection shader can help if you want a sharper image to start with before doing additional glow and blur effects.

❏   Edge detection shaders can also be used to create very artistic images that look like they were painted and not rendered. You just use a very high edge detection amount and add other filters like strain effects or the half-tone shader from Figure 8-1.

All you have to do is to create a simple edge detection filter. The basic idea is here to take several pixels from the original scene map and compare them with the neighboring pixels. In Shader Model 1.1 you can only take four texture inputs, and in Shader Model 2.0 only eight, therefore you are limited on how many pixels you can use in the Pixel Shader. Doing comparisons is also not that easy and not a good thing for Pixel Shader 1.1. Instead just take a center point, multiply it by 2, and then subtract two surrounding points (top and bottom, and left and right). Then take the gray-scale value with the help of the Luminance function of the result and you have your edges.

The following is the basic Pixel Shader code; if you are in Shader Model 2.0 you can do even more texture fetches. If you are unsure how to extend the shader please check out the edge detection shader of Nvidia's FX Composer. You should try to develop the whole shader in FX Composer anyway and then you can work on a C# class if you want to import it into your engine. The variables col1, col2, col3, and col4 are four colors from the scene map through four texture coordinates you passed to the Pixel Shader.

```
return Luminance(
    // Horizontal
    (col1*2.0f-col2-col3)+
    // Vertical
    (col2*2.0f-col1-col4));
```

If you managed to get your shader to work you should see something similar to Figure 8-24.

Figure 8-24

Summary

In this chapter you learned all about post-screen shaders and this concludes your graphics engine for now. Graphics effects are nice and can be a lot of fun to play around with, but this book is about game development and doing graphics work is only a part of it. In the next part of this book you will focus a little bit more on the other aspects like sound, input, and a general game engine. Some of that code was already used in the previous games and especially the Rocket Commander game uses sounds, advanced input classes, and also has a lot of game logic.

Here is a recap of some of the things that post-screen shaders can be used for:

❑ Sky cube mapping (okay, it is a pre-screen shader, but it works similarly).

❑ Rendering textures on top of the scene (blend overlay).

❑ Inverting the scene map (that's easy, just use 1-color).

❑ Turning the scene map into black and white with help of the Luminance function.

❑ Adding screen border effects, in this case to darken down the screen borders for a TV-like effect.

❑ Glowing techniques and how to get them to perform very fast through down-sampling.

❑ HDR faking by using an extra alpha channel in the glow shader. Alternatively you can try using better render targets supporting more than 8 bits per channel and allowing you to save HDR colors in the scene map, which then can later be used for real HDR effects.

❑ Edge detection (well, that was your part).

❑ Menu effects, noise textures in shaders, half-tone effects, and so on.

❑ Color correction including brightness changing, contrast adjustments, and adding colors to influence the overall look of the scene. The sepia effect is also possible with a color-correction post-screen shader.

❑ Motion blur, either per pixel or just for the whole screen. Additional tricks to improve the screen result by rendering a 10×10 screen grid instead of just one screen quad were also discussed.

❑ And many more shaders.

I hope you found these last chapters useful and you were able to create your XNA graphics engine in a short time thanks to the many samples I provided with each chapter. In this chapter you can test out many post-screen shaders with the source code of XnaGraphicEngine, which is now quite a big and powerful engine allowing you to work with shaders, 3D geometry, sprites, post-screen shaders, and many more things without having to worry about any implementation details because it is all handled for you.

Using a multithreaded solution also provided you with great performance results for the Rocket Commander XNA game, but it is harder to program multithreaded.

It is easy now to rely on the graphics engine and stop writing unit tests, but don't do that. It will hurt you later when you try to figure out why menu x does not work the way it should or unit y does this instead of that. With a menu unit test you can quickly find out what's wrong and a unit test for the in-game units is probably also a lot faster to test and debug than going through the whole game, setting everything up, and then waiting for the error to happen again.

More graphics effects, physics, and the racing game are discussed in the last part of this book, but now check out Part III, which also gives you another great game (say hello to my little shoot-'em-up) and you dive a little bit deeper into the details for sound, input, and game logic classes.

Part III: Improving Your Game Engine

9

Adding Sound with XACT

This chapter takes a closer look at XACT. XACT is the name for Microsoft's Cross-Platform Audio Creation Tool, which allows you to create audio projects for the Windows and Xbox 360 platforms. It is actually the only way to play sounds in XNA. That doesn't matter so much for the Windows platform because you can plug in any other sound engine you want (DirectSound of DirectX, OpenAL, FMod, and so on) and play sound or music this way. It is not that easy on the Xbox 360 because you can only use the XNA Framework here and it is absolutely not possible to use any other framework for playing sound. The reason you can't use anything but XACT is the fact that you cannot use any unmanaged code in XNA, and to play sound or use any low-level hardware on the Xbox 360 you would need unmanaged code to access it. For the same reason you cannot use any other graphics or input engine than the one XNA provides for you.

But XACT isn't all bad; the reason why it was implemented into XNA is to make sure it is possible to use the same sound content and sound playback code for both the Windows and the Xbox 360 platforms. For example, the Xbox 360 supports only XMA compression; the PC uses other compression formats for sound and music like MP3, OGG, ADPCM, and many other custom compression formats, but only ADPCM is supported in XACT. Voice over IP applications often use their own proprietary sound compression format because the human voice can be compressed better than music, for example. Sound effects are very short and small anyway, but you as a game developer usually want the highest possible quality for sound effects and therefore sound effects are often uncompressed or use lossless compressions. Music, on the other hand, takes up a lot of space. If your game is on a DVD or you have plenty of hard disk space you can waste, you could just store the music as uncompressed wav files or directly on the CD or DVD. For XNA games this is not an option because you can't access the DVD on the Xbox 360, and wasting a few hundred MB for just the music is not a good idea for your game.

In the past with DirectX or Managed DirectX applications you would most likely use DirectSound for the sound playback or use other frameworks like OpenAL or commercial sound engines like FMod. Even with these frameworks you will still have to do a lot of custom code; you have to decide which sound format is the best for you and you will have to worry about sound compression yourself. Additionally, you must implement a way to play music yourself too. For example,

DirectSound is really not usable for music — it just supports .wav files — but if you want to play MP3 or OGG music files, you have to use other frameworks like DirectShow, Windows MCI, ActiveX sound play-back codecs or other free and commercial frameworks and sound engines. Yes, you are right, this sounds like a lot of work. The actual code to play back sounds or music is very simple for most games. It gets a little bit more complicated if you want to use complex 3D sound calculations and if you want to support surround sound, but it is still way easier to program these things than to develop your 3D engine.

No DirectSound

I'm assuming that most of you have worked with DirectSound before and when you write your first game in XNA you will notice that the sound namespace is very different from DirectSound of DirectX. Take a quick look how DirectSound was used in Managed DirectX. First, you had to initialize the `DirectSound` device:

```
soundDevice = new DirectSound.Device();
soundDevice.SetCooperativeLevel(form, CooperativeLevel.Priority);
```

Now you can load all the sounds, but it can be a little bit more complicated to make sure you have multiple sound buffers and to catch the case when the file does not exist, which would cause DirectSound just to throw an `InvalidOperationException` with no additional error message. In the Managed DirectX Rocket Commander code, the following code was used to make sure all sound files exist and to make sure you can play back sounds multiple times:

```
if (File.Exists(Directories.SoundsDirectory + "\\" + filename) ==
  false)
{
  Log.Write("Sample " + filename + " was not found!");
  loaded = false;
  return;
} // if (File.Exists)

BufferDescription bufferDesc = new BufferDescription();
bufferDesc.StaticBuffer = true;
bufferDesc.ControlPan = true;
bufferDesc.ControlVolume = true;
bufferDesc.ControlFrequency = true;

buffer = new SecondaryBuffer[setNumberOfSimultaneousSounds];
channelVolume = new float[setNumberOfSimultaneousSounds];
channelPanning = new float[setNumberOfSimultaneousSounds];

buffer[0] = new SecondaryBuffer(
  Directories.SoundsDirectory + "\\" + filename,
  bufferDesc,
  Sound.Device);
defaultFrequency = buffer[0].Frequency;

for (int i = 1; i < buffer.Length; i++)
  buffer[i] = buffer[0];
```

```
    try
    {
      for (int i = 1; i < buffer.Length; i++)
        buffer[i] = buffer[0].Clone(Sound.Device);
    } // try
    catch { } // catch
```

And finally, the following is the code required to play the sound effect. Additionally, you can set the volume and panning of each sound buffer channel thanks to the code in the constructor of the `Sample` class (`ControlPan`, `ControlVolume`, `ControlFrequency`, and so on). The extra code to manage all the sound buffers and the properties for each sound (volume, panning, frequency) are not shown here because there is a lot of code in the `Sample` class of Rocket Commander. Take a look if you are interested further.

```
    // Make sure to start at position 0
    buffer[currentBufferNum].SetCurrentPosition(0);
    // And play the sound
    buffer[currentBufferNum].Play(0, BufferPlayFlags.Default);
```

In XNA you no longer need a `Sample` class and you can extend the `Sound` class to support everything you need, including the `MusicManager` of Rocket Commander, the `Sample` class, and everything else in the Sound namespace of Rocket Commander.

Because of the structure of XACT, which is discussed in a short while, you have to load the XACT project and the used wave and sound banks yourself. But don't worry; the code for that is very simple. You already used XACT in the first chapters for all the arcade games there.

```
    audioEngine = new AudioEngine("YourSoundProject.xgs");
    waveBank = new WaveBank(audioEngine, "Wave Bank.xwb");
    soundBank = new SoundBank(audioEngine, "Sound Bank.xsb");
```

And that's it; all you have to do to play a sound now is to call:

```
    soundBank.PlayCue(soundName);
```

Looks much easier, doesn't it? You might ask about all the extra functionality you had to implement for DirectSound. No, it is not missing, but you have to think differently about sound in XNA. Sound files are no longer managed completely by the custom code of your game. Instead the XACT sound project contains all the predefined sound parameters for you. Instead of modifying each sound volume yourself or changing the pitching to reuse existing sounds yourself, you could set all this inside of the XACT tool. This is especially useful to make sure all sound effects are at the same volume level and to make sure the music is not too loud. You can even specify that certain sounds are only allowed to be played once (like the background music) or if it is allowed to play multiple instances of the same sound for firing sounds or explosions. You learn more about this later in this chapter.

Handling .wav Files

For both DirectSound and XACT all your sound files must be in the .wav file format, especially for all sound effects. If you have different sound files in other formats, you have to convert them first. For example, MP3 files are not supported and you cannot play them in DirectSound or just drop them into your XACT project. You have to convert them to .wav files first. Please also note that certain .wav files are not supported in XACT and you will get a warning message that the format is not supported when you add the sound files into a wave bank in XACT.

It is not easy to make sure a music file is in the correct format and that it can be compressed the best way possible in XACT for both the Xbox 360 and the Windows platform (see Figure 9-1).

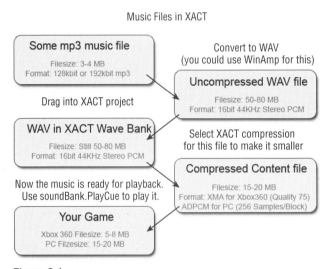

Figure 9-1

Just convert all your sounds to 16-bit 44 KHz Stereo PCM wav files to make sure you can compress them. Even if your music is only mono, you still have to save it in stereo and if you have 8-bit PCM files, don't try to use them. Convert to 16-bit and stereo or else XACT will not allow you to compress the sound files correctly. For 8-bit files you will get the error message shown in Figure 9-2, and mono files compress badly. You will also lose quality for your 16-bit stereo files, but choosing the right XMA and ADPCM compression level for you might tweak the sound quality a little bit.

Figure 9-2

Please note that music files are not really supported by XACT and it is a much better tool for sound effect files than for music files. For the PC platform using ADPCM files for your music might not make much sense if you have MP3 files and already have some code to play them back. On the Xbox 360 platform you currently have no choice but to use XMA compression and XACT for your music files.

You can use compression for your sound effects too, but I recommend that you try to use high compression ratios. For a PC game it is also very uncommon to use heavily compressed sound files; instead you will just use files of lower quality (22KHz mono) because loading them is much faster, and using MP3 files for sounds is impractical because the CPU would have to decompress them every time you play them or you would have to decompress all files at the start of your game, which could take a while. In most cases adding a few extra MB to your game will not affect much, but if you are an optimization freak like I am and you want to make sure the game is as small as possible without losing any feature or noticing any quality drop, you will still try to compress all the files with various options until everything is small and still sounds right.

I also compressed all texture files of all games in this book several times and used different formats to find out which one was the optimal format for each texture. For example, menu and interface graphics are compressed very well with the PNG format because it stores the bitmap in a lossless manner, but PNG files are just too big for model textures or landscape textures. In these cases DDS files are used, which also have the advantage of saving video memory, which is another important point for the Xbox 360. Don't waste your main memory, disk space, or video memory — all of them are very rare on a console.

As an example, the Rocket Commander game from the previous chapter uses about 15 sound files (see Figure 9-3) and with compression enabled the game is nearly 1 MB smaller on the Xbox 360. Not much, but every bit counts.

Enough talk about the basics and file formats; next you create your first sound project in XACT.

Name	Size	PC Format	PC Compressed	PC Ratio	Xb Format	Quality	Xb Compressed	Xb Ratio	Uses	Loop	Notes	Rate	Bi
Speed	137.244	ADPCM	37.520	27%	XMA	80	??	??		N		22050	16
Victory	164.238	ADPCM	44.940	27%	XMA	80	??	??		N		22050	16
Whosh1	10.038	ADPCM	2.730	27%	XMA	80	??	??		N		22050	16
Whosh2	12.150	ADPCM	3.290	27%	XMA	80	??	??		N		22050	16
Whosh3	22.578	ADPCM	6.160	27%	XMA	80	??	??		N		22050	16
Whosh4	45.140	ADPCM	12.320	27%	XMA	80	??	??		N		22050	16
Bomb	56.304	ADPCM	15.539	28%	XMA	80	??	??		N		22050	16
Click	12.504	ADPCM	3.569	29%	XMA	80	??	??		N		44100	16
Defeat	174.598	ADPCM	47.740	27%	XMA	80	??	??		N		22050	16
Explosion	75.280	ADPCM	20.580	27%	XMA	80	??	??		N		22050	16
ExtraLife	33.726	ADPCM	9.240	27%	XMA	80	??	??		N		22050	16
Fuel	65.422	ADPCM	17.920	27%	XMA	80	??	??		N		22050	16
Health	104.232	ADPCM	28.490	27%	XMA	80	??	??		N		22050	16
Highlight	28.276	ADPCM	7.979	28%	XMA	80	??	??		N		44100	16
RocketMotor	66.132	ADPCM	18.060	27%	XMA	80	??	??		N		44100	16

16 Waves (0 unused)

Figure 9-3

Using XACT

XACT used to be a tool just for Xbox 360 developers and you could not get it easily. You would have to be a certified Xbox 360 developer and have access to the XDK (Xbox Development Kit). Not an easy thing even if you are a professional game developer and have worked many years in the industry, if you ask me.

But all that has changed. Microsoft decided to include XACT in the DirectX SDK a year ago and though not many have used it for PC-only games, XACT becomes important now for XNA game development. It is the only way to get any sound files for XNA on the Xbox 360. You don't have to install the DirectX SDK to get access to the XACT tool; it is also included in the XNA Game Studio Express Installation. You can find it under Start ➪ All Programs ➪ Microsoft XNA Game Studio Express ➪ Tools ➪ XACT Auditioning Utility. If you use another version of XACT please make sure that it is supported by XNA; for example, the August 2006 DirectX SDK has XACT 2.0 too, but it saves content files in version 40. The October 2006 DirectX SDK and the XNA Framework use version 41 content files, which are not compatible with previous versions. If you load older XACT sound projects you might get very strange errors like files are missing or just get an `InvalidOperationException`. Future versions might also behave differently. To make sure your XACT project is supported, check the content version in the .xap file (which is just a simple text file; you can open it with any text editor you want).

The .xap file is structured in a simple way and looks similar to xml files. The version numbers are a little bit confusing, but you just have to check for version 13 (which is content version 41 of the XACT tool and can be checked in its About dialog box; see Figure 9-4). Older versions like 11 or 12 (of older DirectX SDKs) are not supported. This issue can also happen to you if you open up an early XNA project from the XNA beta times (August till October 2006), which still used the old XACT tool.

```
Signature = XACT2;
Version = 13;
Options
{
}
Global Settings
{
[...]
```

Figure 9-4

If you just want to make a simple change to some sound volume of a sound file inside your XACT project inside Visual Studio, you can just open the .xap file in the text editor of Visual Studio and edit the value yourself instead of minimizing Visual Studio, searching for the .xap file, opening it, searching for the correct location where the volume is stored, and then changing the value with the XACT tool.

The best thing that can happen to you as a game developer for sounds is when you have someone that does the sound effects and music for you. Try to explain the XACT tool to this person and you won't have to worry much about sound, volumes, and formats anymore. That's business for the sound guy. Unfortunately, most small teams don't have a dedicated person for sound and if you program on your own, make your own graphics and other game content files, you will also have to make your own sound effects. Try to use existing sound effects or freely available sounds at first and exchange them later. For music it often makes sense to choose similar music, maybe even music from your MP3 library, just for testing and presenting your game. For the final version you will need your own music, of course; you can't just use someone else's music and put it in your game. Some music files are free to use, but most music you hear every day is not free to use. Getting sound effect files is a little bit easier. For some simple sound effects you are also allowed to use the sound effect files of the example games from this book. I also suggest that you search for free sound effect sites on the Internet if you don't have any of your own sound effect files or know anyone that can help you out.

To make things a little bit more interesting here you are going to create the sound project for the game at the end of Part III in this book: XNA Shooter, which is a simple shoot-'em-up style game with cool 3D graphics, sound effects, and keyboard, mouse, and Xbox 360 controller support (which is discussed in detail in the next chapter).

Creating Projects

After you open the XACT tool you will see a new empty project (see Figure 9-5). It does not contain any sound files, wave or sound banks yet, but certain variables and settings are already created for you in each new project:

❑ The project tree, which always contains the same root elements. You cannot change it.

❑ Two default categories: Default and Music, which you can use to mark your sound files as sound effects or music files to make your sound files behave differently.

❑ One global variable, SpeedOfSound, which is always 343.5 and 4 cue instance variables for the Distance, Doppler Shift, Number of Cue Instances, and Orientation Angle. All these variables are only important for 3D sounds, which are sadly not possible in XNA yet. More about this issue will be discussed when you write the code to play back sound effects.

❑ A global effect path preset with nothing in it.

❑ All the other root elements are empty. You have to create the child elements for each of them yourself by either clicking on the toolbar or just right-clicking on the element and selecting New. For example, "New Wave Bank" creates a new wave bank.

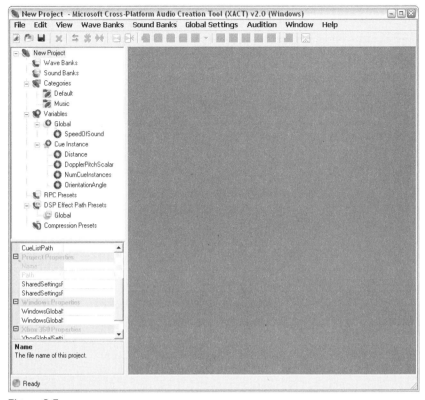

Figure 9-5

To get any wav files into your new XACT project you have to create a wave bank first, which stores all the wav files into a wave bank, and is then loaded and used by your game. This is more work than just loading wav files yourself, but the idea behind XACT is to give the sound artist more flexibility in setting all kinds of sound parameters himself instead of nagging the programmer every time he wants to tweak some sound effect. This will not help you much when you have to do the XACT work and the programming yourself anyway, but XACT gives your project at least a little bit of organization for your sound files and you always know where you can change any sound parameters without having to go into your game code. The disadvantage of using XACT is that you can no longer dynamically load sound files; all content files (like compiled models) have to be created and loaded when you start your game, and nothing can be added while the game is running. This inflexibility was very annoying to me at first because I always add stuff dynamically while writing and debugging my unit tests, but once I got used to it, it was fine. I now create all sound files and the XACT project early in the project and use only existing sounds in the unit tests. Later the sound project is changed from time to time.

Creating Your Wave Bank

To create a wave bank for your project you can either right-click Wave Banks and select "New Wave Bank," use the menu, or you can use the toolbar icon for creating a wave bank (eighth entry, the orange-white rectangle with the wave effect; see Figure 9-5). The wave bank is just the storage for all the sound files you want to use. You can even have different wave banks; for example, if you have multiple levels in your game and you only want to load the wave files for the current level, you could separate the wave files and optimize your game this way. All projects of this book and all other projects I ever made only contain one wave bank, and other than separating the music files and sound files to support streaming the music files, I really don't think it is important to have multiple wave banks, and you will probably never need them either.

After you have created your wave bank you can drag and drop wav files into it or alternatively use the "Insert Wave Files" entry from the context menu. Figure 9-6 shows all the sound files you are going to use for the XNA Shooter game imported into your newly created XACT project.

As you can see all sound files are still unused, which is indicated by the italic red font. As soon as you add these wave files to a sound bank, they become green. But before you do that you should make sure all of the files have the correct settings. By default no compression is chosen and most of the sound files are pretty small; except for the music file, all sound effects are below 1 MB data. The music file, which takes a whopping 36 MB of disk space, is 3 1/2 minutes long and in the format discussed previously (16-bit 44KHz Stereo PCM).

If you want to compress the music sound file, click it and select your desired compression preset in the wave properties panel. It currently shows <none>, but if you click the drop-down list, it has no other

Figure 9-6

options for you. You have to create a compression preset first and then you can use it for any wave file you want (or just assign it to the whole wave bank). XACT works similarly with other presets too. For example, if you want to create a custom variable for a sound effect, you have to create it first in the variables section and then you can select and use it in the sound bank.

Compressing Music Data

To create a new compression preset click Compression Presets and select "New Compression Preset" (see Figure 9-7). Now enter a name for your compression; in this case you just want to create a music compression schema. The notes field is just for you and is never used anywhere outside the XACT tool. Lots of other panels also have note fields and optional parameters you will not need. You will probably find XACT very confusing when using it for the first time. I didn't like it at first either, but after a while you get used to it and you have to remember that this is the only way to get any sound files onto the Xbox 360 with XNA. If you create a Windows-only game, you can still use DirectSound or other sound engines, which might be simpler to use or have other advantages. Finally, set Windows compression (only ADPCM is available) with 128 samples per block (the default). Higher values will make the file smaller, but you can lose a little quality. Thirty-two samples per block is the highest ADPCM quality, but the file is about 30% bigger.

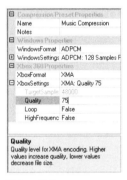

Figure 9-7

For the Xbox 360 you can only select XMA, but the compression is much better here. You might wonder why there are so many options when you can only choose one compression anyway. Well, that's XACT and we all can just hope that we get more compression formats in the future. XMA is fine for the Xbox 360; sometimes it produces file sizes that are a little too big, but it sounds good and works great. But ADPCM for the Windows platform is just unusable. It sounds worse than MP3 files and it is 4–5 times bigger. WMA or MP3 support would be great here.

Unfortunately, XACT does not show the resulting file size for XMA right away. You have to compile the project first, and then it shows you how compressed each wave is in the XMA format for the Xbox 360. To compile the project you can click the last toolbar button or just press F7. By default the project will compile to the Windows platform and you will still not see the XMA compression results. To finally get there you have to switch to the Xbox 360 output in the View menu, then compile the XACT project, and your wave bank will show the file sizes for the Xbox 360 too (the PC Compression rates are always shown and they are always in the same ratio; 27% for the default ADPCM setting).

The following table shows the compression ratios for the `XnaShooterGameMusic.wav` file (36 MB uncompressed).

Compression	File Size	Compression Rate
Uncompressed	36 MB	100%
MP3 with 192kbit	4.8 MB	13%
MP3 with 128kbit	3.1 MB	8.5%
AccPlus with 48kbit, similar to MP3 192kbit	1.2 MB	3%
AccPlus with 24kbit, similar to MP3 96kbit	0.6 MB	1.6%
OGG with 160kbit	3.8 MB	11%
XACT ADPCM 32 samples per block	12.5 MB	34%
XACT ADPCM 128 samples per block (default)	9.9 MB	27%
XACT ADPCM 512 samples per block	9.3 MB	26%
XACT XMA 100% Quality	14.3 MB	40%
XACT XMA 90% Quality	8.9 MB	25%
XACT XMA 75% Quality	5.5 MB	15%
XACT XMA 60% Quality (default)	4.7 MB	13%
XACT XMA 30% Quality	3.5 MB	10%
XACT XMA 10% Quality	2.9 MB	8%

The lower-quality XMA files look very similar to the MP3 in size, but the quality is much worse. I would not recommend using any XMA file with very low compression settings. Use 50% or higher; the file size is still very similar with 60% (the default setting) and 75% is one of my favorite settings because for very good quality settings the file stays very small (below 15%, similar to MP3 with 192kbit, and also sounds similar). If you just have a game without music or with just one track this all will not matter to you, but if you have 10+ music tracks in your game you want to think twice about the compression settings and explore all possibilities.

After setting the new compression for the music file you should now get file sizes of around 5–6 MB for the Xbox directory and 10 MB for the Win directory (see Figure 9-8). For the Rocket Commander XNA project these file sizes are almost twice as much because you use two music files there. In later games of this book more music is used and the file sizes go up even more.

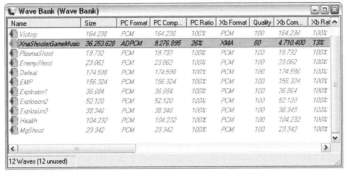

Figure 9-8

Sound Banks

Although you can compile the project and even load it in your XNA game, you can't use any sound yet because the XACT project just contains wave files right now. But for playback you need sound cues, which have to be created in a sound bank first. Again you have the opportunity to create multiple sound banks here, but you probably will never need to do that.

The simplest way to get all the wav files working is to drag them over to your sound bank. But wait, where is the sound bank? You don't have one yet. Similarly to the wave bank you have to create it first. You can do this by clicking the Sound Banks entry or clicking the second orange icon in the toolbar (the one with the orange wave going over the orange-white box on the right side). The new sound bank is just named "Sound Bank"; if you just have one wave bank and one sound bank, just leave the default names. If you have multiple wave or sound banks you should name them properly so you can find them more easily.

To drag all wave files from the wave bank over to your sound bank you should position the windows in a way that allows you to see both of them completely. The sound bank window consists of two parts: the sound names on the top and the cue names on the bottom. Select all files from the wave bank and drag them over to the sound names section of the sound bank now (see Figure 9-9). Each sound here can get additional settings like changing the volume, frequency (pitch), or applying other variations or effects. You can add the same wave file multiple times and give it different sound names. For more complex games you can even mix several wave files in multiple tracks and blend them on top of each other, then for playback this "mix" is used instead of a wave file. To add more than one track to a sound name just drag another file on top of it and XACT will automatically create a second track for it. However, you will not use this feature in this chapter.

While you are editing the sounds in the sound bank you should make sure that the music (XnaShooterGameMusic) uses the category Music instead of Default (you can edit that in the sound properties panel on the left side). I usually also tell the music category to play sounds softer than the default sounds because I want the music to be more in the background. In your game you can use the music category to control the volume of the music if you like. Additionally, you probably want to make sure only one music file is played at a time (maybe you call a `StartMusic` method several times or you just have multiple music files and you don't want to stop and restart them yourself).

For optimal music playback you should put all music files you want to play at a certain part of your game randomly into one sound bank entry (for example, `MenuMusic` and `GameMusic`; see Rocket Commander XNA as an example). Then click "Play Wave" on the right side of the sound bank window when the music sound entry is selected. Here you can force to loop this sound; some sounds are already looped, but for music it is always best to force it to make sure all music files work fine.

Finally you have to make sure only one music file is played at a time, and if another music file is selected a nice fade-over effect would also be nice. Luckily, XACT provides all that for you. You could now set instance limiting and fade in/out durations for each single music file or you could be cleverer and just set it once for the `Music` category (see Figure 9-10). By default `LimitInstances` is set to false; once you set it to true the properties below it become active. If you try to play another music item now after one music item is already started, an exception is thrown because `BehaviorAtMax` is set to `FailToPlay`. Change it to `Replace` for the correct behavior for music playback. For the rest of the settings see Figure 9-10.

Figure 9-9

Figure 9-10

Cue Variables

If you want to you can compile the project again now, but in your XNA code you still have no access to any sound effects. XNA allows you to access only sound cues, which have to be created first. This step is quite easy — just select all sound names and drag them down to the cue section of the sound bank window. The names are automatically taken from the filenames, but you can rename any entry if you like. I usually rename the music files to make access in XNA a little easier.

Another cool feature you can use for your XNA Shooter game is to assign multiple sound effects to one single sound cue. You'll use this feature for the explosion sound effect. You have three explosion wave files, but for simplicity you just want to tell XACT to play an explosion and it should randomly choose between one of the explosions for you. To do that remove the Explosion2 and Explosion3 sound cues from the cue list again by selecting them and pressing the Del key. Now rename the Explosion1 cue to just Explosion. Finally, drag both the Explosion2 sound name and the Explosion3 sound name onto the Explosion sound cue. You should now see what's shown in Figure 9-11. Tip: To make editing a little easier, make the sound bank window bigger or maximize it. XACT sometimes messes with you and when scrollbars appear and disappear all the time you might drop entries to the wrong location or duplicate items unwillingly (happens to me all the time).

Figure 9-11

You might also notice that I renamed the game music sound cue to just `GameMusic` to make it easier to enter the name in your XNA code. Also make sure all the other sound cue names are named in an easy to remember way.

After compiling the project again you can use the XACT project in XNA now and access all the sound cues. Please note that you don't have to compile the XACT project yourself all the time in XACT; XNA will automatically do that for you if you add the .xap project file to your XNA Game Studio project. Alternatively you can also just add the compiled files and load them yourself in XNA. It does not matter how you do it, but the .xap file in your XNA project is certainly the most comfortable solution. When using XACT, however, I recommend pressing F7 to compile the project a lot in a similar way you would test a newly written unit test all the time until it works fine.

Other Effects

XACT allows you to set other effects and sound parameters, which is especially useful for 3D sound effects, where you can set all kinds of parameters for your sound effects. Combined with a little custom programming you can do very powerful things like changing sound effects depending on the location they are played at, and automatically detecting halls from 3D geometry or open space. Your engine might also distort effects if they are played under water or after the player has been hit by a grenade. The possibilities are endless.

For this little game you won't need any special effects, but as an example I will show you how to create a custom variable that allows you to change the frequency (pitch) of a sound effect during run-time. Changing it directly in XACT is easy, but you don't have direct access to these settings in XNA. You have to expose a public cue variable first, and you must make sure the sound uses this custom variable.

This is not just for fun. For both the Rocket Commander XNA and the game in the last part of this book you need this effect to distort the motor sound of the rocket or the car you are currently driving with depending on the current speed.

To create your new cue instance variable click "Cue Instance" and select "New Cue Instance Variable" from the popup menu. You can type in anything you want here and use whatever values you like; they are not bound to anything yet. In this case you call the new variable `Pitch` and allow a range of –100 to +100; the rest of the properties can stay as they are (see Figure 9-12).

Name	Scope	Control	Initial Value	Value	Min	Max	Type
OrientationAngle	CueInstance	Local	0	0	-180	180	Public
DopplerPitchScalar	CueInstance	Local	1	1	0	4	Public
SpeedOfSound	Global	Local	343,5	343,5	0	1000000	Public
NumCueInstances	CueInstance	Monitored	0	0	0	1024	Public
Distance	CueInstance	Local	0	0	0	1000000	Public
Pitch	CueInstance	Local	0	0	-100	100	Public

Figure 9-12

Next you have to make sure XACT does something useful with this variable. You can set it now and assign it to any sound effect, but it will do nothing but store the value yet. In this case you can use the existing parameters of the RPC Presets (Runtime Parameter Control), but the selections are very limited right now (you can only change the Volume, Pitch, and Reverb Send Level, whatever that is). Maybe more options will come in the future. For example, it is not possible to set the panning for Rocket Commander XNA, which was used in the Managed DirectX version to fake 3D sound effects. If XACT would support 3D sounds, this would not matter because you could easily do real 3D sound calculations, but sadly the 3D listener was dropped after the first XNA beta. It is possible to set 3D sound parameters in XACT and you could use them in native XACT projects, but XNA does not support it yet (not funny if you had implemented it before like I did and then everything stops working).

Anyway, for changing the pitch of a sound effect, you can easily use a new RPC Preset. Just click RPC Presets and add a new RPC Preset; call it RPC Pitch or just leave the default name. Select `Sound::Pitch` as the parameter and use the newly created `Pitch` variable. Now you can drag the left and right points in the graph below to let –12 equal –100 of your `Pitch` variable and +12 equal +100 (see Figure 9-13).

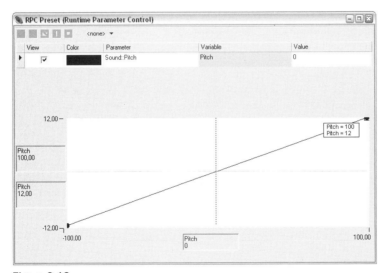

Figure 9-13

The final thing you have to do before this preset can be used is to assign all sounds to the preset that should be able to use this new variable. To do that just drag a sound file from the sound bank (don't use a wave or cue, they won't work) onto the PRC Preset.

The following code can be used to start a sound cue and change the pitch cue variable dynamically. If you just want to set a static pitch value don't go through this trouble; just create a new cue in XACT and set different pitch values. But for motor sounds you have to change the pitch dynamically and therefore you have to go through all this trouble.

```
rocketCue = soundBank.GetCue("RocketMotor");
rocketCue.Play();
// Set the global volume for this category
```

```
motorsCategory.SetVolume(MathHelper.Clamp(volume, 0, 1));
// Set pitch from -55 to +55 (little more than half the max values)
rocketCue.SetVariable("Pitch", 55 * MathHelper.Clamp(pitch, -1, 1));
```

As you will see in a second the rest of the Sound class is even easier and you will probably spend most of the time in XACT and then code your Sound class in a matter of minutes.

In the preceding example you can also see a way to change the volume for a category. Changing the volume of a cue directly is not supported by default, but you could create a volume cue variable the same way you just created the pitch variable to set custom volume values to your sound cues.

Sound Class

Creating the sound class is really simple. You already saw several sound classes in the first chapters and sound cue playback is easy. To make your life even easier you can define an enum with all the sound cue names in it. This way you make sure that every sound cue really exists and you don't mistype any sound. Another great advantage of this approach is IntelliSense, which will now show you all the available sound cues that are hidden in the XACT project if you don't have an enum like this. Spending two minutes to write this enum is the most valuable thing you can do for sound playback in XNA. Playing a sound cue is easy now with help of the Play method in the Sound class.

```
/// <summary>
/// Play
/// </summary>
/// <param name="soundName">Sound name</param>
public static void Play(string soundName)
{
  if (soundBank == null)
    return;

  try
  {
    soundBank.PlayCue(soundName);
  } // try
  catch (Exception ex)
  {
    Log.Write("Playing sound " + soundName + " failed: " +
      ex.ToString());
  } // catch
} // Play(soundName)

/// <summary>
/// Play
/// </summary>
/// <param name="sound">Sound</param>
public static void Play(Sounds sound)
{
  Play(sound.ToString());
} // Play(sound)
```

You can also make the string version private to only allow the `Sounds` enum version. In case the sound bank could not be initialized in the constructor (for example, if the file is missing) this method will immediately return and you are not able to play any sounds. A log file error was already reported in the constructor if that happened. Then you just call `PlayCue` to play and forget about the sound cue. In case this fails you log an error message, but you don't throw the exception down to the caller because you always want to have the sound be played and not to interrupt your program logic just because some sound file is missing or some effect did not work out.

As you saw before you can also use the `GetCue` method to remember a sound cue and then do multiple things with it. This is also useful if you want to stop the cue yourself instead of waiting until it is finished playing. As an example, this is used to stop music playback:

```
someSoundCue = soundBank.GetCue("SomeSound");
someSoundCue.Play();

...

someSoundCue.Stop(AudioStopOptions.Immediate);
```

Though most of the `Sound` class is the same for most of the projects in this book, take a look at the differences and the special functionality because the basic playback code was already discussed (see Figure 9-14).

Figure 9-14

The first thing you will notice is the different sound cue names in the `Sounds` enum. Both Rocket Commander XNA and the Racing Game use the custom pitch cue variable discussed a minute ago. The XNA Shooter game does not use anything special; you just start the music at the beginning of the game, and then play all sound effects as you need them and that's it.

To make typing in the code to play sounds more comfortable, several helper methods were created. For example, `PlayExplosionSound` just replaces the following code making it faster and easier to write the code required to play this sound effect:

```
Sound.Play(Sound.Sounds.Explosion);
```

For music playback two additional methods are added, which also keep track of the music cue in case you want to stop or restart the music: `StartMusic` and `StopMusic`.

There is also a unit test in each sound class to check if the sound playback works the way you want it to, which is also used to check if all sounds have the proper volume settings. This is the unit test from the Rocket Commander XNA `Sound` class:

```
/// <summary>
/// Test play sounds
/// </summary>
public static void TestPlaySounds()
{
  TestGame.Start(
    delegate
    {
      if (Input.MouseLeftButtonJustPressed ||
        Input.GamePadAJustPressed)
        Sound.Play(Sounds.Bomb);
      else if (Input.MouseRightButtonJustPressed ||
        Input.GamePadBJustPressed)
        Sound.Play(Sounds.Click);
      else if (Input.KeyboardKeyJustPressed(Keys.D1))
        Sound.Play(Sounds.GameMusic);
      else if (Input.KeyboardKeyJustPressed(Keys.D2))
        Sound.Play(Sounds.MenuMusic);
      else if (Input.KeyboardKeyJustPressed(Keys.D3))
        Sound.Play(Sounds.Explosion);
      else if (Input.KeyboardKeyJustPressed(Keys.D4))
        Sound.Play(Sounds.Fuel);
      else if (Input.KeyboardKeyJustPressed(Keys.D5))
        Sound.Play(Sounds.Victory);
      else if (Input.KeyboardKeyJustPressed(Keys.D6))
        Sound.Play(Sounds.Defeat);
      else if (Input.KeyboardKeyJustPressed(Keys.D7))
      {
        Sound.PlayRocketMotorSound(0.75f);
        Sound.ChangeRocketMotorPitchEffect(0.5f);
      } // else if
      else if (Input.KeyboardKeyJustPressed(Keys.D8))
        Sound.StopRocketMotorSound();
```

```
        TextureFont.WriteText(2, 30,
          "Press 1-8 or A/B or left/right "+
          "mouse buttons to play back sounds!");
    });
} // TestPlaySounds()
```

Finally, the Update method is called automatically by the Update method of your BaseGame class inside the graphics engine. The Update method just makes sure that all parameters, looping, and timing values are updated inside XACT for you.

Rocket Motor Sound

Take a quick look at the Rocket Motor sound from Rocket Commander XNA. You already saw all the code required for this to work, but it might be nice to see it all thrown together and compatible with the Rocket Commander engine, which was written for DirectSound initially, but works fine with XACT now too:

```
/// <summary>
/// Play rocket motor sound
/// </summary>
public static void PlayRocketMotorSound()
{
  // Get new cue everytime this is called, else we get Xact throwing
  // this: The method or function called cannot be used in the manner
  // requested.
  rocketMotorSound = soundBank.GetCue(Sounds.RocketMotor.ToString());
  // Plays the sound looped, set in XACT
  rocketMotorSound.Play();
  // Make motor category a little silent
  motorCategory.SetVolume(0.86f);
} // PlayRocketMotorSound(volume)

/// <summary>
/// Change rocket motor pitch effect
/// </summary>
/// <param name="pitchFactor">Pitch factor</param>
public static void ChangeRocketMotorPitchEffect(float pitchFactor)
{
  rocketMotorSound.SetVariable("Pitch",
    55 * MathHelper.Clamp(pitchFactor - 1, -1, 1));
} // ChangeRocketMotorPitchEffect(pitchFactor)

/// <summary>
/// Stop rocket motor sound
/// </summary>
public static void StopRocketMotorSound()
{
  rocketMotorSound.Stop(AudioStopOptions.Immediate);
} // StopRocketMotorSound()
```

To start the rocket sound you just call the PlayRocketMotorSound method after a mission starts, then you modify it during the flight with the help of the ChangeRocketMotorPitchEffect method:

```
// Adjust rocket playback frequency to flying speed
Sound.ChangeRocketMotorPitchEffect(0.66f + speed * 0.9f);
```

And finally `StopRocketMotorSound` can be called to stop the rocket sound when you die or the mission is over.

The gear sound logic in the racing game works in a similar way, but it is a little bit more complicated because you have 13 different gear motor sounds and not just one rocket motor sound like in Rocket Commander XNA. Check out the `Sound` class of the racing game for more details.

Whoosh, What Was That?

The original Rocket Commander game used its own 3D sound calculation formula and used the volume and panning properties of a DirectSound sample to achieve the correct effect for the player. In XNA it's sadly not possible to change the panning. All sounds are played the way they are created and set in XACT. For 3D sounds you should use real 3D sound code anyway and in the XNA beta 1 I wrote some code to play 3D sounds and have a 3D listener object moving around the 3D world.

This 3D listener object is now missing from XNA; you can't use 3D sound effects currently. Hopefully this will change in the future and I will certainly update the code for the games in this book when 3D sounds are possible again, but for now you can only play back sounds in mono; there's no stereo or surround sound support.

In case you can use X3DAudio and X3DAudioListener (the classes might have different names; it is just important that you can somehow set and play 3D audio and that you can position yourself with the help of the 3D listener class), the following code could be used to play 3D sounds after you set all important cue variables:

```
// Setup 3D listener for 3D sound
Sound.Listener = new X3DAudioListener(
  zAxis, yAxis, cameraPosition, movementVector);
```

Now set the emitter for each sound you want to play in your 3D world and play the 3D audio instances. Currently there is no C# code available to do this and if you are still puzzling about this when XNA finally supports it some time in the future, you can check out the following link to see how the X3DAudio classes are used in C++. The ideas will be the same in C#, but hopefully much easier to write.

```
http://msdn.microsoft.com/library/default.asp?url=/library/en-us/directx9_c/
audio_xact_overview_x3daudio.asp
```

Menu Sounds

To finish this chapter here are some quick tips for menu sounds:

❑   Use helper methods like `PlayMenuHighlight` or `PlayMenuClick` to play menu sound effects instead of using the `Sounds` enum.

❑   If you want to play certain menu sounds at different volumes, for example a loud highlight sound for major buttons and a more silent highlight sound for smaller controls, then create two sound cues in XACT instead of writing your own custom volume code, which is more work and not necessary at all.

❑ Try to write helper methods to find out if the mouse was moved over a control this frame and reuse this code or method for all controls to unify the highlight or mouse click code. This way you don't have to play click or highlight sounds yourself for every custom button method you use in your game.

❑ Make sure you also support the Xbox 360 controller and the keyboard. Writing a mouse-only game makes no sense on the Xbox 360 because you have absolutely zero mouse support in XNA for your Xbox 360.

❑ Play highlight sounds when navigating through menu entries and play click sounds when the user clicks the gamepad or presses space or Enter on the keyboard to go into the current menu selection.

Challenge: Create Your XACT Project

The challenge for this chapter is simple; just create your own XACT project like the one that was shown in this chapter. It is important that you feel comfortable in XACT, otherwise you will spend a lot of time rewriting code that is not necessary or you have to search for functionality in XACT that is hidden somewhere you have never looked before.

Additionally, write your own Sound class for the XACT project you created and start with the unit test first. Then implement the constructor and load the XACT project and the wave and sound banks. Finally, implement the Play methods to make your unit test work. As an example of how it's done you can check out the XnaShooterSoundProject for this chapter and the TestSounds unit test in there.

That's it; you are now an experienced XACT user. For more details about XACT you can also visit the official XACT forum, which contains many tips and you can ask all the XACT experts for help if you run into trouble with your game code and XACT:

    http://forums.microsoft.com/MSDN/ShowForum.aspx?ForumID=323

If available at the time you are reading this book try to use X3DAudio and check if there is a newer version of Rocket Commander XNA available to show how it's done.

Summary

In this chapter you learned all about sound effects in XNA. XACT is the tool you have to use, no matter if you think it is great or you are annoyed by it. XACT allows you to play sound effects and even music on the Xbox 360 and Windows with the help of the XNA Framework.

Here are all the important points about XACT you learned in this chapter:

❑ XACT is the only way to play sounds on the Xbox 360 with XNA.

❑ The XACT tool might be annoying at first, but once you get used to it you'll enjoy the new cool features. For example, using the fade in and fade out settings for music items is much cooler to use than having to write your own fade in and out code.

❏   MP3, OGG, or ACC compression or other custom compression formats are not supported by XACT. The only two formats supported are ADPCM for the Windows platform and XMA for the Xbox 360 platform.

❏   XMA is a good and useful compression format for the Xbox 360, but ADPCM is not really useful. If you have the time and you want smaller sound files on Windows, implement DirectAudioVideoPlayback from the DirectX SDK into your engine or use other external sound engines for the Windows part of your game.

❏   I recommend 75% quality for XMA and 128 or 256 samples per block for ADPCM. Whatever you choose you have to live with the fact that the Windows version of your game will probably be twice as big as the Xbox 360 version in XNA just because of the sound files and the bad ADPCM compression.

❏   Make sure your Sound class is easy to use and accessible from everywhere.

❏   Use the Sounds enum to quickly access and play all available sound cues.

❏   Write helper methods for code you call often.

❏   Setting custom cue variables is first configured in XACT and then programmed into your XNA code. SetVariable is the method for all the dirty cue instance variable modifying.

The next chapter discusses the Input class for handling the keyboard, the mouse, and the Xbox 360 gamepad controller devices, which is already in the graphics engine you wrote, but all the methods have not been discussed in detail. Additionally you will learn about the menu system and other UI (user interface) code that directly interacts with the Input class. For example, sounds are played by the UI code automatically every time you hover over a control or if you click a control. For custom controls you have to do all the checking and handling yourself. You will also learn more about the XNA Shooter game, which will then be completed in Chapter 11.

10

Player Input and the User Interface

This chapter takes a closer look at the Input class that was used so many times now. Then it discusses the ways to implement a good graphical user interface (GUI) for XNA Shooter. Handling the user input is very simple in XNA because thanks to the Input namespace, you can easily get the mouse, keyboard, and gamepad states with just three lines of code:

```
mouseState = Mouse.GetState();
keyboardState = Keyboard.GetState();
gamePadState = GamePad.GetState(PlayerIndex.One);
```

If you don't have the XNA Input namespace added to the file you are currently working on, go with the text cursor over Mouse, Keyboard, or GamePad and press Ctrl+., which automatically adds the following line to your using directives:

```
using Microsoft.Xna.Framework.Input;
```

Now you can use these states and check if the gamepad is connected at all, if the space key is pressed on your keyboard, or where the mouse position is currently. This is exactly what you did in the first and second chapter when you wrote your first XNA game.

The more complex your games become, the more often you will have to repeat the same code over and over again. Like the classes in the graphics engine you often do not add more functionality, but instead you make the existing functionality easier to use. For example, the Texture class was used to store the XNA texture, the texture size, whether or not it has alpha, and it also contains many useful methods to render the texture directly on the screen with the help of the SpriteHelper class.

All this is possible with the standard XNA Framework too, but you will have to write more code. If you just want to put one single texture on the screen it would not make sense to write all these helper classes, but if you write many projects and use hundreds of textures you will probably thank yourself for all the helper classes you wrote earlier. Only by simplifying the texture, shaders, and materials is it possible to write complex graphics code in a few lines of code, as you can see in the unit tests of the graphics classes.

The same logic applies to the Input class too. The advantages are not that obvious, but you will notice after a while that writing new UI (user interface) code for your custom buttons or menu controls gets much easier thanks to the many helper classes including the Input class.

Just writing a helper class is kind of boring, and you already know how to use this Input class because you already used it so many times. To get something useful done for your next game, XNA Shooter, you will also program all the UI classes and see the menu logic for the more advanced games shown in this book. The idea here is to reuse the existing Rocket Commander XNA game screen classes for newer projects. Some classes have to be removed and you might need a new class here and there, but the overall program logic is pretty much the same.

The game itself shows the user interface (ammunition, health, points, and so on) in the Mission class just like Rocket Commander did. For more complex games, like the racing game in the next part of this book, the game logic and the UI rendering code is separated into more classes. Like for unit testing you should always make sure that writing your game code is as simple as possible, but not simpler. It does not make sense to write 30 helper classes if all you want to do is to output "Hello World" on the screen.

Game UI and especially menu UI is a big topic for games. There was a time a few years back when almost every game had very complex menu animations or even 3D graphics, but it was very hard to use. You should try to keep things simple, not only for you as the programmer, but also for the user. You learn about a good menu design at the end of this chapter.

Input Class

The Input class has many properties to easily access all the most-used keyboard, mouse, and gamepad key states (see Figure 10-1). The class also provides some helper methods to manage keyboard input and typing in text, but you will probably not need most of the code in the Input class for your first game projects. It becomes more useful the bigger your game grows and the more UI code you have in it. The most important method is the Update method, which has to be called every frame (done automatically from the BaseGame class at the beginning of each frame in the Update method there).

Please note that all the mouse functionality is missing if you run XNA on your Xbox 360, and you can't even get the mouse states when you compile for the Xbox 360 (the class is just missing). So you have to comment out all your mouse code just to make the game run on the Xbox 360. That is not funny, especially if you have hundreds of mouse calls all over the place in your project. A much better solution is to completely hide the mouse state (make it private) and only access the mouse parameters through properties in the Input class. As you can see in Figure 10-1, you have access to the Gamepad and Keyboard states directly in case you want to check another key or button yourself, but for the mouse, you can only access the properties the Input class gives you. Now all these properties return just what you would expect on the PC, but on the Xbox 360 they all return false or just the virtual mouse position. You can set and get the mouse position the same way as on the PC, but the user does not control it directly.

Now the same code for mouse, keyboard, and gamepad input can be used on both platforms. XNA had the goal to have 98% of the code behave the same way; go to 100% for your engine.

Figure 10-1

For example, the A button of the Xbox 360 gamepad or the cursor keys for the keyboard are used very often. It is far easier to write code like the following to allow navigating through the menu entries with the up/down keyboard keys. Additionally supporting the gamepad up/down cursor or even controlling the menu with the gamepad left thumb stick is easier to do with these helper properties. If you had to write all the state checking yourself every time you need to check if a key or button is currently pressed and was not pressed before, you would probably go crazy after a while.

```
// Handle GamePad input, and also allow keyboard input
if (Input.GamePadUpJustPressed ||
  Input.KeyboardUpJustPressed)
{
  Sound.Play(Sound.Sounds.Highlight);
  selectedButton =
    (selectedButton + NumberOfButtons - 1) % NumberOfButtons;
} // if (BaseGame.GamePadLeftNowPressed)
```

```
else if (Input.GamePadDownJustPressed ||
  Input.KeyboardDownJustPressed)
{
  Sound.Play(Sound.Sounds.Highlight);
  selectedButton = (selectedButton + 1) % NumberOfButtons;
} // else if
```

For example, the `GamePadUpJustPressed` method does the following:

```
/// <summary>
/// Game pad up just pressed
/// </summary>
/// <returns>Bool</returns>
public static bool GamePadUpJustPressed
{
  get
  {
    return (gamePadState.DPad.Up == ButtonState.Pressed &&
      gamePadStateLastFrame.DPad.Up == ButtonState.Released) ||
      (gamePadState.ThumbSticks.Left.Y > 0.75f &&
      gamePadStateLastFrame.ThumbSticks.Left.Y < 0.75f);
  } // get
} // GamePadUpJustPressed
```

The code uses the current gamepad state, which is assigned at the beginning of each frame, and the gamepad state from the last frame to check if any button state has changed. As you can see, if you had to write this code again and again every time you wanted to check if the gamepad up cursor was pressed, you would go crazy. Copy and paste works fine for the first one or two times, but if you use the same code over and over again, write a helper method or property to let it do the work for you. In the future when you write more UI code it will become much easier to check all input states and work with many different input devices.

The Update Method in the Input Class

The `Update` method does nothing really complicated, but it is the most important part of the `Input` class because all the last frame states are copied over from the previous states and then you get each new state for the keyboard, mouse, and gamepad input. To help out with relative mouse movement there is some extra code to handle it. Relative mouse movement is something that is not supported in XNA unlike the `DirectInput` classes from DirectX, which allow you to get relative mouse data instead of the absolute mouse positions like (–3.5, +7.0) instead of position (350, 802).

```
/// <summary>
/// Update, called from BaseGame.Update().
/// Will catch all new states for keyboard, mouse and the gamepad.
/// </summary>
internal static void Update()
{
#if XBOX360
  // No mouse support on the XBox360 yet :(
  mouseDetected = false;
```

```
#else
  // Handle mouse input variables
  mouseStateLastFrame = mouseState;
  mouseState = Microsoft.Xna.Framework.Input.Mouse.GetState();

  // Update mouseXMovement and mouseYMovement
  lastMouseXMovement += mouseState.X - mouseStateLastFrame.X;
  lastMouseYMovement += mouseState.Y - mouseStateLastFrame.Y;
  mouseXMovement = lastMouseXMovement / 2.0f;
  mouseYMovement = lastMouseYMovement / 2.0f;
  lastMouseXMovement -= lastMouseXMovement / 2.0f;
  lastMouseYMovement -= lastMouseYMovement / 2.0f;

  if (MouseLeftButtonPressed == false)
    startDraggingPos = MousePos;
  mouseWheelDelta = mouseState.ScrollWheelValue - mouseWheelValue;
  mouseWheelValue = mouseState.ScrollWheelValue;

  // Check if mouse was moved this frame if it is not detected yet.
  // This allows us to ignore the mouse even when it is captured
  // on a windows machine if just the gamepad or keyboard is used.
  if (mouseDetected == false)
    mouseDetected = mouseState.X != mouseStateLastFrame.X ||
      mouseState.Y != mouseStateLastFrame.Y ||
      mouseState.LeftButton != mouseStateLastFrame.LeftButton;
#endif

  // Handle keyboard input
  keysPressedLastFrame = new List<Keys>(keyboardState.GetPressedKeys());
  keyboardState = Microsoft.Xna.Framework.Input.Keyboard.GetState();

  // And finally catch the XBox Controller input (only use 1 player)
  gamePadStateLastFrame = gamePadState;
  gamePadState = Microsoft.Xna.Framework.Input.GamePad.GetState(
    PlayerIndex.One);

  // Handle rumbling
  if (leftRumble > 0 || rightRumble > 0)
  {
    if (leftRumble > 0)
      leftRumble -= 1.5f * BaseGame.MoveFactorPerSecond;
    if (rightRumble > 0)
      rightRumble -= 1.5f * BaseGame.MoveFactorPerSecond;
    Microsoft.Xna.Framework.Input.GamePad.SetVibration(
      PlayerIndex.One, leftRumble, rightRumble);
  } // if (leftRumble)
} // Update()
```

You might notice the code for the gamepad rumbling at the end of the Update method, which allows you to use the following method to let the gamepad rumble for a while without having to worry about it anymore. The Update method will automatically reduce the rumbled effect if GamePadRumble is not called again in the next frame. You can also use a weaker rumble effect for smaller events. Playing XNA Shooter is a lot more fun with rumbling enabled.

```
/// <summary>
/// Game pad rumble
/// </summary>
/// <param name="setLeftRumble">Set left rumble</param>
/// <param name="setRightRumble">Set right rumble</param>
public static void GamePadRumble(
  float setLeftRumble, float setRightRumble)
{
  leftRumble = setLeftRumble;
  rightRumble = setRightRumble;
} // GamePadRumble(setLeftRumble, setRightRumble)
```

Mouse Rectangles

The Input class also has some methods to help you detect if the mouse is over a UI element like a menu button. Use the following method to check if the mouse is hovering over a UI element. The method will also automatically play the highlight sound for you if you just entered this rectangle.

```
/// <summary>
/// Mouse in box
/// </summary>
/// <param name="rect">Rectangle</param>
/// <returns>Bool</returns>
public static bool MouseInBox(Rectangle rect)
{
#if XBOX360
  return false;
#else
  bool ret = mouseState.X >= rect.X &&
    mouseState.Y >= rect.Y &&
    mouseState.X < rect.Right &&
    mouseState.Y < rect.Bottom;
  bool lastRet = mouseStateLastFrame.X >= rect.X &&
    mouseStateLastFrame.Y >= rect.Y &&
    mouseStateLastFrame.X < rect.Right &&
    mouseStateLastFrame.Y < rect.Bottom;

  // Highlight happened?
  if (ret &&
    lastRet == false)
    Sound.Play(Sound.Sounds.Highlight);

  return ret;
#endif
} // MouseInBox(rect)
```

As an example you can use the code to allow selecting your main menu elements like in Figure 10-2. As I said before try to keep it simple. A menu should just show all important parts of the game. The background texture should also be a nice picture from your game — some artwork or custom-made from your skilled graphics artist (if you have one).

Title ─────▶ **Your Game**

Start Mission

Not inside any UI rect

Highscores

Menu Background Texture

Options

Mouse entered
Start Mission rect

Credits

Exit

Figure 10-2

To get this to work you would use some code similar to the following code snippet:

```
// Render background
game.RenderMenuBackground();

// Show all buttons
int buttonNum = 0;
MenuButton[] menuButtons = new MenuButton[]
  {
    MenuButton.Missions,
    MenuButton.Highscore,
    MenuButton.Credits,
    MenuButton.Exit,
    MenuButton.Back,
  };
foreach (MenuButton button in menuButtons)
  // Don't render the back button
  if (button != MenuButton.Back)
  {
    if (game.RenderMenuButton(button, buttonLocations[buttonNum]))
    {
      if (button == MenuButton.Missions)
        game.AddGameScreen(new Mission());
      else if (button == MenuButton.Highscore)
        game.AddGameScreen(new Highscores());
      else if (button == MenuButton.Credits)
        game.AddGameScreen(new Credits());
```

```
        else if (button == MenuButton.Exit)
          quit = true;
      } // if
    buttonNum++;
    if (buttonNum >= buttonLocations.Length)
      break;
  } // if

// Hotkeys, M=Mission, H=Highscores, C=Credits, Esc=Quit
if (Input.KeyboardKeyJustPressed(Keys.M))
  game.AddGameScreen(new Mission());
else if (Input.KeyboardKeyJustPressed(Keys.H))
  game.AddGameScreen(new Highscores());
else if (Input.KeyboardKeyJustPressed(Keys.C))
  game.AddGameScreen(new Credits());
else if (Input.KeyboardEscapeJustPressed)
  quit = true;

// If pressing XBox controller up/down change selection
if (Input.GamePadDownJustPressed)
{
  xInputMenuSelection =
    (xInputMenuSelection + 1) % buttonLocations.Length;
  SelectMenuItemForXInput();
} // if (Input.GamePad)
else if (Input.GamePadUpJustPressed)
{
  if (xInputMenuSelection <= 0)
    xInputMenuSelection = buttonLocations.Length;
  xInputMenuSelection - ;
  SelectMenuItemForXInput();
} // if (Input.GamePad)
```

If you have more controls like in your options screen to enable or disable checkboxes, handle slide bars, or edit boxes, the code will get a little bit more complicated and before you have to copy and paste the same code over and over again you should introduce a UI class to handle all the UI code for you. If you just have to use an edit box once, you could also write the code directly into the Options class like I did for Rocket Commander XNA. But the code should be refactored if you use it multiple times. Handling text boxes is also a little bit more complicated in XNA because you have to implement your own keyboard input methods for text.

Entering Text in XNA

You might also have noticed that there is no keyboardStateLastFrame variable in the Input class, because unlike the MouseState and GamePadState you cannot use the KeyboardState struct again the next frame; the data is no longer valid. The reason this is happening is because the KeyboardState struct uses an internal list for all the keys, which is used in the next frame again and overwritten to all the new keyboard key states when you call Keyboard.GetState. To fix this issue you just keep your own list of keys, which is cloned every time you assign it from the last frame keys. Using the constructor of the generic List class will automatically clone all elements for you.

Using this list works almost the same way as using the keyboard state directly. As an example, take a look at the `KeyboardSpaceJustPressed` property of the `Input` class:

```
/// <summary>
/// Keyboard space just pressed?
/// </summary>
/// <returns>Bool</returns>
public static bool KeyboardSpaceJustPressed
{
  get
  {
    return keyboardState.IsKeyDown(Keys.Space) &&
      keysPressedLastFrame.Contains(Keys.Space) == false;
  } // get
} // KeyboardSpaceJustPressed
```

The rest of the `Input` class is very similar to all the code you already saw except for the keyboard input text methods I mentioned a minute ago. To get the keyboard input for text boxes the same way as you would with a normal Windows text box, the following unit test was written:

```
/// <summary>
/// Test keyboard chat input
/// </summary>
public static void TestKeyboardChatInput()
{
  // Better version with help of Input.HandleKeyboardInput!
  string chatText = "";
  TestGame.Start("TestKeyboardChatInput",
    null,
    delegate
    {
      TextureFont.WriteText(100, 100,
        "Your chat text: " + chatText +
        // Add blinking |
        ((int)(BaseGame.TotalTime / 0.35f) % 2 == 0 ? "|" : ""));
      Input.HandleKeyboardInput(ref chatText);
    },
    null);
} // TestKeyboardChatInput()
```

The unit test just displays the `chatText` string and a blinking | sign behind it. Then the `HandleKeyboardInput` method is used to allow the user to type in new chat text. Take a look at the `HandleKeyboardInput` method:

```
/// <<summary>
/// Handle keyboard input helper method to catch keyboard input
/// for an input text. Only used to enter the player name in the
/// game.
/// </summary>
```

```
/// <param name="inputText">Input text</param>
public static void HandleKeyboardInput(ref string inputText)
{
  // Is a shift key pressed (we have to check both, left and right)
  bool isShiftPressed =
    keyboardState.IsKeyDown(Keys.LeftShift) ||
    keyboardState.IsKeyDown(Keys.RightShift);

  // Go through all pressed keys
  foreach (Keys pressedKey in keyboardState.GetPressedKeys())
    // Only process if it was not pressed last frame
    if (keysPressedLastFrame.Contains(pressedKey) == false)
    {
      // No special key?
      if (IsSpecialKey(pressedKey) == false &&
        // Max. allow 32 chars
        inputText.Length < 32)
      {
        // Then add the letter to our inputText.
        // Check also the shift state!
        inputText += KeyToChar(pressedKey, isShiftPressed);
      } // if (IsSpecialKey)
      else if (pressedKey == Keys.Back &&
        inputText.Length > 0)
      {
        // Remove 1 character at end
        inputText = inputText.Substring(0, inputText.Length - 1);
      } // else if
    } // foreach if (WasKeyPressedLastFrame)
} // HandleKeyboardInput(inputText)
```

The method uses two other helper methods in the Input class. First, IsSpecialKey is used to see if the key can be used for the chat text or if it was just an F1, cursor, Delete, Enter, and so on key, which will not be added directly to the chat text. Then you handle the special case for the Backspace key. You could also extend the code to handle the Enter or Delete keys in your text boxes if you need that in your game.

The next problem is that you can't just add keys to your input text; the first problem is that the A key would add A to the input text string regardless of whether the user pressed the Shift key. Then there are special keys like +, -, {, and so on, which would show up as "Plus", "Minus", "OemOpenBrackets" in your input text. To help you out with that it would be nice if XNA would provide you with the real key meaning, but it does not; you have to do it yourself with the help of the KeyToChar helper method in the Input class:

```
/// <summary>
/// Keys to char helper conversion method.
/// Note: If the keys are mapped other than on a default QWERTY
/// keyboard, this method will not work properly. Most keyboards
/// will return the same for A-Z and 0-9, but the special keys
/// might be different. Sorry, no easy way to fix this with XNA ...
```

```
/// For a game with chat (windows) you should implement the
/// Windows events for catching keyboard input, which are much better!
/// </summary>
/// <param name="key">Keys</param>
/// <returns>Char</returns>
public static char KeyToChar(Keys key, bool shiftPressed)
{
  // If key will not be found, just return space
  char ret = ' ';
  int keyNum = (int)key;
  if (keyNum >= (int)Keys.A && keyNum <= (int)Keys.Z)
  {
    if (shiftPressed)
      ret = key.ToString()[0];
    else
      ret = key.ToString().ToLower()[0];
  } // if (keyNum)
  else if (keyNum >= (int)Keys.D0 && keyNum <= (int)Keys.D9 &&
    shiftPressed == false)
  {
    ret = (char)((int)'0' + (keyNum - Keys.D0));
  } // else if
  else if (key == Keys.D1 && shiftPressed)
    ret = '!';
  else if (key == Keys.D2 && shiftPressed)
    ret = '@';
[etc. about 20 more special key checks]

  // Return result
  return ret;
} // KeyToChar(key)
```

With that method the HandleKeyboardInput method works now the way you expect it to and your unit test can be started and tested. There are even more unit tests in the Input class; check them out to learn more about the available properties and methods.

Game Screens

In Figure 10-2 you already saw an example for a simple main menu, but your games contain more than just the game screen itself and a menu. You will usually need a credits screen to make you famous, have an options screen to let the user comfortably set all settings and change the screen resolution, and it is always good to have a help screen in the game explaining the basic game principle (see Figure 10-3).

Most game screens use a special background texture to show most of the information on the screen. In the Mission selection screen you can select one of the four missions and then start the game. The other screens just show some information and only the options screen allows the user to change anything. All game screens return to the main menu after you press Back.

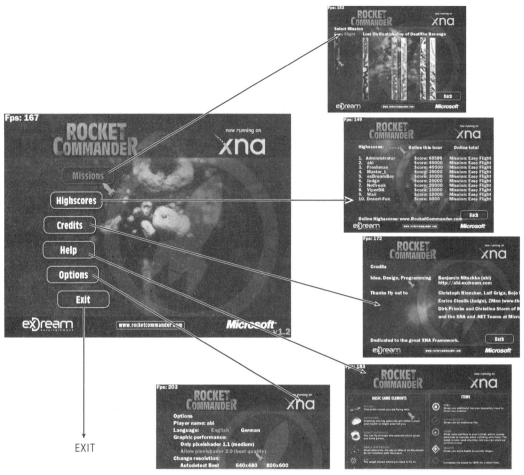

Figure 10-3

To handle all game screens automatically you use a stack of game screens in your main game class (see Figure 10-4). This allows you to use even more complex menu systems with several levels where you can always return to the previous screen. In case you want to return to the main menu, just remove all entries on the stack except for the last one. Another trick I often use for demos is to add another game screen before the main menu is added just to show a demo "buy this game now" screen when the user exits the game. The class itself is only a couple of lines and you only need to add one extra line to your main class. Most game screen classes are very simple too.

GameScreen Stack in Rocket Commander XNA

Figure 10-4

Why is this game screen stack so great? Well, all you have to do is to derive all your game screen classes from IGameScreen (see Figure 10-5) and then you can use the following code to render and handle them automatically. The Render method of each game screen class returns true if you are finished with it and you will return to the previous screen. After all game screens have been removed you can exit the game.

```
// No more game screens?
if (gameScreens.Count == 0)
{
  // Then quit
  Exit();
  return;
} // if (gameScreens.Count)

// Handle current screen
if (gameScreens.Peek().Render())
{
  // Play sound for screen back
  Sound.Play(Sound.Sounds.ScreenBack);
  gameScreens.Pop();
} // if (gameScreens.Peek)
```

Figure 10-5

Help Screen

As a very simple example for a game screen class, here is the complete code of the `Help` class in the `GameScreens` namespace. Other game screen classes are not much more complex except for the `Mission` class, which handles the whole game.

```
/// <summary>
/// Help
/// </summary>
class Help : IGameScreen
{
  #region Properties
  /// <summary>
  /// Name of this game screen
  /// </summary>
  /// <returns>String</returns>
  public string Name
  {
    get
    {
      return "Help";
    } // get
  } // Name
  #endregion

  #region Run
  /// <summary>
  /// Run game screen. Called each frame.
  /// </summary>
  /// <param name="game">Form for access to asteroid manager</param>
  public bool Run(RocketCommanderGame game)
  {
    // Render background
    game.RenderMenuBackground();

    // Show helper screen texture
    game.helpScreenTexture.RenderOnScreen(
      new Rectangle(0,
      174 * BaseGame.Height / 768,
      BaseGame.Width,
      510 * BaseGame.Height / 768),
      new Rectangle(0, 0, 1024, 510));

    if (game.RenderMenuButton(MenuButton.Back,
      new Point(1024 - 210, 768 - 140)) ||
      Input.KeyboardEscapeJustPressed)
      return true;

    return true;
  } // Run(game)
} // class Help
```

That's it. Looks pretty simple, doesn't it? Please take a look at the game screen classes yourself if you want to learn more about them. Some of them also have unit tests to show the behavior and use cases of each game screen.

In-Game User Interface

In this section I want you to follow all the steps I took to make the In-Game UI for the XNA Shooter game. The UI is not very complex, but you will encounter several issues anyway. The following elements are displayed in the shoot-'em-up game:

❑   Mission Time: Minutes and Seconds showing you how long you played

❑   Current Score: You get points for shooting, killing, and collecting items and weapons

❑   Highscore you have to beat to become number one

❑   Your current health; if you lose all of it, you die

❑   Current weapon you are firing with and number of EMP bombs you can throw

Figure 10-6 shows all of these elements together on the screen with help of the following textures:

❑   HudTop.png for the top bar on the screen, showing time, score, and highscore

❑   HudButtom.png for the bottom counterpart, showing health and the current weapons

❑   GameFont.png, the game font you already used in several games in this book

❑   NumbersFont.png for the numbers on the top part; looks cooler than the default font

After the new class to display the numbers from the NumbersFont.png texture was implemented, and thanks to the Texture class and the RenderOnScreen methods, adding the In-Game UI isn't too hard anymore.

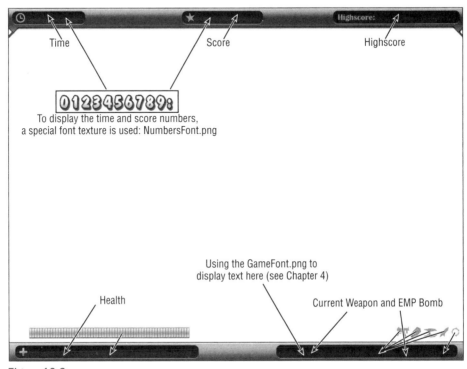

Figure 10-6

The NumbersFont.png texture is handled in the NumbersFont class and it is very similar to the TextureFont class from Chapter 4, but much simpler because you only have 11 rectangles here, 10 for the numbers 0 to 9 and one for the column for displaying times.

```
private void RenderHud()
{
  // Render top hud part
  hudTopTexture.RenderOnScreenRelative4To3(0, 0,
    hudTopTexture.GfxRectangle);
  // Time
  BaseGame.NumbersFont.WriteTime(
    BaseGame.XToRes(73), BaseGame.YToRes(8), (int)Player.gameTimeMs);
  // Score
  BaseGame.NumbersFont.WriteNumberCentered(
    BaseGame.XToRes(485), BaseGame.YToRes(8), Player.score);
  // Highscore
  BaseGame.NumbersFont.WriteNumberCentered(
    BaseGame.XToRes(920), BaseGame.YToRes(8), Highscores.TopHighscore);

  // Render bottom hud part
  Rectangle bottomHudGfxRect = new Rectangle(0, 24, 1024, 40);
  hudBottomTexture.RenderOnScreenRelative4To3(0, 768 - 40,
    bottomHudGfxRect);
  // Health
  Rectangle healthGfxRect = new Rectangle(50, 0, 361, 24);
  hudBottomTexture.RenderOnScreenRelative4To3(50, 768 - 31,
    new Rectangle(healthGfxRect.X, healthGfxRect.Y,
    (int)(healthGfxRect.Width * Player.health), healthGfxRect.Height));
  // Weapon and Emps!
  Rectangle weaponMgGfxRect = new Rectangle(876, 0, 31, 24);
  Rectangle weaponGattlingGfxRect = new Rectangle(909, 0, 27, 24);
  Rectangle weaponPlasmaGfxRect = new Rectangle(939, 0, 33, 24);
  Rectangle weaponRocketsGfxRect = new Rectangle(975, 0, 24, 24);
  Rectangle weaponEmpGfxRect = new Rectangle(1001, 0, 23, 24);
  TextureFont.WriteText(BaseGame.XToRes(606),
    BaseGame.YToRes(768 - 20) - TextureFont.Height / 3, "Weapon: ");

  // Show weapon icon!
  Rectangle weaponRect =
    Player.currentWeapon == Player.WeaponTypes.MG ? weaponMgGfxRect :
    Player.currentWeapon == Player.WeaponTypes.Gattling ?
    weaponGattlingGfxRect :
    Player.currentWeapon == Player.WeaponTypes.Plasma ?
    weaponPlasmaGfxRect : weaponRocketsGfxRect;
  hudBottomTexture.RenderOnScreenRelative4To3(
    715, 768 - 31, weaponRect);
  // And weapon name
  TextureFont.WriteText(BaseGame.XToRes(717+weaponRect.Width),
    BaseGame.YToRes(768 - 20) - TextureFont.Height / 3,
    Player.currentWeapon.ToString());
  TextureFont.WriteText(BaseGame.XToRes(864),
    BaseGame.YToRes(768 - 20) - TextureFont.Height / 3, "EMPs: ");
  // Show emp icons if we have any
  for (int num = 0; num < Player.empBombs; num++)
    hudBottomTexture.RenderOnScreenRelative4To3(
      938 + num * 23, 768 - 31, weaponEmpGfxRect);
} // RenderHud()
```

This solution works fine on the PC, but as soon as you start the game (or the TestHud unit test I wrote before even writing the RenderHud method) on the Xbox 360 connected to a TV screen you will see that the HUD is not completely visible, or worse, almost not visible at all.

If you have never developed a game on a console connected to a TV set before, this may be a new issue for you because on a PC monitor you can always use 100% of the visible area since there is no safe region. Well, on most TV screens you do not see 100% of the screen, more like 90%, which means about 10% of the width and height are not visible at the screen borders (see Figure 10-7).

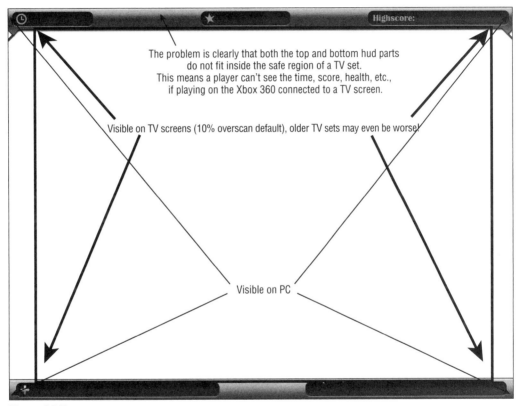

Figure 10-7

You might ask why XNA does not put everything inside this safe region automatically. Well, it is not that easy. The TV set receives the full signal, and depending on the input cables and the model of the TV set, you see different results. These are some examples I have encountered:

❑   PC connected to a monitor with a VGA or DVI cable lets you see 100%

❑   Xbox 360 connected through a VGA cable to a PC monitor lets you see 100% too (or close to 100% if the resolution is not the native one)

❑   Xbox 360 connected to an old-style monitor with SCART: around 92% visible

❏ Xbox 360 connected through Component cables to my new Dell 24″ Monitor (yeah HDTV): around 93%–95% visible (depends on the resolution)

❏ Some old TV sets (according to the XNA docs and tips on the Web) have a save region of 80%–90%, but I never saw the 80% case; that is probably the worst-case scenario

As you can see it is not just 90% on the Xbox 360 and you don't have to worry about it. The results on the screen can be very different in many different situations, which can neither be checked by your game nor the XNA Framework. The only thing for sure is that on the PC you can be sure that 100% of all screen pixels are visible, which is the reason why many PC games use the borders of the screen to display UI elements and other information. If you take a look at Xbox 360 (or any console games for that matter) you will notice that they often have a simpler interface and they never show any information at the very screen borders.

You can't just put the HUD bars in the 90% safe region because if the user sees more it will look very wrong because you have no graphic behind the 90% region, and if the user sees even less you still have the same problem as before. Instead of continuing to work around this issue you should stop here and rethink the problem. It is just not a good idea to have UI elements as shown in Figure 10-6 for an Xbox 360 game. The best solution is to change the UI graphics and put them in the safe region if running the game in a situation where the user cannot see 100% of the screen like starting it on the Xbox 360. Figure 10-8 shows how to change the HUD graphics to have them work on both the PC, where you put them at the screen borders, and on the Xbox 360, where they are put in the inner 92% (still visible with a safe region of 90%, gets hard to read if only 85% or less are visible, but I never saw this worst-case scenario; most TV sets are around 90%–95%).

Figure 10-9 shows the final screen layout of XNA Shooter after going through all the steps of this chapter. Please check out the `RenderHud` method in the `Mission` class for more details. It was mainly developed for widescreen resolutions and to look good on the Xbox 360, but even with smaller resolutions on the PC it looks ok like on the screenshot. To test the menu and game screens from this chapter run the sample game project for this chapter, which is still based on the XnaGraphicEngine project you started in Chapter 5, but you have some new and updated game classes now.

Tips

From my experience there are a couple of things you have to remember when developing XNA games on the Xbox 360. All of these issues are not a big deal on the PC, but they can cost some extra time until you get them right. One of the main problems is that if you develop your game on the PC only and then test it on the Xbox 360 only at the end, a lot of things may go wrong (bad performance on the .NET Compact Framework; UI elements at the border of the screen, which are just not visible on some TVs; bad Xbox 360 controller support, which is the main input device for Xbox 360s; and so on). Please read more about these issues on my blog if you are interested.

❏ **Test, test, and test.** This is the most important tip. Write unit tests and constantly test them on your PC *and* your Xbox 360. I keep two projects open at the same time (both of them use the same files, but I only develop the PC solution and use the Xbox 360 solution for deploying and testing only). Almost all of my classes have unit tests and I constantly test them until they are completed.

Figure 10-8

Figure 10-9

❑ **Don't use foreach loops, especially not in tight render loops.** This may sound a little crazy because it does not matter on a PC game and today's CPUs are fast enough to handle the creation and deletion of many thousands of objects each frame, which most games don't even need. But on the compact framework you will spam the memory even with things like foreach loops because a new enumerator instance is created every time you start a foreach loop. After a while there will be a lot of dead objects, which have to be collected. This can take some time and slow down your game immensely. The PC version might run at over 200 frames, but your Xbox 360 version is stuck at something like 30–40 frames. Avoiding creation of new data each frame and avoiding foreach loops (just replace them with normal for loops; it is mostly just one line of extra code) can improve your performance by a factor of 100% or more.

❑ **In Arena Wars (the first .NET game I developed), I never created any data during the game.** All objects were created at the beginning of each mission and they were reused (which was no big deal since the game principle did not allow an infinite number of units; it always stayed around the same because you get your money back from dead units to build new units). This approach was taken to reduce the Garbage Collector performance impact that could happen on slow computers in .NET 1.1. In later projects I did not care so much about creating new objects and I coded just the easy way because unit tests drive you into a direction to quickly develop solutions, which work and are tested, but may not be the best in other situations like for the Xbox 360 .NET Compact Framework. That is ok because you can now use the unit tests to check if other solutions work just they way you expect them to work. For XNA Shooter and XNA Racer (and a couple of other new game projects) I now make sure that most of the game data is created at the beginning of each level and not dynamically during the game. This makes writing the code far easier and allows you to refactor it much more freely allowing you to improve both the overall code design and the execution speed. I advise you to always take the "clean code" approach first and think about optimizations in the beginning, but do not evolve important code around ugly optimized code that is hard to manage early in the project. Thanks to many improvements that have been made in .NET 2.0 the performance of the Garbage Collector, reusing existing objects and Exception Handling is now much better while we also have much faster computers today.

❑ **Save-Regions on TVs can be problematic.** Just Google for Xbox 360 screenshots and you will notice that the GUI (graphical user interface) looks a lot different from most PC games. PC games often have UI at the screen border showing you tips, little buttons, and other not so important things. If you do that in your Xbox 360 game all of these UI elements may be cut off on a regular TV. For the XNA Shooter I had to rework all the UI elements because they just did not fit on a TV screen and it was not practical to put them in a bar (like the Windows task bar) because it looks so different on the PC and certain TV monitors. Instead I put all UI elements in floating bars, which will be adjusted depending on the screen the user is looking at.

The important thing is to keep the important UI element in this inner 90% (or 93% if you want to be close to the edges) rectangle. This means instead of using a full 1920x1080 pixel resolution you only use 90% of it (1728x945). Or just start rendering UI elements at about 5% of the screen (x coordinate: 96, y coordinate: 54). These pixel locations obviously depend on the screen resolution; just calculate them in your main class and use them whenever you render UI.

For more information about the .NET Compact Framework and how it is best used for the XNA Framework on the Xbox 360, please read the following great article by the .NET compact framework team, which you'll find at http://blogs.msdn.com/netcfteam/archive/2006/12/22/managed-code-performance-on-xbox-360-for-the-xna-framework-1-0.aspx.

Cameras

Handling the input and managing the game screens is important and you will look at a more professional game and a more complete looking game after you have implemented all the game screens, even if your background textures are still placeholders.

For the game itself, especially if it is in 3D and if you can move around freely in the game world, you need a camera class. Chapter 5 introduced the `SimpleCamera` class to move around and zoom in a simple 3D environment. More interesting and useful are the camera classes in the Rocket Commander game (`SpaceCamera` class) and the one in the racing game (`ChaseCamera` class). The camera required for XNA Shooter can be pretty simple; you can just reuse the `SimpleCamera` class and move the look at target position through the level.

Figure 10-10 shows a comparison of all camera classes used in this book. The `SpaceCamera` class is discussed here, and in a few chapters you are going to check out the `ChaseCamera` class too. Thanks to the `GameComponent` class the `SimpleCamera` is derived from you should be able to add new camera classes yourself with ease.

Figure 10-10

Space Camera

The SpaceCamera class is a lot more complex than the SimpleCamera class, and even the ChaseCamera class for the racing game looks simpler. The main reason for the complex code of the SpaceCamera class is the fact that it was the first space camera class I ever wrote and getting the Quaternion math is not that easy. The camera class also supports three modes for the menu camera, for the in-game camera, and a free camera mode for unit tests. The SpaceCamera of Rocket Commander XNA is a little bit simpler because the Quaternion math was removed and the controlling of the rocket is a little bit simplified by just allowing pitch and yaw rotations. The roll rotation around the z axis of the rocket is now handled by the engine automatically, which makes it easier to fly around and not get disoriented. The main reason for this change is to allow the player to control the rocket nicely with the Xbox 360 controller, which is harder than in the original Rocket Commander game that also supports the Xbox 360 controller.

Take a quick look at the most important method in SpaceCamera that handles all the player input and updates the camera position each frame:

```
/// <summary>
/// Handle player input for the game.
/// This is where all the input happens in the game.
/// </summary>
private void HandlePlayerInput()
{
  if (Player.lifeTimeMs < Player.LifeTimeZoomAndAccelerateMs)
  {
    float speedPercentage =
      Player.lifeTimeMs / (float)Player.LifeTimeZoomAndAccelerateMs;
    // Use quadradric product for better speed up effect
    Player.SetStartingSpeed(speedPercentage * speedPercentage);

    // Always move forward
    Translate(Player.Speed * BaseGame.MoveFactorPerSecond *
      Player.MovementSpeedPerSecond, MoveDirections.Z);
    if (Player.gameTimeMs < 100)
    {
      yawRotation = 0;
      pitchRotation = 0;
      pos = Vector3.Zero;
    } // if
  } // if
```

The preceding code increases the speed of the rocket in Rocket Commander and it also resets the rotation and position values if the game just started. Next you do some checking if the game is over and handle the special case to allow moving. Then the mouse and keyboard input is handled. This is pretty much the original code from the very first version I implemented for the SpaceCamera class; all the other code was added later to add more input devices:

```
#region Mouse/keyboard support
if (Input.MouseXMovement != 0.0f ||
  Input.MouseYMovement != 0.0f)
{
  float xMovement = Input.MouseXMovement;
  float yMovement = Input.MouseYMovement;
  Rotate(RotationAxis.Yaw, -xMovement * rotationFactor);
```

```
      Rotate(RotationAxis.Pitch, -yMovement * rotationFactor);
} // if (Mouse.left.Pressed)

// Use asdw (qwerty keyboard), aoew (dvorak keyboard) or
// cursor keys (all keyboards?) to move around.
// Note: If you want to change any keys, use Settings!
if (Input.Keyboard.IsKeyDown(moveForwardKey) ||
  Input.Keyboard.IsKeyDown(Keys.Up) ||
  Input.Keyboard.IsKeyDown(Keys.NumPad8))
{
  float oldPlayerSpeed = Player.Speed;
  Player.Speed += 0.75f * BaseGame.MoveFactorPerSecond;
} // if
if (Input.Keyboard.IsKeyDown(moveBackwardKey) ||
  Input.Keyboard.IsKeyDown(Keys.Down) ||
  Input.Keyboard.IsKeyDown(Keys.NumPad2))
{
  float oldPlayerSpeed = Player.Speed;
  Player.Speed -= 0.75f * BaseGame.MoveFactorPerSecond;
} // if

if (Player.speedItemTimeout > 0)
{
  Player.speedItemTimeout -= BaseGame.ElapsedTimeThisFrameInMs;
  if (Player.speedItemTimeout < 0)
  {
    Player.speedItemTimeout = 0;
    // Reduce to max. possible speed
    if (Player.Speed > Player.MaxSpeedWithoutItem)
      Player.Speed = Player.MaxSpeedWithoutItem;
  } // if
} // if

// Adjust current speed by the current player speed.
float moveFactor = Player.Speed * maxMoveFactor;
float slideFactor = maxSlideFactor;

// Always move forward
Translate(+moveFactor, MoveDirections.Z);

// Slide
if (Input.Keyboard.IsKeyDown(moveLeftKey) ||
  Input.Keyboard.IsKeyDown(Keys.Left) ||
  Input.Keyboard.IsKeyDown(Keys.NumPad4))
{
  consumedAdditionalFuel = true;
  Translate(-slideFactor, MoveDirections.X);
} // if
if (Input.Keyboard.IsKeyDown(moveRightKey) ||
  Input.Keyboard.IsKeyDown(Keys.Right) ||
  Input.Keyboard.IsKeyDown(Keys.NumPad6))
{
  consumedAdditionalFuel = true;
  Translate(+slideFactor, MoveDirections.X);
} // if
```

```
// Up/down
if (Input.Keyboard.IsKeyDown(Keys.F))
{
  Translate(+slideFactor, MoveDirections.Y);
} // if
if (Input.Keyboard.IsKeyDown(Keys.V))
{
  Translate(-slideFactor, MoveDirections.Y);
} // if
#endregion
```

To support the Xbox 360 controller the following code was added in the beginning of 2006 just one day before the game was released. Implementing XInput was very easy and I'm glad XNA uses XInput for all the input classes. The general idea to have all input devices in one namespace is very good in XNA; the only problematic part there is the missing mouse class for the Xbox 360 runtimes. Even if the class is not supported, Microsoft should implement a dummy class to have the code at least compile without having to change all input code that optionally uses a mouse. Well, you fixed that with your own Input class anyway.

Here's the Xbox 360 controller code in Rocket Commander XNA:

```
#region Input support for the XBox360 controller
// 2006-03-09: Added Input support
rotationFactor = 3.0f * BaseGame.MoveFactorPerSecond;

// Change camera rotation when right thumb is used.
if (Input.GamePad.ThumbSticks.Right.X != 0.0f ||
  Input.GamePad.ThumbSticks.Right.Y != 0.0f)
{
  float xMovement = Input.GamePad.ThumbSticks.Right.X;
  float yMovement = Input.GamePad.ThumbSticks.Right.Y;
  Rotate(RotationAxis.Yaw, -xMovement * rotationFactor);
  Rotate(RotationAxis.Pitch, yMovement * rotationFactor);
} // if (Mouse.left.Pressed)

// Use left thumb for moving around
if (Input.GamePad.ThumbSticks.Left.Y != 0)
{
  float oldPlayerSpeed = Player.Speed;
  Player.Speed += 0.75f * Input.GamePad.ThumbSticks.Left.Y *
    BaseGame.MoveFactorPerSecond;

  // Only decrease fuel if change happened
  if (oldPlayerSpeed != Player.Speed)
    consumedAdditionalFuel = true;
} // if

// Slide
if (Input.GamePad.ThumbSticks.Left.X != 0)
{
  consumedAdditionalFuel = true;
```

```
      Translate(slideFactor * Input.GamePad.ThumbSticks.Left.X * 2,
        MoveDirections.X);
    } // if
    #endregion
  } // HandlePlayerInput()
```

You can see all the code that used a lot of helper methods like `Rotate` and `Translate` and made heavy use of the `Input` class properties and some helper values from the `BaseGame` class like `MoveFactorPerSecond`.

`Translate` moves the current camera along the x, y, or z axis. The x axis is used for sliding to the left and right, which can be done with the A and D keys or the cursor keys in Rocket Commander. The y axis allows you to move up and down and the z axis allows you to move forward and backward. In Rocket Commander the z axis is the most important and you fly with very high speed moving on this axis.

```
  /// <summary>
  /// Translate into x, y or z axis with a specfic amount.
  /// </summary>
  /// <param name="amount">Amount</param>
  /// <param name="direction">Direction</param>
  private void Translate(float amount, MoveDirections direction)
  {
    Vector3 dir =
      direction == MoveDirections.X ? XAxis :
      direction == MoveDirections.Y ? YAxis : ZAxis;
    pos += dir * amount;
  } // Translate(amount, direction)
```

Finally, the `Rotate` method is used to rotate the camera around. Yaw rotates you left and right and pitch allows you to rotate up and down. The original Rocket Commander used a Quanternion here and it allowed you to roll around the rocket too. In Rocket Commander XNA the rocket is automatically aligned for you to make it easier on the Xbox 360.

```
  /// <summary>
  /// Rotate around pitch, roll or yaw axis.
  /// </summary>
  /// <param name="axis">Axis</param>
  /// <param name="angle">Angle</param>
  private void Rotate(RotationAxis axis, float angle)
  {
    if (axis == RotationAxis.Yaw)
      yawRotation -= angle;
    else
      pitchRotation -= angle;
  } // Rotate(axis, angle)
```

All camera classes have unit tests to test them out. Make sure you test them if you try to create your own camera class or run into troubles.

Challenge: Write a Free Camera Class

You already learned everything there is to know to handle input devices. Optional input devices like an Xbox 360 Wheel Controller are supported automatically as a gamepad in the `Input` class. You could, for example, play Rocket Commander XNA with an Xbox Wheel Controller if you like. It will be unnatural, but it works and it looks funny.

You also have a lot of game screens classes and you will try to reuse them for the next games. The XNA Shooter game, for example, uses almost the same menu structure as Rocket Commander XNA, just more simplified. In the next chapter you learn more about the XNA Shooter game.

Your task for this chapter is to write your own free camera class. You could implement a free camera in 3D space, allowing you to move to any direction you want. Just exchange the `SimpleCamera` class in `BaseGame` and replace it with your camera class; then you can test all unit tests that show 3D data to test out your camera. If you are unsure about how to start, check out the existing code in the `SpaceCamera` class, which provides most functionality for this kind of camera handling.

Alternatively, you could implement a shooter camera, which also allows you to freely rotate and move around, but you stay on the ground. You could even improve this camera and do simple collision tests with the ground allowing you to go up or down when the underground allows it. If you want to do this I recommend that you write a unit test that shows some objects and a ground plane first to test out your camera class.

Summary

You learned a lot about input devices and how to handle them in XNA. The Xbox 360 controller code is the easiest, but most PC users will not have an Xbox 360 controller and many games are not optimal for this kind of controller. For example, strategy or 3D shooter games work much better with a mouse and keyboard setup instead of using a gamepad. The sad thing about XNA is that the mouse device is not supported on the Xbox 360, so all mouse code you implement on the PC version of your game will not work on the Xbox 360. Keyboard devices are supported on both platforms, but Xbox 360 users will usually just have the Xbox 360 controller. This means you have to implement all three input devices for all your games if you want them to run on both platforms correctly. Thanks to your new `Input` class this is not a difficult job.

Then you learned about the game screen classes, and with help of the game screen stack it is easy to execute all game screen classes derived from the `IGameScreen` interface. For example, the Rocket Commander game uses the following game screen classes (most other games in this book behave similarly):

- Main Menu
- Mission Selection
- Mission (the game itself)
- Highscores

❑   Credits

❑   Help

❑   Options

Finally, many camera classes were discussed and it was your job to implement another one. You really have a powerful graphics engine now. Writing a complete game with it is still not a piece of cake, but you can get the job done much faster now and it will be more fun writing a game like XNA Shooter, as you can see in the next chapter.

11

Creating XNA Shooter

In this chapter I want to guide you through the creation of XNA Shooter, a little shoot-'em-up game, which is actually quite fun to play. It looks and feels better than the usual boring arcade games thanks to many cool effects, nice looking 3D models and a 3D landscape in the background with houses and plants, real-time shadow mapping, a cool sound track, and nice sound effects. I did not really expect to get such a great game out of it when I started programming XNA Shooter (as you can probably guess from the name, which is not that great). But after I added shadow mapping, which is also used in the racing game in the last part of this book, the background and the 3D buildings looked very nice. The nice UI from the previous chapter and some cool post-screen shaders (see Chapter 8) also help.

This chapter allows you to follow every step that was made to create XNA Shooter. The basic game was coded in two to three days and only some of the more advanced classes like the `EffectManager` and the shadow mapping needed some additional tweaking. Shadow mapping is one of those things that is not only hard to implement at first, but you can spend days or even weeks tweaking it over and over again to make it look a little better and fix some issues (and there are always issues). XNA Shooter is completely based on the XnaGraphicEngine from Chapter 5 and on Rocket Commander XNA from Chapter 8. Only in this way is it even possible to create such a good looking game in that short timeframe.

It was not so much work to create the 3D models because I already had most of them from older projects. Thanks to the simple camera, which is fixed and always looks down on the ground, some 3D classes like rendering sky cube maps or lens flares could be ignored. The camera also simplifies the way you can do the shadow mapping because you always see about the same 3D area in size.

The game logic itself is handled in four classes:

❑   The `Player` class, which you already know from the Rocket Commander game. It is even simpler here because you only need to keep track of the current time, score, health, and weapons.

❑   The `Unit` class handles all enemy units; it updates their positions and AI and renders them on the screen.

❏　The `Projectiles` class is used to keep track of all the weapon projectiles you or any enemy unit shoot out. This includes plasma balls, your rockets, fireballs, or enemy rockets. Instant weapons like the MG or Gatling-gun do not have projectiles; they hit the target immediately and you see the effects directly on the screen.

❏　And finally the `Item` class is used to drop items after killing transporter or rocket frigate ships and allowing the player to pick them up by flying over them. Items can be health, EMP bombs, or simply one of the four weapon types.

The game logic is a little bit more complex than for the Rocket Commander game, but after you go through all these classes you can see that the code in the `Mission` class is really easy and after you put everything together the game is almost complete. Just a little bit of play testing and fixing bugs and the game is good to go.

Putting It All Together

You saw some bits and pieces of XNA Shooter in the previous two chapters. Before you can start you need all files in the XNA Shooter project, which has to be created first. The project needs all the sound effects together with the XACT project, and all the usual files like shaders, standard textures for fonts, testing, the menu, and so on. Finally, after adding the .x files for the 3D models and their textures you can go ahead and test them out with help of the unit tests you have in the `Texture`, `Shader`, and `Model` classes.

Figure 11-1 shows the new project, which is just called XnaShooter, after performing the following actions:

❏　Creating a new Windows XNA Game project in XNA Game Studio Express with the name "XnaShooter."

❏　Dragging in all source code files from the Rocket Commander XNA project, which was based on the XnaGraphicEngine. The following files were removed because you won't need them in XnaShooter, sorted by namespaces:

　　❏　Game namespace: `Asteroid.cs`, `BaseAsteroidManager.cs`, `GameAsteroidManager.cs`, `Level.cs`, `PhysicsAsteroidManager.cs`, `SmallAsteroid.cs`, and `SpaceCamera.cs`

　　❏　GameScreens namespace: `Help.cs`, `MissionSelection.cs`, and `Options.cs`

　　❏　Graphics namespace: `AnimatedModel.cs` and `LensFlare.cs`

　　❏　Shaders namespace: `ParallaxShader.cs` and `PreScreenSkyCubeMapping.cs`

❏　`Game1.cs` was also removed and the `RocketCommanderGame` class was renamed to `XnaShooterGame`.

❏　The `RocketCommanderXna` namespace that is used in all files is replaced with the `XnaShooter` namespace.

❏　Most code from the `Mission.cs`, `Player.cs`, `MainMenu.cs`, and `XnaShooterGame.cs` had to be commented out in order to allow compiling the project.

Figure 11-1

Sounds

The source code files are important, but without any textures, sounds, and 3D models you would not have a real game. Because the XnaShooter XACT project was already discussed in Chapter 9, it is the first thing you are going to add to your new project. The only file that has to be in your project is the XnaShooter.xap file, but it uses many .wav files. I tend to add all these .wav files to the project too because I like to see which files are used directly in the project.

After the XACT project is added to the Sounds namespace you can change the Sound class and test all the sounds with help of the TestPlaySounds unit test. The unit test does not cover all sounds, but the most important sound effects are tested here. Some sounds like GameMusic and Explosion are using more than one sound file. This means if you play the Explosion sound one of three explosion sound files is randomly selected and played. There is no special code required for this to work; everything is set up in XACT.

```
public static void TestPlaySounds()
{
  TestGame.Start(
    delegate
    {
      if (Input.MouseLeftButtonJustPressed ||
        Input.GamePadAJustPressed)
        Sound.Play(Sounds.Defeat);
      else if (Input.MouseRightButtonJustPressed ||
        Input.GamePadBJustPressed)
        Sound.Play(Sounds.Victory);
      else if (Input.KeyboardKeyJustPressed(Keys.D1))
        Sound.Play(Sounds.GameMusic);
      else if (Input.KeyboardKeyJustPressed(Keys.D2))
        Sound.Play(Sounds.EnemyShoot);
      else if (Input.KeyboardKeyJustPressed(Keys.D3))
        Sound.Play(Sounds.Explosion);
      else if (Input.KeyboardKeyJustPressed(Keys.D4))
        Sound.Play(Sounds.Health);
      else if (Input.KeyboardKeyJustPressed(Keys.D5))
        Sound.Play(Sounds.PlasmaShoot);
      else if (Input.KeyboardKeyJustPressed(Keys.D6))
        Sound.Play(Sounds.MgShoot);
      else if (Input.KeyboardKeyJustPressed(Keys.D7))
        Sound.Play(Sounds.GattlingShoot);
      else if (Input.KeyboardKeyJustPressed(Keys.D8))
        Sound.Play(Sounds.EMP);

      TextureFont.WriteText(2, 30,
        "Press 1-8 or A/B or left/right mouse buttons to play back "+
        "sounds!");
    });
} // TestPlaySounds()
```

User Interface

The UI and menu textures should be added now. The previous chapter talked quite a bit about handling the input, the UI, and the game screen's logic, so just add the required files (MainMenu.png, MouseCursor.dds, and GameFont.png) and take a look at the game screen logic (see Figure 11-2). Implementing the main menu and the other game screens should not take long. It is very similar to the Rocket Commander game, but several complicated screens like the Options and Mission Selection screens were removed because they were not really necessary for XnaShooter.

You already learned about the in-game UI for XnaShooter, and the game logic for the whole game is discussed at the end of this chapter. For the menu you only have three screens and all of them are easy to implement. The Main Menu just shows four menu buttons, which add a new game screen on the stack to allow you to return to the main menu after quitting the newly added game screen. The Highscore list is a stripped-down version of the Rocket Commander Highscore screen just showing a local highscore because there is no network support for an online highscore in XNA. Last but not least, the Credits screen just shows a bunch of text plus the Back button.

Figure 11-2

Take a quick look at the `MainMenu Run` method, which handles the main menu and the four buttons to the other game screens:

```
// Render background
game.RenderMenuBackground();

// Show all buttons
int buttonNum = 0;
foreach (MenuButton button in menuButtons)
  // Don't render the back button
  if (button != MenuButton.Back)
```

```
    {
      if (game.RenderMenuButton(button, buttonLocations[buttonNum]))
      {
        if (button == MenuButton.Missions)
          game.AddGameScreen(new Mission());
        else if (button == MenuButton.Highscore)
          game.AddGameScreen(new Highscores());
        else if (button == MenuButton.Credits)
          game.AddGameScreen(new Credits());
        else if (button == MenuButton.Exit)
          quit = true;
      } // if
      buttonNum++;
      if (buttonNum >= buttonLocations.Length)
        break;
    } // foreach if

// Hotkeys, M=Mission, H=Highscores, C=Credits, Esc=Quit
if (Input.KeyboardKeyJustPressed(Keys.M))
  game.AddGameScreen(new Mission());
else if (Input.KeyboardKeyJustPressed(Keys.H))
  game.AddGameScreen(new Highscores());
else if (Input.KeyboardKeyJustPressed(Keys.C))
  game.AddGameScreen(new Credits());
else if (Input.KeyboardEscapeJustPressed)
  quit = true;
```

Textures

In addition to the menu, mouse, and game font textures you need a bunch more textures for the game. First of all there are the HUD textures you already saw in the previous chapter and the new NumbersFont.png texture for some colorful numbers you are going to display on the top HUD bar. Then there are also many effect textures you need for the effect system discussed later in this chapter. It is hard to explain which texture is used for which part of the game; please just take a look at Figure 11-3 for a quick explanation on how each texture is used in XNA Shooter.

All these texture files have to be added to the project, but the content importer settings are not all the same. Some files like the mouse cursor, the main menu, and the game font should not be compressed with the DXT compression format (used in dds files). They should stay uncompressed in 32bpp (bits per pixel), but other textures like the explosion effects need compression to become smaller. For example, the BigExplosion effect consists of about 30 textures with the size 128x128. Without compression this would be about 2 MB of texture data just for one explosion effect.

With DXT5 compression you can get it down to half an MB, allowing you to implement several explosion effects and still save disk and video memory space. To support the alpha channel of the explosion textures the DXT5 compression format has to be used instead of DXT1, which would compress even better.

The game has about 3 MB of textures, where 1 MB is just for the two explosion effects and another MB goes to the menu graphics. The rest of the textures are used for the visual effects, the HUD, and fonts. Effect systems can be much more complex with many little particles acting together to form cool big explosions. Sometimes effects are even combined with a physics engine and allow you to let the particles, smoke, and explosion pieces interact with the 3D environment and even with each other.

Figure 11-3

For the XnaShooter game the simple effect system is sufficient; all effects are hard coded, but it is very easy to change them or to add new effects using the existing textures. Just add another Add method and test it with help of the TestEffects unit test in the EffectManager class.

3D Models

The game uses a lot of 3D models (see Figure 11-4). I just started with a ship and some effects, but after a while I noticed that the game would be no fun without at least 3–4 different enemy units that behave differently. The units in XNA Shooter are very different:

❏ OwnShip is the model for your own ship. It allows you to shoot with an MG, Plasma, Gatling-Gun, or the Rocket Launcher. Additionally you can fire EMP bombs to kill everything on the screen. Your ship is the fastest one in the game, but when the screen gets filled with enemy units, that won't help you; you have to kill everything before the enemies can overwhelm you.

❏ Corvette is the basic enemy unit; it shoots two small MGs mounted on the left and right side of the ship. It does not have many hitpoints and the weapon is very weak. The main advantage this unit has is the fact that the weapon hits you instantly if you are in the shooting direction of the Corvette. If the screen fills up with many Corvettes you will constantly lose energy if you don't kill them fast enough.

❑ Small-Transporter is a little ship that carries supplies. There's a 25% to 50% chance these ships have something useful for you, especially health items, which are useful if you are low on health, and EMP bombs can be collected after you kill these transporters. They carry all the other items too, allowing you to switch your weapon after collecting new weapon items. Transporters do not shoot, but you should not collide with them. They are small and have even fewer hitpoints than the Corvette ship.

❑ The Firebird is a very powerful unit because it shoots fireballs directly at you. It even calculates the position you are currently flying to forcing you to constantly evade the incoming fireballs. It has more hitpoints than the other smaller ships and it is a little bigger. Do not collide with Firebirds; they can immensely reduce your energy. Often only an EMP can help you if too many Firebirds are on the screen.

❑ The Rocket-Frigate is the biggest ship in the game. Originally I also wanted to create a Boss-Enemy at the end of the level, but it was too much work creating the 3D model and implementing the additional game logic. It should not be hard to add a Boss-Enemy and more levels to the game if you are really interested in developing a shoot-'em-up game. The Rocket-Frigate fires rockets, similar to the rockets your own ship can fire, but they are a lot smaller and do not inflict as much damage. In addition to the heavy armor and high amount of hitpoints this unit has, the main advantage of the rockets that are fired by the Rocket-Frigate is the homing ability of the rockets, which will always follow your ship until they run out of fuel. Handling just one Rocket-Frigate is no big problem. If you are skilled enough to evade the incoming rockets and are able to still hit the Rocket-Frigate, it will be demolished after a short while. It becomes a lot harder if you have to deal with multiple Rocket-Frigates at the end of the mission. Make sure you have a heavy weapon and EMP bombs on your ship to prepare for these situations.

❑ Asteroids are not really a unit; they just fly around and block your way. They cannot shoot, but if you collide with them you lose a high amount of hitpoints. They are almost indestructible with normal weapons, but with help of EMP bombs you are able to take them out. You have probably noticed that I stole this model from the Rocket Commander game.

The units are very important for your game, but without the items it would be no fun and without the background objects it would look too boring. The items give you back health or EMP bombs or allow you to change the weapon to the four available weapons: MG, Plasma Gun, Gatling-Gun, and the Rocket Launcher.

The background objects do not interact with the game at all; they just sit in the background and receive shadows. First the LandscapeBackground.X model is rendered and repeated for the mission. Later in this chapter you learn more details about the creation process and the level generation. After rendering the landscape all buildings and plants are rendered on top of it. Because the center of the landscape model forms a valley that has the same height at all locations you can easily add the buildings and plants here. All the objects are randomly added and generated as you fly through the level. You can also add more objects if you want to. It is very easy to change the landscape models list; just add another model and it will automatically be generated on the ground.

Animated Textures

You already used animated textures before in the Rocket Commander game, but you never learned how to implement them. Basically you just have a bunch of textures, which are changed every 1/30 of a second. In XNA Shooter two animated textures are implemented for the two explosion effects used when units explode. You could just load the 30 textures for each explosion effect and handle them yourself, but because you need that code more than once it should be abstracted to a new class: `AnimatedTevaxture` (see Figure 11-5).

Figure 11-4

Figure 11-5

The constructor of `AnimatedTexture` is very similar to the `Texture` constructor, but you also check for additional textures with the help of the filename. The big explosion has sequential texture names like `BigExplosion0001.dds`, `BigExplosion0002.dds`, `BigExplosion0003.dds`, and so on. The following code in the constructor is used to load all these filenames into the internal `xnaTextures` array. Please note that in the original Rocket Commander code (Managed DirectX) dds files were loaded, but in XNA you should load the already compiled .xnb files, which is the only way to load textures on the Xbox 360 (the Windows platform, however, also supports loading directly from dds files).

```
// Ok, now load all other animated textures
List<XnaTexture> animatedTextures =
   new List<XnaTexture>();
animatedTextures.Add(internalXnaTexture);
int texNumber = 2;
while (File.Exists(filenameFirstPart +
   texNumber.ToString("0000")+".xnb"))
{
   animatedTextures.Add(BaseGame.Content.Load<Texture2D>(
      filenameFirstPart + texNumber.ToString("0000")));
   texNumber++;
} // while (File.Exists)
xnaTextures = animatedTextures.ToArray();
```

With the help of the `Select` method you can now select any of the loaded textures, and the rest of the class behaves exactly the same as the original texture class. This means you can select and render textures on the screen or pass the texture to shaders because the internal `xnaTexture` field is assigned to the correct selected texture. You can also just call `GetAnimatedTexture` to access any animated texture number yourself.

```
/// <summary>
/// Select this animated texture as the current texture
/// </summary>
/// <param name="animationNumber">Number</param>
public void Select(int animationNumber)
{
   if (xnaTextures != null &&
      xnaTextures.Length > 0)
   {
```

```
      // Select new animation number
      internalXnaTexture =
        xnaTextures[animationNumber % xnaTextures.Length];
    } // if
  } // Select(num)
```

Billboards

You now have all the content in place for your XNA Shooter game. You still need to think about a way to display all this new content. You do not have any rendering code for the landscape and all the objects on it yet and you don't have code to display the new effects in your 3D environment. In Rocket Commander you just displayed the explosion, the only effect you had there, directly on the screen. In your new game it would not look very convincing to put all effects directly on top of the screen. Having the effects directly in your 3D scene as 3D polygons has several advantages:

❏ You don't need to calculate the 2D position and size for every 3D effect. When using 3D polygons they will be transformed to the screen like everything else.

❏ Thanks to the depth buffer it is possible to render effects in front of and behind of other 3D objects. This way flare and smoke effects behind the ship engines look correct even if parts of the ship or other 3D objects are in front.

❏ If you sort the effects back to front you can render them on top of each other with alpha blending turned. This way many effects are combined to give greater looking 3D effects.

To be able to render 3D effects directly on the screen, billboards are usually used. Billboards are just 3D quads (two triangles) showing the texture. Sometimes special graphic card features like point sprites can be used. In any case the billboards should be visible when you view them. But as with any 3D polygons, if they face in the wrong direction you can't see them or they get distorted and smaller (see Figure 11-6).

For some effects this behavior is good; for example, a 3D explosion ring would look correct from the front and the sides except maybe from a 90 degree angle, when it almost disappears. Most other effects, however, are not designed to look good from the side. Explosions, light effects, fire and plasma balls, and so on are all effects that are captured from the front, but they look similar or just like it from all other sides too. Take the fireball effect as an example. A fireball should look like a ball from all directions; it should not be distorted, become small, or disappear if you look from the other side. To achieve that you have to make sure you always look the effect in the eye, so to speak. This is accomplished by always rotating the effect polygons in a way that faces directly to the viewer. The Billboard class helps you achieve this task (see Figure 11-7).

The most important methods of the Billboard class are the Render methods that put the billboards into the billboards list, which is finally rendered when you call RenderBillboards at the end of each frame. There are six overloads of the Render method, but you can also call the RenderOnGround methods to render billboards on the xy plane. One of the Render methods even allows you to specify the right and up vectors, which span the billboard vectors. This way you can randomly align explosion rings for the ship explosion in addition to the other explosion effects.

Viewing Polygons

Directly in Front

From the Side

From the Top

From the Left
Almost not visible

From the Back
(not visible when Culling is on)

Figure 11-6

Figure 11-7

Before you take a look at the Render methods, check out the unit test of the Billboard class, which shows you how to use this class:

```
Billboard.Render(plasma,
  new Vector3(-40.0f, 0.0f, 0.0f), 5.0f,
  BaseGame.TotalTimeMs * (float)Math.PI / 1000.0f,
  Color.White);
Billboard.Render(fireball,
  new Vector3(-40.0f, +50.0f, 0.0f), 5.0f, 0,
  Color.White);
Billboard.RenderOnGround(ring,
  new Vector3(-25.0f, 0.0f, -100.0f), 5.0f, 0, Color.White,
  vecGroundRight, vecGroundUp);
// etc.

// Render all billboards for this frame
Billboard.RenderBillboards();
```

In the Render methods the vecRight and vecUp vectors are used to construct the billboard polygons. These vectors can be directly extracted from the view matrix you currently use. Thanks to the BaseGame class it is easy to extract these vectors, which is automatically done every time you call RenderBillboards through the CalcVectors helper method.

```
/// <summary>
/// Calc vectors for billboards, will create helper vectors for
/// billboard rendering, should just be called every frame.
/// </summary>
public static void CalcVectors()
{
  // Only use the inverse view matrix, world matrix is assumed to be
  // Idenity, simply grab the values out of the inverse view matrix.
  Matrix invViewMatrix = BaseGame.InverseViewMatrix;
  vecRight = new Vector3(
    invViewMatrix.M11, invViewMatrix.M12, invViewMatrix.M13);
  vecUp = new Vector3(
    invViewMatrix.M21, invViewMatrix.M22, invViewMatrix.M23);
} // CalcVectors()
```

Take a quick look at one of the Render methods of the Billboard class:

```
/// <summary>
/// Render 3D Billboard into scene. Used for 3D effects.
/// This method does not support rotation (it is a bit faster).
/// </summary>
/// <param name="tex">Texture used for rendering</param>
/// <param name="lightBlendMode">Blend mode for this effect</param>
/// <param name="pos">Position in world space</param>
/// <param name="size">Size in world coordinates</param>
/// <param name="col">Color, usually white</param>
public static void Render(XnaTexture tex, BlendMode lightBlendMode,
  Vector3 pos, float size, Color col)
{
```

```
      // Invisible?
      if (col.A == 0)
        return;

      TextureBillboardList texBillboard =
        GetTextureBillboard(tex, lightBlendMode);
      Vector3 vec;
      int index = texBillboard.vertices.Count;
      vec = pos + ((-vecRight + vecUp) * size);
      texBillboard.vertices.Add(
        new VertexPositionColorTexture(
        vec, col, new Vector2(0.0f, 0.0f)));
      vec = pos + ((-vecRight - vecUp) * size);
      texBillboard.vertices.Add(
        new VertexPositionColorTexture(
        vec, col, new Vector2(0.0f, 1.0f)));
      vec = pos + ((vecRight - vecUp) * size);
      texBillboard.vertices.Add(
        new VertexPositionColorTexture(
        vec, col, new Vector2(1.0f, 1.0f)));
      vec = pos + ((vecRight + vecUp) * size);
      texBillboard.vertices.Add(
        new VertexPositionColorTexture(
        vec, col, new Vector2(1.0f, 0.0f)));

      texBillboard.indices.AddRange(new short[]
        {
          (short)(index+0), (short)(index+1), (short)(index+2),
          (short)(index+0), (short)(index+2), (short)(index+3),
        });
    } // Render(tex, pos, size)
```

As you can see, four vertices are constructed and added to the vertices list for this billboard type. Each texture and light blend mode combination gets its own `TextureBillboardList`. Then indices for the two polygons that form a screen quad are added to the indices list. Both the vertex and index buffers from the `TextureBillboardList` are then rendered together with the texture and the effect shader in the `RenderBillboards` method.

Landscape Rendering

The landscape in XNA Shooter is just a simple 3D model with just one 1024x1024 texture. However, landscape rendering is not an easy topic. You will spend a whole chapter in the next part of this book just to render the landscape and the tracks for the upcoming racing game.

But I did not want to spend so much time for this simple shoot-'em-up game just for the landscape rendering in the background with which you don't even interact in the game. So instead of implementing a landscape engine to render many thousands of polygons, put tile-able textures on these polygons and maybe even implement alpha blending between the different ground texture types. I just took the easy road and used a finished 3D model for the whole landscape. It is just enough to fit on one screen and it does not allow you to scroll to the left or right, but that is not required for this game; you just move up.

The mission is about 60 of these landscape parts long and you simply put them on top of each other, always showing just the current one and the next. It does not fit together perfectly because the lighting on the borders is hard to fix (texture has to fit, normal map has to fit, 3D model normals have to fit), but it is good enough for our purpose.

In this section I want to show you the necessary steps to create such a background model because I'm not the only one who uses this easy technique to get something on the screen quickly (for example, one game modification of Rocket Commander called Canyon Commander uses a similar technique to show 3D canyons).

Base Texture and Normal Map

Before you start with any 3D data or height-map for the background landscape, you should have an idea of what is displayed in the background. My idea was just to have desert sand in the middle and rocks at the sides, which form a little canyon. I quickly grabbed two textures that would fit and threw them together into the `BackgroundRock.dds` texture (see Figure 11-8). To be honest I did not really think of the sand part at first and I thought just having a rock texture was sufficient, but it looked boring and was too repetitive.

Landscape Background Texture Creation

Rocks

Sand

Also mixed in some other textures and removed the contrast a bit for better normal mapping effects later. The color range is also a little bit changed. Textures are blended softly.

The sand texture was a little bit too close so I tiled it 2×2 times to make it appear farther away.

LandscapeRocks.dds

Figure 11-8

The normal map is mixed together in a similar way, but for these two textures I did not have a normal map at first. I used the Nvidia Photoshop plugins to generate normal maps from the two base textures. You have to play around a little bit with the values until it looks good and sometimes you have to repaint the base texture to fix wrong places. The diffuse textures that are used here have no information about the height or normals in it, so the only thing this normal map generator plugin can do is to convert the image to a grayscale format and generate normals from this fake height map.

Sometimes it looks ok, other times it is just plain wrong to generate normals this way. It would be much better if these textures were created by an artist who also provides normal maps or at least height maps with them, but you will not always have this luxury. Sometimes just the diffuse texture exists and if you take a photo with your camera height and normal map, data is not recorded either. Again, try to keep things simple here. You create more complex landscape textures and normal maps in the next chapter for the more complex racing game. Figure 11-9 shows the normal maps mixed together. You will notice that the normals for the rocks use a stronger normal map than for the sand, and that is good because you want to have the rocks appear curvier than the sand on the ground. But even the sand has some variations in it (added on top of the relatively plain sand texture) to get a little bit better lighting from the normal mapping shader used in the game.

Landscape Background Normal Maps

RocksNormal

SandNormal

Note: Our game only used DXT5 compressed textures and even this hand-made normal map has to be converted to this format. Use the NormalMapCompressor tool for this job.

Uncompressed NormalMap

LandscapeRocksNormal.dds

Figure 11-9

Height Map

With the diffuse and normal texture in place you can now display the landscape background on a simple polygon, but it would not look very convincing or even appear to be 3D this way. You need some real height for the cliffs and the canyon in the middle. To create this canyon I used 3D Studio Max (but you can use whatever 3D content creation tool you feel comfortable with or ask someone who knows how to use these tools if you don't want to create 3D models yourself) and I created a simple plane object on the xy ground (z pointing up) with 64x64 intersection points forming 63*63*2 = 7938 polygons. I used 63 because each polygon needs a start and end position and multiplied by two because each landscape quad is formed from two triangles (see Figure 11-10).

To give each height point another z value than the default 0.0 you could drag them up or down in your 3D modeling program, but I'm not skilled or patient enough to create a landscape this way. A much easier approach is to use a height texture and then displace all height points of your plane according to this height map. Height maps are also often used for geological landscape maps, so it is not very hard to find some cool looking height maps on the Internet, even from other planets.

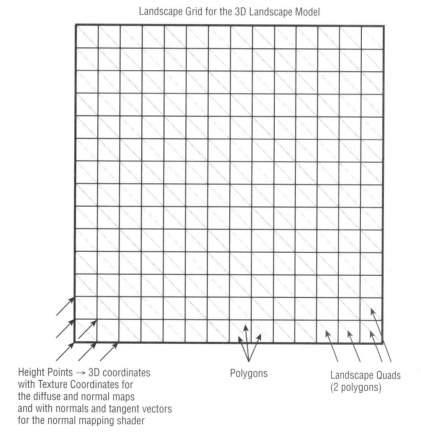

Landscape Grid for the 3D Landscape Model

Height Points → 3D coordinates
with Texture Coordinates for
the diffuse and normal maps
and with normals and tangent vectors
for the normal mapping shader

Polygons

Landscape Quads
(2 polygons)

Figure 11-10

Luckily for us 3D Studio Max has a simple modifier called `Displace`, which does just what you need (not easy to find, but once you know where it is, it becomes very useful). From here you can add your newly created height map (I painted it myself; not spectacular, but it works) to the 3D model (see Figure 11-11).

Nothing happens now; you might ask why that is. Well, Max has many settings and it is not always easy to find out which one is responsible for what. Just play around with the settings until something changes. In this case you need to adjust the Strength setting at the top. Set it to something between 30 and 40 to see a result like the one shown in Figure 11-12.

The final action you have to do in 3D Studio Max is to assign the diffuse and normal textures to a new normal mapping shader material. Then you can assign this material to your 3D model (see Figure 11-13) and export it. It is now ready to be used in your game.

This landscape is now rendered from the top in the game and you will only see the valley and the inner borders of the cliffs. The landscape rendering was tested with support of 16:9 widescreen resolutions, which means on 4:3 resolutions some parts of it might not always be visible. All the action happens in the middle anyway. After you add the 3D buildings and plans in the game everything is up and ready for some shoot-'em-up action.

Figure 11-11

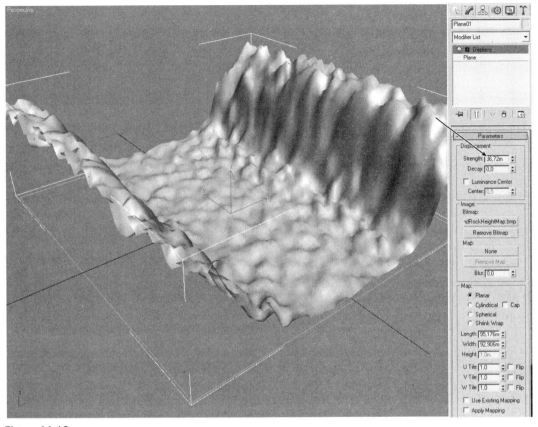

Figure 11-12

Check out the unit test in the `Mission` class to see how this landscape model is rendered in the game. For just taking a look at the 3D model you can also use the unit test in the `Model` class, which shows all used models in the game.

Adding Objects

The landscape looks nice (at least better than a simple xy plane), but it is still kind of empty. To make it a little bit more exciting the buildings and plants you saw earlier are added to it. Check out the `TestRenderLandscapeBackground` unit test at the end of the `Mission` class, which just calls `RenderLandscapeBackground` of the `Mission` class. This method takes the current level position as a parameter and always shows only the current and the next landscape part to ensure you always have 3D models in front of you even when you move up. The player will not notice this because the current landscape part is replaced with the next if you move up enough and a new landscape part is generated at the top until you are done with the level.

Figure 11-13

The more interesting code is the object generation, which takes the array of loaded models and randomly adds new objects to the visible landscape object list. Plants are randomly placed and rotated, but buildings only appear on the left and right side and they are only rotated in 90 degree steps to fit better together.

```
// From the GenerateLandscapeSegment method:
List<MatrixAndNumber> ret = new List<MatrixAndNumber>();
int numOfNewObjects = RandomHelper.GetRandomInt(
  MaxNumberOfObjectsGeneratedEachSegment);
if (numOfNewObjects < 8)
  numOfNewObjects = 8;

for (int num = 0; num < numOfNewObjects; num++)
{
  int type = 1+RandomHelper.GetRandomInt(NumOfLandscapeModels-1);
  // Create buildings only left and right
  if (type <= 5)
  {
```

```
int rotSimple = RandomHelper.GetRandomInt(4);
float rot = rotSimple == 0 ? 0 :
  rotSimple == 1 ? MathHelper.PiOver2 :
  rotSimple == 1 ? MathHelper.Pi : MathHelper.PiOver2 * 3;
bool side = RandomHelper.GetRandomInt(2) == 0;
float yPos = segmentNumber * SegmentLength + 0.94f *
 RandomHelper.GetRandomFloat(-SegmentLength / 2, SegmentLength / 2);
Vector3 pos = new Vector3(side ? -18 : +18, yPos, -16);

// Add very little height to each object to avoid same height
// if buildings collide into each other.
pos += new Vector3(0, 0, 0.001f * num);
ret.Add(new MatrixAndNumber(
  Matrix.CreateScale(LandscapeModelSize[type]) *
  Matrix.CreateRotationZ(rot) *
  Matrix.CreateTranslation(pos),
  type));
} // if
else
{
  ret.Add(new MatrixAndNumber(
    Matrix.CreateScale(LandscapeModelSize[type]) *
    Matrix.CreateRotationZ(
    RandomHelper.GetRandomFloat(0, MathHelper.Pi * 2)) *
    Matrix.CreateTranslation(new Vector3(
    RandomHelper.GetRandomFloat(-20, +20),
    segmentNumber * SegmentLength +
    RandomHelper.GetRandomFloat(
    -SegmentLength / 2, SegmentLength / 2), -15)),
    type));
} // else
} // for
```

The `ret` list is then returned to the caller, which saves it to the requested landscape part. The full `GenerateLandscapeSegment` code also adds all enemy units, checks for colliding landscape objects, and prevents objects from being too close to each other.

If you execute the `TestRenderLandscapeBackground` unit test you should see the landscape and the ground objects like in Figure 11-14. Note that the shadow map generation is not discussed in this chapter; please read the last part of this book for more information about shadow mapping techniques. You can also just check out the `ShadowMappingShader` class if you are interested now.

XNA Shooter Game

It is time for some action now. You have all the 3D models, all effect files and textures, and your sound effects ready to be used, and you don't have to worry about the landscape background anymore because it already works fine. The landscape itself is below the surface (z is below 0); this means you can easily add all your game objects at the z height 0.0, which makes adding effects, collision checking, and testing a little bit easier for the game.

Figure 11-14

You can now add your own ship in the landscape rendering method of the `Mission` class and control it in the `Player` class. Rendering just requires the following lines of code:

```
Player.shipPos =
  new Vector3(Player.position, AllShipsZHeight) + levelVector;
AddModelToRender(
  shipModels[(int)ShipModelTypes.OwnShip],
  Matrix.CreateScale(ShipModelSize[(int)ShipModelTypes.OwnShip]) *
  Matrix.CreateRotationZ(MathHelper.Pi) *
  Matrix.CreateRotationX(Player.shipRotation.Y) *
  Matrix.CreateRotationY(Player.shipRotation.X) *
  Matrix.CreateTranslation(Player.shipPos));

// Add smoke effects for our ship
EffectManager.AddRocketOrShipFlareAndSmoke(
  Player.shipPos + new Vector3(-0.3f, -2.65f, +0.35f), 1.35f,
  5 * Player.MovementSpeedPerSecond);
EffectManager.AddRocketOrShipFlareAndSmoke(
```

```
Player.shipPos + new Vector3(0.3f, -2.65f, +0.35f), 1.35f,
5 * Player.MovementSpeedPerSecond);
```

All the scaling and rotation is just done to get the ship to the correct size and to rotate it correctly. The z rotation lets it point upwards and the x and y rotations let the ship wiggle when moving to the sides or up and down. Then two flare and smoke effects are added where your ship engine is. The EffectManager is discussed in a minute.

Game Logic

The code to control your ships is located in the Player class, where most of the other game logic is handled for you including firing your weapons, moving the ship, getting points for killing ships, and handling items:

```
// From Player.HandleGameLogic:
// [Show victory/defeat messages if game is over]

// Increase game time
gameTimeMs += BaseGame.ElapsedTimeThisFrameInMs;

// Control our ship position with the keyboard or gamepad.
// Use keyboard cursor keys and the left thumb stick. The
// right hand is used for fireing (ctrl, space, a, b).
Vector2 lastPosition = position;
Vector2 lastRotation = shipRotation;
float moveFactor = mouseSensibility *
  MovementSpeedPerSecond * BaseGame.MoveFactorPerSecond;
// Left/Right
if (Input.Keyboard.IsKeyDown(moveLeftKey) ||
  Input.Keyboard.IsKeyDown(Keys.Left) ||
  Input.Keyboard.IsKeyDown(Keys.NumPad4) ||
  Input.GamePad.DPad.Left == ButtonState.Pressed)
{
  position.X -= moveFactor;
} // if
if (Input.Keyboard.IsKeyDown(moveRightKey) ||
  Input.Keyboard.IsKeyDown(Keys.Right) ||
  Input.Keyboard.IsKeyDown(Keys.NumPad6) ||
  Input.GamePad.DPad.Right == ButtonState.Pressed)
{
  position.X += moveFactor;
} // if
if (Input.GamePad.ThumbSticks.Left.X != 0.0f)
{
  position.X += Input.GamePad.ThumbSticks.Left.X;// *0.75f;
} // if

// Keep position in bounds
if (position.X < -MaxXPosition)
  position.X = -MaxXPosition;
if (position.X > MaxXPosition)
  position.X = MaxXPosition;
```

```
// [Same for Down/Up changes position.Y, see Player.cs]

// Calculate ship rotation based on the current movement
if (lastPosition.X > position.X)
  shipRotation.X = -0.5f;
else if (lastPosition.X < position.X)
  shipRotation.X = +0.5f;
else
  shipRotation.X = 0;
// [Same for shipRotation.Y, see above]

// Interpolate ship rotation to be more smooth
shipRotation = lastRotation * 0.95f + shipRotation * 0.05f;
```

HandleGameLogic first checks if the game is over and displays a message on the screen telling you if you have won or lost. Then the current game time is increased. After that your ship control is handled, and then the weapon firing and items are handled at the end of the method together with some code that gives you scores for killing enemy units.

You allow input from the keyboard and gamepad input devices. The mouse is not supported because tweaking it is hard for a shoot-'em-up game and I personally don't like controlling a shoot-'em-up game with the mouse; it feels wrong. With the help of the MaxXPosition and MaxYPosition constants you make sure that your ship does not move outside the visible screen area and the shipRotation is calculated based on the movement you made. If no movement was made it will slowly get back to zero.

The following lines show how the firing is handled. Additional details can be found in the Player class.

```
// Fire?
if (Input.GamePadAPressed ||
  Input.GamePad.Triggers.Right > 0.5f ||
  Input.Keyboard.IsKeyDown(Keys.LeftControl) ||
  Input.Keyboard.IsKeyDown(Keys.RightControl))
{
  switch (currentWeapon)
  {
    case WeaponTypes.MG:
      // Shooting cooldown passed?
      if (gameTimeMs - lastShootTimeMs >= 150)
      {
        // [Shooting code goes here ...]

        shootNum++;
        lastShootTimeMs = gameTimeMs;
        Input.GamePadRumble(0.015f, 0.125f);
        Player.score += 1;
      } // if
      break;
    case WeaponTypes.Plasma:
      // [etc. all other weapons are handled here]
      break;
  } // switch
} // if
```

As soon as you press the A button or the right trigger on the gamepad or the Ctrl keys on the keyboard you enter the firing code, but the weapon will not fire until you reach the next cool-down phase (each weapon has different cool-down times). Then the weapon firing and weapon collision detection is handled and `lastShootTimeMs` is reset to the current game time waiting for the next cool-down phase.

After handling the weapons the only thing left is to create the winning and losing conditions. You achieve victory if you successfully reach the end of the level and you lose if you run out of hitpoints before that happens.

```
if (Player.health <= 0)
{
  victory = false;
  EffectManager.AddExplosion(shipPos, 20);
  for (int num = 0; num<8; num++)
    EffectManager.AddFlameExplosion(shipPos+
      RandomHelper.GetRandomVector3(-12, +12));
  Player.SetGameOverAndUploadHighscore();
} // if
```

The rest of the game logic is part of the enemy units, the items, and the weapon projectiles, which are all handled in their own separate classes that are described at the end of this chapter.

3D Effects

Back to the 3D effects. You already learned a lot about them and thanks to the `Billboard` class it is not hard to render textures in 3D now. The effects are now handled at a higher level; you worry about the effect length, animation steps, and fading them in and out. All the 3D polygon generation and rendering is handled by the `Billboard` and `Texture` classes. All effects are managed through the `EffectManager` class (see Figure 11-15), which allows you to add new effects from anywhere in the code thanks to the many static `Add` methods.

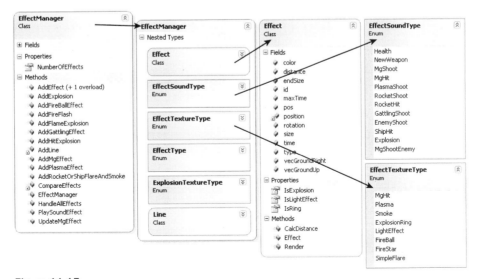

Figure 11-15

You can see the many fields in the inside `Effect` class, which are used to allow you to create many different kinds of 3D effects. Explosions are optimized differently than light effects. For example regular effects are just blended out with an alpha value, but for light effects this does not work because if the alpha value was modified the effect would get darker and look very strange. Instead of doing light effects just get smaller at the end of their. The other enums help you to quickly identify effect types and to add them easily through the `AddEffect` method.

The best way to learn about the `EffectManager` class is to just look at the `TestEffects` unit test at the end of the class. Then add new effects here and implement them after changing the unit test or just write new unit tests for more effects.

```
public static void TestEffects()
{
  TestGame.Start("TestEffects",
    delegate
    {
      // No initialization code necessary here
    },
    delegate
    {
      // Press 1-0 for creating effects in center of the 3D scene
      if (Input.Keyboard.IsKeyDown(Keys.D1) &&
        BaseGame.EveryMs(200))
      AddMgEffect(new Vector3(-10.0f, 0, -10),
        new Vector3((BaseGame.TotalTimeMs % 3592) / 100.0f, 25, +100),
        0, 1, true, true);

      if (Input.Keyboard.IsKeyDown(Keys.D2))
      {
        AddPlasmaEffect(new Vector3(-50.0f, 0.0f, 0.0f), 0.5f, 5);
        AddPlasmaEffect(new Vector3(0.0f, 0.0f, 0.0f), 1.5f, 5);
        AddPlasmaEffect(new Vector3(50.0f, 0.0f, 0.0f), 0.0f, 5);
      } // if (Input.Keyboard.IsKeyDown(Keys.D2])

      if (Input.Keyboard.IsKeyDown(Keys.D3))
      {
        AddFireBallEffect(new Vector3(-50.0f, +10.0f, 0.0f), 0.0f, 10);
        AddFireBallEffect(new Vector3(0.0f, +10.0f, 0.0f),
          (float)Math.PI / 8, 10);
        AddFireBallEffect(new Vector3(50.0f, +10.0f, 0.0f),
          (float)Math.PI * 3 / 8, 10);
      } // if (Input.Keyboard.IsKeyDown(Keys.D3])

      if (Input.Keyboard.IsKeyDown(Keys.D4))
        AddRocketOrShipFlareAndSmoke(
          new Vector3((BaseGame.TotalTimeMs % 4000) / 40.0f, 0, 0),
          5.0f, 150.0f);

      if (Input.Keyboard.IsKeyDown(Keys.D5) &&
        BaseGame.EveryMs(1000))
        AddExplosion(Vector3.Zero, 9.0f);
      // etc.
```

```
      // Play a couple of sound effects
      if (Input.Keyboard.IsKeyDown(Keys.P) &&
        BaseGame.EveryMs(500))
        PlaySoundEffect(EffectSoundType.PlasmaShoot);
      // etc.

      // We have to render the effects ourselfs because
      // it is usually done in RocketCommanderForm (not in TestGame)!
      // Finally render all effects before applying post screen shaders
      BaseGame.effectManager.HandleAllEffects();
    });
  } // TestEffects()
```

Unit Class

Maybe this class should be called EnemyUnit because it is only used for the enemy ships; your own ship is already handled in the Player class. Originally I wanted to unify all units (your own ship and the enemy ships) in this class, but they behave very differently and it only made the code more confusing and complicated. In more complex games you should maybe create a base class for units and then derive it once for enemy units and once for your own and friendly player ships (for example, for multiplayer code, where you want to make sure that all the other players get the same ship movement you do locally on their machines). Anyway, take a look at the class in Figure 11-16.

Figure 11-16

The class uses many fields internally to keep track of each unit's hitpoints, shoot times, position values, and so on, but from the outside the class looks very simple; it just has one method you have to call every frame: Render. The constructor just creates the unit and assigns the unit type, position, and all the default hitpoints and damage values to it (from constant arrays inside the class — more complex games should load these values from xml files or other external data sources that can be changed easily).

As always you should check out the unit test to learn more about this class:

```
public static void TestUnitAI()
{
  Unit testUnit = null;
  Mission dummyMission = null;

  TestGame.Start("TestUnitAI",
    delegate
    {
      dummyMission = new Mission();
      testUnit = new Unit(UnitTypes.Corvette, Vector2.Zero,
        MovementPattern.StraightDown);
      // Call dummyMission.RenderLandscape once to initialize everything
       dummyMission.RenderLevelBackground(0);
      // Remove the all enemy units (the start enemies) and
      // all neutral objects
      dummyMission.numOfModelsToRender = 2;
    },
    delegate
    {
      // [Helper texts are displayed here, press 1-0 or CSFRA, etc.]

      ResetUnitDelegate ResetUnit = delegate(MovementPattern setPattern)
        {
          testUnit.movementPattern = setPattern;
          testUnit.position = new Vector2(
            RandomHelper.GetRandomFloat(-20, +20),
            Mission.SegmentLength/2);
          testUnit.hitpoints = testUnit.maxHitpoints;
          testUnit.speed = 0;
          testUnit.lifeTimeMs = 0;
        };
      if (Input.KeyboardKeyJustPressed(Keys.D1))
        ResetUnit(MovementPattern.StraightDown);
      if (Input.KeyboardKeyJustPressed(Keys.D2))
        ResetUnit(MovementPattern.GetFasterAndMoveDown);
      // [etc.]

      if (Input.KeyboardKeyJustPressed(Keys.Space))
        ResetUnit(testUnit.movementPattern);

      if (Input.KeyboardKeyJustPressed(Keys.C))
        testUnit.unitType = UnitTypes.Corvette;
      if (Input.KeyboardKeyJustPressed(Keys.S))
        testUnit.unitType = UnitTypes.SmallTransporter;
      if (Input.KeyboardKeyJustPressed(Keys.F))
        testUnit.unitType = UnitTypes.Firebird;
```

```
      if (Input.KeyboardKeyJustPressed(Keys.R))
        testUnit.unitType = UnitTypes.RocketFrigate;
      if (Input.KeyboardKeyJustPressed(Keys.A))
        testUnit.unitType = UnitTypes.Asteroid;

      // Update and render unit
      if (testUnit.Render(dummyMission))
        // Restart unit if it was removed because it was too far down
        ResetUnit(testUnit.movementPattern);

      // Render all models the normal way
      for (int num = 0; num < dummyMission.numOfModelsToRender; num++)
        dummyMission.modelsToRender[num].model.Render(
          dummyMission.modelsToRender[num].matrix);
      BaseGame.MeshRenderManager.Render();
      // Restore number of units as before.
      dummyMission.numOfModelsToRender = 2;

      // Show all effects (unit smoke, etc.)
      BaseGame.effectManager.HandleAllEffects();
    });
} // TestUnitAI()
```

The unit test allows you to press C, S, F, R, or A to change the unit type to the five available units: Corvette, Small Transporter, Firebird, Rocket-Frigate, and Asteroid. By pressing 1-0 you are able to change the AI behavior of this unit. Speaking about AI here is a little bit crazy because all the AI does for the unit is to handle the movement differently. The unit just follows certain movement patterns and is in no way intelligent. For example, the GetFasterAndMoveDown movement code looks like this:

```
case MovementPattern.GetFasterAndMoveDown:
  // Out of visible area? Then keep speed slow and wait.
  if (position.Y - Mission.LookAtPosition.Y > 30)
    lifeTimeMs = 300;
  if (lifeTimeMs < 3000)
    speed = lifeTimeMs / 3000;
  position += new Vector2(0, -1) * speed * 1.5f * maxSpeed * moveSpeed;
  break;
```

Other movement patterns are even simpler. The name of each movement pattern should tell you enough about the behavior. In the game you randomly assign a movement pattern to each new unit. You could also create a level with predefined positions and unit values including the movement AI for a shoot-'em-up game, but I wanted to keep things simple. The rest of the unit test just renders the unit and the background landscape. It was used to create the whole Unit class and it should cover everything except the shooting and dying of units, which is tested easier directly in the game.

Projectile Class

While we are speaking about units shooting around, the code required to let the Corvette shoot is not so complicated because it immediately hits you if you are below it when it shoots (it just checks its and your x and y position and acts accordingly). Corvettes just shoot into the emptiness most of the time.

All other units do not fire instant weapons; instead projectiles like rockets, fireballs, or plasma balls are fired. These projectiles stay active for a short while and fly toward their target position. The `Projectile` class (see Figure 11-17) helps you manage these objects and simplifies the weapon logic because you can now just shoot a projectile and forget about it. The projectile will handle collisions with any enemy ships themselves and after it runs out of fuel or goes out of the visible area, it is removed too.

There are three different projectiles in XNA Shooter and they all behave a little differently:

❑ Plasma projectiles are only fired from your own ship and you fire them only if you currently have the Plasma weapon. Plasma projectiles are fast and inflict more damage than the MG can, but the Gatling-Gun and the Rocket Launcher are more powerful, although they have their disadvantages too.

❑ Fireballs are fired from enemy Firebird ships and they fly slowly toward you. They do not change direction, but the enemy Firebird's AI shoots them a little bit ahead of you, so you always have to evade them.

❑ Rockets are used by both you and the enemy Rocket Frigate ship. Your rockets are bigger and inflict more damage, but they just fly straight ahead. Enemy rockets are more intelligent and will adjust their target to your ship position, constantly making it much harder to evade them.

Figure 11-17

Compared to the `Unit` class `Render` method, the `Projectile` class `Render` method is not very complex. The most interesting part is the collision handling after updating the position and rendering the projectile in the `Render` method.

```
public bool Render(Mission mission)
{
  // [Update movement ...]

  // [Render projectile, either the 3D model for the rocket or just the
  // effect for the Fireball or Plasma weapons]
```

```
// Own projectile?
if (ownProjectile)
{
  // Hit enemy units, check all of them
  for (int num = 0; num < Mission.units.Count; num++)
  {
    Unit enemyUnit = Mission.units[num];
    // Near enough to enemy ship?
    Vector2 distVec =
      new Vector2(enemyUnit.position.X, enemyUnit.position.Y) -
      new Vector2(position.X, position.Y);
    if (distVec.Length() < 7 &&
      (enemyUnit.position.Y - Player.shipPos.Y) < 60)
    {
      // Explode and do damage!
      EffectManager.AddFlameExplosion(position);
      Player.score += (int)enemyUnit.hitpoints / 10;
      enemyUnit.hitpoints -= damage;
      return true;
    } // if
  } // for
} // if
// Else this is an enemy projectile?
else
{
  // Near enough to our ship?
  Vector2 distVec =
    new Vector2(Player.shipPos.X, Player.shipPos.Y) -
    new Vector2(position.X, position.Y);
  if (distVec.Length() < 3)
  {
    // Explode and do damage!
    EffectManager.AddFlameExplosion(position);
    Player.health -= damage / 1000.0f;
    return true;
  } // if
} // else

// Don't remove projectile yet
return false;
} // Render()
```

If this is your own projectile (plasma or rocket) you have to check if it collides with any enemy ship that is currently active. If that happens you inflict the damage this projectile does and the explosion effect is added. You also get some points for this kill (10% of the unit's remaining health). Then true is returned to tell the caller of this method that you are done with this projectile and it can be removed from the currently active projectiles list. This also happens if the projectile goes outside of the visible landscape area.

If the projectile was shot by an enemy unit, the collision checking code is much simpler; you only have to check if it collides with the player ship and then the damage is inflicted the same way. Both your unit and the enemy unit's death is handled by their own Render method. You already saw the defeat condition earlier that is triggered when you run out of health. The enemy unit's death condition looks very similar, and there you also return true to allow removing this unit from the current unit list.

Item Class

Last but not least, the Item class is used to handle all the items in the game. It is very simple as you can see in Figure 11-18, but without it the game would not be half the fun. As you can see from the ItemTypes enum inside the class there are six available items. Four of them are the weapons for your ship and the other two are the health item, which completely refreshes your ship's health, and the EMP bomb, which allows you to kill all units on the screen by pressing the space key. You can stack up to three bombs at the same time.

Figure 11-18

The Render method is similar to the one from the Projectiles class; you just don't kill anyone that collides with this projectile. Instead the player can collect these items and their effect is immediately handled. This means you either get a new weapon or you can get back 100% of your health or you get another EMP bomb.

```
/// <summary>
/// Render item, returns false if we are done with it.
/// </summary>
/// <returns>True if done, false otherwise</returns>
public bool Render(Mission mission)
{
    // Remove unit if it is out of visible range!
    float distance = Mission.LookAtPosition.Y - position.Y;
    const float MaxUnitDistance = 60;
    if (distance > MaxUnitDistance)
        return true;

    // Render
    float itemSize = Mission.ItemModelSize;
    float itemRotation = 0;
    Vector3 itemPos = new Vector3(position, Mission.AllShipsZHeight);
    mission.AddModelToRender(mission.itemModels[(int)itemType],
        Matrix.CreateScale(itemSize) *
        Matrix.CreateRotationZ(itemRotation) *
        Matrix.CreateTranslation(itemPos));
```

```
      // Add glow effect around the item
  EffectManager.AddEffect(itemPos + new Vector3(0, 0, 1.01f),
    EffectManager.EffectType.LightInstant,
    7.5f, 0, 0);
  EffectManager.AddEffect(itemPos + new Vector3(0, 0, 1.02f),
    EffectManager.EffectType.LightInstant,
    5.0f, 0, 0);

  // Collect item and give to player if colliding!
  Vector2 distVec =
    new Vector2(Player.shipPos.X, Player.shipPos.Y) -
    new Vector2(position.X, position.Y);
  if (distVec.Length() < 5.0f)
  {
    if (itemType == ItemTypes.Health)
    {
      // Refresh health
      Sound.Play(Sound.Sounds.Health);
      Player.health = 1.0f;
    } // if
    else
    {
      Sound.Play(Sound.Sounds.NewWeapon);
      if (itemType == ItemTypes.Mg)
        Player.currentWeapon = Player.WeaponTypes.MG;
      else if (itemType == ItemTypes.Plasma)
        Player.currentWeapon = Player.WeaponTypes.Plasma;
      else if (itemType == ItemTypes.Gattling)
        Player.currentWeapon = Player.WeaponTypes.Gattling;
      else if (itemType == ItemTypes.Rockets)
        Player.currentWeapon = Player.WeaponTypes.Rockets;
      else if (itemType == ItemTypes.Emp &&
        Player.empBombs < 3)
        Player.empBombs++;
    } // else
    Player.score += 500;
    return true;
  } // else

  // Don't remove item yet
  return false;
} // Render()
```

The render code just puts the item at the given screen location rotated and scaled correctly. It also adds two light effects to make the item glow a little. If you don't look at the items you might not notice the glow effect, but when it is missing it is a lot harder to detect the items currently flying around.

If you are closer than five units to any item, you automatically collect it. Your ship has a radius of about five units too, which means you can touch the item with any part of your ship. Then the item is handled either giving you health or the new weapon, and after that you even get a little bit of extra score for your heroic act of collecting this item. The item can now be removed. If you did not collide with the item, it stays active until you do or it is no longer visible.

Final Screenshot

Yeah, you finally made it. That was everything you need for your XNA Shooter game; see Figure 11-19 for the result. I hope this chapter was more helpful than Chapter 8 where I did not want to repeat my existing Rocket Commander tutorials, which already explain how to create the original Rocket Commander game.

I hope you enjoy XNA Shooter and you find it useful if you want to create your own shoot-'em-up game. Remember that it was created in only a couple of days and you can probably make it much better, add more levels, enemy ships, or a better AI. Have fun with it.

Figure 11-19

Challenge: Write a Game with Your Engine

A lot of games were already discussed in this book and before you get to your final blockbuster game I want you to think about creating your own little game with your existing engine. You saw all the important steps in this chapter, from creating the project based on the Rocket Commander XNA engine to the XNA Shooter engine, that is even more powerful (except you want to make a space game, of course). You probably have some great game idea in your head already and you should not wait any longer to start this game idea if you haven't done so already.

It took me more than half the time to implement all the additional helper classes for XNA Shooter; even more if I put the shadow mapping in, which had to be adjusted quite a lot to look good in the game. Coding the game itself was a lot more fun and having to play it over and over again was also a lot of fun, especially at the end when all the effects and units were correctly implemented.

If you have a really big game idea and not some kind of a simple arcade game you should try to build a prototype first because doing a MMORPG (which stands for Massive Multiplayer Online Role Playing Game) like World of WarCraft alone is just impossible and you might spend years before you realize that you can never get as big as those monster games. When I give advice to beginners and game programmers this is my number one tip: Start with a small game and work your way up. This does not mean you have to create Tetris or a Jump'n'Run game first if all you want to do is to create an RPG (role playing game), but try to implement only one small part of your game idea (maybe running around with your hero and slaying or shooting at some simple monsters) and go from there.

Writing games is not easy today. It has gotten a lot easier thanks to XNA and many useful tutorials you can find on the Internet, but getting everything together and working is often underestimated. Try to get your first game working (including UI, input, the menu, and some simple game logic) and then think about your next monster project instead of the other way around. This is the number one reason why more than half of all game projects on the Internet are canceled before they are halfway done.

Anyway, good luck with your game project. Feel free to contact me and tell me about it, especially if it is based on one of my game engines.

Summary

In this chapter you learned all about the XNA Shooter game. It not only introduced 3D effects, billboards, simple landscape rendering, and handling the game logic with all the new game classes, but it also prepared you for the more advanced racing game project you are going to encounter next.

Your graphics engine is now capable of rendering textures, 3D models, 3D effects, shaders, handling sound effects with XACT, and it handles the user input and all game classes easily for you. You are also very familiar with some of the game classes by now. The Player class for handling most of your own game logic has been proven worthy in the Rocket Commander XNA and in the XNA Shooter games. Other aspects of the game programming world like the landscape rendering and shadow mapping were also introduced for the first time in this chapter, but you learn about those advanced topics in the next chapters in greater detail.

Part IV of this book is devoted completely to a cool looking racing game. You are going to create a beautiful 3D landscape for the game and generate tracks from spline data. Additionally you are going to take a tour through the world of physics for games, which was already handled a little bit by the Rocket Commander game, but the racing game needs a much more complex model. Finally, you are going to learn about the game logic in the racing game and how to fine-tune such a big project.

Part IV: Writing a Racing Game

12

Generating Landscapes and Tracks

To create the last big game for this book, the XNA Racing Game, you have to go through some more advanced topics in the next chapters.

This chapter covers the whole landscape generation and render techniques as well as the track data for the roads in all levels. The next chapter takes a closer look at the physics engine required for the racing game. In the final chapter you learn all about the game screens, game logic, and fine-tuning of the racing game and get some final tips about game development. The game that is covered in this book is a complete racing game, but it only shows you one track and a simplified game principle. The complete XNA Racing Game is available as a starter kit for the XNA Framework by Microsoft. The complete game covers more missions, more cool features, several cars, more cool looking 3D objects, and a whopping 10 video tutorials, which you can download and watch to learn more. This book covers all the basics to allow you to create a cool game like the racing game, but I wanted to cover more than just one game (maybe you don't like racing games so much; for this reason this chapter and the next one are interesting even if you don't really want to do a racing game) and a book would probably be too short to cover everything about the racing game anyway.

Before you go ahead designing your little racing game you should think a little bit about what exactly the game should be capable of. Thanks to the many available racing games, especially on the console platforms, it is not very hard to figure out what these games need. Most racing games have great looking cars and show nice scenery around the road itself. The games themselves are often very simple, but the game designers take great care in fine-tuning the controller input and adding small features to make the racing games more fun.

After you are sure in which direction your game is heading, you can think about the required 3D models, textures, effects, and other data like the landscape and track data, which will become very important for your game. I spent more than half the development time just getting the landscape rendering and track generation right. You will see later in this chapter why there was so much work involved and why several new shaders for the landscape and road rendering were required.

When I say "much work," I mean relatively speaking. Keep in mind that the racing game was developed in a few weeks and is similar to Rocket Commander in that it's a nice looking game, but you cannot compare it to an AAA game title that took years and many people to develop. Console games especially are developed by big game companies with 100 people or more. For being just one guy I think I have done a nice job, however.

The time is over when one man could code, design, and test his game in a few days or weeks like in the seventies or eighties (see Figure 12-1). But wait, there is XNA now and it is possible again to create your own games in short time frames. And if you think about it, the past was not really friendly to game developers. You had to implement your own routines to even get a pixel on the screen. I'm better off not mentioning that this most likely involved a lot of assembly machine code just to get it to work on one single hardware configuration.

Figure 12-1

Game Comparisons

I would say most racing games can be split up into three main categories. Sometimes games fall into multiple categories. You could, of course, think of many more categories and if you add various similar games like kart games, motor truck games, motor bicycle games, futuristic games, and so on, you could create many more categories, but I want to keep things simple here and talk only about classic racing games:

❏ **Realistic racers:** Racing simulations and typical racing games like Gran Tourismo, Colin McRae Rally, Test Drive, and Formula One would be examples of realistic racing games. These games are all about realism and giving the player the impression that they are really driving a racing car. At fairs these games are often shown with wheel controllers, sometimes in stage cars with monitors, in special racing chairs, or with multiple monitors or other devices attached to enhance the realism aspect. The basic game principle for these games is to beat the fastest lap time, but it gets more complicated with many available cars and sometimes added game modes.

❏ **Street racers:** Underground racers like Need for Speed, Midnight Club, Street Racing, or Juiced have become popular in the past years. The basic game principle is still the same, but the realism is not so important anymore. It is more like watching a movie; everything has to be cool, gangster-style, and you need tuned cars and cool music for this kind of game. They are very popular, especially on the console platforms.

❏   **Fun racers**: Arcade racers like Trackmania, Wipeout, and Carmageddon that are no longer focusing on being real would fall into this category. They are all about having fun and having crazy tracks or modified cars, which can shoot or do other crazy things. You could even count all crazy racing games like Crazy Taxi or Grand Theft Auto in this category, which are not really racing games anymore; you just drive around with cars to get somewhere else. The mission is not to drive around, but much rather to accomplish certain goals. You would also not call an adventure game a 3D shooter just because it is in 3D, but there are adventure elements in some shooter games as well, so what the heck.

Some games like Project Gotham Racing would fall into more than one category. They are more realistic than street racers, but they are not really as much of a simulation like Grand Tourismo or Formula One because you can also tune your cars and you drive through streets. Need for Speed, on the other hand, is no longer realistic; you can't crash your car, no matter how fast you drive into a wall, and you can drive over other cars, escape the police, damage public property, and so on. The game falls much more in the underground and street racer aspect.

The next sections take a quick look at some racing games that fall into these genres that exist and that could be implemented with the XNA Racing Game engine.

Gran Tourismo

Most realistic racing games like this one are for some reason PlayStation games like Gran Tourismo, Formula One, Enthusia Professional Racing, Colin McRae Rally, and many more. Most games are also available on the PC platform, and sometimes also on the Xbox platform, but not often. You will find a lot more street racers and fun racers on the Xbox than on the PlayStation.

Anyway, I do not know much about these games and I usually fall asleep before completing the first lap. Better ask my brother about details here. I can just leave you with a nice picture of Gran Tourismo (see Figure 12-2).

Figure 12-2

For the Xbox 360 the most popular game in this category is probably Project Gotham Racing, which is a little fun to play thanks to the additional street racer angle of the game, but even here I do not get very far; after a couple of missions it is always the same over and over again. But I must say that the game is done very well and I would expect that the other classic racing games also evolve a little bit into street racer style of games since the recent popularity. And it is obviously more fun to have some additional game modes instead of just driving around in circles, but hey, that's what racing games are all about.

Need for Speed

Need for Speed is an extremely popular game by EA Sports and many versions of the game exist. I can't count them all, so I will not even bother. The latest two games are Need for Speed Underground (2005, see Figure 12-3) and Need for Speed Carbon (2006). Usually all Need for Speed games come out for all the latest console platforms and even for the PC, which makes them less of a system seller, but nevertheless an incredibly well selling game over all platforms combined.

Games like these have great graphics and also a lot of details in the background. Additionally you get some extra game modes and bonus points for drifting around or achieving special tricks. You are also able to tune your car, paint directly onto it, or apply stickers, which is highly anticipated by the car tuning scene.

Figure 12-3

Trackmania

And finally there are the fun racers where I choose Trackmania to represent them all. I will leave the crazy racing games out because they are often not a pure racing game, but more like a mixture between a shooter and a racing game.

In Trackmania (see Figure 12-4) you have to reach the finish line, but there are several checkpoints at which you can see your current time and whether or not you improved since the last time you passed this checkpoint. It is not always easy to reach the goal and sometimes tracks are only as long as a few seconds, but the game is designed in a way that you constantly want to beat your own times or your opponents' times if you play together with some friends in a multiplayer game. You often reach the bronze medal, but you also want the silver or gold medal for this track, which can only be achieved by driving 1–2 seconds faster than before. And after a while you see yourself playing the same track 30 times just to get that extra second. It is a highly addictive and very successful game for its genre.

Other than the basic game principle the tracks are really defining Trackmania. You don't see many games with that many loopings and opportunities to fly around in the level with your car or driving up walls just to fall into the right spot somewhere else. The levels are also very different and you could play Trackmania just for a few minutes to test out a track or even for hours trying to solve all singleplayer tracks.

Figure 12-4

XNA Racing Game

Let's talk about the direction your racing game is going to be. Before the street racers became popular it was either realistic games or fun games and I always liked the fun games much more because just driving a car like in Test Drive was always boring to me. But many people like the realistic racing games. My little brother is a great fan of all realistic and street racing games, or else I would not know anything about them at all except for seeing them in magazines or at game fairs.

Anyway, the racing game I want to develop is more like a fun racer because creating realistic graphics is really hard. It is ok to mix in a little bit of the street racer and underground racer genres, but only to make the game look and sound cooler. The game principle I liked the most recently is Trackmania, which just lets you drive through crazy tracks with loopings, ramps, holes in the road, and so on. The game principle is still to get to the finish line as fast as possible, but I like the fact that getting there becomes a lot harder. Just driving slowly forward will not get you through any loopings or above certain ramps. And if you fall out of the track you have to start over. It is much more like an arcade game than an old-fashioned racing game driving in circles.

The recent release of Trackmania (Sunrise and Nations) also has great graphics. They may not be as good looking or realistic as the other racers mentioned here, but that does not matter so much for a fun racer like this one. Some of the techniques used are still very nice and a game like Trackmania has to solve many difficulties like handling so many road pieces and seeing far into the level. In games like Need for Speed or Project Gotham Racing you hardly see ever more than the current road piece plus the next curve.

You are going to face the same problems, and therefore I want to make sure that both the landscape rendering and the track rendering is as fast as possible and that you can optimize landscape objects to skip away if a certain frame limit is reached.

Landscape Rendering

You already saw a simplified way to generate a 3D landscape with help of an .X model in the previous chapter. There you created the diffuse texture first and then created a normal map from that and finally you added a simple height map to generate the canyon for the XNA Shooter game.

For this game you are still going to use a very simplified approach to render the landscape because the development time was so short and developing a highly sophisticated landscape rendering engine alone can take months. The landscape engine in Arena Wars, for example, supports very big landscapes, but it was never used in the game, and it was a lot of work to get it optimized on the many available hardware configurations, especially because 24 different ground texture types are supported there.

To keep things simple in the racing game only one very big ground texture is used, but you also have a normal map for it and an additional detail texture to add a little detail in case you look very closely at the ground, which can happen in the game if you stay still and are close to the landscape ground. Originally I created a 4096×4096 texture, but it was very hard to constantly update a texture this big and have to manage a normal map for it too. Uncompressed this texture is about 64 MB just for the diffuse texture, and another 64 MB for the normal map. Now imagine you have 10 or more layers of each of these textures when creating them and a computer with only about 1 GB of RAM. The story does not end nicely. Even compressed as a DXT5 texture the 4096×4096 normal map was still about 12 MB and the loading process alone was too annoying when I was developing the landscape class with the help of the unit test in there. What finally stopped me from using 4096×4096 textures ever again in XNA was the content pipeline, which almost takes forever to convert textures this big into the .xnb content files.

I went down to 2048×2048 textures, which look almost as good as the 4096×4096 ones, but only take up 1/4 of the space and loading time. The normal map was even reduced to 1024×1024 a little later because it did not make much of a visual difference. Another reason to not use that big of a texture size is the Xbox 360, which has a limited amount of video memory (64 MB) and you should not load too much stuff or too big textures, or the performance will go down. Instead of creating a super-sized texture I added the detail texture to make the landscape look better when zooming in. The rendering texture to accomplish this is discussed in the next pages.

Textures

First you need a height map and an idea of how big your landscape will be. I initially wanted each landscape texel (1 pixel of a texture) to be 1 meter (3.3 feet) and by having a 4096×4096 texture the whole landscape would be 4x4 km big (about 2.5x2.5 miles). Even after the texture was reduced to 2048×2048 the landscape size stayed the same; now each texel is 2×2 meters.

So where do you get this many height values for your landscape? Just painting them yourself will probably not look very good and you don't have a good program for that and certainly not enough time to write a custom landscape height-map editor. A good idea is to search for height maps on the Internet and try to use existing height-map data from one of the many sources that provide it (geological organizations, NASA, which even has height-map data for other planets, and so on).

For the racing game I tried to get some mountains and I mixed them in together. It was good enough for testing, but later I needed mountains around the landscape and I had to modify the landscape height map a bit to create a big mountain in the middle and mountains around the border of the landscape. The final height map result can be seen in Figure 12-5. Please note that the LandscapeGridHeights.png height map that is used for the game in the Landscapes directory has a size of only 257×257 pixels because the grid that is generated in the Landscape class only generates 257×257 vertices (which are already 66,049 vertices) for the 256*256*2 polygons (which are around 130,000 polygons). Having more polygons would slow down rendering too much, but handling 130,000 polygons is not a big problem for today's graphic cards and the Xbox 360 handles it fine too (still several hundred frames per second).

Figure 12-5

You may notice flat areas on the height map, which are used for city areas where it is simpler to have all the buildings and objects generated at the same height as well as the palms at the side of the road. The white area in the middle is the big mountain and you can see the gray to white areas around the border of the map, which show the mountains at the border to hide the fact that you have nothing behind them.

This height map is now used together with a little bumpy grain texture to generate the normal map. Additionally you could also mix in the diffuse map as you did in the last chapter, but I changed the diffuse map so often for this landscape that the normal map is not really affected anymore by the diffuse texture. Figure 12-6 shows the used diffuse and normal maps for the landscape in the game.

Please note that I changed these textures a lot until I got them this way and I'm not completely pleased with them, but you have to stop sometime, especially if you don't have more time to improve the landscape. The normal map, for example, looks really great from a far distance, but more closely it doesn't have many variations and it could maybe be improved to fit better to the diffuse texture. Anyway, it looks fine in the game and I have not heard any complaints yet.

Landscape Textures in the Racing Game

Landscape.dds | LandscapeNormal.dds (Note: Looks reddish if compressed)

Figure 12-6

Finally, a detail map is also added for when you look closely at the landscape. You will not notice the detail map after a while, but Figure 12-7 shows the difference quite convincingly between using a detail map and not using it. You will never go without a detail texture ever again if you have such a big landscape and allow zooming in like you do for the racing game.

Rendering

If you open up the Racing Game project you can see a lot of the classes from the previous chapters, but also two new namespaces, which are discussed in this chapter: Landscapes and Tracks. There is just one class in the Landscapes namespace called Landscape (see Figure 12-8), which is responsible for rendering the landscape, all objects on it, all the tracks and track objects, and basically everything in the game except your own car. In the Mission class you are just calling the Render method of this class to perform all the rendering. For shadow mapping several helper methods are available. More details about the shadow mapping are discussed in Chapter 14.

Improving the Landscape with a Detail Texture

Zoomed in part of the Landscape

LandscapeDetail.dds (512×512, grayscale)

The final result, what the player will see. Now that is much better.

Figure 12-7

Figure 12-8

All landscape objects are generated at the creation time of the Landscape class, especially in the constructors of the Track classes, which are used inside the Landscape class. You will take a quick look at some of the used 3D models in a second.

The first thing you have to do to be able to render your landscape is to generate it first in the constructor. Before you take a look at that you should check out the TestRenderLandscape unit test of the Landscape class in the same way the unit test was written before the class was implemented. You may also notice the other unit test, GenerateLandscapeHeightFile, which generates a level file for the landscape height map the same way you had to generate a special content file for Rocket Commander XNA levels because loading bitmap data is not possible on the Xbox 360.

```
/// <summary>
/// Test render landscape
/// </summary>
public static void TestRenderLandscape()
{
  TestGame.Start("TestRenderLandscape",
    delegate
    {
      RacingGame.LoadLevel(RacingGame.Level.Beginner);
      RacingGame.Landscape.SetCarToStartPosition();
    },
    delegate
    {
      if (BaseGame.AllowShadowMapping)
      {
        // Generate shadows
        ShaderEffect.shadowMapping.GenerateShadows(
          delegate
```

```
    {
      RacingGame.Landscape.GenerateShadow();
      RacingGame.CarModel.GenerateShadow(
        RacingGame.Player.CarRenderMatrix);
    });

    // Render shadows
    ShaderEffect.shadowMapping.RenderShadows(
      delegate
      {
        RacingGame.Landscape.UseShadow();
        RacingGame.CarModel.UseShadow(
          RacingGame.Player.CarRenderMatrix);
      });
  } // if (BaseGame.AllowShadowMapping)

  BaseGame.UI.PostScreenGlowShader.Start();
  BaseGame.UI.RenderGameBackground();

  RacingGame.Landscape.Render();
  RacingGame.CarModel.RenderCar(0, Color.Goldenrod,
    RacingGame.Player.CarRenderMatrix);

  // And flush render manager to draw all objects
  BaseGame.MeshRenderManager.Render();
  if (BaseGame.AllowShadowMapping)
    ShaderEffect.shadowMapping.ShowShadows();

  BaseGame.UI.PostScreenGlowShader.Show();

  TestGame.UI.WriteText(2, 50, "Number of objects: "+
    RacingGame.Landscape.landscapeObjects.Count);
  });
} // TestRenderLandscape()
```

The unit test does a lot of things; it even shows the car and all landscape objects. Even the track and all the shadow mapping and post-screen shaders are tested here to make sure they work fine together with the landscape. If you just want to test the landscape itself, just call Render of the Landscape class; that's already enough to test the landscape rendering.

The LoadLevel method of the RacingGame class, which is actually the main class for this game, loads one of the levels. All levels currently use the same landscape, which means you don't have to reload it. But you should check out the code for generating the landscape vertices anyway. The landscape constructor does the following things:

❑ Loads the map height data from the level file and builds tangent vertices with it

❑ Generates and smoothes normals for the whole landscape, and also regenerates the tangents with the new normals.

❑ Sets the vertex buffer with these vertices

❑ Calculates the index buffer (very similar to the landscape triangles you saw in the last chapter)

❑ Sets the index buffer for the landscape rendering

❑ Loads and generates all track data for the current level, including all landscape objects

❑ And finally, adds additional objects like the city ground planes to give the city objects a better looking ground texture.

The most important part of the constructor is the tangent vertex generation from the height-map data, which goes through all 257×257 points of the height map and generates vertices for you:

```
// Build our tangent vertices
for (int x = 0; x < GridWidth; x++)
  for (int y = 0; y < GridHeight; y++)
  {
    // Step 1: Calculate position
    int index = x + y * GridWidth;
    Vector3 pos = CalcLandscapePos(x, y, heights);
    mapHeights[x, y] = pos.Z;
    vertices[index].pos = pos;

    // Step 2: Calculate all edge vectors (for normals and tangents)
    // This involves quite complicated optimizations and mathematics,
    // hard to explain with just a comment. Read my book :D
    Vector3 edge1 = pos - CalcLandscapePos(x, y + 1, heights);
    Vector3 edge2 = pos - CalcLandscapePos(x + 1, y, heights);
    Vector3 edge3 = pos - CalcLandscapePos(x - 1, y + 1, heights);
    Vector3 edge4 = pos - CalcLandscapePos(x + 1, y + 1, heights);
    Vector3 edge5 = pos - CalcLandscapePos(x - 1, y - 1, heights);

    // Step 3: Calculate normal based on the edges (interpolate
    // from 3 cross products we build from our edges).
    vertices[index].normal = Vector3.Normalize(
      Vector3.Cross(edge2, edge1) +
      Vector3.Cross(edge4, edge3) +
      Vector3.Cross(edge3, edge5));

    // Step 4: Set tangent data, just use edge1
    vertices[index].tangent = Vector3.Normalize(edge1);

    // Step 5: Set texture coordinates, use full 0.0f to 1.0f range!
    vertices[index].uv = new Vector2(
      y / (float)(GridHeight - 1),
      x / (float)(GridWidth - 1));
  } // for for (int)
```

You can see that this code generates the vertices in five steps. First, the position vector is calculated. Then all edge vectors are calculated for constructing the normal from three cross products and assigning the tangent. Finally, the texture coordinates are assigned, but you flip x and y to make xy rendering easier later, but still having the correct texture map alignment the same way it looks as a bitmap. The vertices list is already generated when it is defined because you only support 257×257 height-map grids. The `CalcLandscapePos` helper method that is used here is quite simple and just extracts a height vector from the height-map data:

```
private Vector3 CalcLandscapePos(int x, int y, byte[] heights)
{
  // Make sure we stay on the valid map data
  int mapX = x < 0 ? 0 : x >= GridWidth ? GridWidth - 1 : x;
  int mapY = y < 0 ? 0 : y >= GridHeight ? GridHeight - 1 : y;
```

```
    float heightPercent = heights[mapX+mapY*GridWidth] / 255.0f;

    return new Vector3(
      x * MapWidthFactor,
      y * MapHeightFactor,
      heightPercent * MapZScale);
  } // CalcLandscapePos(x, y, texData)
```

With all the vertices and indices generated now you can finally render the landscape with the help of the
`LandscapeNormalMapping.fx` shader. You will not believe how easy that is now. The following lines
of code will render 130,000 polygons with the `LandscapeNormalMapping` shader using the landscape
diffuse map, the normal map, and the additional detail map:

```
// Render landscape (pretty easy with all the data we got here)
ShaderEffect.landscapeNormalMapping.Render(
  mat, "DiffuseWithDetail20",
  delegate
  {
    BaseGame.Device.VertexDeclaration =
      TangentVertex.VertexDeclaration;
    BaseGame.Device.Vertices[0].SetSource(vertexBuffer, 0,
      TangentVertex.SizeInBytes);
    BaseGame.Device.Indices = indexBuffer;
    BaseGame.Device.DrawIndexedPrimitives(
      PrimitiveType.TriangleList,
      0, 0, GridWidth * GridHeight,
      0, (GridWidth - 1) * (GridHeight - 1) * 2);
  });
```

The `ShaderEffect` class from Chapter 7 allows you to render the landscape material with the specified
technique using the `RenderDelegate` code for rendering.

The `Render` method of the `Landscape` class also renders the track and all landscape objects. The track
rendering is discussed for the rest of this chapter. We will not talk about all the landscape models used in
the game because there are so many. Check out the `TestRenderModels` unit test of the `Model` class to
view them all; a quick overview is shown in Figure 12-9.

Some Models of the Racing Game

| Palm2.X | PalmSmall.X | SignWarning.X | Windmill.X | OilTanks.X | SignLeft.X |

Figure 12-9

Optimizing Tips

Handling landscape engines is not easy. Even if you have developed a great looking landscape engine that supports many different shaders and texture sets, you might find yourself worrying about performance for a while. On the other hand, if you already have a great performing landscape engine like the one from the racing game or the shoot-'em-up game from the last chapter, you might want to improve the visual quality of it without affecting the performance too much. It is a tricky challenge getting a landscape engine just right for your game. As I told you earlier, in the past I tried to create a more complex landscape and graphics engine than actually required for a game like Arena Wars. It was possible to create huge landscapes 100 times as big as the ones that were finally used, but it did not make sense after a while optimizing these cases when the game never utilizes these features.

Instead you should focus on what the game is doing. Take the racing game as an example. It is much easier to have one fixed landscape, which is always the same. Testing is easier and you can reuse existing parts of the landscape and the locations of many objects for other levels too without having to redesign everything. The landscape is also big enough (4096×4096 meters) for many different tracks because the first level only shows you a small part of it (maybe 20%–30%).

There are three disadvantages to a more-or-less fixed landscape rendering technique like used here and in the last chapter:

❑   You can't just change the size of the landscape that easily. It will involve a lot of work just to make it smaller or bigger. If you are already using 4096×4096 textures you can probably not go up anymore to improve the texture quality, and if your game is very close to the ground it may still look very blurry even with extra detail textures.

❑   Changing the diffuse texture map is really hard. You not only have to mix all different texture types together yourself, but it is also hard to see the result and it involves a lot of testing. To make things worse the bigger the mega-texture gets, the slower the development time gets.

❑   The landscape engine is just not powerful enough to handle advanced effects like adding craters or extra textures (tracks, roads, leaves, riffs, and so on) to the ground and you can't even change the visual appearance dynamically. This means the landscape will always look the same. If you wanted to build a level editor you would need a more dynamic solution that would allow you to change the texture types and a way to mix them together automatically.

The best way to get around these issues is to use a landscape rendering technique called *splatting*, which basically takes a bunch of textures and renders them based on a texture map that uses the same resolution as the height map onto the landscape. Because it would not look very good to have different ground textures sitting side by side, you need a smooth interpolation between them. You could either fade from tile to tile, but that would still look too harsh, or you could save percentage values for each texture type.

The landscape is rendered separately for all ground texture types and you should make the lowest one completely opaque to make sure you can never look through the landscape. Then the other ground types are alpha blended on top of the previous ones until you are done with all of them (see Figure 12-10).

You can also use an alpha texture for blending or just blend softly with color values (see the example in Figure 12-10). Because you will use shaders in XNA you might also want to combine four (pixel shader 1.1) or even eight (pixel shader 2.0) textures together into one shader pass to optimize performance. If your landscape engine needs to handle more textures, however, you will need multiple passes until every

Landscape Texture Splatting Techniques

No alpha blending—just the textures side-by-side

Tile-based alpha blending—tiles still visible, but easier to render

Softly blending through interpolated alpha values—
does not always fit

Customized application of an alpha mask for each blending—
can look the best

Figure 12-10

thing is rendered. Sometimes it can even be faster not to render all textures on top of each other, but just the ones that are visible. It becomes harder when you have to generate the vertex and index buffers, but if you really have a lot of textures, like 20 or 30 different ground types, the performance will greatly increase because each ground texture type is used only 10% or less and it does not make sense to render it all the time.

Whichever technique you choose, I strongly suggest you start with something simple like just rendering a big landscape with one texture type tiled over it and then improve it later when your game is more than just a landscape engine. You might also want to make sure your landscape can always be rendered at several hundred frames to make sure the game still runs fast enough after you add all the landscape models, 3D units, and effects plus the game logic into it.

There are many more tips and tricks about creating good landscapes. You could implement precalculated lighting and huge landscape shadows; there are also many opportunities for great looking shaders, especially if you have water involved. Grass could be done with fur shaders. The 3D appearance of rocks and cliffs could be enhanced with parallax or even offset mapping. If you are interested in these topics please pick up a good shader book like the *Game Programming Gems* or *ShaderX*, or search the Internet for many tips and tricks as well as tutorials.

Figure 12-11 shows the final appearance of the landscape in the racing game after also applying the post-screen shaders, the in-game HUD, and the sky cube mapping (see Chapters 5 and 6 for more information about these kinds of shaders if you have forgotten about them).

Figure 12-11

Tracks

Except for the HUD the game does not really look like a racing game right now. More like a fantasy RPG thanks to the glow and color-correction post-screen shaders. The road track and the car itself are currently missing to make it look like a racing game. Just putting the car somewhere in your landscape might look funny, but you don't want to drive around on the ground, especially since the landscape does not look so good from this zooming level (1 landscape texel for 2x2 meter, so the whole car stays on 2 texels).

The idea for this game was to create some tracks like the ones from Trackmania, but after investigating Trackmania and the editor in the game you can see how complex the rendering process is in the game. Instead of just rendering the track as one piece and adding landscape objects like I wanted to do, Trackmania levels are constructed with many different road building blocks, which fit together perfectly. This way you can put three loopings after each other without having to paint or construct them yourself. The disadvantage of this technique is that you are limited by the available building blocks, and from the developer's point of view you really will have a lot of work creating hundreds of these building blocks, not to mention all the levels you need to test them out.

So this idea was thrown out of the window in seconds. I returned to my original approach of creating just a simple 2D track and adding a little height to it through the landscape height map. I wanted to use a bitmap with the track painted on it as a white line and then import it into the game extracting all bitmap positions and building 3D vertices from it. But after playing around with this idea it was very clear that the track heavily depends on the landscape ground, and doing things like loopings, ramps, and crazy curves was just not possible or at least very hard to implement additionally to the bitmap track.

So again another idea flew out the window (hopefully I did not hit anyone with it). To get a better understanding of how a track might look I used 3D Studio Max and played around with the spline functions there to create a simple circle track with just four points (see Figure 12-12). Rotated by 90 degrees to the left, this looked almost like looping and much more appealing as a fun racer than the bitmap approach.

Figure 12-12

I had to get this spline data out of 3D Studio Max and somehow into my engine. This way I could make the creation process of the tracks very easy by just drawing a 3D spline in Max and exporting it into the racing game engine. The hard part would be to generate a useful track out of this data because each spline point is just a point, and not a road piece with orientation, a road width, and so on.

Before spending more time trying to figure out the best way to generate tracks and before you can start importing this spline data into your game, you should make sure that this idea even works.

Unit Testing to the Rescue

This is a great time again to do some heavy unit testing. Start with the first simple unit test of the new `TrackLine` class, called `TestRenderingTrack`, which just creates a simple spline like the one from 3D Studio Max and displays it on the screen:

```
public static void TestRenderingTrack()
{
  TrackLine testTrack = new TrackLine(
    new Vector3[]
    {
      new Vector3(20, -20, 0),
      new Vector3(20, 20, 0),
      new Vector3(-20, 20, 0),
      new Vector3(-20, -20, 0),
    });

  TestGame.Start(
    delegate
    {
      ShowGroundGrid();
      ShowTrackLines(testTrack);
      ShowUpVectors(testTrack);
    });
} // TestRenderingTrack()
```

`ShowGroundGrid` just displays some grid lines on the xy ground plane to help you see where the ground is. I wrote this method a while back for the models class; it is just reused here. `ShowTrackLines` is the important method here because it shows all the lines and interpolated points that have been generated for you through the constructor of the `TrackLine` class. Finally the `ShowUpVectors` method shows you in which direction the up vector points for every position on the track. Without the up vector you will not be able to generate the right and left side of the road correctly. For example, in curves the road should tilt and for loopings you need the up vectors pointing to the center of the loop and not just upward.

The `ShowTrackLines` helper method just shows each point of the track connected through white lines. When you execute the `TestRenderingTrack` unit test you can see a screen like the one in Figure 12-13.

```
public static void ShowTrackLines(TrackLine track)
{
  // Draw the line for each line part
```

```
    for (int num = 0; num < track.points.Count; num++)
        BaseGame.DrawLine(
            track.points[num].pos,
            track.points[(num + 1)%track.points.Count].pos,
            Color.White);
} // ShowTrackLines(track)
```

Fps: 1878

Figure 12-13

The track almost looks like a road thanks to the red up vectors and the green tangent vectors. All you have to do now is to tweak the track generation code and maybe test out a couple more splines. In the TrackLine class you can see several of my test tracks I created all by adding a couple of 3D points by hand, and more tracks are available through the Collada files used later to import track data from 3D Studio Max into your engine.

Before you take a look at the spline interpolation code in the constructor you can also test out a simple looping by just switching the x and z values of the track points (see Figure 12-14). To make the spline look more round I've also added four new points. The new `TestRenderingTrack` unit test now looks like the following:

```
public static void TestRenderingTrack()
{
  TrackLine testTrack = new TrackLine(
    new Vector3[]
    {
      new Vector3(0, 0, 0),
      new Vector3(0, 7, 3),
      new Vector3(0, 10, 10),
      new Vector3(0, 7, 17),
      new Vector3(0, 0, 20),
      new Vector3(0, -7, 17),
      new Vector3(0, -10, 10),
      new Vector3(0, -7, 3),
    });
  // [Rest stays the same]
} // TestRenderingTrack()
```

Fps: 2025

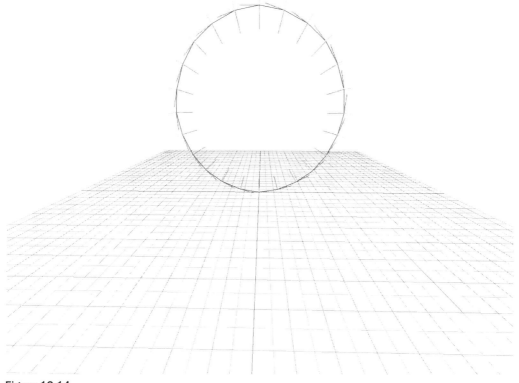

Figure 12-14

Interpolating Splines

You might ask how you even get all these points from just passing in four or eight input points and how these points are interpolated so nicely. It all happens in the `TrackLine` constructor, or to be more precise, in the protected `Load` method, which allows you to reload the track data anytime you need it to be regenerated. The `Load` method will not look very easy when you see it for the first time and it is the main method for all the track loading, track data validation, interpolation, and up and tangent vector generation. Even the tunnels and neutral landscape objects are generated here from the helpers you can pass to this method.

The `Load` method does the following things:

- ❑   It allows reloading, which is important for loading levels and starting over. Any previous data is killed automatically if you call `Load` again.

- ❑   All data is validated to make sure you can generate the track and use all the helpers.

- ❑   Each track point is checked to see if it is above the landscape. If not, the point is corrected and the surrounding points are also lifted up a bit for a smoother road. This way you can easily generate a 3D track in Max without having to worry about the actual landscape height that is used later when the track is put on top of the landscape.

- ❑   Loopings are simplified by just putting two spline points on top of each other. The loading code automatically detects this and replaces these two points with a full looping of nine points, which are interpolated to even more points to generate a very smooth and correct looking looping.

- ❑   Then all track points are interpolated through a Catmull-Rom spline interpolation method. You take a closer look at that in a second.

- ❑   Up and tangent vectors are generated and interpolated several times to make the road as smooth as possible. The tangent vectors especially should not suddenly change direction or flip to the other side, which would make driving on this road very hard. This code took the longest time to get it right.

- ❑   Then all helpers are analyzed and the road width for each track position is saved and will be used later when the actual rendering happens in the `Track` class, which is based on the `TrackLine` class.

- ❑   Texture coordinates for the road texture are also generated here because you store the track points as a `TrackVertex` array to make the rendering easier later. Only the u texture coordinate is stored here; the v texture coordinate is then later just set to 0 or 1 depending on whether you are on the left or right side of the road.

- ❑   Then all the tunnel helpers are analyzed and the tunnel data is generated for you. Basically the code here just constructs a few new points for later use. They are used to draw the tunnel box with the tunnel material in the `Track` class.

- ❑   Last but not least, all landscape models are added. They are also saved together with the track data to form a complete level with everything you need. Additional landscape objects are also automatically generated in the `Track` class; for example, palms and lanterns at the side of the road.

When I started developing the `TrackLine` class the constructor only generated the new interpolated points from the input points through the Catmull-Rom spline helper method. The code looked like this and can still be found in the `Load` method:

```
// Generate all points with help of catmull rom splines
for (int num = 0; num < inputPoints.Length; num++)
{
  // Get the 4 required points for the catmull rom spline
  Vector3 p1 = inputPoints[num-1 < 0 ? inputPoints.Length-1 : num-1];
  Vector3 p2 = inputPoints[num];
  Vector3 p3 = inputPoints[(num + 1) % inputPoints.Length];
  Vector3 p4 = inputPoints[(num + 2) % inputPoints.Length];

  // Calculate number of iterations we use here based
  // on the distance of the 2 points we generate new points from.
  float distance = Vector3.Distance(p2, p3);
  int numberOfIterations =
    (int)(NumberOfIterationsPer100Meters * (distance / 100.0f));
  if (numberOfIterations <= 0)
    numberOfIterations = 1;

  Vector3 lastPos = p1;
  for (int iter = 0; iter < numberOfIterations; iter++)
  {
    TrackVertex newVertex = new TrackVertex(
      Vector3.CatmullRom(p1, p2, p3, p4,
      iter / (float)numberOfIterations));

    points.Add(newVertex);
  } // for (iter)
} // for (num)
```

More Complex Tracks

The unit tests are nice to get everything up and running, but the more complex the tracks get, the more difficult it is to even generate them by typing in the 3D position for each spline point. It would be much easier to use the data from exported splines of 3D Studio Max, which allows you to construct and modify the spline positions easier.

Take a look at the expert track for the expert level in the XNA Racing Game in Figure 12-15. The track alone contains about 85 points, which are interpolated to about 2,000 track points resulting in about 24,000 polygons for the road alone. Additional data for the guard rails and additional road 3D models are also generated later in the game. Constructing a track like this one and tweaking it is just not possible without a nice editor and you can be glad that you can use Max for that. Maybe in the future I will implement a little track editor for the game that at least allows you to create simple tracks directly in the game.

Exporting this data was not as easy as I initially thought. .X files do not support splines and .FBX files also do not help. Even if they would export the splines you would still have to do a lot of work extracting the track data before you could use it in the game because it is not possible to get any vertex data from imported models in XNA. I decided to go with the currently very popular Collada format, which was built to allow exporting and importing 3D content and 3D scenes from one application to the next. The main advantage of Collada over other formats is the fact that everything is stored as xml data and you can quickly see which data is used for what purpose just by looking at the exported file. You don't even need to look at any documentation; just search for the data you need and extract it (in this case you are looking for the spline and helper data, the rest is not important for you).

Collada is not really a good export format for a game because it usually stores way too much information and the file sizes are a lot bigger than binary file formats because xml data is just a bunch of text. For that reason and because I was not allowed to use any external data formats for the XNA Starter Kit, all the Collada data is converted to the internal level data format in the TrackImporter class. Using your own data format speeds up the loading process and makes sure no one can figure out how to construct his own levels. Hey, wait a second; don't you want people to create their own tracks? Damn, I really want this to be easier and it is not good that you even need 3D Studio Max to construct or change the levels. I really have to implement some other way to import or build tracks in the game later.

Figure 12-15

Importing the Track Data

To make the loading of Collada files a little bit easier several helper classes are used. First of all the `XmlHelper` class (see Figure 12-16) really helps you out with loading and managing xml files.

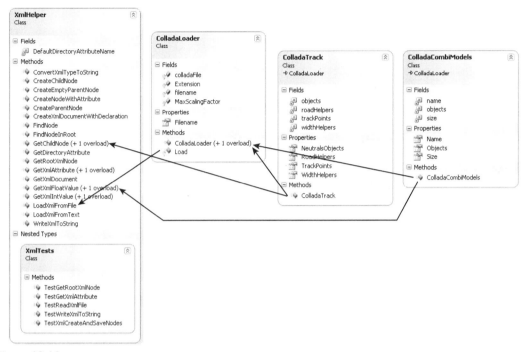

Figure 12-16

The `ColladaLoader` class is just a very short class that loads the Collada file (which is just an xml file) for you and lets the derived classes use the `XmlHelper` methods more easily.

❑ `ColladaTrack` is used to load the track itself (`trackPoints`), but also all helper objects like the `widthHelpers` to make the road bigger and smaller and the `roadHelpers` for tunnels, palms, lanterns, and other objects on the side of the road. Finally all additional landscape objects are loaded to be displayed as you drive close enough to them (because there can be a lot of landscape objects in the scene).

❑ `ColladaCombiModels` is a little helper class to load and display multiple models at once by just setting one combo model that contains up to 10 models with relative positions and rotation values in them. For example, if you want to set a city block of nine buildings, just use the `Buildings.CombiModel` file or if you need a bunch of palms plus a few stone models use the `Palms.CombiModel` file.

To learn more about the loading process you can use the unit tests in the `TrackLine` and `Track` classes, but more importantly check out the `ColladaTrack` constructor itself:

```
public ColladaTrack(string setFilename)
  : base(setFilename)
{
  // Get spline first (only use one line)
  XmlNode geometry =
    XmlHelper.GetChildNode(colladaFile, "geometry");
  XmlNode visualScene =
    XmlHelper.GetChildNode(colladaFile, "visual_scene");

  string splineId = XmlHelper.GetXmlAttribute(geometry, "id");
  // Make sure this is a spline, everything else is not supported.
  if (splineId.EndsWith("-spline") == false)
    throw new Exception("The ColladaTrack file " + Filename +
      " does not have a spline geometry in it. Unable to load " +
      "track!");

  // Get spline points
  XmlNode pointsArray =
    XmlHelper.GetChildNode(geometry, "float_array");
  // Convert the points to a float array
  float[] pointsValues =
    StringHelper.ConvertStringToFloatArray(
    pointsArray.FirstChild.Value);

  // Skip first and third of each input point (MAX tangent data)
  trackPoints.Clear();
  int pointNum = 0;
  while (pointNum < pointsValues.Length)
  {
    // Skip first point (first 3 floating point values)
    pointNum += 3;
    // Take second vector
    trackPoints.Add(MaxScalingFactor * new Vector3(
      pointsValues[pointNum++],
      pointsValues[pointNum++],
      pointsValues[pointNum++]));
    // And skip thrid
    pointNum += 3;
  } // while (pointNum)

  // Check if we can find translation or scaling values for our
  // spline
  XmlNode splineInstance = XmlHelper.GetChildNode(
    visualScene, "url", "#" + splineId);
  XmlNode splineMatrixNode = XmlHelper.GetChildNode(
    splineInstance.ParentNode, "matrix");
  if (splineMatrixNode != null)
    throw new Exception("The ColladaTrack file " + Filename +
      " should not use baked matrices. Please export again " +
      "without baking matrices. Unable to load track!");
```

```
XmlNode splineTranslateNode = XmlHelper.GetChildNode(
  splineInstance.ParentNode, "translate");
XmlNode splineScaleNode = XmlHelper.GetChildNode(
  splineInstance.ParentNode, "scale");
Vector3 splineTranslate = Vector3.Zero;
if (splineTranslateNode != null)
{
  float[] translateValues =
    StringHelper.ConvertStringToFloatArray(
    splineTranslateNode.FirstChild.Value);
  splineTranslate = MaxScalingFactor * new Vector3(
    translateValues[0], translateValues[1], translateValues[2]);
} // if (splineTranslateNode)
Vector3 splineScale = new Vector3(1, 1, 1);
if (splineScaleNode != null)
{
  float[] scaleValues = StringHelper.ConvertStringToFloatArray(
    splineScaleNode.FirstChild.Value);
  splineScale = new Vector3(
    scaleValues[0], scaleValues[1], scaleValues[2]);
} // if (splineTranslateNode)

// Convert all points with our translation and scaling values
for (int num = 0; num < trackPoints.Count; num++)
{
  trackPoints[num] = Vector3.Transform(trackPoints[num],
    Matrix.CreateScale(splineScale) *
    Matrix.CreateTranslation(splineTranslate));
} // for (num)

// [Now Helpers are loaded here, the loading code is similar]
} // ColladaTrack(setFilename)
```

Getting the spline data itself is not very hard, but getting all the translation, scaling, and rotation values is a little bit of work (and even more complicated for the helpers), but after you have written and tested this code (there are several unit tests and test files that were used to implement this constructor) it is very easy to create new tracks and get them into your game.

Generating Vertices from the Track Data

Just getting the track points and helpers imported is only half the story. You already saw how complex the TrackLine constructor loading is and it really helps you out generating the interpolated track points, and building up vectors and the tangents. Even the texture coordinates and all the helpers and landscape models are handled here. But you still only have a bunch of points and no real road your car can drive on. To render a real road with the road textures (see Figure 12-17) you need to construct renderable vertices first for all the 3D data that forms your final road, including all the other dynamically created objects like the guard rails. The most important texture is the road texture itself, but without the normal map it looks boring in the game. The normal map adds a sparkly structure to the road and makes it shiny when looking toward the sun. The other road textures for the road sides and background (RoadBack.dds) and for the tunnels (RoadTunnel.dds) are also important, but you won't see them that often.

Road Textures

Road.dds   RoadBack.dds   RoadTunnel.dds

RoadNormal.dds   RoadBackNormal.dds   RoadTunnelNormal.dds

Figure 12-17

The class that handles all these textures as road materials, as well as all the other road data like the road cement columns, the guard rails, and the checkpoint positions, is the `Track` class, which is based on the `TrackLine` class. The `Landscape` class is used to render the track and all the landscape objects together with the landscape, which is finally everything you need to put the car on the road and start driving straight ahead. You still need physics to stay on the road and to collide with the guard rails, but that is covered in the next chapter.

So the `Track` class is responsible for all the road materials, generating all vertices as well as the vertex and index buffers, and finally for rendering all the track vertices with the help of the shaders you use in the game. Most materials use the Specular20 technique of the `NormalMapping` shader for a nice shiny road, but the Diffuse20 technique is also quite popular for the tunnels and other non-shiny road materials.

The unit test to render the track is quite simple; all you want to do is to render the track. There is not much else you have to verify here:

```
public static void TestRenderTrack()
{
  Track track = null;
```

```
TestGame.Start(
  delegate
  {
    track = new Track("TrackBeginner", null);
  },
  delegate
  {
    ShowUpVectors(track);
    track.Render();
  });
} // TestRenderingTrack()
```

As you can see you can still use the protected ShowUpVectors helper method from the TrackLine class because you derived the Track class from it. The Render method is also similar to the first render code you had in the previous chapter for the landscape rendering in the Mission class.

```
public void Render()
{
  // We use tangent vertices for everything here
  BaseGame.Device.VertexDeclaration = TangentVertex.VertexDeclaration;
  // Restore the world matrix
  BaseGame.WorldMatrix = Matrix.Identity;

  // Render the road itself
  ShaderEffect.normalMapping.Render(
    roadMaterial, "Specular20",
    delegate
    {
      BaseGame.Device.Vertices[0].SetSource(roadVb, 0,
        TangentVertex.SizeInBytes);
      BaseGame.Device.Indices = roadIb;
      BaseGame.Device.DrawIndexedPrimitives(
        PrimitiveType.TriangleList,
        0, 0, points.Count * 5,
        0, (points.Count - 1) * 8);
    });

  // [etc. Render rest of road materials]
} // Render()
```

Well, that does not look very complicated. Take a look at the code that generates the road vertex and index buffers. The private GenerateVerticesAndObjects helper method is where all the magic happens:

```
private void GenerateVerticesAndObjects(Landscape landscape)
{
  #region Generate the road vertices
  // Each road segment gets 5 points:
  // left, left middle, middle, right middle, right.
  // The reason for this is that we would have bad triangle errors if the
  // road gets wider and wider. This happens because we need to render
  // quads, but we can only render triangles, which often have different
  // orientations, which makes the road very bumpy. This still happens
  // with 8 polygons instead of 2, but it is much better this way.
```

```
// Another trick is to not do so many iterations in TrackLine, which
// causes this problem. Better to have a not so round track, but at
// least the road up/down itself is smooth.
// The last point is duplicated (see TrackLine) because we have 2 sets
// of texture coordinates for it (begin block, end block).
// So for the index buffer we only use points.Count-1 blocks.
roadVertices = new TangentVertex[points.Count * 5];

// Current texture coordinate for the roadway (in direction of
// movement)
for (int num = 0; num < points.Count; num++)
{
  // Get vertices with the help of the properties in the TrackVertex
  // class. For the road itself we only need vertices for the left
  // and right side, which are vertex number 0 and 1.
  roadVertices[num * 5 + 0] = points[num].RightTangentVertex;
  roadVertices[num * 5 + 1] = points[num].MiddleRightTangentVertex;
  roadVertices[num * 5 + 2] = points[num].MiddleTangentVertex;
  roadVertices[num * 5 + 3] = points[num].MiddleLeftTangentVertex;
  roadVertices[num * 5 + 4] = points[num].LeftTangentVertex;
} // for (num)

roadVb = new VertexBuffer(
  BaseGame.Device,
  typeof(TangentVertex),
  roadVertices.Length,
  ResourceUsage.WriteOnly,
  ResourceManagementMode.Automatic);
  roadVb.SetData(roadVertices);

// Also calculate all indices, we have 8 polygons for each segment
// with 3 vertices each. We have 1 segment less than points because
// the last point is duplicated (different tex coords).
int[] indices = new int[(points.Count - 1) * 8 * 3];
int vertexIndex = 0;
for (int num = 0; num < points.Count - 1; num++)
{
  // We only use 3 vertices (and the next 3 vertices),
  // but we have to construct all 24 indices for our 4 polygons.
  for (int sideNum = 0; sideNum < 4; sideNum++)
  {
    // Each side needs 2 polygons.
    // 1. Polygon
    indices[num * 24 + 6 * sideNum + 0] = vertexIndex + sideNum;
    indices[num * 24 + 6 * sideNum + 1] =
      vertexIndex + 5 + 1 + sideNum;
    indices[num * 24 + 6 * sideNum + 2] = vertexIndex + 5 + sideNum;

    // 2. Polygon
    indices[num * 24 + 6 * sideNum + 3] =
      vertexIndex + 5 + 1 + sideNum;
    indices[num * 24 + 6 * sideNum + 4] = vertexIndex + sideNum;
    indices[num * 24 + 6 * sideNum + 5] = vertexIndex + 1 + sideNum;
  } // for (num)
```

```
      // Go to the next 5 vertices
      vertexIndex += 5;
   } // for (num)

   // Set road back index buffer
   roadIb = new IndexBuffer(
      BaseGame.Device,
      typeof(int),
      indices.Length,
      ResourceUsage.WriteOnly,
      ResourceManagementMode.Automatic);
      roadIb.SetData(indices);
   #endregion

   // [Then the rest of the road back, tunnel, etc. vertices are
   // generated here and all the landscape objects, checkpoints, palms,
   // etc. are generated at the end of this method]
 } // GenerateVerticesAndObjects(landscape)
```

Good thing I wrote so many comments when I wrote this code. The first part generates a big tangent vertex array with five times as many points as the track vertices you get from the TrackLine base class. This data is directly passed into the vertex buffer for the road and then used to construct the polygons in the index buffer. Each road piece gets eight polygons (four parts with two polygons each) and therefore the index buffer needs 24 times as many indices as you have track points. To make sure you are still able to properly access all these indices you have to use int values here instead of short values I would usually use for index buffers because they reduce the memory size by half. But in this case for the roads you can have many more than just 32,000 indices (2000 road pieces from the expert track example times 24 is already 48,000 indices). You need many iteration points for your road because it is not hand-crafted, but automatically generated, which can lead to overlapping errors if you don't have enough iterations and don't generate the road smoothly enough (see Figure 12-18).

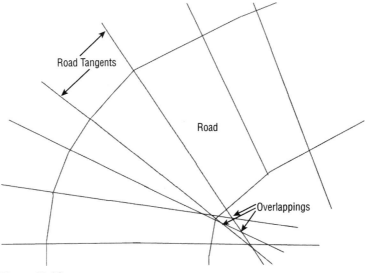

Figure 12-18

You might ask why four parts are generated for each road segment, and the reason for that was not because I enjoy throwing more polygons at the poor GPU. This technique is used to improve the visual quality of the road, especially in curves.

Figure 12-19 explains this problem much better than I can do with words. As you can see two polygons that form an uneven quad are not always the same size, but they still use the same amount of texels. On the right you can see an extreme situation where the bottom-right part of the road is heavily distorted and does not look good anymore.

This problem can be fixed by dividing the road into multiple parts. You use four parts for each segment in the racing game to make the road look much better.

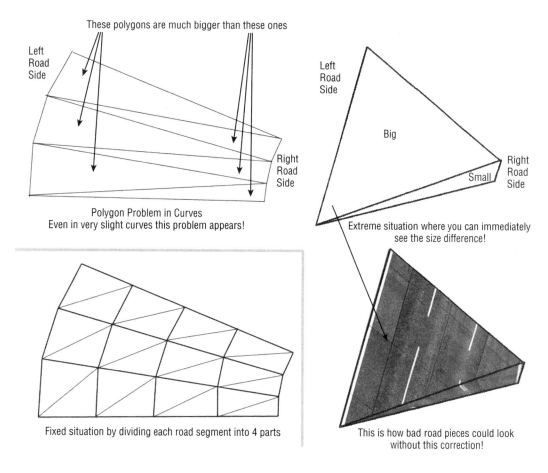

Figure 12-19

Final Result

That was really a lot of work to get the landscape and road rendering right, but now you have a really good portion of the game ready; at least the graphical parts are good to go. There are of course many smaller tricks and tips you can find in the classes of the `Tracks` namespace. Please check out the unit tests to learn more about rendering the road back sides, the loopings, and tunnels.

Figure 12-20 shows the final result of the `TestRenderTrack` unit test of the `Track` class.

Figure 12-20

Together with the landscape rendering from the first part of this chapter you have a pretty nice rendering engine now. Together with the pre-screen sky cube mapping shader for the background, the landscape and the road rendering looks quite good (see Figure 12-21). The post-screen glow shader of the game also makes everything fit together even better, especially if you have many landscape objects in the scene too.

Figure 12-21

Challenge: Create a New Unit Test Track

This chapter handled a lot of complex issues and you are probably as exhausted reading this as I am writing it, so I want to give you an easy task this time. Go into the TrackLine class and add a new unit test for a simple track. You just have to add a bunch of vectors and test them until you think the track looks good enough.

Figure 12-22 shows an example of such a custom track. Please note that I inverted the screenshot to be better visible in this book. You could also use an invert post-screen shader as described in Chapter 8.

If you have some energy left, try to import a track from 3D Studio Max through the TrackImporter class and then test it in the Track or Landscape class. Anyway, enjoy the landscape and track rendering code. Hopefully it is also useful for other game projects.

Fps: 1783

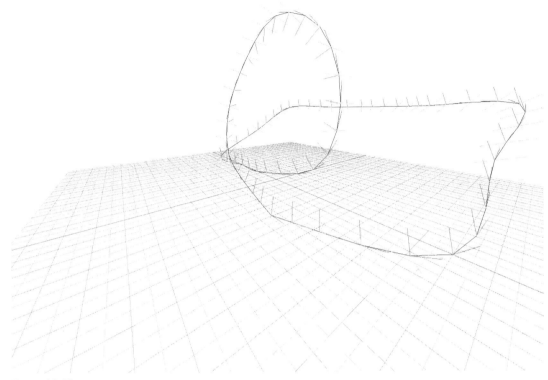

Figure 12-22

Summary

In this chapter you learned a lot about rendering complex 3D objects like the landscape, the track, and the many 3D models used to create the levels in the racing game you are creating here. It will hopefully be useful for other games too, but there are a couple of things you might want to remember when creating landscapes for games:

❑ Always figure out first how the player looks at the landscape in the game later. It does not make sense to have a great looking landscape, which only looks good at a close distance and only covers 50×50 meters if in reality you need huge terrains for strategy, role playing, or racing games. You need something bigger for these kinds of games and this means you either have to repeat textures or have clever rendering techniques combining detail textures with big textures, or use splatting to "paint" the landscape ground this way.

❑ Splatting is a great technique for huge terrains. Most games go with texture splatting and use many different ground textures and additional special textures, tracks, and so on for great looking terrains. If you don't have much development time or if you don't really need huge terrains you might find simpler solutions like the one from the last chapter, which was ok for a shoot-'em-up kind of game.

❑ Additional layers, shaders, and effects, especially water shaders and shadow mapping, can be a very time-consuming task. I intentionally left out water from the game because in my last couple of projects it always took several weeks to get great looking water and I know myself — if it does not look good I will keep fixing it, even if I really don't have time for that.

❑ There are many tips and tricks you can learn from other people; good resources are many tutorials on the Internet and books like the *Game Programming Gems* or *ShaderX* series.

For the track generation you have similar rules, and the rule to create unit tests first is always important. Always test your performance, especially if you get into high polygon areas like you did this chapter, with more than 130,000 polygons just for the landscape and up to 24,000 polygons for the road plus maybe 50,000 polygons for additional road data like guard rails, tunnels, and the cement columns the road stands on. This means even without any additional landscape objects you already have more than 200,000 polygons each frame, which means to even achieve a frame rate of 100 frames per second you need to push more than 20 million polygons per second to the GPU just for the landscape and the track. The car has about 25,000 polygons and the landscape objects all have several thousand polygons too, which means that you can end up with several million polygons per frame if you have 1000 landscape objects or more in the scene. This may sound like a lot, but if you take a look at the screenshots from the TestRenderLandscape unit test you can see that you have almost 2000 objects in all of them.

You can probably guess that the GPU will not be able to push 2–3 million polygons each frame to the screen and still run at over 60 frames per second on the Xbox 360. On the PC it is even worse because 75 Hz is the most-used screen refresh rate and the GPU of most players is much slower, not able at all to handle that much 3D geometry each frame. To make sure the game still runs great even on mid to low spec PCs, the following tricks are used:

❑ Never render anything that is not visible. Well, the landscape and the track are always visible, so you can't just skip them. But many of the landscape models might be behind you or just not in your field of view and can be easily skipped. Another trick is to skip any models that are just too far away to be noticed anymore. Especially smaller 3D models can be skipped after 100 meters. This is the biggest performance gain in the whole game. Check out the Model class and the Render method to learn more about this trick.

❑ Render the GPU-heavy data at the beginning of each frame. This way you can prepare the landscape models and other rendering data while the GPU is still working with the many landscape and track polygons.

❑ Always sort rendering by shaders. You already saw in the previous games how the MeshRender-Manager is used and how it can greatly improve the performance. In the many performance tests I did with the racing game (see the Model class for some of them) I constantly improved the performance of the MeshRenderManager class. Especially for many objects of the same type using the same shader the performance can be really astonishing in the engine. Check out the TestRenderManyModels unit test, which pushes more than 100 million polygons to the GPU on the Xbox 360 (and your PC if your GPU is fast enough).

❑ Use short shaders! In the original Rocket Commander game everything used the `ParallaxShader`, which just has a few extra instructions compared to the `NormalMapping` shader, but it will still take more time to render a parallax mapped 3D object than just a normal mapped 3D object. For that reason you only use normal mapping in the racing game and it does not make any visual difference. Only the landscape uses a more complex shader to add the detail map effect (see Figure 12-7; it is really worth the effort).

Okay, before your brain explodes with all this new knowledge, relax for a while. Chapter 13 is about physics and involves a lot of math. By the time you read Chapter 14, the final chapter, you will finally be able to put everything together for the racing game — and you can drive a few test rounds!

13

Physics

Physics in games has become quite popular in recent years. It is not like older games do not have any physics, but recently many shooter games have complex physic systems that are only possible through the immense increase in computing power and multi-core systems. Even hardware PPUs (physics processing units) are available today, similar to GPUs that just handle graphics. These processors are just for calculating physics.

The games that use physics the most are first-person shooters, especially if you have a lot of freedom and allow the player to walk around freely and interact with the scenery. One of the most popular games that used a lot of innovative physics techniques and also involved physics in the game play and mission design was Half-Life 2, which came out at the end of 2004.

Half-Life 2 uses the commercial physics engine Havok internally, but there are several other physics frameworks, which are discussed in a short while. Sadly none of them will work on the Xbox 360 with the XNA Framework because they all use unmanaged code, which is not allowed on the Xbox 360 when you develop games with XNA. On the PC you can use whatever you like, and this chapter discusses which framework might be the best to use right now. The Racing Game you are currently developing will not make use of any advanced physics framework for that reason and because it is a lot of work implementing and testing such a powerful framework, aside from the fact that most of them cost a lot of money to license. In Half-Life 2 the engineers spent several years tweaking and fine-tuning the physics until they were pleased with the result.

Physics always comes along with some heavy mathematics. It is certainly possible to use a physics framework or apply a simple formula like the famous $F = m * a$ without knowing much about physics or math, but as soon as you want to develop your own physics system for your game, you will need at least a basic understanding of Newton's laws of motion. Having a physics formula book nearby or at least Google at your fingertips for help is also a good idea. Figure 13-1 shows a typical example of a physics problem involving several objects, transmitting forces, gravity, and so on.

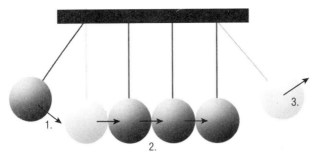

1. Gravity pulls first ball down and pushes it towards the other balls through the attached string.
2. The force gets transmitted through the balls until it reaches the last ball, where the force can be used to lift up the last ball.
3. The last ball flies up, all the other balls stay still. After a while gravity reverses the direction of the ball and the game begins again.

Figure 13-1

When you talk about physics you just have to mention Isaac Newton, the apple, and the tree. You know the story. Physics has evolved quite a bit since then and there are many theories about the extremely small world of atoms, quarks, electrons, and so on and of course the macro cosmos, the solar system, stars and planets, and so on. But for most games you are happy to use just a bunch of simple physics formulas to help you accelerate and decelerate objects. It is just not practical to work on a smaller scope due to limited processing power and because it just has to look good, you don't need every virtual atom to behave like in the real world.

While formulas like Newton's laws of motion will be heavily used, you are going to spend most of the time with collision issues, just like for the Rocket Commander game from Chapter 8. At least physics are fun and thanks to unit testing you can quickly try out things until they work, but be aware — you can spend a lot of time with physics and it is hard to see the results of your work if the world of your game does not allow much interaction. It is nice to have real physics for a puzzle game, but if all you can do is click on objects to be removed, you really don't need a complex physics engine. Just fake it!

Newton's Laws of Motion

Let's take a quick look at the important laws of motion by our friend Isaac Newton. Check out Figure 13-2 to see these physics laws in action:

❑ First Law — Objects stay in motion unless some external force interacts with them. This is really easy because all objects that can move usually have a movement vector or some velocity value anyway. Just don't change that value unless you apply some force on it to slow it down, accelerate it, or change the direction. That's it.

❑ Second Law — When you do apply an external force, it means you can accelerate or decelerate an object, or if you have more than one dimension (well, you have three for 3D games) you can also change the direction the object is moving. In that case you just work with vectors instead of scalar values and all vector components (x, y, and z) will be changed instead of just one simple value. Because masses for your objects will always be constant (at least in most games I know of) you can use the simplified $F = m * a$ formula, where "a" is the acceleration defined by the change of velocity divided by the change of time: $a = dv/dt$.

❑ Third Law — Each action has an equal and opposite reaction. This means if you have a force like the gravity of the earth acting on an object, there is a reacting force of the object applying the same force on the earth in opposite direction. Because the earth has a much greater mass than some small object like a stone or apple it will not matter much to the earth if it is acting on it. But if you take a much bigger object like the sun, the gravity of the earth is even much smaller than the one from the sun. Good thing our earth is always in motion rotating around the sun keeping it in orbit, the same way the moon is orbiting around the earth.

Newton's Laws on Steroids, er, I mean, Asteroids!

First Law

Objects just stay in motion until some force changes that (gravity, collisions, explosions). In RC this is just the movement vector, which will stay the same and be used every frame to update each asteroid's position.

Second Law

m=Mass of Rocket
a = Resulting acceleration
F = Acceleration Force through the Rocket Booster
$F = m*a$
$a = F/m$
F=Collision Force
Movement after collision
Mass 1
Mass 2
Incoming movement

Each applied force on an object changes its momentum, which means the object either accelerates, decelerates, or changes direction. In the case of a collision, all the momentum of both objects builds the collision Force, which is then used to either break the objects or give the force back to them and let them bounce off in opposite directions.

Third Law

Moon
Gravity of Earth acting on Moon
Earth
Gravity of Moon acting on the Earth, much smaller force, but we can still see it in our oceans' high and low tides

For every action there is an equal reaction pointing in the opposite direction. This means that the same way the earth pulls on the moon, the moon pulls on the earth. Since the masses are very different, the effect is much greater on the moon. But even a simple moving asteroid from the first example has an opposite force of the movement, or else it would get faster and faster and then would not comply with the first law.

Figure 13-2

One of the things Newton thought about when he wrote his "Principia Mathematica" showing these laws of motion for the first time was his law of universal gravitation, which explains the planetary movement and why the moon orbits the earth and the earth orbits the sun. Pretty exciting stuff back then, but today every school kid can calculate this, at least if they pay attention in physics class. Computers are more powerful than just giving them one planet moving around another one. In Rocket Commander you already saw thousands of asteroids interacting with each other. They don't apply gravity on each other and they just collide and bounce off each other, but adding more reality to the unit tests there by adding gravity would not be a big challenge.

Keep It Simple

Because physics is a big topic and can require your full attention when you implement physics into your game, you should try to keep things simple. Often you don't even have to know which formula is the correct one — just find something that works. For example, you don't have to code anything to follow the first law of motion, and the third law can be ignored too most of the time because you are only interested in forces that change motion for your objects.

Before you dive deeper into the world of physics and take a quick look at the available physics engines, you should make sure you know exactly what you need for your Racing Game. There is no need to implement a highly complex physics engine allowing you to stack boxes and throw them over, if all you need is to be able to just drive around with your car and stay on the road. I really wish I would have had more time for implementing physics into the Racing Game, but the game had to be completed and I had quite a lot of other projects I was working on at the time. For that reason the Racing Game only uses a simple approach to physics and the collisions are handled in a very simplified way. But it works, and even though it stills requires a lot of fine-tuning and special care as you can see in the next chapter, you can get your car on the road and drive around.

Figure 13-3 shows the basic physics requirement for the Racing Game. Because you do not interact with any other object in the world and no landscape object has physics, you can fully turn your attention to the car and don't have to worry about anything else.

These rules are implemented in a few lines of code, but it gets harder to tweak all the values and let the car interact correctly with the road:

```
// [From CarPhysics.cs]
// Handle car engine force
float newAccelerationForce = 0.0f;
if (Input.KeyboardUpPressed ||
  Input.Keyboard.IsKeyDown(Keys.W) ||
  Input.MouseLeftButtonPressed ||
  Input.GamePadAPressed)
  newAccelerationForce +=
    MaxAccelerationPerSec;
// [etc.]

// Add acceleration force to total car force, but use the current
// car direction!
carForce +=
  carDir * newAccelerationForce * (moveFactor * 85);// 70);//75);

// Change speed with standard formula, use acceleration as our
// force, gravity is handled below in the ApplyGravity method.
float oldSpeed = speed;
Vector3 speedChangeVector = carForce / CarMass;
// Only use the amount important for our current direction
// (slower rotation)
if (speedChangeVector.Length() > 0)
{
  float speedApplyFactor =
    Vector3.Dot(Vector3.Normalize(speedChangeVector), carDir);
```

```
   if (speedApplyFactor > 1)
     speedApplyFactor = 1;
   speed += speedChangeVector.Length() * speedApplyFactor;
 } // if (speedChangeVector.Length)
```

1. Our car engine pushes the car forward as we step on the gas.
2. Wind, road friction, etc., pull the car back and slow it down. We can also brake the car ourselves.
3. Gravity pulls the car down and keeps the car on the road. If we drive fast enough, we might stay in the air for a few seconds through the momentum of the car until gravity pushes us down again.

Figure 13-3

The code is maybe a little bit more complicated than it was when I implemented the solution the first time with the help of the unit test of the `CarPhysics` class, but it still basically increases the speed of the car when you accelerate through the keyboard up keys or the equivalent input keys and buttons. To allow letting the car drift into a different direction than you are actually heading I split up the car direction and the movement vector. Speed was used to update the length of the movement vector, but I ran into many problems and to simplify the problem I just use a scalar value for the speed now. This way it is also very easy to just drive backwards a little bit with the help of negative speed vectors while the car is still pointing forward.

Because your track is not just going straight ahead you need to rotate your car with the help of the left and right keyboard cursors or the gamepad, or even by using the mouse. Figure 13-4 shows the basic rules for the rotation of your car, which is very simple and implemented in just a few lines of code. To make rotations more smooth the last rotation value is still used, but reduced a bit.

```
// First handle rotations (reduce last value)
rotationChange *= 0.825f;// 75f;

// Left/right changes rotation
if (Input.KeyboardLeftPressed ||
  Input.Keyboard.IsKeyDown(Keys.A))
  rotationChange += MaxRotationPerSec * moveFactor / 2.5f;
```

```
else if (Input.KeyboardRightPressed ||
  Input.Keyboard.IsKeyDown(Keys.D) ||
  Input.Keyboard.IsKeyDown(Keys.E))
  rotationChange -= MaxRotationPerSec * moveFactor / 2.5f;
else
  rotationChange = 0;

if (Input.MouseXMovement != 0)
  rotationChange -=
    (Input.MouseXMovement / 15.0f) *
    MaxRotationPerSec * moveFactor;

// Rotate dir around up vector

// Interpolate rotatation amount.
virtualRotationAmount += rotationChange;

// Smooth over 200ms
float interpolatedRotationChange =
  (rotationChange + virtualRotationAmount) *
  moveFactor / 0.225f;// / 0.200f;
virtualRotationAmount -= interpolatedRotationChange;
// We can't rotate our car ourself if it is currently not on the ground
if (isCarOnGround)
  carDir = Vector3.TransformNormal(carDir,
    Matrix.CreateFromAxisAngle(carUp, interpolatedRotationChange));
```

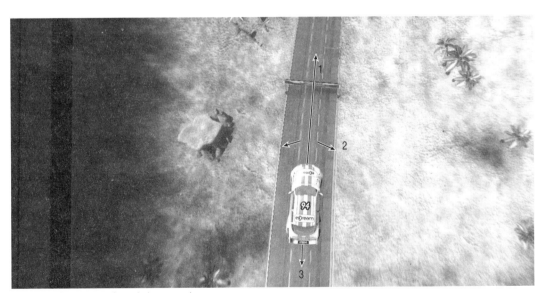

1. Forward movement through the car engine
2. We can turn the car left and right or just crash into the guard rail when a curve comes. Anyway we will stay on the road because gravity pulls us down. Only if we manage to fly above the guard rails, we die. We can also fall out of the track in loopings.
3. Friction through wind and the road, or if the player brakes himself.

Figure 13-4

A more complex way to handle the car physics makes sense if you have more than a few weeks' time to develop your game, and if you really want more realistic calculations you could use more constants and forces to get the car behavior more realistic than I did. But my solution works too and it did not take much time to implement it.

If you want to check it out please use the `TestCarPhysicsOnPlaneWithGuardRails` unit test in the `CarPhysics` class. The unit test started out very simple with just the car and a plane rendered on the ground, which is rendered with the help of the new `PlaneRenderer` class. Later the guard rails and collision checking and response were added, which are discussed later in this chapter. This is an earlier version of the unit test before it was renamed to `TestCarPhysicsOnPlaneWithGuardRails` just showing you my test environment for handling the basic car physics. Figure 13-5 shows the result. Testing is done with the normal keys and input devices the game uses for controlling the car (up, down, left, right, and so on).

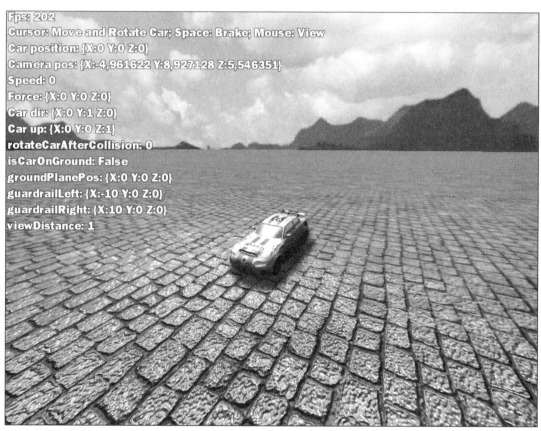

Figure 13-5

```
static public void TestCarPhysicsOnPlane()
{
    PlaneRenderer plane = null;

    TestGame.Start("TestCarPhysicsOnPlane",
```

```
      delegate
      {
        plane = new PlaneRenderer(Vector3.Zero,
          new Plane(new Vector3(0, 0, 1), 0),
          new Material("CityGround", "CityGroundNormal"), 500.0f);

        // Put car on the ground and use standard direction and up vectors
    RacingGame.Player.SetCarPosition(
          new Vector3(0, 0, 0),
          new Vector3(0, 1, 0),
          new Vector3(0, 0, 1));
      },
      delegate
      {
        // Test slow computers by slowing down the framerate with Ctrl
        if (Input.Keyboard.IsKeyDown(Keys.LeftControl))
          Thread.Sleep(75);

        Matrix carMatrix = RacingGame.Player.UpdateCarMatrixAndCamera();

        // Generate shadows, just the car does shadows
        ShaderEffect.shadowMapping.GenerateShadows(
          delegate
          {
            RacingGame.CarModel.GenerateShadow(carMatrix);
          });

        // Render shadows (on both the plane and the car)
        ShaderEffect.shadowMapping.RenderShadows(
          delegate
          {
            RacingGame.CarModel.UseShadow(carMatrix);
            plane.UseShadow();
          });

        BaseGame.UI.RenderGameBackground();
        // Show car and ground plane
        RacingGame.CarModel.RenderCar(0, Color.White, carMatrix);
        plane.Render();

        // Just add brake tracks (we don't render the landscape here)
        RacingGame.Landscape.RenderBrakeTracks();

        // Render all 3d objects
        BaseGame.MeshRenderManager.Render();

        // Add shadows
        ShaderEffect.shadowMapping.ShowShadows();
        RacingGame.Player.DisplayPhysicsValuesAndHelp();
      });
  } // TestCarPhysicsOnPlane()
```

Gravitation

Just driving around on a plane surface is easy to do, but not really fun, especially since the Racing Game allows you to drive crazy tracks with loopings, tunnels, hard curves, and so on. The collision detection and response techniques are discussed later in this chapter, but you can add gravity relatively quickly to your current `TestCarPhysicsOnPlane` unit test and fine-tune it a little bit more later.

You are just going to make a very simple change to the `TestCarPhysicsOnPlane` unit test by simply putting the car 10 meters above the ground in the initialization code. It should fall down now, but because you have not implemented any real physics yet (only the car controlling, accelerating, and steering was done until now) it just stays in the air (see Figure 13-6).

Figure 13-6

```
// Put car 10m above the ground to test gravity and ground plane!
RacingGame.Player.SetCarPosition(
  new Vector3(0, 0, 10),
  new Vector3(0, 1, 0),
  new Vector3(0, 0, 1));
```

The `Player` class is derived from the `ChaseCamera` class, which is again derived from the `CarPhysics` class. This way all the car controlling, physics, player logic, and so on can be handled and accessed from one single place: the `Player` class. The `ChaseCamera` has two modes, similar to the modes of the `SpaceCamera` class from Rocket Commander:

❑ The Free Camera Mode is usually used for all unit tests. Sometimes you have to change it for unit tests like the one you are currently working on to allow the same controller features as in the game.

❑ Default Chase Car Game Camera is used for the game. Either used for the menu or replays to chase the camera behind the car and of course in the game to show and control the car.

Use the following lines in the initialization code to make sure the game camera is used and you don't use any zoom-in time like in the game, so you can see the car falling down at the beginning:

```
// Make sure we are not in free camera mode and can control the car
RacingGame.Player.FreeCamera = false;
RacingGame.Player.ZoomInTime = 0;
  RacingGame.Player.SetCameraPosition(new Vector3(0, -5, 8));
```

The rest of the unit test can stay the same; the actual gravity computation happens in the `Update` method of the `CarPhysics` class, which calls the `ApplyGravity` method:

```
/// <summary>
/// Apply gravity
/// </summary>
private void ApplyGravity()
{
  // Fix car on ground
  float distFromGround = Vector3Helper.SignedDistanceToPlane(
    carPos, groundPlanePos, groundPlaneNormal);
  isCarOnGround = distFromGround > -0.1f;

  // Use very hard and instant gravity to fix if car is below ground!
  float moveFactor = BaseGame.MoveFactorPerSecond;
  float maxGravity = Gravity * moveFactor;

  // Use more smooth gravity for jumping
  float minGravity = -Gravity * moveFactor;

  if (distFromGround > maxGravity)
  {
    distFromGround = maxGravity;
    gravitySpeed = 0;
  } // if (distFromGround)
  if (distFromGround < minGravity)
  {
    distFromGround = minGravity;
    gravitySpeed -= distFromGround;
  } // if (distFromGround)

  carPos.Z += distFromGround;
} // ApplyGravity()
```

This code basically just reduces the z position value of the car position until you reach the ground. Because the car might be lower than the road when you drive uphill or because of some precision error, the z position value is also corrected to reset the car back to the road level.

For tweaking the many constants are used, which are all defined at the very beginning of the `CarPhysics` class. These are the first three constants; changing the `CarMass`, for example, gives you control if the car is very heavy and almost glued to the ground or if it is as light as a feather and can fly a long time until gravity kicks in again:

```
#region Constants
/// <summary>
/// Car is 1000 kg
/// </summary>
const float CarMass = 1000;//1000.0f;

/// <summary>
/// Gravity on earth is 9.81 m/s^2
/// </summary>
const float Gravity = 9.81f;

/// <summary>
/// Max speed of our car is 275 mph.
/// While we use mph for the display, we calculate internally with
/// meters per sec since meter is the unit we use for everthing in the
/// game. And it is a much nicer unit than miles or feet.
/// </summary>
public const float MaxSpeed =
  275.0f * MphToMeterPerSec;

/// <summary>
/// Convert our meter per sec to mph for display.
/// 1 mile = 1.609344 kilometers
/// Each hour has 3600 seconds (60 min * 60 sec).
/// 1 kilometer = 1000 meter.
/// </summary>
public const float MeterPerSecToMph =
  1.609344f * ((60.0f*60.0f)/1000.0f),
  MphToMeterPerSec = 1.0f / MeterPerSecToMph;

// [etc.]
```

You probably saw a couple of times now that I use meters instead of feet, inches, yards, miles, or whatever crazy formats there are in the U.S. Sorry, the rest of the world uses meters and it is an easier unit system for measuring and setting constants. I don't even know constants like gravity in other unit systems and you can see that whenever I have other formats like Mph (Miles per hour) I use helper constants to convert from one format to the next. You can also use Google to convert from one format to another. Just type in "1500 meters as miles" and you will get the value in miles.

The new `TestCarPhysicsOnPlane` unit test allows you to control the car and it handles gravity correctly (see Figure 13-7). It also handles displaying the brake tracks on the ground after you suddenly try to stop the car.

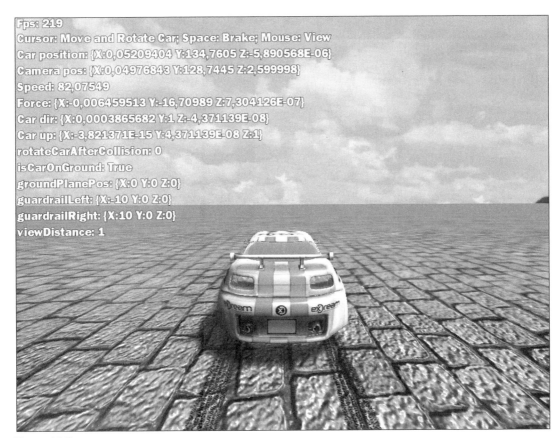

Figure 13-7

Physics Engines

With all this new knowledge about the basics of physics you can now compare existing physics engines a little easier. After these basics are handled and after making sure you have the correct constants defined and feel comfortable in your unit system, you should think a little bit about the requirement for your game. Physics engines can often do a lot of different things and while many physics demos and tutorials look pretty cool, they cannot be used for most games. Having a bunch of boxes on top of each other and kicking them over is fun the first time, but not many games even allow direct control of boxes to push them around, and after a while it really gets boring seeing boxes fall over. It is like being in kindergarten again.

But not all demos are just a bunch of boxes. There are many good examples showing you specific features of physics engines, but my point is that most games only need certain features. First-person shooter games can probably use most of the features from physics engines and you can see that by just looking at the released games in the past couple of years. Almost all first-person shooters have some kind of physics implemented, whereas other games like role playing games, strategy games, and so on have either no physics or just rudimentary physics, often only used to improve the visual effects a little bit, but not game logic itself.

I personally don't like physics in strategy games, because they are not implemented very well and do not improve the game. They often just add better visuals and have as a side effect that your units can die if some big building collapses or falls over your units. It is like playing chess while an earthquake is going on; it really destroys the game principle and you would not be able to make any clever moves anymore because everything is just shaking and falling over. Maybe it will take time until the developers figure out how to use physics decently in the game play and in a way that makes the game still predictable and not luck-based.

What I really like are physics for explosions, effects, and for improving the visual quality. There are several games that have really nice simulations for water, explosion, and smoke effects that interact with the surrounding environment, and so on.

As I said before you will not be able to use any of the physics engines on the Xbox 360 when using XNA because all of them are based on unmanaged code, which is just not supported in XNA. On the Windows platform you can use whatever you like, but even here most engines do not have a proper .NET interface that allows you to easily use and handle physics directly in your game. The possibilities for .NET are discussed when you go through the engines in a second. Anyway, take a quick look at some of the features of physics engines available today:

❑   Forces like gravity, friction, kinetic and contact friction, buoyancy, and so on.

❑   Basic physics objects support for defining and handling boxes, spheres, cylinders, plates, and so on. Often these engines also support connected objects and more complex predefined models like cars, planes, hovercrafts, ships, and so on to allow you to quickly play around with them.

❑   Checking for collisions between many objects, especially if they are not just spheres. This is usually the main place for optimizations because collision calculations are used very often and require checking a lot of objects, bounding spheres, and even polygon-based checks.

   The Rocket Commander game shows a good solution on how to check many collisions that are optimized with the help of sectors to achieve great performance.

❑   Collision response, which is executed when a collision was detected. Either you let the objects bounce off each other (like in Rocket Commander), or you can even damage or break them (collision force is transformed to kinetic energy and breaks up your models). Games usually use predefined 3D models for explosions, wrecks, and broken parts because it would really be hard to generate this data in real time, but the result is still great looking if the 3D artist does a good job.

❑   Projectile physics can help you for bullets, rockets, and other projectiles that are fired. You saw how projectiles are used in the last chapter and if you have a physics engine that handles projectiles too, you would just add the projectile to it and allow using physics parameters and maybe adding special behavior depending on the 3D surroundings (for example, bullets are slower under water).

❑   Even complete particle systems can be done with physics and as I said earlier I really like effect systems that can make good use of a physics engine, but effect systems are already a lot of work.

❑   There are many more features a physics engine can have like supporting rigid body simulators, rag-doll physics for characters falling down, deformable objects like clothes, flags, fluids, and other complex bodies.

PhysX

PhysX is the name for the physics engine and SDK by AGEIA, which was formerly known as NovodeX SDK, but PhysX is also the name of the PPU (physics processing unit) also developed by AGEIA. The PhysX PPU is the world's first card devoted just to calculating physics on the PC and can be used in any game that uses the PhysX SDK. Currently there are not many games around that support the PhysX engine, but many engines and upcoming games have already licensed the PhysX SDK and the most popular step was done by Sony licensing PhysX for its Playstation 3 console game development.

Even without having the PPU the engine is really powerful and the developers have been doing physics engines for a long time now. They are probably the number two behind the Havok engine, which is more widely used, not only in games, but also in 3D content creation programs like 3D Studio Max. While the idea is nice to offload the heavy lifting for physics calculations to a special card, the PPU is just too expensive ($250–$300) and not many people will have this card. Most people who buy a physics card like this will probably be developers or artists that can benefit from the card in the content creation process, but you can't expect your gamers to have this card in order for your game to work. But PhysX also performs well on the CPU, and thanks to multi-core systems it runs well on today's hardware too, but not as crazy good as the PPU.

Not so many games use PhysX right now; you can only find a handful of games using the engine. Examples are Ghost Recon, Gothic 3, Joint Task Force, and most recently Gears of War (Xbox 360). But there are many future titles and engines like the Unreal Tournament 2007 game and the Unreal 3 engine, Splinter Cell, Monster Madness, and so on.

PhysX focuses a lot on games, game engines, and handling effects, the game logic that uses physics, and having a lot of cool looking examples and tutorials. Their main advantage is that they have the PPU hardware to run a lot faster than all the other physics engines and PhysX also uses a more unified architecture to handle all physic calculations the same way.

You can find more information about PhysX on the official website at `http://www.ageia.com`.

Havok

Havok is the name of the very popular and widely known Havok Game Dynamics SDK (currently at version 4, released in 2006) and also the name of the company that develops this SDK. It was founded in 1998 and the first SDK (v 1.0) was released in 2000. More than 100 games use the Havok physics engine today and the most famous ones are games like Half-Life 2 and the Source engine by Valve, which is used by many other mods based on Half-Life. Havok is mainly used by first-person shooter games, but some other game genres also have been using the Havok engine.

Havok is available on many platforms including the PC (Windows and Linux) and almost every console that came out since it was released (Xbox, Xbox 360, PS 2, PS 3, WII, Game Cube). It is written in C/C++ and is very portable to any system that allows compiling C code. For you as a .NET developer there is not much support; there may be wrappers out there, but I have not heard of any .NET game or engine that uses Havok.

This physics engine is not only used in games, but it is also available in 3D Studio Max, which uses the middleware internally and is quite popular in the 3D artist community for simulating physics effects. In previous versions it was implemented as a plug-in named reactor, but in recent versions it is implemented into the basic version of 3D Studio Max. Havok was even used in the movie production of the *Matrix* trilogy.

Havok supports two major physics operations. Effect physics are used for anything that does not affect the game play and they can even be offloaded to a GPU that supports Shader Model 3.0 like the GeForce 7x and 8x series, especially if the GPU is fast. And then there are game physics, which are calculated on the CPU. Havok is the main competitor of PhysX and proves that you can do really great things without having an extra PPU; even the Half-Life 2 game from 2004 proved that it was possible to have pretty good physics in a game and even how to improve the game play through physics.

You can find more information about Havok on the official website at `http://www.havok.com/`.

ODE

ODE stands for Open Dynamics Engine and unlike PhysX and Havok is not a commercial engine, which may be more interesting to most beginner developers or teams that just don't have the kind of money to use a big commercial physics engine.

ODE is an open source physics engine, which uses the BSD license (or LGPL if you like that). It was started in 2001 and some games have been developed with it already, but it is not as feature-complete as PhysX or Havok and certainly not that successful.

ODE basically supports rigid body dynamics and collision detection. You will still have a lot of work to do for more advanced physics, but ODE gives you a nice basic framework, which gives you all the basic geometries (like boxes, spheres, cylinders, and so on) and physics calculations you need to do some basic physics demos. There are also frameworks that have been built on top of ODE or use ODE.

Now comes the cool part: ODE has a nice .NET wrapper called ODE.NET, which can be found on the following website. There are several samples available and it is always nice to see some .NET code between all these physics engines, which are all just using C++ code and only give you C++ samples. The samples show basic physics problems like stacking boxes and pushing them over, and rag-doll physics and controlling some basic objects like cars or toys are also presented on ODE.NET at `http://www.thejamesrainenetwork.co.uk/ode/ode.html`.

You can also take a look at the official website of ODE. If it is down, check out the Wikipedia entry about the Open Dynamics Engine at `http://www.ode.org/`.

Other

There are many other physics engines available and I certainly do not know about all of them. Maybe there are even other useful engines that can be used in .NET, but I have not found any other wrappers that were as useful as ODE.NET yet.

Here are a couple of other physics engines I have encountered:

❑ Newton Game Dynamics is a free physics engine with really nice samples and a good documentation. It can be used for hobby and commercial use and it supports the Windows, Mac, and Linux platforms.

A free engine like this one is nice. I remember seeing a .NET wrapper for this engine some-where a year ago, but the source code for the base engine is not available. This makes it very hard to implement it into .NET or to change anything if you want to improve the engine. ODE, on the other hand, is highly customizable to your every need. Check it out at `http://www` `.newtondynamics.com/`.

❑ Tokamak Game Physics is another nice physics engine that is completely free to use for both non-commercial and commercial projects. It also has quite a few samples and tutorials, but again, there is no source code available for the core engine itself, just for the samples. Sadly this engine has not been updated for almost two years now and it seems that the developers do not care anymore; the forum is completely overrun by spam. The last news entry was March 2005. I implemented a simple .NET wrapper a few years back and played around with the engine a little bit, but I never found the time to get any further. Today I would probably just use one of the other available engines, especially ODE.NET since it already works with .NET. Visit `http://www.tokamakphysics.com/`.

❑ Physics and Math Library (also called Game Physics Engine) is a German-based engine that was originally developed for a book. It focuses on implementing many of the available features of the commercial engines like Havok and PhysX. It is free to use, but I could not find many screenshots or forum discussions. It is hard to tell if an engine like this is really worth the effort you would probably put into it (making it run in your project and maybe even porting it to .NET), but the project looks pretty promising. The website is `http://game-physics-engine.info/`.

❑ nV Physics Engine (also called The Physics Engine) has a nice website and some screenshots on it (which is always good for a website presenting a product). It looks promising but all samples are C++ again and you probably don't even have access to the source code. The website is `http://www.thephysicsengine.com/`.

❑ Bullet Physics Library is yet another free physics engine, this time hosted by sourceforge.net and it includes the full source code, which is nice. The author worked at Havok before and the engine is already used by several engines, especially open source engines and the 3D modeler tool Blender 3D. It also supports the latest file formats and has several advanced features already. The website is `http://www.continuousphysics.com/Bullet/`.

❑ There are probably many more physics engines, especially smaller ones. Try to search for some-thing specific when you encounter a certain problem and don't really need a full-blown physics engine.

As you can see there are many physics engines available, but it is not easy to use them in .NET. This doesn't have much to do with XNA; it is just annoying that you can't use them on the Xbox 360 because all of them are developed in C++ and use unmanaged code, which means no-no for the Xbox 360 when using XNA.

But even if you don't use a physics engine in the end, just by checking them out and playing around with the many available samples and tutorials you can get a clearer picture what is possible with a physics engine and which parts will probably be hard to re-implement if you do it yourself. You don't really need a complex physics engine in the Racing Game. Well, it would be nice to have good solid foundation, but because implementing physics engines is so hard in .NET and because I want the game to run on the Xbox 360 too, you are back to doing it yourself again.

Implementing Physics

Time to dive a little bit deeper into the implementation of the physics required for your Racing Game. You saw some of the features of the many powerful physics engines available today, but because it is not easy to implement them and because they are not written in .NET you are going to continue implementing physics in your own way.

You handled some of the car controlling and simple gravity at the beginning of the chapter. The thing you are currently missing is an accurate collision detection system for your car. The car should be stopped when you crash into one of the guard rails. You are also going to check some of the more complex situations like driving through loopings. Loopings are actually not hard to implement. Thanks to the track generation code from the last chapter they can be added to your tracks quite easily by just putting two of the spline points on top of each other, and when driving along the road the loopings are almost handled automatically if your physics system for the car is handling all the car forces correctly.

Handling Loopings

Before you continue with the hard stuff (collision detection and response, which is actually most of the code in the `CarPhysics` class), please take a look at Figure 13-8, which shows in a simplified way how the forces act on your car when you drive through a looping.

Handling Loopings in a Racing Game

A   Car Engine Force
B   Gravity always pulls us down
C   Momentum from the previous movement
D   Current resulting force for the car

Figure 13-8

If you just put the car on the top part of the looping without applying any forces, gravity (red) will pull it down and you will not be able to even move or drive the car because you will lose contact with the road immediately. So to even get to the top part of the looping the car must be always be pushed toward the road, which is upwards at the top of the looping. This force must be stronger than the gravity or else your car will lose contact with the road and begin to fall down again (see Figure 13-9). It is important that you have enough momentum to keep the car on the road. Momentum is the force the car had from the car's previous movement forces in the current time frame you are looking at.

Situations Where the Car Is Too Slow for Loopings

Situation 1: Car is too slow to even get up to the first part of the looping. Gravity is stronger than the decreasing momentum and the car engine together. Finally the car stops and falls down again (basically rolls/slides back).
Situation 2: Car was fast enough to get up the looping, but it is too slow now to keep pushing it towards the road (upwards). Gravity is stronger and will pull the car down. If this happens before reaching the top, the car will probably fall down and crash upside down. If it happens after reaching the top or almost reaching it, we still have a chance to fall back on the road again.

A Car Engine Force
B Gravity always pulls us down
C Momentum from the previous movement
D Current resulting force for the car
E Crashes into the road again here

Figure 13-9

If you just drive straight up a wall (with a ramp in front of it to get some momentum first), the gravity pulls you down and after a while you are going to lose all of the momentum and finally fall down. Because a looping is always changing the direction of the car, you are able to keep the car on the road relatively easy. Beating gravity is no big deal if you have a centrifugal force that is stronger than the gravity. Figure 13-10 shows you an example of just circling around a ball attached to a string. Even with a slow swinging force you will be able to let the ball fly in circles and the faster you go, the less you will even notice the gravity the ball usually has. It will just get harder to keep the string in your hand because the ball is pulling on it stronger and stronger thanks to the centrifugal force.

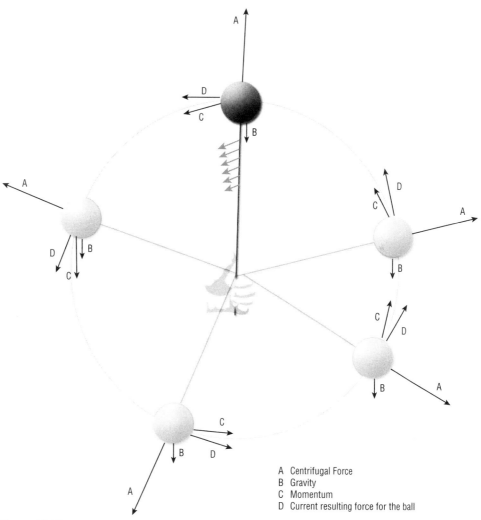

Centrifugal Force on a Rotating Ball Attached to a String

A Centrifugal Force
B Gravity
C Momentum
D Current resulting force for the ball

Figure 13-10

You can see the centrifugal force pushes the ball away from the hand and the gravity is relatively slow in comparison to that force when you move the ball fast enough. The momentum will keep the ball in the circulating motion even if you stop moving your hand.

Spring Physics

Most formulas for your game are simplified and the car movement is not as complex as it could be. You do not care much about the car engine, about any of the car internals or use. It is possible to implement many more parameters to use the power, rpm, starting and stalling forces, better braking and friction formulas, and so on. For a more detailed description about car physics please check out the following link at `http://www.racer.nl/reference/carphys.htm`.

Because of your simplified car logic many of these resulting effects are not implemented like pitching the car backwards when you accelerate and forward when you brake. But you still can implement something like this in a simplified way yourself.

All car wheels are connected to springs on the car allowing the car to stay more stable on the road even if you drive over smaller bumps on the road. When you accelerate the wheels push the car forward but it takes a while until enough movement energy is able to move the huge mass of the car itself. The effect becomes even more apparent when you suddenly stop the car. The wheels stop, but the car itself is still in motion and the still moving car mass pulls the entire car forward and tilts the car a little bit (see Figure 13-11).

Pitch Effect of a Car When Accelerating or Braking

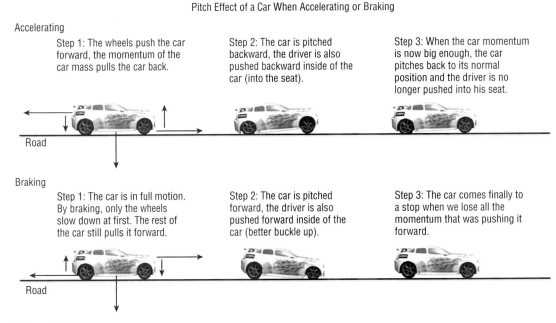

Accelerating

Step 1: The wheels push the car forward, the momentum of the car mass pulls the car back.

Step 2: The car is pitched backward, the driver is also pushed backward inside of the car (into the seat).

Step 3: When the car momentum is now big enough, the car pitches back to its normal position and the driver is no longer pushed into his seat.

Road

Braking

Step 1: The car is in full motion. By braking, only the wheels slow down at first. The rest of the car still pulls it forward.

Step 2: The car is pitched forward, the driver is also pushed forward inside of the car (better buckle up).

Step 3: The car comes finally to a stop when we lose all the momentum that was pushing it forward.

Road

Figure 13-11

Gravity always pushes you down, but different parts of the car, especially the wheels and the rest of the car, behave differently. The wheels are attached to springs on the car allowing the car to pitch forward and backwards, which will happen when you accelerate or decelerate and even if you just stay on a road that is not straight (if you drive uphill, the car will be pulled backwards).

You do not really have a representation of the springs and you don't even render the wheels the way they are shown in Figure 13-11. The car wheels will go into the ground if the car is pitched, but because you don't see the car from the side you will not notice it in the game. The chase camera is always behind the car and you are going to see most of the pitch effect just from the top of and behind the car.

Because the effect is relatively simply described you can just pitch the car whenever the speed changes for it:

❑   When accelerating, pitch the car backwards — the faster you are accelerating, the bigger the pitch angle is going to be.

❑   When braking, pitch the car forward — this pitch effect is usually stronger than the accelerating pitch effect because you brake much faster than you accelerate the car.

You already saw this behavior in the last game, XNA Shooter, where your own ship was rotated horizontally and vertically when you moved in either direction. The same formula can be used for the car too. To fix the problem that the wheels and the rest of the car would disappear into the road, you are going to limit the effect:

```
// Calculate pitch depending on the force
float speedChange = speed - oldSpeed;

// Limit speed change, never apply more than 8 mph change per sec.
if (speedChange < -8 * moveFactor)
  speedChange = -8 * moveFactor;
if (speedChange > 8 * moveFactor)
  speedChange = 8 * moveFactor;
carPitch = speedChange;
```

When the car is not changing its speed the car pitch value will stay 0 and behave correctly, and if you are accelerating or decelerating the car also behaves the correct way. But even after applying a better smoothing formula the effect does not look very convincing. In the real world the car would pitch forward and then backwards swinging out until the springs of the cars lose all of their forces to their friction.

All you need now is to let the car swing forward and backwards with a simple spring formula. The SpringPhysicsObject class (see Figure 13-12) of the Racing Game helps you with that. It calculates the position of a single object with a certain mass attached to a spring with a specific spring constant. This position swings up and down, but it slows down through the friction constant also used in this class. You are going to use a big mass and a strong friction. This results in a slow pitch effect for the car and the pitch effect becomes weaker very quickly. You don't want the car to bounce around like crazy.

This helper class is directly used in the `CarPhysics` class and initialized with the `CarMass` constant, 1.5 for the friction and 120 for the spring constant (both relatively high values). The initial position for the virtual spring object is 0 (car in its normal state):

```
/// <summary>
/// Car pitch physics helper for a simple spring effect for
/// accelerating, decelerating and crashing.
/// </summary>
SpringPhysicsObject carPitchPhysics = new SpringPhysicsObject(
    CarMass, 1.5f, 120, 0);
```

Figure 13-12

To update the current virtual spring object position when the car changes the speed you can use the `ChangePos` helper method:

```
carPitchPhysics.ChangePos(speedChange);
```

And finally you just call `Simulate` with the current time factor for this frame to simulate the pitch behavior, then when rendering you are going to use the pos value of this class to get the current pitch value:

```
// Handle pitch spring
carPitchPhysics.Simulate(moveFactor);
```

The interesting part of the `SpringPhysicsObject` class is obviously the `Simulate` method; all the other methods just set some values. To understand what the spring formula does you have to know about the restoring force for the spring by applying Hooke's law to the well-known $F = m^*a$ formula.

Hooke's law describes how stress is directly proportional to strain by using a constant pressure value. This way elasticity, spring, stress, and strain physics can be described.

If you want to read more about Hooke's law please read a good formulary book or check out the Internet. Wikipedia and Wolfram Research (`http://scienceworld.wolfram.com`) have great articles about many physics problems.

You are just going to use the simple spring formula $F = -k*x$ where F is the restoring force that pulls the object attached to your spring back or forward and k is the spring constant. Figure 13-13 describes this formula and the effect it has over time on the spring object you are going to use for the car pitch effect.

When no force is acting on the object and it is in the initial position (0) it will just stay that way. But if you pull it down the spring expands and forces the object back to its initial position. When it reaches the position 0 again, the spring restoring force is also back to zero, but the speed of the attached object is still fast and its momentum still pushes it up. The spring restoring force becomes negative now and prevents the object from moving up anymore when it reaches its highest position of 1. Now the restoring force is –1 and that pulls the object down again and when it is at the bottom position, the game starts from the beginning again.

The only thing that slows you down is friction, which should be very strong in your case to make sure the car does not bounce around too much. Please also note that you are ignoring gravity here and it is not really important for your car pitch effect because the car handles gravity itself, and for the spring effect you can safely ignore the gravity because it pulls everything down to the same direction anyway and does not affect any calculations.

The code to make this all work is in the `Simulate` method and you should be able to quickly understand it with the help of the knowledge you just acquired:

```
/// <summary>
/// Simulate spring formular using the timeChange.
/// The velocity is increased by the timeChange * force / mass,
/// the position is then timeChange * velocity.
/// </summary>
public void Simulate(float timeChange)
{
    // Calculate force again
    force += -pos * springConstant;
    // Calculate velocity
    velocity = force / mass;
    // And apply it to the current position
    pos += timeChange * velocity;
    // Apply friction
    force *= 1.0f - (timeChange * friction);
} // Simulate(timeChange)
```

The `SpringPhysicsObject` class can be found in the `Game Physics` namespace (see Figure 13-13). If you want to add more physics classes and try to implement more physics behaviors, you should do it in this namespace. This way it gets easier when you try to reuse some of the physics in future projects; just copy over and use the physics namespace.

Collision Detection

The final task for this chapter is to do the collision detection for the car and the guard rails. The car cannot collide with any other cars because you are the only car on the road and I made sure that there are no other objects on the road you could collide with. Collision detection and especially the response would be a lot more complex if you allowed other objects on the road. For example, having lanterns, signs, trash cans, and so on on the road would mean that you would have to kick them away with your car if you hit them. Then again these objects need to collide with each other and also with the surrounding world.

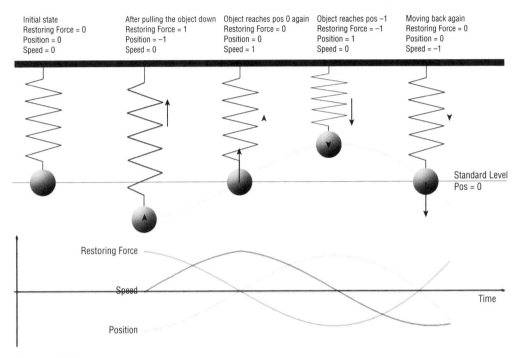

Figure 13-13

If you have a good physics engine this would be possible, but it is still a lot of work to tweak these objects, the general physics constants, and constantly test all the different kinds of collisions that can occur. It would probably be fun to implement such techniques and play around with them, but since I don't even have a full-blown physics engine for XNA, even getting the basics up and running would take longer than the whole project took.

The principles for collision detection and collision response are still the same, but you can simplify them to your needs and only involve the car and the guard rails. Because the guard rails are indestructible the only object that is affected by any collision is your car.

The biggest part of the physics in the Rocket Commander game was the asteroid-to-asteroid collision detection and optimization. The collision response is not very complex and thanks to the many unit tests even the basic collision detection could be done in a very simple way.

PhysicsAsteroidManager

For example, the `TestAsteroidPhysicsSmallScene` unit test of the `PhysicsAsteroidManager` class in Rocket Commander shows a good way to test collision detection. The unit test allows you to press 1–7 to test out various scenarios and shows the result of an asteroid collision event.

Figure 13-14 shows this unit test in action by using two asteroids of the same size flying toward each other and bouncing off in opposite directions after the collision happens. The method SetupScene is used to set the asteroids to their initial positions while the unit test itself handles all the collision testing.

```
case 2:
    // Collide with crazy movement vectors
    AddAsteroid(new Vector3(-35, +19, 8) * (-2),
        12.5f, asteroidModel.ObjectSize,
        new Vector3(-35, +19, 8));
    AddAsteroid(new Vector3(+15, 40, 14) * (-2),
        12.5f, asteroidModel.ObjectSize,
        new Vector3(+15, 40, 14));
    break;
```

The TestAsteroidPhysicsSmallScene unit test then calls the HandleSectorPhysics method, which checks all asteroids in a certain sector and does a simple bounding spheres test if they are too close to each other and if you should handle such a collision case.

The method not only checks the asteroids from your own sector, but also all asteroids from all surrounding sectors, which could very well collide with one of your own asteroids. Even with the very good sector optimization there are still several thousand collision detection checks going on in Rocket Commander each frame and it gets slower the more asteroids you have. For this reason it is a good thing that Rocket Commander XNA now uses multiple threads to handle the physics and the rendering code in two different threads.

Figure 13-14

The collision detection adds up the radiuses of both asteroids and checks if they are smaller together than physically possible. If so, a collision has occurred and you have to handle it. The following code just shows the collision test for one single sector. The code for testing all surrounding sectors is similar, but a lot longer.

```
// Only check this sector! Crosscheck with any other asteroid in
// this sector.
foreach (Asteroid otherAsteroid in thisSectorAsteroids)
  if (asteroid != otherAsteroid)
  {
    float maxAllowedDistance =
      otherAsteroid.collisionRadius +
      asteroid.collisionRadius;

    // Distance smaller than max. allowed distance?
    if ((otherAsteroid.position -
      asteroid.position).LengthSq() <
      maxAllowedDistance * maxAllowedDistance)
    {
      HandleAsteroidCollision(asteroid, otherAsteroid);
    } // if (otherAsteroid.position)
  } // foreach if (asteroid)
```

The `HandleAsteroidCollision` method now handles a collision and it moves the asteroids away from each other so they don't intersect with each other:

```
// Put both circles outside of the collision
// Add 1% to add a little distance between collided objects!
otherAsteroid.position = middle +
  otherPositionRel * otherAsteroid.collisionRadius * 1.015f;
asteroid.position = middle +
  positionRel * asteroid.collisionRadius * 1.015f;
```

Then the method reflects both movement vectors of the two asteroids away from the collision plane (the purple line in Figure 13-14) by using the total collision force and applying it to the masses of the asteroids. This way a smaller asteroid gets pushed away by a bigger asteroid with a far greater force than the other way around. Check out the unit tests to see this behavior in action.

The method is actually quite long and does a lot of extra checking, calculates masses and directions, and even adds rotation speed to the asteroids, but the code for handling the collision looks basically like this:

```
// Normalize movement
Vector3 asteroidDirection = asteroid.movement;
asteroidDirection.Normalize();
Vector3 otherAsteroidDirection = otherAsteroid.movement;
otherAsteroidDirection.Normalize();

// Get collision strength (1 if pointing in same direction,
// 0 if 90 degrees) for both asteroids.
float asteroidCollisionStrength = Math.Abs(Vector3.Dot(
  asteroidDirection, asteroidNormal));
float otherAsteroidCollisionStrength = Math.Abs(Vector3.Dot(
  otherAsteroidDirection, otherAsteroidNormal));
```

```
// Calculate reflection vectors from the asteroid direction and the
// normal towards the reflection plane.
Vector3 asteroidReflection =
  ReflectVector(asteroidDirection, asteroidNormal);
Vector3 otherAsteroidReflection =
  ReflectVector(otherAsteroidDirection, otherAsteroidNormal);

// Make sure the strength is calculated correctly
// We have also to correct the reflection vector if the length was 0,
// use the normal vector instead.
if (asteroidDirection.Length() <= 0.01f)
{
  asteroidCollisionStrength = otherAsteroidCollisionStrength;
  asteroidReflection = asteroidNormal;
} // if (asteroidDirection.Length)
if (otherAsteroidDirection.Length() <= 0.01f)
{
  otherAsteroidCollisionStrength = asteroidCollisionStrength;
  otherAsteroidReflection = otherAsteroidNormal;
} // if (otherAsteroidDirection.Length)

// Ok, now the complicated part, everything above was really easy!
asteroid.movement = asteroidReflection *
  // So, first we have to reflect our current movement speed.
  // This will be scaled to 1-strength to only account the reflection
  // amount (imagine a collision with a static wall). In most cases
  // Strength is close to 1 and this reflection will be very small.
  ((1 - asteroidCollisionStrength) * asteroidSpeed +
  // And finally we have to add the impuls, which is calculated
  // by the formula ((m1-m2)*v1 + 2*m2*v2)/(m1+m2), see
  // http://de.wikipedia.org/wiki/Sto%C3%9F_%28Physik%29 for more help.
  (asteroidCollisionStrength *
  (Math.Abs(asteroidMass - otherAsteroidMass) * asteroidSpeed +
  (2 * otherAsteroidMass * otherAsteroidSpeed)) / bothMasses));

  // Same for other asteroid, just with asteroid and otherAsteroid
  // inverted.
  otherAsteroid.movement = otherAsteroidReflection *
    // Same as above.
    ((1 - otherAsteroidCollisionStrength) * otherAsteroidSpeed +
    (otherAsteroidCollisionStrength *
    (Math.Abs(otherAsteroidMass - asteroidMass) * otherAsteroidSpeed +
    (2 * asteroidMass * asteroidSpeed)) / bothMasses));
```

Car Collision

Thanks to the preceding code I already knew how to check if the car collides with one of the guard rails.
I would just build two collision planes, one for each guard rail, and then I would check if any of the four
wheels collide with these collision planes. Because the car is not just a sphere and can't be handled as
easily as the asteroids, all four sides have to be checked, but just checking the four wheel positions (or at
least the most outer parts of the car) still allows you to do the basic collision detection (see Figure 13-15).

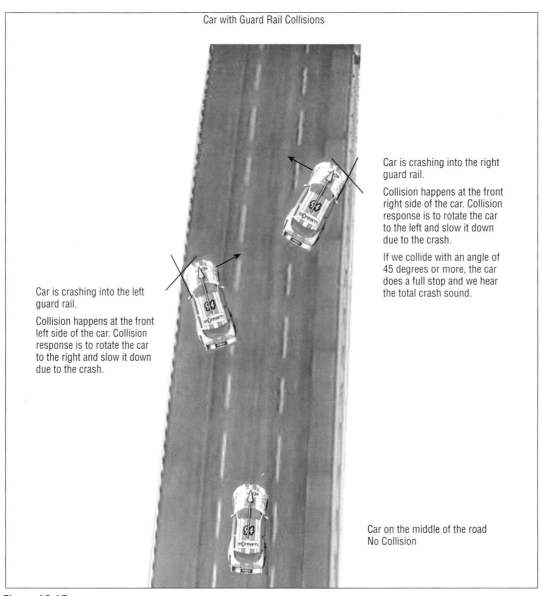

Car with Guard Rail Collisions

Car is crashing into the right guard rail.

Collision happens at the front right side of the car. Collision response is to rotate the car to the left and slow it down due to the crash.

If we collide with an angle of 45 degrees or more, the car does a full stop and we hear the total crash sound.

Car is crashing into the left guard rail.

Collision happens at the front left side of the car. Collision response is to rotate the car to the right and slow it down due to the crash.

Car on the middle of the road
No Collision

Figure 13-15

The code for these collision checks can be found in the `ApplyGravityAndCheckForCollisions` method of the `CarPhysics` class. The code basically goes through all four car corners and checks if any of them are not between the collision planes (see the two lines on either side of the road in Figure 13-15). The four car corners are defined by calculating the car corners based on actual car length and width values:

```
// Check all 4 corner points of our car.
Vector3 carRight = Vector3.Cross(carDir, carUp);
Vector3 carLeft = -carRight;
```

```
// Car dimensions are 2.6m (width) x 5.6m (length) x 1.8m (height)
// Note: This could be improved by using more points or using
// the actual car geometry.
// Note: We ignore the height, this way the collision is simpler.
// We then check the height above the road to see if we are flying
// above the guard rails out into the landscape.
Vector3[] carCorners = new Vector3[]
{
  // Top left
  pos + carDir * 5.6f/2.0f - carRight * 2.6f/2.0f,
  // Top right
  pos + carDir * 5.6f/2.0f + carRight * 2.6f/2.0f,
  // Bottom right
  pos - carDir * 5.6f/2.0f + carRight * 2.6f/2.0f,
  // Bottom left
  pos - carDir * 5.6f/2.0f - carRight * 2.6f/2.0f,
};
```

The collision test is now relatively easy thanks to all the helper values that have been calculated before in this method:

```
// Check for each corner if we collide with the guard rail
for (int num = 0; num < carCorners.Length; num++)
{
  // Hit any guardrail?
  float leftDist = Vector3Helper.DistanceToLine(
    carCorners[num], guardrailLeft, nextGuardrailLeft);
  float rightDist = Vector3Helper.DistanceToLine(
    carCorners[num], guardrailRight, nextGuardrailRight);

  // If we are closer than 0.1f, thats a collision!
  if (leftDist < 0.1f ||
    // Also include the case where we are farther away from rightDist
    // than the road is wide.
    rightDist > roadWidth)
  {
    // Handle collision with left guard rail here
  } // if (leftDist < 0.1f)

  if (rightDist < 0.1f ||
    // Also include the case where we are farther away from leftDist
    // than the road is wide.
    leftDist > roadWidth)
  {
    // Handle collision with right guard rail here
  } // if (rightDist < 0.1f)
} // for (num)
```

The final part of the collision handling is now to respond to this collision event. But before you do that you should set some field in your unit test to show you that your collision detection code works. Or just set a breakpoint inside the "if" statement blocks to see if you ever reach the conditions.

Now all you have to do is to play the crash sound and rotate the car around depending on which of the four car corners had the collision. The car will also be slowed down and you let the camera wobble a bit to notify the player that he just crashed. If the collision was straight ahead (0–45 degrees to the wall), you immediately stop the car and play the total crash sound:

```
// Force car back on the road, for that calculate impulse and
// collision direction (same stuff as in Rocket Commander).
Vector3 collisionDir =
  Vector3.Reflect(carDir, guardrailRightNormal);

float collisionAngle =
  Vector3Helper.GetAngleBetweenVectors(
    carLeft, guardrailRightNormal);

// Flip at 180 degrees (if driving in wrong direction)
if (collisionAngle > MathHelper.Pi / 2)
  collisionAngle -= MathHelper.Pi;

// Just correct rotation if collison happened at 0-45 degrees (slowly)
if (Math.Abs(collisionAngle) < MathHelper.Pi / 4.0f)
{
  // Play crash sound
  Sound.PlayCrashSound(false);

  // For front wheels to full collision rotation, for back half!
  if (num < 2)
  {
    rotateCarAfterCollision = +collisionAngle / 1.5f;
    speed *= 0.935f;//0.85f;
    if (viewDistance > 0.75f)
      viewDistance -= 0.1f;//0.15f;
  } // if (num)
  else
  {
    rotateCarAfterCollision = +collisionAngle / 2.5f;
    //slowdownCarAfterCollision = 0.8f;
    speed *= 0.96f;//0.9f;
    if (viewDistance > 0.75f)
      viewDistance -= 0.05f;//0.1f;
  } // else

  // Shake camera
  ChaseCamera.SetCameraWobbel(0.00075f * speed);
} // if (collisionAngle)

// If 90-45 degrees (in either direction), make frontal crash
// + stop car + wobble camera
else if (Math.Abs(collisionAngle) < MathHelper.Pi * 3.0f / 4.0f)
{
  // Also rotate car if less than 60 degrees
  if (Math.Abs(collisionAngle) < MathHelper.Pi / 3.0f)
    rotateCarAfterCollision = +collisionAngle / 3.0f;
```

```
    // Play crash sound
    Sound.PlayCrashSound(true);

    // Shake camera
    ChaseCamera.SetCameraWobbel(0.005f * speed);

    // Just stop car!
    speed = 0;
} // if (collisionAngle)

// For all collisions, kill the current car force
carForce = Vector3.Zero;

// Always make sure we are OUTSIDE of the collision range for
// the next frame. But first find out how much we have to move.
float speedDistanceToGuardrails =
    speed * Math.Abs(Vector3.Dot(carDir, guardrailLeftNormal));

if (rightDist > 0)
{
    float correctCarPosValue = (rightDist + 0.01f +//0.11f +
        0.1f * speedDistanceToGuardrails * moveFactor);
    carPos += correctCarPosValue * guardrailRightNormal;
} // if (rightDist)
```

With this code you are now able to test the `TestCarPhysicsOnPlaneWithGuardRails` unit test and fine-tune the crashing into the guard rails. The code for the game is a little bit more complex, but the same rules apply and all the collision code and physics calculations are exactly the same as you use for the unit test.

Challenge: Figure out the Road Collision

In the previous chapter I let you off easily, so this time it should be a little harder. Your job is to check out the `CarPhysics` class and to figure out how the same physics code and collision detection is actually used in the Racing Game itself to keep the car on the road and how it handles the collision with the guard rails, which are not just straight lines like in the unit test.

The best thing for this job would be to write a unit test that renders the road and lets you control the car the same way you controlled it in the `TestCarPhysicsOnPlaneWithGuardRails` unit test and the same way it is actually handled in the game itself. But you can also use the game to test the physics by setting a breakpoint in the `Update` method of the `CarPhysics` class and then stepping through the code to see how the variables change. Figure 13-16 shows such a unit test in action.

You can of course also try to improve the physics or maybe even try to implement a physics engine if you are really eager to extend the game and add more features. At least on the Windows platform this can be an opportunity to change the game play, add effects, and to handle more complex collision scenarios.

For a little tip if you don't know where to look or how the road can even use the same simple collision logic as the simple plane unit test does, please look at the UpdateCarMatrixAndCamera method of CarPhysics and the GetTrackPositionMatrix of the Track class. The track matrix transforms the current road piece into a space that can be used in the exact same way you used the car matrix in the simple plane collision unit test.

Figure 13-16

Summary

Physics are an important part of games today, but you saw that it is not easy to get even an existing physics engine implemented into an XNA game. But you can still implement physics your own way to make sure that the game runs on the Xbox 360 too, where unmanaged code is not allowed.

There are many topics in physics and it is certainly not easy to implement them all yourself, and even with a good physics engine you still have to do a lot of fine-tuning and testing. However, if you compete with another game that has great physics and uses it in a way that does not destroy the game play or the fun of the game, the other game will be superior if you only have very basic rules. But you should also be aware of the work associated with physics and you can probably guess by this chapter's length and position in this book that physics is not the easiest topic, especially for beginners. Though this chapter did not cover all possibilities that physics engines might cover you did take a nice tour through available physics engines. If you are interested in reading more about physics, there is a lot of information available both on the Web and in many good books and series of books like the *Game Programming Gems*.

The Racing Game and the game logic and how everything else is handled in the game is discussed in the next chapter. Other games of this book also used a little bit of physics, but you could get away with ignoring many other issues. For example, the XNA Shooter only handles ship, unit, and projectile movements and handles simple collisions by checking distances. But the game works and that is what counts in the end. In the same manner you only implemented what was necessary for the Racing Game — nothing more, and nothing less.

In this chapter you learned about the following topics, which are all used in the Racing Game:

❑ Newton's Laws of Motion may be old, but they are still useful and allow you to quickly implement simple physics into your game. You also saw that the famous $F = m * a$ formula was used several times and it is the most important formula you need for most physics calculations.

❑ Always keep the problems as simple as possible; split them up into smaller problems and write unit tests to figure out what to do next. You also won't end up implementing any unnecessary code that will not be used later anyway.

❑ You learned all about the physics engines that are available today. PhysX and Havok are the major players here, but they are both commercial engines and you can't just plug them into XNA and expect them to work on your Xbox 360 because they use unmanaged code, which is not supported or even allowed on the Xbox 360 with XNA. Because they cost a lot of money you will probably be better off using one of the free alternatives, which have great samples and tutorials, but suffer from the same lack of .NET support. ODE.NET is a nice solution because a lot of work has already been done, and though it just supports some basic features, it is still a very powerful physics engine that can save you months of work.

❑ Then you went step by step through the problems you encounter in a Racing Game like driving through loopings, handling spring physics, and how to handle collision detectionRacing Game. A more complex collision detection system was used in Rocket Commander, but the collisions themselves were pretty simple due the fact that you only checked if the bounding spheres collide.

❑ After detecting a collision it must be handled, and when the collision detection is accurate you will spend most of the time tweaking this code to make sure the collision feels real. In the Racing Game I did not have much time to fine-tune a lot, but the basic rules are implemented and it should be possible for anyone that is interested to improve the game and maybe add more physics collisions and calculations.

In Chapter 14, the last chapter in this book, you learn all about the Racing Game and how to create modifications, which will be pretty exciting.

14

Fine-Tuning and "Modding" the Racing Game

You are almost at the end of this book; just one chapter left now. You are finally going to learn about all the details of the Racing Game here. In this chapter you learn all about the game screens used in the racing game and the game logic, the scoring system, and everything else you need for the game itself. Most of the rendering techniques for the landscape and the track were already discussed in Chapter 12, but this chapter shines a little more light on the whole shadow mapping thing. Thanks to the previous chapter, where everything about the game physics and car controlling were discussed, you should now be able to plug this code and start actually testing out the game itself.

The whole purpose of this chapter is to get you familiar with the racing game and the underlying code. At the end of this chapter you should know everything to create your own game modifications (better known as *mods*) of the racing game. A game modification can be as simple as just changing a couple of graphics and 3D models or it can change the whole game logic in a way that it is no longer a racing game. The Rocket Commander game, for example, was also mod-able, but the game logic and the rendering code itself were pretty much fixed. You could more or less just change the models and add a little bit of game logic. Though most Rocket Commander mods looked quite different (see Figure 14-1), the game logic was always similar. The game principle in Rocket Commander is always to fly around and avoid colliding with certain objects (like asteroids) while also collecting items such as health, fruits, pizza pieces, and so on. Some mods had an even faster game speed; other mods were much slower and focused on solving puzzles like collecting the correct ingredients or fruits (Pizza Commander and Fruit Commander). The good thing about creating mods in Rocket Commander was that it was relatively easy to change the original game. If there are just a couple of different 3D models it is simple to change them. It was also not hard to change the game logic because you would only have to worry about the `Mission` and the `Player` classes; the rest of the classes were just used for the menu and graphics rendering engine.

Rocket Commander Mods

Name: Rocket Commander
Development time: 4 weeks (whole game)
Game: Avoid asteroids, collect items, fly fast.
First .NET 2.0 game ever.
Game was made to help beginners programming
games in .NET, but the game is also fun.
Over 120,000 online played games in 2006.

Name: Flower Commander
Development time: 4 hours
Game: Collect flowers instead of avoiding asteroids.
The rest of the game stayed the same.
Code changes were pretty easy.
First Mod ever.

Name: Fruit Commander
Development time: Less than a week
Game: Keep your vitamin levels (A, B, and C) up.
Collecting fruits gives you more vitamins and health.
Collecting bad fruits will reduce health.
Quite a lot of UI, 3D model, and code changes.

Name: Canyon Commander
Development time: Maybe 2 weeks
Game: Fly through the canyons and collect items.
Game principle is still similar, but the game looks very
different. The landscape rendering technique is also
quite impressive and put together cleverly.
Not many changes in the UI or game logic, but a lot of
new code for the landscape rendering through 3D
models.

Figure 14-1

The latest mod (at the time of this writing) is Canyon Commander, and it shows that the graphics and game play can be changed quite a lot without much effort. The mod was created by a .NET beginner in Canada and this was his first game project. Quite impressive I would say.

The racing game of this chapter, on the other hand, is a little bit more complex and allows even greater game changes. There is no reason why it should not be possible to take the code and 3D models and make a completely different game out of it. Landscape engines can be found in strategy or role-playing games, but even outdoor shooters or adventures could greatly benefit from an existing landscape rendering engine. It would, however, be a little bit more work to make a total mod and to change the whole game logic and even removing the code responsible for generating the roads when you don't need it for your mod.

It is obviously a lot easier to stay in the same genre and just change a couple of 3D models and maybe tweak some of the game parameters. This is what you are going to do at the end of this chapter with the Speedy Racer mod, but you are free to implement your own game ideas yourself by then. The Speedy Racer mod exchanges the car model and also makes the road much wider and simpler to drive on, but it greatly increases the car speed. This mod is discussed in detail at the end of this chapter.

Game Concept

Before you get to the game screens and the game logic of the racing game itself, take a quick look at the original concept of the game so you can understand why certain implementations were made and why other parts are missing from the game. Some parts of the game were added later after most features from the concept were implemented. One example of this would be the shadow mapping, which is always a complex part of a game engine because you can spend a lot of time fine-tuning it until it looks right. Other things had to be skipped or were intentionally left out because they were just too complex to implement in such a short time frame. The best example here would be the obstacles on the road (for example, columns) into which the player could crash if he did not drive carefully (see Figure 14-2).

The main problem with this idea was to set the obstacle columns effectively. There is no level or track editor for the game as you learned in Chapter 12. All tracks are generated from splines and it would be hard to even set those obstacles in 3D Studio Max. It would cause even more problems game testing these objects and updating the collision checking system for these obstacles. In an earlier test version I used the road columns that the road stays on (see Figure 14-3) to test out this obstacle idea, but it did not look very convincing and driving on the road was already hard enough. A much better solution was to add destructible objects like road signs, traffic lights, trash cans, and so on, but as you already saw in the last chapter the physics engine is not capable of handling many different objects. It just checks for any collision between the car and the guard rails and does a couple of physics calculations, and that's it.

After a couple of unit tests I decided to drop the idea and concentrate on the rest of the game. I also added tunnels and an easy way to set palms, signs, lanterns, and so on near the road and added a nice technique to automatically add landscape objects to each level near the roads.

The following text is directly from the initial game concept that was made in August 2006 way before the Racing Game was developed later in 2006. Please be aware that it was written before the first XNA beta came out and I did not know many details about XNA in general.

Figure 14-2

Basic Racing Game Objects

Figure 14-3

Game Idea

The Racing Game is a simple 3D racing game. The player will see his car in the front and can directly control it with an Xbox 360 Controller (Xbox) or the mouse and keyboard (PC). The main goal in the game is to drive as fast as possible to the finish line circumventing all obstacles in the way. Crashes do not hurt the player, but the car will lose all its speed and the total time for completing the track will be much higher. The player can't lose a game; he only can take a long time to complete a track. There are 3 tracks with different difficulty settings and a highscore list for each of the tracks. (Note: Neither multiple tracks, nor the high-scores or trophies are implemented in this racing game version for this book; please check out the XNA Framework Racing Game Starter Kit for more details and additional features of the game plus more mods.)

The graphics for this game (see Figure 14-4) are oriented on games likes Trackmania, Grand Tourismo, Need for Speed, and similar games. Obviously these games took a very long time to develop and have highly polished graphics, which is not possible in this short timeframe, so the main focus for this game is to create a simple and easy to learn racing game with just the basic features. The main graphics theme is located in the city (showing streets, some simple buildings, and some trees). The underground is done with the help of a simple 2D graphic, the tracks are auto-generated from a 2D image (using points in certain intervals), and for additional difficulty a height-map is used to create hills and make the track more difficult. (Please note that this idea was abandoned and instead real 3D data is now imported into the game.)

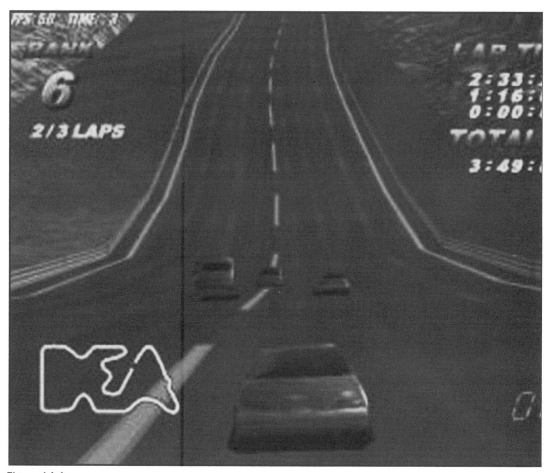

Figure 14-4

In the game there are no other cars around (like in Trackmania), which keeps the code simple and only requires collision checking with objects in the level. The game consists in the basic version just of a main menu, three simple single-player tracks, and a highscore list for each of the tracks (time dependent).

More graphics sets (snow, desert, grassland, and so on), more tracks, and maybe even mods or multiplayer game code could be made at a later point (for example, by the XNA community).

Due to the short development time everything is cut down to the basic idea of controlling the car and driving through the tracks. A simple physics system is also implemented and collision with static objects in the scene is checked each frame. All other ideas are left out of the basic game. This simplifies not only the game play, but also the understanding of the techniques and the code.

The game is viewed from behind, showing the car in the front, the track in the middle, and some more objects and the sky far away. The sky is implemented with a sky cube map.

The concept goes on and talks about the development time, all the features, and which project files are used, how shaders are going to work, and which effects and sounds are used. Then it gets a little bit more interesting again when the concept discusses the technology to be used.

The XNA Racing Game Starter Kit will be programmed in C# using .NET 2.0 and XNA using XNA Game Studio Express (similar to Visual C# Express with DirectX). A big plus is using the XNA API and managed code in general, which helps to write very easy to read code, which executes powerful functionality like loading textures, using shaders, or displaying models with just one line of code.

The graphics are all .dds files. All models (Car, Trees, Effects, and so on) are modeled with 3D Studio Max 8 and exported into Microsoft DirectX .X files. Models will not use animations for easier understanding of the underlying code (Note: And as I later found out XNA does not even support animated models out of the box).

The game will not use any existing engine or additional complicated framework. Non-game programmers would not be familiar with it and this would only confuse anyone wanting to take a look at the source code. The game consists basically of these parts:

❏ Helper classes for texture loading, model loading, game screen handling, managing XNA, handling controls, and so on.

❏ Shader class to support rendering models (mainly the car) and the landscape with shader effects. (Note: I quickly found out that I underestimated the amount of landscape objects required to make the road and the landscape look at least somewhat decent.)

❏ Pre- and post-screen shader class to help you with rendering the sky and adding effects like glow, motion blur, and color correction.

❏ Main menu class for starting a game, checking the highscores, and for quitting the game.

❏ Highscore game screen for showing the highscores and maybe even submitting them to an online server. Highscores are also saved locally, which can be viewed with this class as well. (Note: Because XNA does not support any networking and I wanted to use the same code for the PC and the Xbox 360 version I left out the sending the highscores to an online server.)

❏ Mission class to play the game.

That was almost the entire concept and I started coding as soon as I had the first XNA beta in my hands. Of course there were many more problems during the development of the project, but thanks to unit testing and updating the concept from time to time it was not hard to keep track of the general game idea. The hardest parts were definitely getting the landscape and track code working (see Chapter 12) and the physics from Chapter 13. The shadow mapping is probably also not an easy thing for most inexperienced programmers, but I just implemented a shadow mapping engine into another engine a few months back, and by looking at the unfinished racing game I was sure that it would never look very good without implementing some kind of shadows.

Additional Features

If you take a look at the class overview of the whole racing game (see Figure 14-5), it looks quite complex, especially if you think about the short development period. The biggest help was the Rocket Commander project, which allowed me to quickly test out ideas, models, and rendering techniques with the help of its unit tests and code I added early in the development process. Later when the XNA engine was standing on its own feet I could move code over and continue testing in the new engine. For example, I found out early that my idea to generate the tracks from 2D images was not very clever and caused more problems than it solved. Implementing the basic tracks was not very hard, but when I needed access to 3D vertices I was happy to have some Managed DirectX code from the Rocket Commander game that allowed me to load .x files and use their vertices to generate an early track. Sadly XNA does not support accessing or loading the vertices of imported 3D models; you could write you own content importer, but that was too much work since at the time I just wanted to test some tracks. I later changed the way tracks are imported and added many features to it (tunnels, road widths, road objects, palms, and so on). Tracks are now directly exported in 3D Studio Max into the Collada format and then imported in the game engine into a binary format (for quicker loading).

The following features were imported from previous projects (mostly from Rocket Commander):

❏   Helper classes like the Log class for debugging, the versatile StringHelper class or other important classes like the RandomHelper, Vector3Helper, or ColorHelper classes.

❏   The graphics engine was written from the ground up, but the basic ideas for handling textures, materials, models, fonts, and lines through special classes, which extend the functionality of XNA classes, was taken from Rocket Commander. Most classes in XNA are much simpler and did not do much at the beginning like the Model class, which just loaded an XNA model and displayed it with a couple lines of code. But later the model rendering was improved a lot for higher performance (which is discussed later in this chapter) and the internal logic for the model class changed completely. Models were no longer rendered directly; instead, the shaders and meshes for each used 3D model were collected and rendered at the end of the frame together with all other meshes that use the same shader, material, and mesh data. This way the rendering performance was improved by 200%–300% on the Xbox 360. And thanks to the abstraction to the special model class none of the code that used models had to be changed, it just got faster!

❏   The game screen logic was stolen 100% from Rocket Commander. I really like the idea behind it and it is very simple to implement.

❏   Shaders and other graphical classes like the ParallaxMapping, PostScreenGlow, PreScreenSkyCubeMapping, and the LensFlare class were imported from Rocket Commander too, but after a while only the LensFlare and Sky shader were left because all the other shaders changed too much. Instead of writing a new shader for every new material, a more general ShaderEffect class was written and all the shaders are now derived from it. This simplified some shaders and made classes like NormalMapping or ParallaxMapping obsolete because they work now directly from the ShaderEffect class, which can handle all the used shader parameters. The PostScreenGlow shader was derived from PostScreenMenu, which is a new shader just for the menu.

❏   For unit testing a similar approach was taken, but both NUnit and TestDriven.NET were left out to simplify the development on the Xbox 360 and because TestDriven.NET does not work with the Express editions of Visual Studio anyway.

Racing Game Class Overview (Early Version)

Figure 14-5

There are of course several new features in the game, which are not even in the game concept like the shadow mapping, which uses the following classes:

❑ `RenderToTexture`: While this class was implemented for the post-screen shaders anyway, it had to be improved to support rendering shadow maps, which require different surface formats for better precision. This means that for normal render targets you can just use the same format the back buffer uses. This is most likely `R8G8B8X8`, which means that 8 bits are used for all the color channels and 8 bits are reserved because alpha does not make sense for the back buffer, and 32 bit in total is better than 24 bit, which makes it much harder to read pixel data on 32-bit platforms.

Anyway, for shadow maps you need more precision per pixel and you don't really need colors. Each pixel of a shadow map should be just a depth value between 0 and 1 and have as much precision as possible. Good formats are `R32F` or `R16F` if the first one is not available. But these formats have to be initialized differently and the `RenderToTexture` class handles this for you. It also decides based on the options the user selected if the shadow map is 2048×2048 in size, or 1024×1024 or just 512×512 for slower computers. It also supports fallback to a 32-bit color format if both `R32F` and `R16F` are not available.

❑ `ShadowMapBlur`: This class helps you to blur the shadow map. The technique used here is similar to the glow technique for the `PostScreenGlow` shader. It takes the input data and blurs it in two steps. The blur not only makes the shadows much softer and appear more realistic, but it also fixes certain shadow mapping artifacts, which are just blurred away.

This trick was not used in the XNA Shooter game because it will not look good if you have a lot of smaller objects in the background and a lot of overlapping shadow areas and non-shadow areas. In this racing game it looks much better; the shadows on the car especially have fewer artifacts and appear much smoother. All the other landscape objects are mostly distant and their shadows do not overlap with other objects. This allows you to use even nicer blur values.

❑ ShadowMapShader: This is the main class for shadows. It initializes all the required render targets, used textures, the shadow mapping shader, and it handles the ShadowMapBlur class. More about the shadow mapping technique is discussed later in this chapter.

Other game features like loopings and the landscape rendering engine you saw already in Chapter 12 were also not in the game concept. They just evolved from the early unit tests of the TrackLine and Track classes and they made the game more fun.

I do not really remember why the game concept does not talk about the game screens. It just says that the main menu should allow starting a mission, viewing the highscores, and quitting the game. The game ended up with a highly complex game screen namespace (see Figure 14-5), which supports many more game screens than planned. Please note that some of the game screens are not implemented in the code for this chapter (for example, the track or car selection screens); they are only used in the full Racing Game Starter Kit for the XNA Framework. The main reason here is that you only have one track and one car and it would not make much sense to implement those screens if there is nothing to select anyway. You can find a more complex version of the racing game and more information about the game in general at http://www.xnaracinggame.com, the official website for the game.

Game Screens

The racing game features many different game screens, which are all managed by the RacingGame class by the gameScreens stack variable. This section describes most game screens used in the game and exactly what they do. Most game screen classes are fairly simple, but others are a little bit more complex and feature a unit test, which can be used to learn more about the class. For example, the Credits screen is fairly simple and just displays a background texture, but the Main Menu is more complex and has all the buttons to get to the other game screens. The Options screen introduces many new controls, which had to be tested, and there is obviously a unit test in this class to help you out with that process.

All game screen classes are derived from the interface IGameScreen (see Figure 14-6), which you probably will remember from the Rocket Commander game in Chapter 8. It is pretty much the same class, but it was made a little bit simpler. You now only have one method left called Render, which takes no parameters and returns a Boolean value. The code is actually the same as you used in the XNA Shooter game. If a game screen Render method call returns true it means you are done with this class and can return to the previous game screen until you run out of game screens and exit the game. Usually game screens return false because the user does not immediately quit them again after joining a game screen.

Figure 14-6

Because of this simple interface all the game screen classes in the class diagram view look just the same; they all just have a `Render` method and not much else. Some classes have some private helper methods, but they are mostly very simple. Some of the more complex game screens have unit tests for testing if all elements are aligned correctly and function they way the should. Not even the `GameScreen` class, which handles the complete game, is that complex. Unlike XNA Shooter or Rocket Commander all the game code is handled and rendered in the landscape and model classes. The game logic is handled in the `Player` class, which is a little bit more complex, but you already learned all about the underlying physics of the `CarPhysics` class and the `ChaseCamera` class in the last chapter.

Take a look at Figure 14-7 for a basic overview of all the game screens used in this version of the racing game. The most complex class is obviously the `Mission` class, which handles the game play and game logic. It does not contain all the game code, however; some of it is handled in the player classes and the `RacingGame` main class also handles a bit of the general game content.

Splash Screen

The splash screen (see Figure 14-8) is one of the easier classes; it basically just sits around and waits for the user to press start on his gamepad. Space or Esc on the keyboard or the left mouse button will let the player also continue if he does not have a game pad. The only thing for this class that is even remotely interesting is the code to let the "Press start to continue" text blink.

```
/// <summary>
/// Render splash screen
/// </summary>
public bool Render()
{
  // This starts both menu and in game post screen shader!
  BaseGame.UI.PostScreenMenuShader.Start();

  // Render background and black bar
  BaseGame.UI.RenderMenuBackground();
  BaseGame.UI.RenderBlackBar(352, 61);

  // Show Press Start to continue.
  if ((int)(BaseGame.TotalTime / 0.375f) % 3 != 0)
    BaseGame.UI.Logos.RenderOnScreen(
      BaseGame.CalcRectangleCenteredWithGivenHeight(
        512, 352 + 61 / 2, 26, UIRenderer.PressStartGfxRect),
        UIRenderer.PressStartGfxRect);

  // Show logos
  BaseGame.UI.RenderLogos();

  // Clicking or pressing start will go to the menu
  return Input.MouseLeftButtonJustPressed ||
    Input.KeyboardSpaceJustPressed ||
    Input.KeyboardEscapeJustPressed ||
    Input.GamePadStartPressed;
} // Render()
```

GameScreen Classes in the Racing Game

Figure 14-7

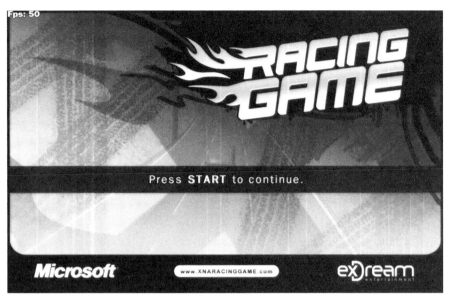

Figure 14-8

The `RenderMenuBackground` method is a little bit more complex. It is used to show the menu background behind the splash screen, which shows the car driving through one of the tracks. The car is controlled by the computer and the camera just follows it. The code for that is not very complex:

```
// [From RenderMenuTrackBackground(), which is called by
// RenderMenuBackground(), both located in the UIRenderer class]

// [Some code to calculate carPos, carMatrix, etc.]

// Put camera behind car
RacingGame.Player.SetCameraPosition(
   carPos + carMatrix.Forward * 9 - carMatrix.Up * 2.3f);

// For rendering rotate car to stay correctly on the road
carMatrix =
   Matrix.CreateRotationX(MathHelper.Pi / 2.0f) *
   Matrix.CreateRotationZ(MathHelper.Pi) *
   carMatrix;

RacingGame.Landscape.Render();
RacingGame.CarModel.RenderCar(
   randomCarNumber, randomCarColor, carMatrix);
```

Thanks to the `Render` method of the `Landscape` class and the `RenderCar` method of the `Model` class you do not have to worry about rendering the landscape, track, or anything else here. The camera matrix makes sure you look at the correct position and the car advances through the track through the car matrix variable.

All other menu game screens also use the `RenderMenuBackground` method to render the game in the background, but it can be less visible in some game screens because you put darker textures in the front (for example, in the Credits screen it is harder to see the background anymore). It is just a background effect, however; you can see more of the game when you actually start playing it.

Main Menu

The Main Menu (see Figure 14-9) is a little bit more complex than most other menu screen classes, but even this class is just about 250 lines of code. Every other game screen can be started from here except the Splash screen, which is only shown initially after starting the application. The most important choices are starting the game and viewing the highscores (the first two buttons).

The coolest feature of this class is the menu button animation. Every button gets a float value between 0 and 1, where 0 is the smallest possible button size and 1 is the biggest button size. When you hover over a button with the mouse or select it with the gamepad or keyboard it gets bigger until it reaches 1.0. When you leave the button, it slowly gets smaller again.

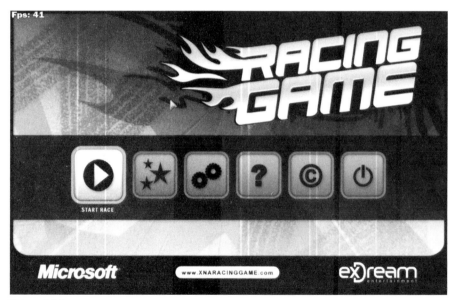

Figure 14-9

The first button is initially set to 1. All other buttons are left at the smallest size (0).

```
/// <summary>
/// Current button sizes for scaling up/down smooth effect.
/// </summary>
float[] currentButtonSizes =
  new float[NumberOfButtons] { 1, 0, 0, 0, 0, 0 };
```

Then in the `Render` method the button selection code and scaling of the buttons is handled. To make sure you do not hover over more than one button at the same time a helper variable is used for the mouse. If no mouse is used to select the menu buttons this variable will never be used.

```
// Little helper to keep track if mouse is actually over a button.
// Required because buttons are selected even when not hovering over
// them for GamePad support, but we still want the mouse only to
// be applied when we are actually over the button.
int mouseIsOverButton = -1;

// [a little later in the code ...]

for (int num = 0; num < NumberOfButtons; num++)
{
  // Is this button currently selected?
  bool selected = num == selectedButton;

  // Increase size if selected, decrease otherwise
  currentButtonSizes[num] +=
    (selected ? 1 : -1) * BaseGame.MoveFactorPerSecond * 2;
  if (currentButtonSizes[num] < 0)
    currentButtonSizes[num] = 0;
  if (currentButtonSizes[num] > 1)
    currentButtonSizes[num] = 1;

  // Use this size to build rect
  Rectangle thisRect =
    InterpolateRect(activeRect, inactiveRect, currentButtonSizes[num]);
  Rectangle renderRect = new Rectangle(
    xPos, yPos - (thisRect.Height - inactiveRect.Height) / 2,
    thisRect.Width, thisRect.Height);
  BaseGame.UI.Buttons.RenderOnScreen(renderRect, ButtonRects[num],
    // Make button gray if not selected
    selected ? Color.White : new Color(192, 192, 192, 192));

  // Add border effect if selected
  if (selected)
    BaseGame.UI.Buttons.RenderOnScreen(renderRect,
      UIRenderer.MenuButtonSelectionGfxRect);

  // Also check if the user hovers with the mouse over this button
  if (Input.MouseInBox(renderRect))
    mouseIsOverButton = num;

  // [etc.]
} // for (num)

if (mouseIsOverButton >= 0)
  selectedButton = mouseIsOverButton;
```

Game Screen

The GameScreen class (see Figure 14-10) is the most important game screen because it handles the whole game logic. No game variables are stored here however, and you do not handle anything exclusive here, but all the important parts (landscape, track, car, objects, HUD, and so on) are still rendered and called from here.

Figure 14-10

Most of the player variables are stored in the Player class and all the input and physics are handled in the base classes of the Player class (CarPhysics and ChaseCamera). The Player class also makes use of all the game variables. Most variables are displayed in the UI like the current game time on the in-game HUD and they are updated in the HandleGameLogic method of the Player class.

All the Render methods, even the in-game HUD, are located in the UIRenderer helper class for any UI rendering code and the rest is handled and rendered in the landscape and model classes; even the shadow mapping is mostly done there. All the rendering and game handling is called from here, so this class gives you a good overview of what happens in the game. If you write a game modification, start modifying code here. Comment out code here or in the called methods to quickly see what part of the game is affected by that change.

The first part of the Render method handles all the shadow mapping rendering, which is not very complex because most of it is handled in the landscape class. You just give the data to the shadow mapping class, which renders everything into the shadow map that can then be used directly after rendering the 3D objects to shadow the 3D scene.

```
/// <summary>
/// Render game screen. Called each frame.
/// </summary>
public bool Render()
{
```

```
if (BaseGame.AllowShadowMapping)
{
  // Generate shadows
  ShaderEffect.shadowMapping.GenerateShadows(
    delegate
    {
      RacingGame.Landscape.GenerateShadow();
      RacingGame.CarModel.GenerateShadow(
        RacingGame.Player.CarRenderMatrix);
    });

  // Render shadows
  ShaderEffect.shadowMapping.RenderShadows(
    delegate
    {
      RacingGame.Landscape.UseShadow();
      RacingGame.CarModel.UseShadow(
      RacingGame.Player.CarRenderMatrix);
    });
} // if (BaseGame.AllowShadowMapping)
```

Then the post-screen glow shader is started and all the 3D game content is rendered. This includes the sky cube map, landscape with the track and all 3D models, and finally the car.

```
// This starts both menu and in game post screen shader!
BaseGame.UI.PostScreenGlowShader.Start();

// Render background sky and lensflare.
BaseGame.UI.RenderGameBackground();

// Render landscape with track and all objects
RacingGame.Landscape.Render();

// Render car with matrix we got from CarPhysics
RacingGame.CarModel.RenderCar(
  RacingGame.currentCarNumber, RacingGame.CarColor,
  RacingGame.Player.CarRenderMatrix);

// And flush all models to be rendered
BaseGame.MeshRenderManager.Render();
```

After the MeshRenderManager has rendered all 3D models you can add the shadow mapping effect to the 3D scene. The order of the calls here is important because if the 3D models are not rendered before showing the shadows, the shadows will not have the correct effect on them or will not work at all.

```
// Show shadows we calculated above
if (BaseGame.AllowShadowMapping)
{
  ShaderEffect.shadowMapping.ShowShadows();
} // if (BaseGame.AllowShadowMapping)

// Apply post screen shader here before doing the UI
BaseGame.UI.PostScreenGlowShader.Show();
```

And finally the code for the UI in the game; if you want to get rid of it or change the HUD, here is the place for doing that.

```
// Play motor sound
Sound.UpdateGearSound(RacingGame.Player.Speed,
  RacingGame.Player.Acceleration);

// Show on screen UI for the game.
BaseGame.UI.RenderGameUI(
  (int)RacingGame.Player.GameTimeMiliseconds,
  // Best time and current lap
  (int)RacingGame.Player.BestTimeMs,
  RacingGame.Player.CurrentLap+1,
  RacingGame.Player.Speed * CarPhysics.MeterPerSecToMph,
  // Gear logic with sound (could be improved ^^)
  1+(int)(5*RacingGame.Player.Speed/CarPhysics.MaxSpeed),
  // Motormeter
  0.5f*RacingGame.Player.Speed/CarPhysics.MaxSpeed +
  // This could be improved
  0.5f*RacingGame.Player.Acceleration,
  RacingGame.Landscape.CurrentTrackName,
  Highscore.GetTop5Highscores());

if (Input.KeyboardEscapeJustPressed ||
  Input.GamePadBackJustPressed)
{
  // Stop motor sound
  Sound.StopGearSound();

  // Play menu music again
  Sound.Play(Sound.Sounds.MenuMusic);

  // Return to menu
  return true;
} // if (Input.KeyboardEscapeJustPressed)

return false;
} // Render()
```

Highscores

The Highscores screen (see Figure 14-11) is very similar to the highscores of Rocket Commander, but all the online highscores are missing because no network code or web services were implemented yet. Again, the reason for that is the lack of network support in XNA, but it would be possible to implement that just for the PC version.

There are a couple of helper methods in the Highscore class that, for example, help you to determine the current rank in the game while the player is getting points for driving around the track, but most of these methods were already used in earlier games of this book.

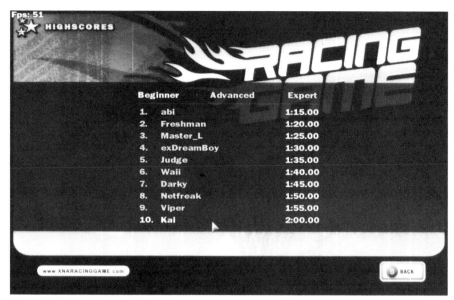

Figure 14-11

The following code is used to render the top 10 highscore players on the screen. You will notice that the code is pretty simple thanks to the many helper methods in the UIRenderer class. If you just want to test the highscore game screen please use the unit test inside the class, which was used to position all the UI elements for this game screen in the same way it was done for most other game screens too. I also cheated a bit and used TestDriven.NET in Visual Studio 2005 and the new cool feature to re-run tests with a hotkey. This way I could practically code, press the hotkey, say "oh no," press Escape, and fix the code until the class worked perfectly. In a matter of minutes most UI code was programmed this way.

```
// Go through all highscores
for (int num = 0; num < NumOfHighscores; num++)
{
  // Show player in white if mouse is over line or else use gray color
  Rectangle lineRect = new Rectangle(
    0, yPos, BaseGame.Width, lineHeight);
  Color col = Input.MouseInBox(lineRect) ?
    Color.White : new Color(200, 200, 200);

  // Fill in text for this line
  BaseGame.UI.WriteText(xPos1, yPos, (1 + num) + ".", col);
  BaseGame.UI.WriteText(xPos2, yPos,
    highscores[selectedLevel, num].name, col);
  BaseGame.UI.WriteGameTime(xPos3, yPos,
    highscores[selectedLevel, num].timeMs, Color.Yellow);
  yPos += lineHeight;
} // for (num)
```

The other game screen classes that are left are Options, Help, and Credits. They are all pretty similar to the highscore class and not really exciting. Options has some nice UI features and allows you to enter text with the help of the Input class and to select one of multiple sliders and drag them around with either the mouse or a gamepad. Use the unit test in the `Options` class to learn more about the features in this class. Both the `Help` and the `Credit` classes just display a texture on the screen, very similar to the `SplashScreen` class you saw earlier.

Finally the exit button quits the game because there will be no other game screens left after the main menu is closed. All other game screens always return to the main menu (even the `SplashScreen` class).

Final Unit Testing and Tweaking

You now have all classes together for the game, but you are not done quite yet. We talked a few times about the `Player` class, but you never saw it called. The reason for this is the fact that XNA separates the update and drawing code. If you look at the `Update` method of the `RacingGame` class, you can finally see the call to the `Player Update` method:

```
/// <summary>
/// Update racing game
/// </summary>
protected override void Update(GameTime time)
{
    // Update game engine
    base.Update(time);

    // Update player and game logic
    player.Update();
} // Update()
```

If you take a look inside the `Player` class, you might wonder why it is so simple. The `Update` method does not do much here; it only handles some additional game logic. In the Rocket Commander game the `Player` class handled almost the whole game logic and input together with the `SpaceCamera` class. The game logic in the racing game seems to be much simpler thanks to the separation of all the game logic code into four different classes, which are all connected to each other (see Figure 14-12).

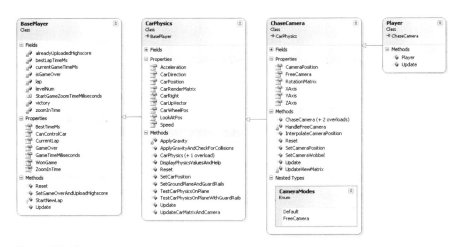

Figure 14-12

❑   BasePlayer — This is the basic game logic class for the game; it holds all the important variables and helper properties to see if the game is over, how long you played, and if you won the game. The whole purpose of this class is to give the derived classes an easy way to access these data because you are not able to control the car anymore if the game is over or the game has not even started yet, because you are still zooming in. Though the BasePlayer class does provide almost everything you need externally (and internally) to know about the current game state, it does not handle much of it. The class will only update the timers; all the rest of the game logic is handled in the derived classes!

```
/// <summary>
/// Update game logic, called every frame. In Rocket Commander we did
/// all the game logic in one big method inside the player class, but it
/// was hard to add new game logic and many small things were also in
/// the GameAsteroidManager. For this game we split everything up into
/// many more classes and every class handles only its own variables.
/// For example this class just handles the game time and zoom in time,
/// for the car speed and physics just go into the CarController class.
/// </summary>
public virtual void Update()
{
  // Handle zoomInTime at the beginning of a game
  if (zoomInTime > 0)
  {
    // Handle start traffic light object (red, yellow, green!)
    RacingGame.Landscape.ReplaceStartLightObject(
      2-(int)(zoomInTime/1000));
    zoomInTime -= BaseGame.ElapsedTimeThisFrameInMs;
    if (zoomInTime < 0)
      zoomInTime = 0;
  } // if (zoomInTime)

  // Don't handle any more game logic if game is over or still zooming
  // in.
  if (CanControlCar == false)
    return;

  // Increase game time
  currentGameTimeMs += BaseGame.ElapsedTimeThisFrameInMs;
} // Update()
```

❑   CarPhysics — This class was already discussed in the previous chapter. It is derived from the BasePlayer class and adds all the physics calculations to the car and the rest of the game. While the Update method updates the internal car values like the direction, position, up vector, the car speed and acceleration, most of the actual physics calculation is done in several helper methods like in the ApplyGravity, ApplyGravityAndCheckForCollisions, and SetGroundPlaneAndGuardRails methods. To get a car matrix for rendering the car and updating the basic look at position for the camera the UpdateCarMatrixAndCamera helper method is used.

For testing the physics in general you should use the two unit tests TestCarPhysicsOnPlane and TestCarPhysicsOnPlaneWithGuardRails in this class, especially if you want to change some of the many constants defined in this class like the car mass, maximum speed, maximum rotation, or acceleration values.

You can find more information about this class in Chapter 13.

❑ ChaseCamera is similar to the SpaceCamera class of the Rocket Commander game or the SimpleCamera class of XNA Shooter. The class is not very complex and it does not have to be because it is derived from the CarPhysics class, which provides you with almost everything you need. It supports two camera modes: Default for the game and the menu and FreeCamera, which is mostly used for unit tests.

The view matrix of the BaseGame class is updated here every frame and if you need access to the camera position or the rotation matrix or a rotation axis, this is the place to look. You probably will not need this class very often because most the important game information like the current car position or game time can be accessed through the properties of the BasePlayer and the CarPhysics classes.

❑ And finally there is the Player class, which is derived from the ChaseCamera class and finally combines all the features of the four classes. If you want to add additional game logic or rules, this is probably the easiest place to do that, but if you don't change the Update methods of the base classes, you will not be able to change much of the behavior of the game. For example, to change the maximum car speed, which is handled directly in the CarPhysics class, it would be easier to change the game logic there, but if you want to add an abort condition or text message after reaching a certain check point or completing a lap, it is probably easier to add that code in the Player class.

Tweaking the Track

You now know how to change the global game logic rules, but most of the game play and levels is defined directly through the level data. As you already saw in Chapter 12 it is not easy to create the tracks and it doesn't get any easier to import the 3D track data into the game because you need to do the following things (see also Figure 14-13):

❑ You need 3D Studio Max to even open one of the tracks and change it. It will probably also work with other 3D modeling programs, but that hasn't been tested yet. In any case as a game programmer you probably will not have these tools.

❑ Next you have to use a Collada exporter in 3D Studio Max, which is not supported out of the box, and getting one for the latest 3D Studio Max version is not always a piece of cake. For example, at the time of this writing there is no working Collada exporter for 3D Studio Max 9; you would have to use 3D Studio Max 8 to export the tracks, which again is not compatible with any .max files saved in 3D Studio Max 9. You can see this is getting more complicated even just speaking about it.

❑ Now you need to import the Collada track data into the game with the help of the unit tests in the TrackImporter class, which will tell you if anything goes wrong, but they don't give you visual feedback.

❑ Finally you will have to test the tracks yourself either by starting and playing the game or using one of the unit tests in the Track or TrackLine classes.

Well, this is not ideal and I will work on an in-game track editor in the future to resolve this issue. Please check the official website for updates of the game and better ways to edit tracks at http://www.xnaracinggame.com.

Importing a Racing Game Track into the Game

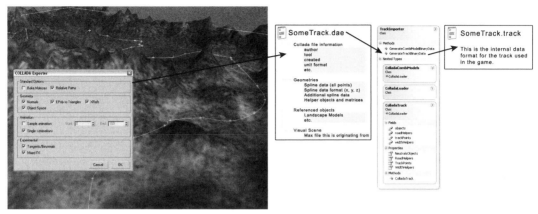

SomeTrack.max file inside 3D Studio Max

Figure 14-13

Currently you can also create tracks the way they are created for some of the unit tests in the `TrackLine` class by just defining a couple of 3D points. To "import" such a track you would just write down each of the points of this track in an array of 3D points and then use the array instead of an imported binary track. You can also create tunnels, road width helpers, and set landscape models, but beyond some unit tests this is not the way to go.

The `TestRenderingTrack` unit test shows how to initialize the `TrackLine` class with a custom array of vectors to create a track. If you just want to quickly play around with some track ideas you might have, I suggest using this unit test first.

```
/// <summary>
/// Test rendering track
/// </summary>
public static void TestRenderingTrack()
{
  TrackLine testTrack = new TrackLine(
    new Vector3[]
    {
      new Vector3(20, 0, 0),
      new Vector3(20, 10, 5),
      new Vector3(20, 20, 10),
      new Vector3(10, 25, 10),
      new Vector3(5, 30, 10),
      new Vector3(-5, 30, 10),
      new Vector3(-10, 25, 10),
      new Vector3(-20, 20, 10),
      new Vector3(-20, 10, 5),
      new Vector3(-20, 0, 0),
      new Vector3(-10, 0, 0),
      new Vector3(-5, 0, 0),
      new Vector3(7, 0, 3),
```

```
            new Vector3(10, 0, 10),
            new Vector3(7, 0, 17),
            new Vector3(0, 0, 20),
            new Vector3(-7, 0, 17),
            new Vector3(-10, -2, 10),
            new Vector3(-7, -4, 3),
            new Vector3(5, -6, 0),
            new Vector3(10, -6, 0),
        });

    TestGame.Start(
        delegate
        {
            ShowGroundGrid();
            ShowTrackLines(testTrack);
            ShowUpVectors(testTrack);
        });
} // TestRenderingTrack()
```

Shadow Mapping

The shadow mapping classes, which were discussed earlier in this chapter, are a prime candidate for tweaking. Not only are there many settings and parameters, but there are also several shaders involved, which have to be fine-tuned for both optimal performance and a good visual quality.

The main unit test that was used throughout the development of the shadow mapping techniques in the racing game is the TestShadowMapping method in the ShadowMapShader class (see Figure 14-14). If you press the Shift key (or A on the gamepad) you can see the shadow map and the two blur passes of the ShadowMapBlur shader. You can replace the car with any other 3D model if you would like to test the shadows of other 3D objects.

Earlier in this chapter you saw in the GameScreen class how to use the ShadowMapShader class. First of all you call GenerateShadows and RenderShadows on all objects you want to include in the shadow map generation process. Please note that both methods are rendering 3D data and you should only render what is necessary here. The data should be visible from the virtual shadow mapping light, and if the object is just receiving shadows like the plate in Figure 14-14, you don't need to include it into the GenerateShadows method call. Just let the shadows be thrown onto it with the RenderShadows method!

```
if (Input.Keyboard.IsKeyUp(Keys.LeftAlt) &&
    Input.GamePadXPressed == false)
{
    // Generate shadows
    ShaderEffect.shadowMapping.GenerateShadows(
        delegate
        {
            RacingGame.CarModel.GenerateShadow(Matrix.CreateRotationZ(0.85f));
        });

    // Render shadows
    ShaderEffect.shadowMapping.RenderShadows(
        delegate
        {
```

```
        RacingGame.CarSelectionPlate.UseShadow(Matrix.CreateScale(1.5f));
    RacingGame.CarModel.UseShadow(Matrix.CreateRotationZ(0.85f));
      });
  } // if
```

After the shadow map has been generated you can start rendering the real 3D content. In this unit test it is basically the same code as the render delegate for `RenderShadows` method executes with the additional call to render the game background sky with help of the sky cube mapping shader. This way you can optimize in the actual game which object will be rendered, which ones will generate shadows, and which ones will receive shadows. If you just generate, render, and apply shadows on every single object in the scene your frame rate would go down terribly. Only about 10%–20% of the visible objects will be included in the shadow map generation in the game code, but for this unit test you just want to test out the shadow mapping on the car and the car selection plate models.

```
if (Input.Keyboard.IsKeyUp(Keys.LeftAlt) &&
    Input.GamePadXPressed == false)
{
    ShaderEffect.shadowMapping.ShowShadows();
} // if
```

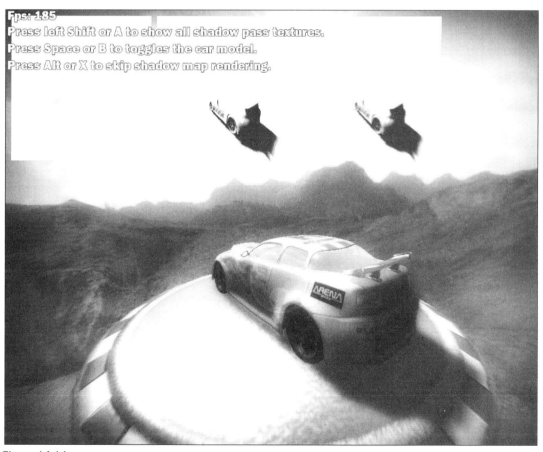

Figure 14-14

With the unit test up and running you can now tweak the shadow mapping code (after it has been written, of course). Most tweaking variables can be found directly in the `ShadowMapShader` class, but some of them like the shadow color for darkening shadowed areas are only defined in the `ShadowMap.fx` shader file and do not change once the shader is loaded.

To see the result of each shadow mapping pass press Shift on your keyboard or the A button on a connected gamepad. The most important render target is the first one, which shows the actual shadow map from the virtual shadow light position. It is displayed in teal because you use a render target surface format of R32F as discussed earlier in this chapter, which just contains the red color channel. All the other color channels are unused and will use the default values of 1.0. If the value in the shadow map is 1.0 (for the farthest possible value) you end up with a completely white color; if you get closer to 0.0 the resulting color will be teal. It is often hard to see the differences in the shadow map. To enhance the values you can multiply it with a fixed constant in the shader and zoom in by moving the virtual shadow light position closer to the look target.

The following variables and constants are the most important ones to tweak; there are a couple more things you can tweak by changing the vertex and pixel shaders in the `ShadowMap.fx` and `PostScreenShadowBlur.fx` shaders. Please note that due the limitations of pixel shader 1.1 most code for shader model 1.1 is pretty much fixed and will not be affected by most of the variables. If you still need support for shader model 1.1 and change some parameters, make sure the shader model 1.1 shader still works. It can by tested by forcing the shader model 1.1 techniques in the shader classes instead of using the techniques ending with 20, which are used for shader model 2.0.

❑ `virtualLightDistance` and `virtualVisibleRange` are used to construct the virtual shadow mapping light and especially the `lightViewMatrix`, which is important for both the shadow map generating and when rendering the shadow map. The virtual light distance is the distance from the shadow mapping look-at position, which is always the current car position, or to be more precise, a position a little bit in front of the car to fit the actual viewing area of the player camera a little bit better. The virtual visible range describes the field of view of the shadow map matrix. It can be a lot different from the view matrix used in the game and it has nothing to do with the view matrix at all.

For example, in the XNA Shooter game a very distant virtual light position is used and a relatively small virtual visible range results in a small field of view for the shadow mapping matrix, almost orthogonal. This way the shadows are always oriented in the same way, but it gets a little bit harder to tweak a shadow map light with a distant light position. In the racing game you do not care so much about a closer virtual light distance because when driving around with your car you won't notice the shadows in the distance so much, and the shadows on the car stay pretty much the same because the position of the car in the resulting shadow map is always the same.

❑ `nearPlane` and `farPlane` are used to tweak the shadow map depth calculation a little bit. If all the shadow map values have a depth value of 20.0 to 30.0 it would not make sense to use the same near and far plane values as in the game (for example, 1.0 and 500) because the shadow map would then get only 2% of the depth buffer precision. For depth buffer values it won't matter so much because you only run into problems if depth values overlap by overlapping geometry, which will not happen very often if the scene is well constructed.

For shadow mapping, on the other hand, you are only looking at depth values that do overlap because you need to test if each pixel in the scene is shadow mapped or not. By using a bad shadow mapping depth buffer precision the whole shadow mapping looks bad. This is also one of the main reasons there are so many other shadow algorithms available, especially stencil shadows, which is the main competitor of shadow mapping in 3D games. With stencil shadows a lot of these problems disappear, but they are often a lot harder to handle and they usually involve rendering a lot more geometry, which can slow down any game that already has a lot of polygons.

The racing game mainly uses the farPlane value, which is fairly low (30–50) and then the nearPlane is automatically generated in the shader code. Earlier versions used a nearPlane value, which was more than half of the farPlane value to improve the depth precision, but then any objects near the virtual light would be skipped from the shadow map generation process. For a better tweaked nearPlane value check out the XNA Shooter game that also uses better code for the virtual light distance and range values.

```
// Use farPlane/10 for the internal near plane, we don't have any
// objects near the light, use this to get much better percision!
float internalNearPlane = farPlane / 10;

// Linear depth calculation instead of normal depth calculation.
Out.depth = float2(
  (Out.pos.z - internalNearPlane),
  (farPlane - internalNearPlane));
```

❑   texelWidth, texelHeight, and the texOffsetX and texOffsetY values are used to tell the shader about the texel sizes used for the shadow map. These values are calculated in the CalcShadowMapBiasMatrix helper method, which puts all these values into a helper matrix called texScaleBiasMatrix, which is then used by the shader to transform all shadow mapping position values to fit the shadow map better.

```
/// <summary>
/// Calculate the texScaleBiasMatrix for converting proj screen
/// coordinates in the -1..1 range to the shadow depth map
/// texture coordinates.
/// </summary>
internal void CalcShadowMapBiasMatrix()
{
  texelWidth = 1.0f / (float)shadowMapTexture.Width;
  texelHeight = 1.0f / (float)shadowMapTexture.Height;
  texOffsetX = 0.5f + (0.5f / (float)shadowMapTexture.Width);
  texOffsetY = 0.5f + (0.5f / (float)shadowMapTexture.Height);

  texScaleBiasMatrix = new Matrix(
    0.5f * texExtraScale, 0.0f, 0.0f, 0.0f,
    0.0f, -0.5f * texExtraScale, 0.0f, 0.0f,
    0.0f, 0.0f, texExtraScale, 0.0f,
    texOffsetX, texOffsetY, 0.0f, 1.0f);
} // CalcShadowMapBiasMatrix()
```

❑   The shadowColor constant in the shader is used to darken down any shadowed areas. Due to the blur effect used after the shadow map is rendered and thanks to the PCF3x3 (precision closer filtering on a 3x3 box) used in PS_UseShadowMap20 the shadow color is interpolated with the surrounding non-shadowed areas. Using completely black shadows (ShadowColor of 0, 0, 0, 0) is often the easiest solution because it fixes many shadow mapping artifacts, but it will not look good if it is bright daylight. In those cases shadowing does not darken everything down to black, there is still ambient color and occlusion lighting left in a realistic 3D scene.

```
// Color for shadowed areas, should be black too, but need
// some alpha value (e.g. 0.5) for blending the color to black.
float4 ShadowColor =
  { 0.25f, 0.26f, 0.27f, 1.0f };
```

❑   depthBias and shadowMapDepthBias are probably the two shadow mapping parameters that were tweaked the most together with the actual shader code that uses them.

```
// Depth bias, controls how much we remove from the depth
// to fix depth checking artifacts. For ps_1_1 this should
// be a very high value (0.01f), for ps_2_0 it can be very low.
float depthBias = 0.0025f;

// Substract a very low value from shadow map depth to
// move everything a little closer to the camera.
// This is done when the shadow map is rendered before any
// of the depth checking happens, should be a very small value.
float shadowMapDepthBias = -0.0005f;
```

The shadowMapDepthBias is added to the shadow map generation code to pull the depth values a little bit closer to the viewer.

```
// Pixel shader function
float4 PS_GenerateShadowMap20(VB_GenerateShadowMap20 In) : COLOR
{
  // Just set the interpolated depth value.
  float ret = (In.depth.x/In.depth.y) + shadowMapDepthBias;
  return ret;
} // PS_GenerateShadowMap20(.)
```

The depthBias value is a little bit more important because it is used in the shadow depth comparison code of the UseShadowMap20 technique. Without the depthBias most shadow mapping pixels that are not really shadowed, but are both used to generate and to receive shadows, have such similar values that they often pop in and out of the shadow map comparisons due to depth map precision errors (see Figure 14-15). Please note that the shadow map blur effect hides these artifacts, but the stronger they are, they more apparent they get and even with a good blur code applied to the shadow map result, it will look wrong in the game, especially when moving the camera around.

```
/ Advanced pixel shader for shadow depth calculations in ps 2.0.
// However this shader looks blocky like PCF3x3 and should be smoothend
// out by a good post screen blur filter. This advanced shader does a
// good job faking the penumbra and can look very good when adjusted
// carefully.
float4 PS_UseShadowMap20(VB_UseShadowMap20 In) : COLOR
{
  float depth = (In.depth.x/In.depth.y) - depthBias;

  float2 shadowTex =
    (In.shadowTexCoord.xy / In.shadowTexCoord.w) -
    shadowMapTexelSize / 2.0f;
```

```
float resultDepth = 0;
for (int i=0; i<10; i++)
  resultDepth += depth > tex2D(ShadowMapSampler20,
    shadowTex+FilterTaps[i]*shadowMapTexelSize) ? 1.0f/10.0f : 0.0f;

// Multiply the result by the shadowDistanceFadeoutTexture, which
// fades shadows in and out at the max. shadow distances
resultDepth *= tex2D(shadowDistanceFadeoutTextureSampler,
  shadowTex).r;

// We can skip this if its too far away anway (else very far away
// landscape parts will be darkenend)
if (depth > 1)
  return 0;
else
  // And apply shadow color
  return lerp(1, ShadowColor, resultDepth);
} // PS_UseShadowMap20(VB_UseShadowMap20 In)
```

Figure 14-15

There are probably a lot more things we could discuss about the shadow mapping techniques used in the game and possible improvements like using better code to construct the virtual light matrices and tweaking certain parameters even better. You did see some of the most important shader code for the shadow mapping, but there are a lot more tricks in the shader code. Additionally there are so many shadow mapping techniques and tricks that can be used today, it would probably fill up another book.

Two of the most exciting shadow map techniques today are the perspective shadow mapping light matrix generation techniques (there are many different variations of it; I wrote some perspective shadow mapping code a year ago and played around with it for some time, but it is really hard to tweak and fine-tune, especially if your game allows many different perspectives). The other exciting technique is variance shadow mapping, which uses two shadow maps instead of one (or two channels) and allows storing much higher precision values this way. I did not have much time to play around with variance shadow mapping and it is a fairly new technique, but early tests showed that you can gain a lot of speed and save memory bandwidth due to much smaller shadow mapping sizes (512×512 looks as good as a 2048×2048 traditional shadow map) and it fixes quite a lot of the shadow mapping problems and artifacts. But again, there are always problems with shadow mapping; some programmers like the famous John Carmack from id Software dislike it so much, they'd rather implement the more complicated stencil shadows and fight with their issues instead of using shadow mapping.

Final Testing on Windows

Well, with all that great code lying around some game testing can now be done. Before you start the game and drive around the track trying to beat the highscores, you should make sure that you have checked out most of the unit tests of the game engine (see Figure 14-16).

If you use the unit tests before even testing out the game you don't have to test any issues with shadow mapping, the physics, the menu, and so on directly in the game. You are going to solve all issues with unit tests instead until they work fine. Then the game will magically run very nicely in the end without you ever testing the game itself; all you did was test smaller unit tests.

Often there are improvements that can be made to the game or you might want to tweak something directly in the game code. You will find yourself tweaking the game code and fixing bugs in the final testing phase of the game, but you should make sure that you don't spend more time always starting the game and testing the issues. For example, if you encounter a bug in some physics calculation or you want to tweak some of the shadow mapping values, you should either use an existing unit test or write a new unit test for the specific issue if it is easier than constantly restarting the game with all its content and submenus. It often just takes a couple of clicks and waiting for the loading and screen transitions, but even that can slow you down.

Some of the Racing Game Unit Tests

- TestCredits.cmd
- TestDraw3DLine.cmd
- TestGamePadInput.cmd
- TestHelp.cmd
- TestHighscores.cmd
- TestKeyboardChatInpu...
- TestLensFlare.cmd
- TestNormalMappingSha...
- TestPlayClickSound.cmd
- TestPostScreenGlow.cm...
- TestPostScreenMenu.cmd
- TestRenderLandscape...
- TestRenderLines.cmd
- TestRenderModel.cm...
- TestRenderTrack.cm...
- TestShadowMapping.cmd
- TestSimpleDiffuseShad...
- TestSimpleSpecularPer...
- TestSingleModel.cmd
- TestSkyCubeMapping.c...
- TestTextureFont.cmd
- TestTextures.cmd
- TestUI.cmd
- TestWriteNumbers.cmd

Figure 14-16

One common trick I always use at the final stage of any game development project is to change the game screen initialization code. This way I end up directly in the game instead of the menu where I might have to set some options first, then select a level and start a custom game. There is no point in doing that over and over again if all you want to test is some issue inside the game itself.

```
// Create main menu at our main entry point
gameScreens.Push(new MainMenu());

// But start with splash screen, if user clicks or presses Start,
// we are back in the main menu.
gameScreens.Push(new SplashScreen());

#if DEBUG
//tst: Directly start the game and load a certain level, this code is
// only used in the debug mode. Remove it when you are done with
// testing! If you press Esc you will also quit the game and not
// just end up in the menu again.
gameScreens.Clear();
gameScreens.Push(new GameScreen());
#endif
```

Because all unit tests should only work in the debug mode and you are not even adding the NUnitFramework.dll assembly in the release mode, you should make sure the game runs fine in the release mode too. Sometimes you also get a little better performance in the release mode, but since most of the performance critical code is probably going to happen inside the XNA Framework, your code will not care if it is run in debug or release mode if it is optimized good enough anyway.

Figure 14-17 shows the racing game in action. There are still things to tweak, but the game runs good and has a good frame rate even in the highest resolution possible on the Xbox 360 (1080p, which is 1920×1050). The final fine-tuning, level design, and game testing took an extra week of work, but that was a lot of fun. It is always good to let the game be played by some people you know, maybe even ones that are not really fans of your game genre. Also make sure the game can be installed easily. No one wants to compile the game himself and find out which assemblies are used the hard way through exceptions. Your installer should contain the compiled game and it should check which frameworks are not installed on a target machine and preferably install them itself. Your game probably needs just the .NET Framework 2.0 (about 30 MB), the latest DirectX version (about 50 MB), and the XNA Framework Redistributables (just 2 MB). On the Xbox 360 there is currently no deployment method available other than compiling the source code and deploying it with XNA Game Studio Express. For the installer used for this game I chose NSIS (Nullsoft Installer Script), which allowed me to build the installer in a way that downloads and installs all these frameworks automatically if the user does not have them installed. After that the game can be started and you can play a while and have fun while trying to get the best highscores.

Final Testing on the Xbox 360

You obviously want your game to run on the Xbox 360 as well and the Racing Game was mainly developed especially for the Xbox 360 platform, because it makes sense to have a racing game on a console, especially if you have a wheel controller like I do.

Figure 14-17

As I mentioned so many times before all the unit tests you write should be tested on both Windows and the Xbox 360 platform, but you will probably forget that from time to time and then at the end of the project when the final test on the Xbox 360 is due you find out that the shadow mapping is not working the same way as on the PC, for example. Well, time to pull out those unit tests (see Figure 14-16) again and test them on the Xbox 360, one by one, until you find a problem.

Because the racing game was the first project I ever did for the Xbox 360 I made quite a few mistakes that I found out about the first time I was able to run it on the Xbox 360 (the first beta of XNA in August did not support the Xbox 360 platform yet, so I was only able to test XNA on the PC for a while). The two major issues were the screen layout in the game and the menu, which did not fit well on all certain TV monitor configurations on the Xbox 360 (we already talked about that earlier in this book) and certain issues with render targets on the Xbox 360, which behave quite differently from the PC.

One of the hardest parts was to get the shadow mapping right on the Xbox 360. There were several issues with resolving the render targets and I used some tricks that are neither allowed nor possible on the Xbox 360, like using several render targets at the same time and reusing the back buffer information after rendering some render targets.

Here is some text from a blog entry from my blog at `http://abi.exdream.com` early in November 2006 when I talked about this issue while I was visiting the XNA Team in the USA:

> Today I worked a lot with the Xbox 360 side of XNA. In the earlier builds I had a lot of problems with testing my starter kit on the Xbox 360, but most of these issues are resolved now. About 99% works the same on the Windows and Xbox 360 platforms, but if you hit that 1% it does still get you angry and pushing your head into the wall. For example a couple of the more advanced shadow mapping shaders work fine on the windows platform, but all kinds of crazy things happen on the Xbox 360, the game crashes, you see black bars all over the screen or the output is just not right.
>
> If you are like me and have not worked with the Xbox 360 before, I can tell you that it is not easy getting used to the way the console uses render targets. You have to resolve them with a little helper method in XNA (or in the Xbox 360 SDK) to get the contents copied over to your texture. This is not required on windows. But even if you take care of that the shaders might behave a little different. For example most of my post screen shaders use the background buffer to mix results and sometimes mix them together several times. This works fine on the windows platform and behaves the same way as it does in DirectX.
>
> But after some discussion with Tom Miller, Matt and Mitch Walker from the XNA Team and debugging a little, it was clear that the background buffer can have garbage data after rendering into render targets. This was very bad for one of the shaders because it requires 2 separate images over several passes and then blends them together at the last pass. I used the back buffer to hold one of them and a render target for the other, but that had to be changed in order to run correctly on the Xbox 360. Good thing this was just one shader, in my bigger game engine I have over 100 shaders and it would not be fun to rethink all of the post screen shaders ^^

Figure 14-18 shows the repositioning code required to make the game look ok on TV monitors attached to the Xbox 360. Because you cannot know what kind of monitor is attached and how much is visible you can end up displaying more or less of the screen borders, but the values used here look good on all systems I've tested the game on.

The safe region (90% visible) is shown as the red border, but even if you see 100% of the screen, the game looks still fine. If your TV set is worse and goes below the 90% visibility you will still see all the important information, but some texts might be cut off.

The following code is used to push the UI elements more into the center than for the PC version, which shows all HUD elements near the screen border:

```
// More distance to the screen borders on the Xbox 360 to fit better
// into the safe region. Calculate all rectangles for each platform,
// then they will be used the same way on both platforms.
#if XBOX360
// Draw all boxes and background stuff
Rectangle lapsRect = BaseGame.CalcRectangle1600(
  60, 46, LapsGfxRect.Width, LapsGfxRect.Height);
ingame.RenderOnScreen(lapsRect, LapsGfxRect, baseUIColor);
```

```
Rectangle timesRect = BaseGame.CalcRectangle1600(
  60, 46, CurrentAndBestGfxRect.Width, CurrentAndBestGfxRect.Height);
timesRect.Y = BaseGame.Height-timesRect.Bottom;
ingame.RenderOnScreen(timesRect, CurrentAndBestGfxRect, baseUIColor);

// [etc.]
```

Figure 14-18

Additional Ideas

The game runs fine now and if you got through the final testing it is ready to be released. But even after that you might not have enough of it and you still might want to try additional ideas or think about future extensions. I often find myself reusing one of my existing engines just to test out new game ideas. It is just so much easier to use an existing engine you are already familiar with than to start from scratch.

This section is about additional ideas I had before even starting the development of the game and during the development time.

More Cars

Having more car models was one of my earlier wishes, but since I'm not a modeler and none of the modelers I know have much time and think it is "fun" to create a couple more car models for my little racing game, I never got beyond the initial 3D car model that was made specifically for the racing game. It was relatively easy to change the appearance of the car by changing the texture a bit and the starter kit version features three different car textures and some code to recolor the cars dynamically, but they all use the same underlying geometry.

The Speedy Racer Game mod, which is shown at the end of this chapter, will also feature another car model (just a free one from the Internet), but having even more different car types would be fun, especially if you give each car different speeds, acceleration, and braking parameters. For a multiplayer game it would also be more fun to have different cars so every player can choose his favorite car type.

But I guess having as many cars as the commercial racing games you saw in Chapter 12 will cost a lot of money to develop and it also takes a lot of time to get them as good as they are done in those games. Hopefully the community will find ways to import new car models, and after a while when there are more game modifications available enough cars can be found to make even better game modifications.

The car rendering code for the racing game is pretty specific; for example, the `Model` class uses a customized render method called `RenderCar` just for rendering the car. If you have more than one car model it would be harder to keep this method up to date and it would probably make more sense to implement the cars with the normal `Render` method.

Online Highscore List

Implementing a call to a web service and getting the top 10 online highscores from there is probably not a big problem. You would add such code in the `Highscore` class and you could even reuse most of the existing code from the Rocket Commander game.

Before you can use web services you will have to add the `System.Web.Services` assembly to your references list, which is only available on the Windows platform. All the web services code you are going to add to the `Highscore` class must be disabled on the Xbox 360 platform.

```
Highscore[] onlineHighscores = new Highscore[10];
Thread onlineGetHighscoreThread = null;

/// <summary>
/// Get online highscores
/// </summary>
/// <param name="onlyThisHour">Only this hour</param>
private void GetOnlineHighscores(bool onlyThisHour)
{
  // Clear all online highscores and wait for a new update!
  for (int num = 0; num < onlineHighscores.Length; num++)
  {
    onlineHighscores[num].name = "-";
    onlineHighscores[num].level = "";
    onlineHighscores[num].points = 0;
  } // for (num)
```

```
      // Stop any old threads
      if (onlineGetHighscoreThread != null)
        onlineGetHighscoreThread.Abort();

      // Ask web service for highscore list! Do this asyncronly,
      // it could take a while and we don't want to wait for it to complete.
      onlineGetHighscoreThread = new Thread(new ThreadStart(
        // Anoymous delegates, isn't .NET 2.0 great? ^^
        delegate
        {
          // See notes above
          try
          {
            string ret = new www.xnaracinggame.com.
              RacingGameService().GetTop10Highscores(onlyThisHour);

            // Now split this up and build the online highscore with it.
            string[] allHighscores = ret.Split(new char[] { ',' });
            for (int num = 0; num < allHighscores.Length &&
              num < onlineHighscores.Length; num++)
            {
              string[] oneHighscore =
                allHighscores[num].Split(new char[] { ':' });
              onlineHighscores[num] = new Highscore(
                oneHighscore[0].Trim(), oneHighscore[2],
                Convert.ToInt32(oneHighscore[1]));
            } // for (num)
          } // try
          catch { } // ignore any exceptions!
        }));

      onlineGetHighscoreThread.Start();
    } // GetOnlineHighscores(onlyThisHour)
```

In order for this code to work you need a web service running at the specified location of the
RacingGameService class. Writing the web service itself is rather trivial, but implementing a nice looking
website that shows all this data to the visitors is quite a bit of work. Maybe this will be done in the future.

More Shaders and Effects

Having more shaders and effects in a game today is always a good thing, at least from the player's
perspective because games look cooler and more different than a few years ago when many games used
similar rendering techniques and looked at least in that regard similar.

One thing you could plug in quite easily would be the parallax mapping shader from the Rocket
Commander game, but you would also need a height map on all materials where you want to use the
parallax shader instead of the standard normal mapping shader.

But adding effects and an effect manager system like for the XNA Shooter game would also be nice (see
Figure 14-19). You currently have no effect at all, not even for a car explosion or crashing into something.

For more examples of some good post-screen shaders go back to Chapter 8. A racing game would
greatly benefit from HDR rendering, especially if you change the lighting situations and drive through
tunnels (as you actually do in the game).

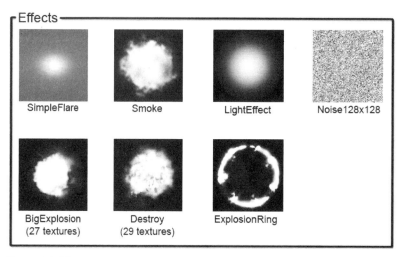

Figure 14-19

The per pixel motion blur effect discussed in Chapter 8 would also be a lot better than the currently implemented whole screen post-processing effect, but it is obviously also a lot harder to implement.

The major thing I would always improve for a racing game mod is to change the color correction factors in the `PostScreenMenu` and `PostScreenGlow` shader classes and the underlying shader code. It will give the whole game a completely different experience without having to change all of the textures yourself.

More Game Modes

More game modes would also be fun. I'm not really a racing game expert, but maybe it would be fun to implement one or more of the common racing game modes you can often find in commercial racing games:

- ❑ Beat the best time: This is the mode you have in the racing game currently. It could also be extended to more players and you would need to add some racing car AI for other players.

- ❑ Be the first: For this game mode you obviously need more than one car and more than one driver. This is the main game mode for most racing games. It is currently not possible because you have no multiplayer and no computer AI code for handling other cars. Even with some AI code you would still need to improve the collision code for the cars, because now you would be able to collide with other cars on the track.

- ❑ Practice mode: Special game mode for some racing games that allow you to train on the tracks before actually going into competition. You can test out tricks and train on certain parts of the track, but this whole game mode only makes sense if you would lose something by training in the competition game mode, which again is not the case in the racing game.

❏ Time Trails: You have to complete the track or certain parts of it in a specified time frame. This way the game can get a lot harder for beginners because it is usually much harder to beat these times instead of just having to complete the track and beating some highscore or not.

❏ Cone Parkour mode or driving lessons mode: You have to drive around cones placed on the road in a certain time frame or by not knocking over to many of them. Other parkours could involve driving on certain sides of the road or following the street signs.

❏ Tricks: This is one of the more popular game modes, especially in the street racer games discussed in Chapter 12. Doing tricks means that you have to drift your car, slide through curves, or maybe even jump through certain parts of the track. Games like Trackmania have other kinds of tricks you have to perform to even complete a track. You do have loopings, but not most of the other advanced mode parts Trackmania has to make it more difficult completing tracks.

❏ Crash mode: Some games have focused on crashing the car into walls and getting points for it or damaging your car as fast as possible. Sounds like fun for the first couple of times, but I never played those games long enough to discuss this any further.

❏ Add weapons to the cars, or at least add items for special abilities. Many arcade racing games have this idea implemented and there are many different game modes that can come out of this idea. Items make even more sense in a multiplayer game where everyone is fighting each other and items help you destroy your enemies or push them aside to let you become the first-place player. Popular examples of these games would be Mario Kart, Wacky Wheels, and games like Micro Machines.

❏ Implement your own game ideas or mix in existing game ideas into a racing game. You could even get rid of the racing part altogether and maybe add something completely different. The sky is the limit.

Multiplayer Mode

For most game modes just discussed it would be a lot more fun if you could play the game together with a couple of friends either in your local area network (LAN) or over the Internet. Because networking code is not possible on the Xbox 360, the multiplayer part would only work on the PC right now with XNA.

The main change you would have to do to the game after implementing the basic code for networking is to change the `Player` class and allow multiple instances of this class. You will also need to handle a list of players and update all the data for each player with help of multiplayer messages. Again, this alone could fill up a book because there are many issues with multiplayer games and many possible ways to implement such code.

As a little example, take a look at Figure 14-20, which shows a couple of such multiplayer network classes working together. The game class holds a list of player objects. Each player receives data from all the other players and adds all received messages to an internal list. Messages are loaded with the help of the `Message` class and the `MessageType` enum.

Figure 14-20

Challenge: Write Your Own Mod!

As the final challenge for this book it is now your task to create your own game modification for the Racing Game. You can implement your own game idea or follow the process of coding the Speedy Racer mod.

As you saw at the very beginning of this chapter, there are quite a lot of mods available for the Rocket Commander game. More than 12 mods were written in 2006 alone and many more game projects were started and I bet more games and mods were made, but the people involved in that were either too shy to share their games or they did not want to mention that they used the Rocket Commander engine. It is of course also possible that I'm just not aware of more game modifications out there, which might be floating around somewhere on the Internet.

The racing game and the XNA Shooter have great potential for modding. Not only are these games less specific than the Rocket Commander game, but they also have more reusable engines, which allows for creating new games more quickly than starting from scratch, even if some of the used technology is not really required for the new game.

If you want to create your own mod and if you already have a certain idea you don't need to read ahead about the Speedy Racer; go ahead and try to implement your own game idea first. In this chapter you learned enough to make incisions into the classes and change whatever you need to make your new game idea work.

Example Game: Speedy Racer

The Speedy Racer mod is not completely described here; it is still your challenge to create such a mod yourself, but I will give you everything you need to get started. If you are really lazy and don't want to code your own mod or Speedy Racer yourself right now you can also just go ahead and install the game from the book CD, but I recommend trying to make the changes to the racing game yourself first before looking at the existing Speedy Racer code.

Step 1: Changing the Car Model

Because the mod had to be created quickly and I could not afford to pay a 3D modeler to make me a nice new car, I searched a little bit on the Internet for 3D models than can be used freely. I found a couple of nice cars, but most of them had too many polygons and others were in strange formats and I found no converters for them. After a while I gave up and just used one of the older 3D models I found earlier. Figure 14-21 shows an early version of this new Speedy Racer Car, which has about 21,000 polygons (compared to the 25,000 polygons of the original car in the Racer Game), but no material data set. I just added some boring red and black materials and the model was good enough to be exported and tested in the game. Later I added normal maps and a little texture mapping to the car model to make it look a little bit better. If you have more time for your project, try to do it better than me.

Figure 14-21

Step 2: Menu Changes

Changing the menu often involves a lot of textures and was always quite a bit of extra work on the Rocket Commander mods. The Racing Game is no different. Changing the menu did take some time, but only background textures and the used colors were changed; all the code could remain the same. Some of the menu logic was even simplified a little bit to avoid having to re-create certain textures again for the new mod.

If you would like to add more game screens, add more buttons to the main menu, or handle more options, and so on, it would probably help the most if you read the part about the game screens in this chapter again and try to figure out where the best place is to put any new code into the game.

Step 3: New Landscape and Objects

The Speedy Racer mod still uses the same landscape data as the original game, but I changed the landscape shader a little bit to make the game a bit more colorful and I changed everything into the blue color range. The shadow mapping and the post-screen shaders were also changed to make the game look a little bit different. See Chapter 8 for more details about the post-screen shaders and how to change them, especially the color correction shader part in `PostScreenMenu.fx` and `PostScreenGlow.fx`.

The following code is from the final post-screen rendering technique of the `PostScreenGlow` shader. You should be able to easily change the code for other visual effects and resulting colors. A good tip with shaders is always to go crazy first and then settle with more decent values. For example, if you want to test a blue look of the game, try adding 25% or even 50% to the blue color value and check the result. Maybe it does not look cool with blue or you like the craziness and settle with a value like 10% (which is a lot) for the blue color component. Or try playing around with the contrast values; there are always some variables you can tweak in most used shaders. The main goal of Speedy Racer was not to make it look highly realistic; it just should look different from the original Racing Game.

```
float4 PS_ComposeFinalImage20(
  VB_OutputPos3TexCoords In,
  uniform sampler2D sceneSampler,
  uniform sampler2D blurredSceneSampler) : COLOR
{
  float4 orig = tex2D(sceneSampler, In.texCoord[0]);
  float4 blur = tex2D(blurredSceneSampler, In.texCoord[1]);

  float4 screenBorderFadeout = tex2D(screenBorderFadeoutMapSampler,
    In.texCoord[2]);
  float4 ret =
    0.75f*orig +
    GlowIntensity*blur+
    HighlightIntensity*blur.a;
  ret.rgb *= screenBorderFadeout;

  // Change colors a bit, sub 20% red and add 25% blue (photoshop values)
  // Here the values are -4% and +5%
  ret.rgb = float3(
    ret.r+0.054f/2,
    ret.g-0.021f/2,
    ret.b-0.035f/2);

  // Change brightness -5% and contrast +10%
  ret.rgb = ret.rgb * 0.975f;
  ret.rgb = (ret.rgb - float3(0.5, 0.5, 0.5)) * 1.05f +
    float3(0.5, 0.5, 0.5);

  return ret;
} // PS_ComposeFinalImage20(...)
```

Step 4: Driving Faster

To drive faster with the car in the game and still have a playable and enjoyable game you need to make two major changes to the game logic:

❏   Make the roads much wider; this way you can drive faster through them. Also try to adjust the up vector for straight roads in a way that makes it easier to drive around curves.

   The code to change the basic road width can be found in the TrackVertex class of the Track namespace; just change the RoadWidthScale value to something crazy like 50 for testing and then settle for some reasonable value.

```
/// <summary>
/// Minimun, maximum and default road width for our track.
/// </summary>
public const float MinRoadWidth = 0.25f,
  DefaultRoadWidth = 1.0f,
  MaxRoadWidth = 2.0f,
  RoadWidthScale = 13.25f;

// [The constants are then used to generate the left and right track
// vertices ...]

/// <summary>
/// Left side track vertex generation, used for the GuardRail class.
/// </summary>
/// <returns>Track vertex</returns>
public TrackVertex LeftTrackVertex
{
  get
  {
    return new TrackVertex(
      pos - RoadWidthScale * roadWidth * right / 2,
      right, up, dir,
      new Vector2(uv.X, 0),
      roadWidth);
  } // get
} // LeftTrackVertex

// [etc.]
```

❏   Make the car drive much faster. This can be done directly in the CarPhysics class by changing the following code. Constantly use the unit tests of this class to test out the new values. If they look ok try them in the real game.

```
#region Constants
/// <summary>
/// Car is 1000 kg
/// </summary>
const float CarMass = 1000;//1000.0f;

/// <summary>
/// Gravity on earth is 9.81 m/s^2
/// </summary>
```

```
const float Gravity = 9.81f;

/// <summary>
/// Max speed of our car is 275 mph.
/// While we use mph for the display, we calculate internally with
/// meters per sec since meter is the unit we use for everthing in the
/// game. And it is a much nicer unit than miles or feet.
/// </summary>
public const float MaxSpeed =
    275.0f * MphToMeterPerSec;

/// <summary>
/// Max. acceleration in m/s^2 we can do per second.
/// We have also to define the max and min overall acceleration we can
/// do with our car (very car specfic, but for this game always the same
/// to make it fair). Driving backwards is slower than driving forward.
/// </summary>
const float MaxAccelerationPerSec = 5.0f,//120.0f,//1000.0f,
    MaxAcceleration = 10.0f,//70.0f,//250.0f,
    MinAcceleration = -6.0f;//-35.0f;//250.0f;//-40.0f;

/// <summary>
/// Friction we have on the road each second. If we are driving slow,
/// this slows us down quickly. If we drive really fast, this does not
/// matter so much anymore. The main slowdown will be the air friction.
/// </summary>
const float CarFrictionOnRoad = 17.523456789f;//15.0f;//2.5f;

/// <summary>
/// Air friction we get if we drive fast, this slows us down very fast
/// if we drive fast. It makes it also much harder to drive faster if
/// we already drive at a very fast speed. For slow speeds the air
/// friction does not matter so much. This could be extended to include
/// wind and then even at low speeds the air friction would slow us
/// down or even influence our movement. Maybe in a game mod sometime.
/// </summary>
const float AirFrictionPerSpeed = 0.66f;//0.225f;//0.33f;//0.42f;

/// <summary>
/// Max air friction, this way we can have a good air friction for low
/// speeds but we are not limited to 190-210mph, but can drive faster.
/// </summary>
const float MaxAirFriction = AirFrictionPerSpeed * 200.0f;

/// <summary>
/// Break slowdown per second, 1.0 means we need 1 second to do a full
/// break. Slowdown is also limited by max. 100 per sec!
/// Note: This would not make sense in a real world simulation because
/// stopping the car usually needs more time and is highly dependant
/// on the speed resulting in longer stopping distances. For this game
/// it is easier and more fun to just always brake the same.
/// </summary>
const float BrakeSlowdown = 1.0f;

// [etc.]
```

Step 5: Adding Items and New Sounds

This part was actually the most work. To make the game more fun I added several items (more speed, focus view, road widener, and so on) and new sounds for them. Check out the files in the mod itself for more information about the new items. The code changes were also a bit of work, but not as much work as creating the items themselves and testing them.

Summary

Phew, that was a long chapter and a long book overall. Just remember this is my first try at writing a book. I hope you liked it and learned a little bit from the example games I made. I'm pretty happy with the many example games in the book; I think the more practical approach to writing games will help out beginners more and give more advanced readers a way to quickly skip existing parts and take a look at the more complex things in the game programming world.

The topics in the book cover almost everything you need for learning XNA and game programming in general, but I have hidden each topic under the current game project of the chapter. For example, the physics chapter would still be helpful with some general physics calculations, but linking it to the racing game makes it so much easier to think about the problems that can happen in your game if you add physics. Even if you want to develop a completely different game that uses other physics calculations you will probably benefit from the approach in general because you write some unit tests first, you test out the available physics engines, and you will probably have some early idea about solving your physics problem after reading the chapter because you see some similarities with problems described there.

I congratulate you for reading through this book, but you should not stop now. Hopefully you are eager to start your own graphics engine projects or use one of the games in this book as a foundation for your next game project.

Here is a short list of the games you encountered in this book and which game programming topics were discussed while developing these games:

- ❏ After Chapter 1, which was only an introduction to the XNA Framework and the first simple game project, you created a Pong game in Chapter 2. Here you learned all the basics for using unit testing properly, planning the whole project, and writing a good game concept. On the technical side you learned how to use sprites, handling the input, playing sounds, and doing some basic 2D collision testing. The game is playable with multiple players on the same screen and that is as far as you get with multiplayer games in this book.

- ❏ In Chapter 3, several very important helper classes were discussed, but just having some helper classes alone is not really a fun game project so a new game was created: Breakout, which uses some of the game logic of Pong, but allows you to play against yourself instead of another player or the stupid AI of Pong.

- ❏ Chapter 4 goes through the usefulness of game components and shows how to program one of my all-time favorite classic games: Tetris. Some of the game component classes developed here and in Chapters 5 and 6 survive until the end of this book, but the general idea to do everything with game components was never adopted by any game in this book. It just wouldn't make any sense.

❏ Part II (Chapters 5–8) focused on developing a basic graphics engine for all the upcoming game projects. Chapter 5 explains how to render models, use unit testing for 3D code, render textures, fonts, and lines on the screen and finally even do some testing on the Xbox 360. Chapters 6 to 8 focus on shaders, a really big and complex topic, but in every chapter you dive a little deeper into the world of shaders. Chapter 8 finally ends with the great Rocket Commander game, which is now ported to the XNA Framework thanks to the graphics engine that was developed in these chapters.

❏ Part III of the book (Chapters 9–11) is all about improving the game engine. You finally learned how to use XACT properly, how to handle all the game screen classes and the game engine in general, and of course all about the UI and the player input class. To make things a little bit more interesting the XNA Shooter game was introduced here, which really looks great and is quite a lot of fun to play. Some of the more advanced topics like shadow mapping are also introduced for the first time, but all the hard stuff is left for Part IV.

❏ Finally, Part IV (Chapters 12–14) focuses on the Racing Game, the complex landscape and track generation code and the physics engine used in the game. You also learned a lot about the game screens and game logic in the game and how to test and tweak a relatively big game project like this one. At the end the cool Speedy Racer mod was written to show how to create your own mod based on the existing game engine.

This chapter also discussed a lot about the final stages in the game development process, which is sadly not reached by many people because most game projects are canceled before they reach even the alpha stage. Many beginners also stop developing their game because they run into some big problem or they are no longer motivated to keep going, especially if the game project is big. Hopefully the games of this book can help such people out and give them a handbook on how to really write games from start to finish, or at least reuse some existing game engine instead of reinventing the wheel and stopping too early.

That's about it for this book. Maybe there will be future endeavors and I also constantly update my blog, so if you want to read more material from me, check it out. I'm also always happy to receive any emails about new game programmers getting started, seeing cool new game projects based on my engines, or getting to know of more mods for one of the games described in this book.

Resources

This book has covered a lot of ground, and I hope you learned enough to develop better games now. The following resources should help you out a little — I've included all the links, books, source code, and games that were mentioned throughout the book.

Links

Here's a list of many important links from the book:

❏ **http://msdn.microsoft.com/directx/xna/**

XNA Developer Center on Microsoft's MSDN page with the XNA Game Studio Forum and the XNA Framework Forum, which are the most active XNA forums you will find on the Internet. You can also download the latest XNA version here, read the FAQ, and see what's new.

❏ **http://blogs.msdn.com/xna/**

XNA Team blog. Bookmark this one to stay up to date with the latest news from the XNA team.

❏ **http://abi.exdream.com**

Official website of the author. You can find more games I made here, as well as Rocket Commander XNA, the XNA Shooter, and the Racing Game from this book and all the documentation and video tutorials I made for them. Additionally I suggest checking out the Rocket Commander Video Tutorials, which were pretty popular on Coding4Fun.

❑ http://www.rocketcommander.com

This is the official website for Rocket Commander, which was released at the beginning of 2006, and was written for Managed DirectX originally. A new version running completely on XNA to support the Xbox 360 was released at the end of 2006.

❑ http://www.xnaracinggame.com

Official website for the racing game talked about at the end of this book.

❑ http://www.xnashooter.com

This is the official website for the XNA Shooter game from Chapter 11 of this book. All the other games of this book can also be found on my blog.

❑ http://en.wikipedia.org/wiki/Microsoft_XNA

Entry on Wikipedia about XNA, constantly updated and contains many links to other topics. On the bottom of the page are a few useful external links.

❑ http://xnadevelopment.com

Nice new site with many links, tutorials, and tips to get you started in the XNA world.

❑ http://xnaresources.com

Another new site with lots of news and some really useful tutorials on tile engines. Also contains a lot of game components you might like.

❑ http://learnxna.com

XNA news site in form of a blog, also contains some video tutorials and focuses on learning XNA and tips and tricks with graphic tools.

❑ http://martinfowler.com

In Chapter 2 unit testing and Agile Methodologies are discussed. If you want to read more about unit testing I recommend reading this website of Martin Fowler, one of the founders of this whole idea.

❑ http://www.nvidia.com

Home of the Nvidia homepage and many free tools like the FX Composer, which is used in Chapter 6. You can also learn a lot about graphic card architecture, special rendering techniques, shaders, and so on from the many samples, tutorials, and documentation that can be found in the developers section.

Code Download Structure

You can download all the code from the book. You can also download other important files that were discussed in the book; for example, in Chapter 2, the concept for the first game is discussed. (The information can be found in a PDF file.) To make your life even easier, I've included executables, which let you start the game or sample code. If you don't have .NET, DirectX, or XNA installed, please use one of the game installers, because they will automatically install all of the files for you. You can also install everything yourself from the Setup folder.

Here's a list of items that you can download:

❑ Readme.txt — Contains additional information about the sample code.

❑ Setup folder — This folder contains all the setup for the frameworks used in the game, namely .NET 2.0, the current DirectX version, and the XNA Framework Redistributable as well as XNA Game Studio Express. If you have not installed anything yet, this is the order you have to install these tools:

    1. Install Visual C# Express from the Internet Shortcut file in the Setup folder first, which will also install the .NET Framework automatically for you.

    2. Install XNA Game Studio Express, which will install the XNA Framework for you also and notify you if you need an updated DirectX version, or just use the Internet Shortcut in the Setup folder.

❑ Executables folder — This directory contains all the precompiled samples and games from all the chapters. For the source code please look at the Chapter 1–14 directories, where all the other content (help files, concepts, textures, sounds, and so on) is located.

❑ Games folder — All games that are presented in the book can be installed through the installers located in this directory. You can also just start the games from the Executables directory, but it often makes more sense to install the games and keep them on your PC.

❑ Folders for Chapter 1 to Chapter 14 — Contain all the source code and samples from the book including all the content files (textures, sounds, fonts, music, and so on). You might also find several additional files like concepts or links that are used in the chapter.

Please note that you can start all projects in either the Windows mode or in the Xbox 360 mode. Because XNA Game Studio Express does not allow switching the project type dynamically (because different assembly references are used) I have created two project files for all projects in this book. The normal project (.csproj) file is always for the Windows platform output, and the projects ending with Xbox360.csproj are used to allow you to deploy and test projects directly on the Xbox 360 console. Both projects actually use the exact same source files and if there are any differences they are marked with the XBOX360 keyword in the source code files, which are used as #if XBOX360 #endif blocks.

For more information and updates you can check the official website for this book at http://www.wiley.com.

You can also check out my blog for more information at http://abi.exdream.com.

Books

Here are some books I have read and reviewed a while back on my blog. They are still very useful and fit perfectly with this book. I recommend these books here for the interested reader who wants to learn more about the many topics in the game programming world. If you have problems finding these books, just type the name in Google and the first match will always return the correct book result.

Graphics and Shader Technologies

- ❑ *Game Programming Gems 5* (and recently 6 and 7 came out) — Like any other *Game Programming Gems* book this one is no exception; it is just great. You can read it from front to back or use it as a reference if you're looking for solution to common game programming problems and even programming problems in general. It covers seven sections — general programming and mathematics to AI and physics and finally to Graphics, Network, and Audio. This one is the most recommended game programming book series.

- ❑ *ShaderX* — Another book series. I read the first three and use them as a reference whenever I look for cool shader effects. The 4th and 5th volumes are as good as the predecessors. Wolfgang Engel is a good editor and I heard him speaking at several developer conferences. This guy knows a lot about shaders.

- ❑ *GPU Gems 2* — Yet another book series. Good stuff for Nvidia developers, but since most shaders work fine on ATI hardware too (except when you tried to write PS3.0 shader when ATI still hadn't any cards for that), it is a good shader book. It covers some nice tricks and can be compared to the *ShaderX* books. Unlike the *Game Programming Gems* or the *ShaderX* books, every page is printed in color and this also makes it a good colorful picture book where I can show effects to my artist guys, who won't even bother to look if it isn't a nice picture.

- ❑ *Shaders for Game Programmers and Artists* — This is one of the first shader books I read, but even for a first book I think it is too shallow. It jumps right into post-screen shaders that are very advanced in my opinion, and then continues with much easier shaders. The book is all about ATI's Render Monkey tool, which I don't like because the output is unusable (I need fx files). It is still a good shader book and may be helpful for artists, beginners, or people who just want an overview of shader technologies.

- ❑ *Programming Vertex & Pixel Shaders* — This book is the best and most complete shader programming book for anyone seriously wanting to go into shader technologies. It is a bit harder to read than the previous one and sometimes way too mathematical instead of just having fun with shaders, but it pays off because you learn all the basic shader technologies you will ever need. This is another book by Wolfgang Engel (like the *ShaderX* books, which are more advanced).

AI Programming

- ❑ *AI Game Engine Programming* — This book goes into a lot of first-person shooter AI problems and discusses useful techniques, not only about AI, but also how to use scripts (Lua), how to write all kinds of state machines, and neural nets. The CD not only contains all the source code and figures, but also a bunch of useful web bookmarks sorted by category. I like that.

- ❑ *Programming Game AI by Example* — This book is a bit more for beginners and intermediate programmers than the rest of the books here. It is still a great book, but it "only" explains how to get into AI programming, and as soon as you are ready to go, the book ends. The book starts with math and physics and does a good job explaining them. Then it goes to state-driven design and continues with game agents. It also covers questions about path finding, fuzzy logic, and scripting. It is written by the founder of www.ai-junkie.com and written really well. My only criticism is the fact that it is a good beginner book. Anyway, I got it together with the previous book at the same price and that's really ok. Maybe it is good for a reference or to tell interns or wannabe AI programmers "Go read that."

❏ *AI Game Programming Wisdom I and II* — Similar to *Game Programming Gems*, this series is all about finding skilled professionals writing chapters and articles, which do really help you out. Steve Rabin is the editor and he also edited the *Game Programming Gems* AI sections; he also is the creator of www.AIWisdom.com. Like the other two AI books I haven't read all of it (I'm so busy, you know), but from what I've seen and read this is a really helpful resource when doing anything related to AI programming.

General Development and Programming

❏ *Refactoring: Improving the Design of Existing Code* — Someone told me when I read this book on the flight to the PDC two years ago that you could probably dry up a cellar with this book. Maybe he is right; this book is all about crazy design pattern and rules. The first couple of chapters are good to read and the rest is more of a reference. Anyway, the idea counts and refactoring is one of the most useful processes today in writing big programs. This very useful book was first released in 1999 and still applies 100%.

❏ *Rapid Development* — This is a good book about software design and keeping schedules, but it is a bit too long and sometimes hard to read (you know I have this problem of reading only half the book and then never finding time to finish it). It was written back in 1996 and the techniques described still apply, but some of the ideas are not as flexible as they could be with all this new technology around (for example, when using Agile Methodologies you have to plan differently). Still it is a very good book and it contains a couple of interesting stories from big products like MS Word and how they never kept their schedule.

❏ *Code Complete 2* — One of the best books ever for any kind of programmer. It is about describing the process of developing software and helps you to find out the most efficient ways to manage your projects. It goes into great detail by explaining which data structures, which routines, which loops, or which strategies are the most useful. It is one of the books I would recommend to both new and experienced programmers. This book just helps anyone and should be on every programmer's desk, not just in their book shelves.

❏ *Managing Agile Projects* — What does Agile Projects mean? It is about scaling and customizing your project depending on the customer feedback. That still sounds too vague? Ok, it means that you don't plan every single bit before writing code, but you cut your project into smaller pieces and only plan the overview and then directly start developing. Now you can present a very early version really fast and with the help of feedback (customers or yourself) you can adjust your project instead of wasting time and resources developing something no one wants. You can also shorten specific parts of your project if you see there is no time left or other parts are more important, which again is not possible if you had planned every bit of your project in advance. It is a technique that goes hand-in-hand with unit testing and refactoring (see the *Refactoring: Improving the Design of Existing Code* book above). This book gives a very broad overview and doesn't really talk about coding, it's just methodologies.

❏ *Maximizing .NET Performance* — I'm a performance freak. In the past I often tried to re-implement existing and working code into assembler code just to see how much faster it could get. Later I found out that it is often much more important to work at a much higher level and rethink a problem until the solution is good enough to run very fast even if not optimized to every bit. This is still true and I still think that most performance problems come from bad coding or sub-optimal algorithms and not because of the language. However, to even think of good solutions you need some knowledge of what is possible, what is fast, and how certain things affect your performance. This book gives you a very useful inside view of .NET and covers a lot of tricks and tips about .NET performance. It is also a good reference book.

❑ *Code Generation in Microsoft .NET* — I first heard of this topic from the DotNetRocks radio show where the author Kathleen Dollard was the guest a few years ago. She talked about code generation using templates and other tricks. I immediately bought this book. It is mostly written in Visual Basic, but a C# conversion exists too. It does a good job explaining how to use code generation with the Code Dom, but does not go into detail about MSIL (which I was more interested in). Anyway, the book is written nicely and I learned a lot from it. The book presents an entire framework for building SQL bindings, stored procedures, and building Win Forms from XML templates. It is also one of the first books on this subject (and maybe still the only one going into the Code Dom instead of MSIL).

Another Useful Title

❑ *Programming in Lua* — This is *the* book for Lua programmers. It is also available for free to download from lua.org. I first read the online version and then bought the book because it is so good and it helps to have a reference. Lua is a very simple script language. But sometimes it is so simple that you just don't know which keyword to use or what to type. Having a few useful code examples every other page is the biggest help ever. With the help of this book I learned Lua in 1–2 days and could do really useful stuff with it (instead of just writing hello like most languages you learn in a short time).

Golden Rules and Tips

Here are some "golden rules" and tips you'll discover in the book.

Tips

❑ You need an Xbox 360 Live Account on your Xbox 360, which must be connected at all times when you develop and test your XNA games.

❑ Make sure your PC and the Xbox 360 are on the same network and they can "see" each other. You can test ping-ing the Xbox 360 IP from your PC or connecting to your PC as a media center from the Xbox 360.

❑ When you create an encryption key in the Settings of the XNA Game Launcher and it is not accepted by your PC because you maybe mistyped it or it contained 0 (the number zero) and O letters, which look almost the same, just try it again. You can always create a new encryption key. See Chapter 1 for details.

❑ If you run into compiler errors from the code in this book, make sure you have all required content in the project and all the classes and used variables are defined correctly for graphics, sounds, and music files.

❑ Read the compiler error message and change the code accordingly. Maybe you are trying to use some obsolete method; either replace it with the new method or just comment it out to see how the rest of the code behaves.

❑ If the compiling works, but the program crashes or throws an exception it is most likely that you have some content file missing or that your graphic hardware does not support at least Shader Model 1.1.

❑ It is important to write down your ideas and to develop a small concept. Just one page of concept can be quite useful.

❑ To solve problems you use a top-down approach and you use unit testing to stay at just the top level without even thinking of the implementation. This way you can quickly adopt ideas from the concept and write them down in unit tests, making it easier to see exactly what methods you have to implement.

❑ Final tips about managing your projects: Think about your problems and divide them into small manageable parts.

❑ Write the tests first and do not think about the implementation. Just write them down like you think the final code should look or like you want to have your game code.

❑ Try to make sure you test as much as possible. For example, the `TestIsInList` method tests both a successful call to `IsInList` and a failure from the `IsInList` call. Spend time with your unit tests, but never more than 50%. You should not have to write 30 checks for a method that has only two lines of code.

❑ Start the test constantly from this point on, even when you think it does not make sense. It will force you to see what has to be done and how far you are in the implementation process. At first the test will not even compile because you haven't implemented anything. Then after implementing empty methods the test should fail because you are not doing anything yet. Later when everything works you'll feel much better.

❑ Whereas you will not test your static unit tests very often, dynamic unit tests can be tested every single time you compile your code (if they all run quick enough). Always try to run all unit tests once a day or once a week to always make sure your latest code changes did not add new bugs or errors.

Golden Rules

❑ **Do not use any external dlls if not required** — While using XNA Game library DLLs is supported, most DLLs you will have on the Windows platform will call System DLLs that are not available on the Xbox 360 or even worse, call unmanaged DLLs with P-Invoke, which is absolutely not supported on the Xbox 360 for security reasons. Also don't use unsafe code or make any attempts to call external code, access devices, or use unsupported features. It will be a waste of time and you are better off just playing by the rules.

❑ **Don't wait with the testing** — In the middle of the project test if your code compiles if you change the output settings to the Xbox 360. Often methods you might get used to might be missing on the Xbox 360. For example, there are no `TryParse` methods in the System.dll on the Xbox 360, and some XNA methods and classes like the `MouseState` classes are even missing and unsupported.

❑ **Don't load content directly** — On the Windows platform it is possible to load textures or shaders directly with the help of the `Texture2D` or `CompiledEffect` constructors. These methods are completely missing from the Xbox 360; you can only load content from the content pipeline. If you use code that dynamically loads or reloads textures or shaders, it will only work on your Windows platform. In that case use the XBOX360 define to exclude this code parts to make the project still compile on the Xbox 360 platform.

❏ **Save games and loading other content** — For save games you can use the Content namespace and the many available helper classes. To load content you will always have to make sure you use the correct path with the help of `StorageContainer.TitleLocation`, which works on the Windows platform too and just uses your output directory there. Loading from other locations on the Xbox 360 results in Access Denied exceptions for IO operations.

❏ **Test resolutions** — The Xbox 360 supports many different resolutions compared to the PC and you should test at least 2–3 different resolutions to make sure the game runs fine with it.

❏ **Allow controlling everything with a gamepad** — Most XNA games I've seen made the mistake of only allowing keyboard input or only gamepad input, which means it runs either only on Windows or only if you have an Xbox 360 controller. Always add support for as many input devices as you can think of and that make sense for your game.

❏ **Debug and unit test on the Xbox 360** — Debugging and unit testing is no different on your console; the same rules apply. It might be a little harder to trace errors and log messages, but stepping through code and testing unit tests works great with XNA. Take advantage of that. By the way: Edit and continue works only on the Windows platform; you can't do that with Xbox 360 games, which can be annoying, but you will probably do the major part of your development on the Windows platform anyway.

Class Overviews

Finally, I've included the class overviews from three of the more complex games described in the book:

❏ Rocket Commander XNA from Chapter 8 (Figure A-1)

❏ XNA Shooter from Chapter 11 (Figure A-2)

❏ And finally the Racing Game from Chapter 14 (Figure A-3)

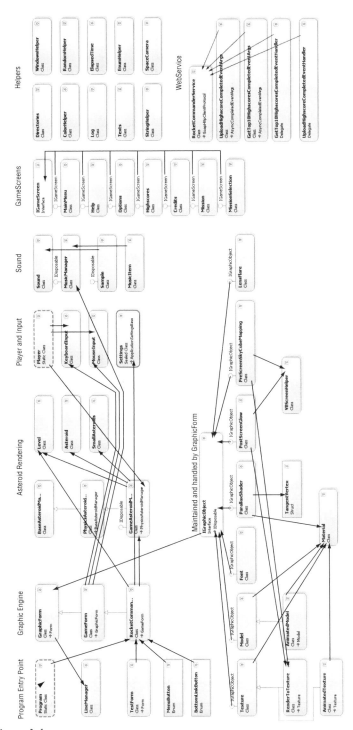

Figure A-1

Appendix A: Resources

Figure A-2

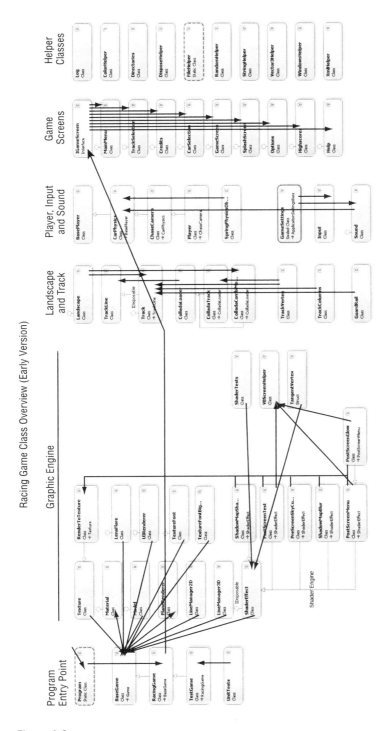

Figure A-3

Index